Praise for *Marketing For Dummies*

"What to do. How to do it. In simple, everyday language. There's never been anything like it."

> — Ira N. Bachrach, President, NameLab, Inc., San Francisco

"A full-service approach to marketing. Alex Hiam delivers strategic thinking in plain English — no translation needed. He takes advantage of the *...For Dummies*® format to offer a comprehensive sourcebook for both the small business person and the corporate marketing manager. Hiam is the premier applied marketing writer of our time, and *Marketing For Dummies* is a great platform for his wisdom and clarity."

> — Dirk Coburn, Chief Marketing Officer,
> The Babson-United Companies

"Throw out all your old marketing books — cancel your MBA classes. This is the one book to have. A valuable reference for people new to marketing and savvy pros as well."

> — Jim Jubelirer, Senior Consultant, Burke Customer
> Satisfaction Associates

Praise for *The Portable MBA in Marketing*

"Alex Hiam and Charles Schewe have developed both an objective and tactical approach that makes global marketing sense: Focus on the customer worldwide; simplify and change strategic planning; drive marketing knowledge and skills to all levels of an organization. I highly recommend this book."

> — Scott H. Creelman, Vice-President-International, Spalding Sports
> Worldwide

"*The Portable MBA in Marketing* breathes life into the conceptual frameworks of marketing with a generous dose of exciting real-world case histories. It's a great introduction to the foundations of marketing and engaging refresher for marketing managers."

> — David G. Fubini, Managing Director, McKinsey & Company, Inc.,
> Boston

"This book not only provides the reader with the basic foundation of marketing but adds to the structures using contemporary issues such as globalization, innovation, quality management, and customer service."

> — Gordon W. Paul, Professor of Marketing, University of Central Florida

"*The Portable MBA in Marketing* has clarity and style . . . it is full of real-world examples that make the conceptual material jump off the pages. This book will sharpen and hone your marketing skills. I guarantee it."

> — Stephen H. Winchell, President, Stephen Winchell & Association,
> A Direct Response Agency

"Engaging, easily digestible concepts built on a sea of real-world examples. . . . Finally, I've received my MBA in Marketing . . ."

> — Bruce R. McBrearty, Transamerica Marketing Services, Inc.

"An energetic, conversational style makes this book an engaging introduction to a corporate focus that will soon transform American business practice."

> — Burrelle's Business Information Center

Praise for *Closing The Quality Gap*

"Alexander Hiam has identified many 'best practices' of U.S. companies that are successful global competitors. His book will be helpful for any manager embarking on a Total Quality Journey."

> — Thomas C. McDermott, President and Chief Operating Officer, Bausch & Lomb

"Closing the Quality Gap drives home the importance of getting management and rank-and-file employees alike to buy into the quest for quality."

> — Jon C. Madonna, Chairman and Chief Executive, KPMG Peat Marwick

"Hiam weaves an entertaining story essential for anyone concerned with the progress of today's business management. This professor believes it should be required reading."

> — Charles D. Schewe, Ph.D., Professor of Marketing, University of Massachusetts at Amherst

"This book fills a gap in management publications by addressing two very important and often overlooked aspects of Total Quality Management: Companies embarking on TQM must do so as part of their business strategy, and they must provide leadership, vision, resources, and untiring support. It will help managers plan their company's TQM journey."

> — Laszlo J. Papay, Director, Market-Driven Quality Assesment, IBM Corporation

"A useful book not only on how total quality might be constructed, but why quality represents an essential transformation of the traditional marketing concept. Without this insight we will not realize the full potential of what quality has to offer."

> — Edward J. Kane, Vice President, Quality, Dun & Bradstreet Corp.

"Leading the continual improvement of quality in your organization will require new knowledge. This book shares the views and insights of those who work inside organizations to lead the acquisition of that knowledge."

> — Paul B. Batalden, M.D., Vice President for Medical Care, Head, Quality Resource Group, Hospital Corporation of America

MARKETING FOR DUMMIES®

by Alexander Hiam

IDG Books Worldwide, Inc.
An International Data Group Company

Foster City, CA ♦ Chicago, IL ♦ Indianapolis, IN ♦ Southlake, TX

Marketing For Dummies®

Published by
IDG Books Worldwide, Inc.
An International Data Group Company
919 E. Hillsdale Blvd.
Suite 400
Foster City, CA 94404
http://www.idgbooks.com (IDG Books Worldwide Web site)
http://www.dummies.com (Dummies Press Web site)

Library of Congress Catalog Card No.: 97-71817

ISBN: 1-56884-699-1

Printed in the United States of America

10 9 8 7 6 5 4 3 2 1

1DD/QT/QW/ZX/IN

Distributed in the United States by IDG Books Worldwide, Inc.

Distributed by Macmillan Canada for Canada; by Transworld Publishers Limited in the United Kingdom; by IDG Norge Books for Norway; by IDG Sweden Books for Sweden; by Woodslane Pty. Ltd. for Australia; by Woodslane Enterprises Ltd. for New Zealand; by Longman Singapore Publishers Ltd. for Singapore, Malaysia, Thailand, and Indonesia; by Simron Pty. Ltd. for South Africa; by Toppan Company Ltd. for Japan; by Distribuidora Cuspide for Argentina; by Livraria Cultura for Brazil; by Ediciencia S.A. for Ecuador; by Addison-Wesley Publishing Company for Korea; by Ediciones ZETA S.C.R. Ltda. for Peru; by WS Computer Publishing Corporation, Inc., for the Philippines; by Unalis Corporation for Taiwan; by Contemporanea de Ediciones for Venezuela; by Computer Book & Magazine Store for Puerto Rico; by Express Computer Distributors for the Caribbean and West Indies. Authorized Sales Agent: Anthony Rudkin Associates for the Middle East and North Africa.

For general information on IDG Books Worldwide's books in the U.S., please call our Consumer Customer Service department at 800-762-2974. For reseller information, including discounts and premium sales, please call our Reseller Customer Service department at 800-434-3422.

For information on where to purchase IDG Books Worldwide's books outside the U.S., please contact our International Sales department at 415-655-3200 or fax 415-655-3295.

For information on foreign language translations, please contact our Foreign & Subsidiary Rights department at 415-655-3021 or fax 415-655-3281.

For sales inquiries and special prices for bulk quantities, please contact our Sales department at 415-655-3200 or write to the address above.

For information on using IDG Books Worldwide's books in the classroom or for ordering examination copies, please contact our Educational Sales department at 800-434-2086 or fax 817-251-8174.

For press review copies, author interviews, or other publicity information, please contact our Public Relations department at 415-655-3000 or fax 415-655-3299.

For authorization to photocopy items for corporate, personal, or educational use, please contact Copyright Clearance Center, 222 Rosewood Drive, Danvers, MA 01923, or fax 508-750-4470.

About the Author

Alex Hiam (pronounced "**High**-am") has had marketing in his blood for many years. He has worked in the marketing departments of a Silicon Valley computer startup and a Fortune 100 company and helps countless clients write marketing plans and solve marketing and sales problems in industries as varied as restaurants, sporting goods, financial services, health care, transportation, and industrial chemicals.

Alex has also investigated customer service and product quality issues for The Conference Board and its all-star membership list, including companies like Corning, Ford, Whirlpool, IBM, and Procter & Gamble.

Alex's credentials include degrees from Harvard and U.C. Berkeley (where he earned an MBA in marketing and strategy), and he taught marketing and advertising as a visiting professor at the School of Management of the University of Massachusetts at Amherst for many semesters. He has authored more than a dozen books on marketing and related topics, including *The Portable MBA in Marketing* (a Fortune Book Club main selection), *The Vest-Pocket Marketer, The Entrepreneur's Complete Sourcebook, The Vest-Pocket CEO*, and *Closing the Quality Gap: Lessons from America's Leading Companies*.

Alex is currently facing a new marketing challenge in his own work. He founded Human Interactions Asessment & Management, a firm specializing in innovative products for trainers, consultants, human resource managers, and marketing/sales managers, and he is now working to build its product lines and establish it as a leading brand. The first two products are already out: *The Portable Conference on Change Management* and a training and planning line for negotiators called *Flex Style Negotiation* (both distributed by HRD Press of Pelham, Mass.). He intends to use *Marketing For Dummies* extensively as he undertakes this new career challenge!

You can reach Alex for professional inquiries at 413-253-3658.

ABOUT IDG BOOKS WORLDWIDE

Welcome to the world of IDG Books Worldwide.

IDG Books Worldwide, Inc., is a subsidiary of International Data Group, the world's largest publisher of computer-related information and the leading global provider of information services on information technology. IDG was founded more than 25 years ago and now employs more than 8,500 people worldwide. IDG publishes more than 275 computer publications in over 75 countries (see listing below). More than 60 million people read one or more IDG publications each month.

Launched in 1990, IDG Books Worldwide is today the #1 publisher of best-selling computer books in the United States. We are proud to have received eight awards from the Computer Press Association in recognition of editorial excellence and three from *Computer Currents'* First Annual Readers' Choice Awards. Our best-selling *...For Dummies*® series has more than 30 million copies in print with translations in 30 languages. IDG Books Worldwide, through a joint venture with IDG's Hi-Tech Beijing, became the first U.S. publisher to publish a computer book in the People's Republic of China. In record time, IDG Books Worldwide has become the first choice for millions of readers around the world who want to learn how to better manage their businesses.

Our mission is simple: Every one of our books is designed to bring extra value and skill-building instructions to the reader. Our books are written by experts who understand and care about our readers. The knowledge base of our editorial staff comes from years of experience in publishing, education, and journalism — experience we use to produce books for the '90s. In short, we care about books, so we attract the best people. We devote special attention to details such as audience, interior design, use of icons, and illustrations. And because we use an efficient process of authoring, editing, and desktop publishing our books electronically, we can spend more time ensuring superior content and spend less time on the technicalities of making books.

You can count on our commitment to deliver high-quality books at competitive prices on topics you want to read about. At IDG Books Worldwide, we continue in the IDG tradition of delivering quality for more than 25 years. You'll find no better book on a subject than one from IDG Books Worldwide.

John Kilcullen
CEO
IDG Books Worldwide, Inc.

Steven Berkowitz
President and Publisher
IDG Books Worldwide, Inc.

Eighth Annual Computer Press Awards ≥1992

Ninth Annual Computer Press Awards ≥1993

Tenth Annual Computer Press Awards ≥1994

Eleventh Annual Computer Press Awards ≥1995

IDG Books Worldwide, Inc., is a subsidiary of International Data Group, the world's largest publisher of computer-related information and the leading global provider of information services on information technology. International Data Group publishes over 275 computer publications in over 75 countries. Sixty million people read one or more International Data Group publications each month. International Data Group's publications include: **ARGENTINA:** Buyer's Guide, Computerworld Argentina, PC World Argentina; **AUSTRALIA:** Australian Macworld, Australian PC World, Australian Reseller News, Computerworld, IT Casebook, Network World, Publish, Webmaster; **AUSTRIA:** Computerwelt Osterreich, Networks Austria, PC Tip Austria; **BANGLADESH:** PC World Bangladesh; **BELARUS:** PC World Belarus; **BELGIUM:** Data News; **BRAZIL:** Annuário de Informática, Computerworld, Connections, Macworld, PC Player, PC World, Publish, Reseller News, Supergamepower; **BULGARIA:** Computerworld Bulgaria, Network World Bulgaria, PC & MacWorld Bulgaria; **CANADA:** CIO Canada, Client/Server World, ComputerWorld Canada, InfoWorld Canada, NetworkWorld Canada, WebWorld; **CHILE:** Computerworld Chile, PC World Chile; **COLOMBIA:** Computerworld Colombia, PC World Colombia; **COSTA RICA:** PC World Centro America; **THE CZECH AND SLOVAK REPUBLICS:** Computerworld Czechoslovakia, Macworld Czech Republic, PC World Czechoslovakia; **DENMARK:** Communications World Danmark, Computerworld Danmark, Macworld Danmark, PC World Danmark, Techworld Denmark; **DOMINICAN REPUBLIC:** PC World Republica Dominicana; **ECUADOR:** PC World Ecuador; **EGYPT:** Computerworld Middle East, PC World Middle East; **EL SALVADOR:** PC World Centro America; **FINLAND:** MikroPC, Tietoverkko, Tietoviikko; **FRANCE:** Distributique, Hebdo, Info PC, Le Monde Informatique, Macworld, Reseaux & Telecoms, WebMaster France; **GERMANY:** Computer Partner, Computerwoche, Computerwoche Extra, Computerwoche FOCUS, Global Online, Macwelt, PC Welt; **GREECE:** Amiga Computing, GamePro Greece, Multimedia World; **GUATEMALA:** PC World Centro America; **HONDURAS:** PC World Centro America; **HONG KONG:** Computerworld Hong Kong, PC World Hong Kong, Publish in Asia; **HUNGARY:** ABCD CD-ROM, Computerworld Szamitastechnika, Interneto online Magazine, PC World Hungary, PC-X Magazin Hungary; **ICELAND:** Tolvuheimur PC World Island; **INDIA:** Information Communications World, Information Systems Computerworld, PC World India, Publish in Asia; **INDONESIA:** InfoKomputer PC World, Komputek Computerworld, Publish in Asia; **IRELAND:** ComputerScope, PC Live!; **ISRAEL:** Macworld Israel, People & Computers/Computerworld; **ITALY:** Computerworld Italia, Macworld Italia, Networking Italia, PC World Italia; **JAPAN:** DTP World, Macworld Japan, Nikkei Personal Computing, OS/2 World Japan, SunWorld Japan, Windows NT World, Windows World Japan; **KENYA:** PC World East African; **KOREA:** Hi-Tech Information, Macworld Korea, PC World Korea; **MACEDONIA:** PC World Macedonia; **MALAYSIA:** Computerworld Malaysia, PC World Malaysia, Publish in Asia; **MALTA:** PC World Malta; **MEXICO:** Computerworld Mexico, PC World Mexico; **MYANMAR:** PC World Myanmar; **NETHERLANDS:** Computer! Totaal, LAN Internetworking Magazine, LAN World Buyers Guide, Macworld Netherlands, Net, WebWereld; **NEW ZEALAND:** Absolute Beginners Guide and Plain & Simple Series, Computer Buyer, Computer Industry Directory, Computerworld New Zealand, MTB, Network World, PC World New Zealand; **NICARAGUA:** PC World Centro America; **NORWAY:** Computerworld Norge, CW Rapport, Datamagasinet, Financial Rapport, Kursguide Norge, Macworld Norge, Multimediaworld Norge, PC World Ekspress Norge, PC World Nettverk, PC World Norge, PC World ProduktGuide Norge; **PAKISTAN:** Computerworld Pakistan; **PANAMA:** PC World Panama; **PEOPLE'S REPUBLIC OF CHINA:** China Computer Users, China Computerworld, China Infoworld, China Telecom World Weekly, Computer & Communication, Electronic Design China, Electronics Today, Electronics Weekly, Game Software, PC World China, Popular Computer Week, Software Weekly, Software World, Telecom World; **PERU:** Computerworld Peru, PC World Profesional Peru, PC World SoHo Peru; **PHILIPPINES:** Click!, Computerworld Philippines, PC World Philippines, Publish in Asia; **POLAND:** Computerworld Poland, Computerworld Special Report Poland, Cyber, Macworld Poland, Networld Poland, PC World Komputer; **PORTUGAL:** Cerebro/PC World, Computerworld/Correio Informático, Dealer World Portugal, Mac*In/PC*In Portugal, Multimedia World; **PUERTO RICO:** PC World Puerto Rico; **ROMANIA:** Computerworld Romania, PC World Romania, Telecom Romania; **RUSSIA:** Computerworld Russia, Mir PC, Publish, Seti; **SINGAPORE:** Computerworld Singapore, PC World Singapore, Publish in Asia; **SLOVENIA:** Monitor; **SOUTH AFRICA:** Computing SA, Network World SA, Software World SA; **SPAIN:** Communicaciones World España, Dealer World España, Macworld España, PC World España; **SRI LANKA:** Infolink PC World; **SWEDEN:** CAP&Design, Computer Sweden, Corporate Computing Sweden, Internetworld Sweden, it.branschen, Macworld Sweden, MaxiData Sweden, MikroDatorn, Natverk & Kommunikation, PC World Sweden, PCaktiv, Windows World Sweden; **SWITZERLAND:** Computerworld Schweiz, Macworld Schweiz, PCtip; **TAIWAN:** Computerworld Taiwan, Macworld Taiwan, NEW ViSiON/Publish, PC World Taiwan, Windows World Taiwan; **THAILAND:** Publish in Asia, Thai Computerworld; **TURKEY:** Computerworld Turkiye, Macworld Turkiye, Network World Turkiye, PC World Turkiye; **UKRAINE:** Computerworld Kiev, Multimedia World Ukraine, PC World Ukraine; **UNITED KINGDOM:** Acorn User UK, Amiga Action UK, Amiga Computing UK, Apple Talk UK, Computing, Macworld, Parents and Computers UK, PC Advisor, PC Home, PSX Pro, The WEB; **UNITED STATES:** Cable in the Classroom, CIO Magazine, Computerworld, DOS World, Federal Computer Week, GamePro Magazine, InfoWorld, I-Way, Macworld, Network World, PC Games, PC World, Publish, Video Event, THE WEB Magazine, and WebMaster; online webzines: JavaWorld, NetscapeWorld, and SunWorld Online; **URUGUAY:** InfoWorld Uruguay; **VENEZUELA:** Computerworld Venezuela, PC World Venezuela; and **VIETNAM:** PC World Vietnam. 3/24/97

Dedication

To Heather, Eliot, Paul, and Noelle.

Acknowledgments

Many thanks to the hundreds of clients and students who have shared my marketing journey. There is always something new to learn, and I have learned a great deal from all of you!

Thanks also to Happi Cramer of Word for Word for her help, and to Charles Schewe for his always-insightful advice. Also, to the many people and buisinesses who answered the call for help and contributed their information and ideas.

Finally, thanks to two remarkably efficient editors at IDG, Jennifer and Tammy, for their many improvements to the book.

Publisher's Acknowledgments

We're proud of this book; please send us your comments about it by using the IDG Books Worldwide Registration Card at the back of the book or by e-mailing us at feedback/dummies@idgbooks.com. Some of the people who helped bring this book to market include the following:

Acquisitions, Development, and Editorial

Project Editor: Jennifer Ehrlich

Acquisitions Editor: Mark Butler

Associate Permissions Editor:
Heather H. Dismore

Copy Editor: Tamara S. Castleman

Technical Editor: Jill Kapron

Editorial Manager: Leah P. Cameron

Editorial Assistants: Chris H. Collins,
Michael D. Sullivan

Production

Project Coordinator: Valery Bourke

Layout and Graphics: Linda M. Boyer,
Dominique DeFelice, Maridee V. Ennis,
Angela F. Hunckler, Todd Klemme,
Brent Savage, Michael A. Sullivan

Proofreaders: Jennifer K. Overmyer,
Joel K. Draper, Nancy Price,
Robert Springer, Karen York

Indexer: Joan Grissits

General and Administrative

IDG Books Worldwide, Inc.: John Kilcullen, CEO; Steven Berkowitz, President and Publisher

IDG Books Technology Publishing: Brenda McLaughlin, Senior Vice President and Group Publisher

Dummies Technology Press and Dummies Editorial: Diane Graves Steele, Vice President and Associate Publisher; Judith A. Taylor, Product Manager; Kristin A. Cocks, Editorial Director

Dummies Trade Press: Kathleen A. Welton, Vice President and Publisher; Stacy S. Collins, Marketing Manager

IDG Books Production for Dummies Press: Beth Jenkins, Production Director; Cindy L. Phipps, Supervisor of Project Coordination, Production Proofreading, and Indexing; Kathie S. Schutte, Supervisor of Page Layout; Shelley Lea, Supervisor of Graphics and Design; Debbie J. Gates, Production Systems Specialist; Tony Augsburger, Supervisor of Reprints and Bluelines; Leslie Popplewell, Media Archive Coordinator

Dummies Packaging and Book Design: Patti Sandez, Packaging Specialist; Lance Kayser, Packaging Assistant; Kavish + Kavish, Cover Design

◆

The publisher would like to give special thanks to Patrick J. McGovern,
without whom this book would not have been possible.

◆

Contents at a Glance

Cartoons at a Glance

By Rich Tennant • Fax: 508-546-7747 • E-mail: the5wave@tiac.net

page 71

page 109

page 366

page 7

page 339

Table of Contents

· ·

Introduction

$\bullet \bullet$

Marketing is the most important thing that you do in business today, even if your job title doesn't have the word *marketing* in it. This is true because marketing, in all its varied forms, is concerned with attracting customers, getting them to buy, and making sure that they are happy enough with their purchase that they come back for more. What could be more important? Ever try to run a business without customers?

I wrote this book to make sure that you have all the resources and expertise I could assemble, in order to do that critical job of marketing as well as you possibly can.

Sure, marketing can be a great deal of fun — it is, after all, the one aspect of business where creativity is not only tolerated but essential to success. In the long run, however, marketing is all about the bottom line. So while I had fun writing this book, and I hope you will enjoy using the book, I also take the subject matter very seriously. Any task that brings you to this book is vitally important, and I want to make sure that the advice you get here helps you perform that task well. While no book can hold all the answers, I believe this one has a great many answers of use to you and all other people who face the challenge of finding and satisfying customers.

About This Book

I anticipate three reactions to this book.

First, many readers will say, "I didn't know marketing was that complicated." Readers will quickly note that a great deal goes into marketing. Marketing encompasses several specialized fields — from advertising to public relations, from selling to strategy, from database management to packaging and product design. How can you possibly be expert at even half of these tasks? Yet at some point, anyone who wears a marketing cap has to handle problems in all of these areas and more. The task can be intimidating, but hopefully this book will help you cope with the need to be an instant expert in all the many facets of marketing.

Second, I hope that readers will say, "I didn't know marketing was that simple." As you read through this book or poke into specific chapters to solve your marketing problems, you find certain themes running throughout. These themes unify the thousands of details and help you be the instant expert you need to be. Some basic principles apply to and unify the specialties that make up the field of marketing. For example, how the *customer* sees your product and its competitors is the key to decisions in as diverse areas as advertising, personal selling, pricing, and planning. (In marketing, this is called *customer perception,* a term you'll use often.) So don't be surprised to find, as you soak up the principles and philosophy of marketing, that you can anticipate more and more of the details. Marketing ought to be based on common sense — at least if it's done well.

Third, I expect many readers to say, "This book doesn't look like other marketing books." I know that it doesn't. In fact, I put a great deal of trouble into rethinking the field and presenting it in a novel manner. When authors present marketing to readers, they generally follow a traditional approach based on what is taught in business schools. I've done so myself (in a book called *The Portable MBA in Marketing*). But that's not what the practitioner — the real-world person with a real-world task or problem — needs. A business school lecture won't help you very much if you have to actually *do* marketing, not just study it. In this book, you will find that every page is about how to do something important or solve some important problem. This book is strictly action-oriented, because that's how you have to be in the real world of marketing.

How This Book Is Organized

Marketing has two basic orientations — you need to employ one or the other of them depending upon the situation. The first is the *thinking orientation*, in which you attempt to gain insights that you can cash in on later through your actions. This orientation is the subject of Parts 1 and 5, so thinking-oriented activities bracket the rest of the book's parts. Starting and ending with the thinking orientation is good whenever you work on marketing tasks.

The second orientation you must adopt is the *action orientation,* in which your focus is on doing rather than thinking. Whether you're drafting a marketing plan, surveying your customers, or designing a new product or advertising campaign, marketers are responsible for getting a lot of things done. But how? Running into unfamiliar problems or unexpected pitfalls happens easily in even the most familiar tasks, so the rest of this book's parts give you blow-by-blow details of how to do a great many marketing jobs well.

Following is a detailed description of each of the book's four parts. See the Table of Contents for the topics of the chapters within each part.

Part I: Designing a Marketing Program

I want you to think about what a marketing program isn't. A marketing program is not the things in a marketing department budget, because that may not encompass all the ways in which your company reaches customers. Nor is a marketing program simply a collection of advertising, sales, and other marketing communications, because these need to be integrated with product and distribution strategies and a great deal more. And all the components of your marketing program need to be focused toward well-defined strategies. Finally, a marketing problem is not worth implementing unless it has some creative ideas to make it stand out from the competition. Read this part to make sure that your program hangs together and adds up to real impact in your marketplace.

Part II: Technical Skills You May Need

Marketers need to do a great deal of research, and they spend a lot of time communicating. This part gives you in-depth coverage of marketing research and marketing communication skills. Dip into this part when you encounter situations that require more research or communications skills than you currently posess. For example, you may encounter situations in which you need to do some research before finalizing an ad. Or situations in which you need some inspiration to help you improve the text of a letter to your customers.

Part III: Using the Components of a Marketing Program

The classic marketing program is said to have four components (the 4 Ps): product, price, placement, and promotions. These are the four areas from which you can draw your tactics. But in the real world of marketing, many more tools are actually available for your use. That's why this part of the book is the longest by far. In this part, you find advice on how to handle those four traditional elements, along with details about everything from the Internet to trade shows, from labeling to billboards, from point-of-purchase advertising to telemarketing. You have a host of options. Use them wisely and use as many of them as you can. You have a tough job convincing customers to choose your products over others, so I recommend approaching the task with the largest toolbox you can carry!

Part IV: The Part of Tens

The Part of Tens is a traditional element of ...*For Dummies* books, and at first I thought it was silly. But as I began to write this part, I realized that this format is perfect for communicating all sorts of essential wisdom that doesn't fit easily into the other parts. I recommend you look at this stuff first unless you are in a great hurry to solve some pressing problem, because this part encapsulates much of the essential philosophy and strategies of good marketing practice. And reading this part will also help you avoid many silly errors that other people keep making.

Icons Used in This Book

Look for these symbols to help you find valuable stuff throughout the text:

Marketing is rapidly going online. This signpost indicates advice or examples concerning how to take advantage of the Internet.

This icon flags specific advice you can try out in your marketing program right away. The icon uses a dollar sign for the filament of the light bulb because the acid test of any great ideas in business is whether it can make you some money.

I didn't include anything technical for its own sake, but sometimes details are present that you do need to worry about, like how to project the response rate on a special offer or mailing. So when I discuss technical matters, this icon flags them.

Running into trouble in marketing is easy because so many mines are just waiting to be stepped on. That's why I've marked them all with this symbol.

All marketing is real world, but this icon means that you will find an actual example of something that worked (or didn't work!) in the real world for another marketer.

Sometimes the right perspective on a problem is essential to success. This icon flags a brief discussion of how to think about the task at hand. Often a basic principle of marketing pops up at this icon to help you handle important decisions.

In marketing, lone rangers don't last long. Successful marketers use a great many supporting services, and often bring in ad agencies, research firms, package designers, retail display designers, publicists, and many other specialists. You can't do it all. Sometimes the best advice I can give you is to pick up your phone and make a call. And this icon marks a spot where I give you some helpful names and numbers.

Where to Go from Here

Anything *bugging* you? Any problems you can't solve? Jobs you don't want to tackle or can't seem to finish? Puzzles you wish you could solve — like why sales are falling in that territory or what to do about an aggressive competitor? A host of marketing issues are always at hand. Grab one off the burner (doesn't matter which one) and use the table of contents, index, or your browsing skills to start working on the problem right away. Odds are that you'll be able to cross one more thing off your to-do list in short order.

Having trouble thinking of a solution for a pressing marketing problem? Don't worry. If you start reading — from the front or absolutely anywhere that catches your eye — you will find yourself reaching for a pad and pen in a hurry. One way or the other, I know that this book will get you into high gear as soon as you dig into it. What are you waiting for? Time to get started!

Part I
Designing a
Marketing Program

The 5th Wave   By Rich Tennant

MARKETING SIGNAGE GUIDELINES

RIGHT
OPHTHALMOLOGIST

WRONG
INTERNIST

RIGHT
Lawyer

RIGHT
TOY STORE

WRONG
TOY FACTORY

WRONG
Marriage Counselor

In this part . . .

Marketing consists of so many different activities — sales, advertising, customer service, the product itself, your pricing and discounts, reputation, strategies, and much, much more. Which of the many elements of marketing are the key to your success? Which should you emphasize? How can you best coordinate all the many elements of marketing into a coherent, powerful, and profitable presence in the marketplace?

If you don't know what the keys to marketing success are for your product and market, don't be alarmed. Nobody does — at least not until they do the kind of careful analysis this part of the book presents.

Oh, and one other thing. Analytical thinking, while key, is not enough. It must be followed by that all-important creative thinking that is needed to add unique touches that make your marketing effort stand out favorably in customers' minds. It don't mean a thing if it ain't got that swing!

Chapter 1

Why You Need a Marketing Program

*Y*ou already know that marketing presents some difficult and puzzling tasks. Otherwise, you probably wouldn't have bought this book. And you will certainly find appropriate answers here because this book is all about the *practice,* not the philosophy, of marketing. If you want (and your schedule demands), you can jump right into the chapter that solves your current problem. That's fine. But you also need to know that a more logical and organized approach to marketing pays off in the long run, and often the short run, too.

This chapter focuses on how to do marketing in an organized, programmatic manner. As a marketer, you face so many key decisions, so many minute details, so many separate budget items — and too many of these are beyond the direct control of the marketing department in most organizations. The result of all this fragmentation is that marketing efforts spring up with every good idea or customer demand, rather like rabbits. In most organizations, hundreds of marketing rabbits are running around, each one in a slightly different direction from any other. As a result, I am afraid the reality is that *marketing is the least efficient and effective of all the major business functions.*

Part of marketing's difficulty lies in the little-recognized fact that most other business functions are, in a sense, part of marketing. That's because everything that touches the customer is marketing. The obvious points of customer contact — like products and advertisements — are easier for marketing to control. But less obvious points of contact — like bills, warranties, service, even the appearance of employees and the ease with which packaging can be opened and discarded — also make up part of the complex marketing picture. These hidden marketing functions make the marketing job even tougher.

Of course, marketers do have the hardest job to start with — they have to find customers and motivate them to buy and rebuy the product. That's not easy! Still, no good reason exists for marketing to operate on the edge of total chaos. Doing the job better is not that hard, really.

All you need is a competent *marketing program*. A marketing program is any coordinated effort to communicate with and persuade customers to purchase, use, and repurchase your product through multiple points of influence.

Whether developed in the context of a formal, month-long planning process, or just sketched on the back of a napkin, the marketing program is guaranteed to help get all those rabbits pulling in the same direction. A good marketing program will increase the bottom-line returns of all your marketing efforts, reveal waste and inefficiencies, and help you achieve breakthrough results. Really! So please, *please,* find the time to read and apply this chapter as soon as you can.

How to Think about Marketing

In marketing, you must plan and coordinate a great many activities in order to reach customers and compel them to purchase, use, and repurchase your product. Even the smallest firms typically have more than a dozen such activities. In mid-sized and large firms, the number is in the hundreds or thousands.

Many separate activities have an impact on customers and their behavior. Some of these activities are actually performed by people with "marketing" in their titles, but many are not. Some of these people are not even on the payroll, because subcontracting of marketing tasks is commonplace.

The marketer's most powerful source of leverage is an appropriate marketing program that coordinates and focuses all the diverse activities of marketing. You can call the development of a program planning, management, vision, or just plain common sense. (And indeed, it goes by different names in different organizations.) Call it what you like, just so long as you *do* it! Unless you think about what marketing goals have to be accomplished and how best to accomplish them, all those many so-called marketing activities won't add up to anything. They certainly won't come together into the coordinated program needed to sway customer purchase decisions in your direction. That is why this book starts with the essentials of creating a marketing program.

You may find this approach surprising, because starting from the "other end" of marketing — the tactics like ads, coupons, and events that occupy the majority of this book — is commonplace.

Starting at the wrong place is why marketing activities often don't add up to a program. The typical marketing activities lack the focus, coordination, and common purpose of a good marketing program. They all pull in different directions, and nothing much is accomplished when the dust settles — except to burn through a budget without producing a decent return.

The typical approach to program development

Take a look at a typical example of program development. Mary Johnson has just been promoted to Marketing Manager for her division of a medium-sized computer software firm. Her boss tells her to put together a plan and budget for marketing their software. (The software is used in bookkeeping by other companies, so Mary needs to convince corporate accountants to purchase the product and its upgrades.)

Mary worked in product development as a Quality Control Officer for two years, and before that she spent a year in sales, calling on big corporate accounts. Quality and sales are two important aspects of marketing. That's why she got the Marketing Manager job. But she has never designed a marketing program before. How well does she do?

Unfortunately, she blows it big time by submitting a budget based on last year's, with just a few modifications. (This is a big mistake, as I show later, because last year's budget was not based on a coherent marketing program. Design a program first, and then write the budget for it!) But who can blame Mary? With only two weeks to submit her budget, she has to scramble to figure out what to do. She starts by looking at last year's budgets (always a mistake unless you are sure that *they* were good!). The budget Mary sees is shown in Table 1-1.

Table 1-1	Marketing Budget
Item	*Cost*
Literature and Brochures for Sales Force	$8,300.00
Executive Entertainment (travel, meals, golf events)	$36,500.00
Advertising (in trade magazines, through AdPro Agency)	$54,769.00
Premium Items (mugs, hats, golf shirts)	$7,454.50
Trade Shows (booths and free samples, three computer shows)	$48,060.00

The budget looks pretty detailed to Mary (although as you'll see, it really needs to be taken to another level of detail). But how should it be modified for next year? She swings by the Sales Manager's office — he's her mentor at the firm, and the person who first hired her. He says, "I'll be honest with you, Mary. Marketing has been tying our hands for years. We need twice that budget for premium items. My sales force usually runs out of gifts half-way through the year. And we ought to replace all our literature because we're introducing a new series of upgrades for all our products next spring. That will probably cost $20,000 if we use four-color printing throughout."

"Are these expenses really necessary?" Mary asks.

"I guarantee we'll sell more if you get those in the budget," her old boss tells her. "And if you don't, well, let's just say everyone will know why we didn't make our sales projections."

"But where will the money come from? I doubt the President will authorize a doubling of the marketing budget."

"That's easy," the Sales Manager told her. "Just cut the unnecessary expenses. Like all that corporate entertainment. The executives just use that as a slush fund. They don't really do any selling, they just hang out at golf clubs with the executives of our client companies, *after* the sales force has made the sale. Those trade shows are a waste, too. Our customers are accountants; they don't go to computer trade shows! But our programmers like to do a few shows, because they can network with their buddies from the computer industry."

If you've ever worked in a company with more than one employee, I think you can guess where this story is going. We're talking politics. By the time Mary is done, she will have heard from all the stakeholders in her budget — except her customers. And depending on who has the most influence, she may bump some of the items up by 5 or 10 percent. If she is lucky, her boss will have enough clout to keep the other items from being cut by the same amount. But the end result will inevitably be remarkably like last year's budget, and it won't have any clear customer-driven rationale. (By the way, if you're thinking, *hey, Mary could never do a customer survey in two weeks,* well, you're not thinking like a marketer yet. It takes only two minutes to pick up the phone and dial up a customer.)

That means that the program, if you can call it a program, will be much like last year's. Just like most companies' marketing budgets generally look alike from year to year (they do, *don't* they?).

Analyzing last year's budget

Think about Mary's program for a minute (you can pull out your last marketing budget and subject it to the same analysis if you have the stomach for it!). What is the focus of this program as revealed by the budget? If you go by the numbers, the program emphasizes display ads in trade magazines. Next in importance is the trade shows, followed by executive entertainment. In order of importance, the list looks like the following:

✔ Print ads in trade magazines

✔ Booths at computer industry trade shows

✔ Executive entertainment of clients (especially on golf courses)

Based on these budget priorities, the marketing department has been using a *marketing mix* (the combination of marketing actions that make up a program) that emphasizes advertising, trade shows, and corporate entertainment.

So the real question is (or should be), "Will this mix of marketing activities do the trick?" Will the mix generate new sales, retain old customers, and fuel the company's growth?

It may *if* you believe two things:

✔ Accountants will see the ads in their magazines, or visit the company's booth at a trade show, and will decide to license the software as a result.

✔ Current customers will buy upgrades, and not defect to competitors, *because of* the executive entertainment.

(I focus on these two assumptions because the key things any program needs to do in order to generate increased sales are *to draw in new customers* and *to retain customers by generating repeat business*. See Figure 1-1.)

But Mary, from the preceding example, is not sure about these assumptions. She doesn't have much information about what motivates her prospective and current customers. Nor will she base a decision on any insights into their behavior. She thinks she just doesn't have the time or data needed to look at this program from the customer's perspective.

We don't have any information about her customers' behavior either, but we can make some educated guesses (as Mary would have had she a little more experience in marketing). Common sense tells us that the assumptions are flawed — and that the program does not focus on the key activities driving customer behavior.

This company depends on *face-to-face selling*. The sales force goes out to write orders and maintain relationships, as Mary knows from her first job. But that activity is not even in the marketing department's budget.

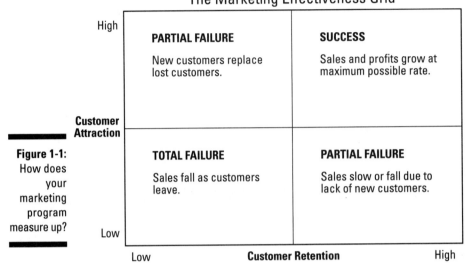

The Marketing Effectiveness Grid

And you can assume that another off-budget item is key to the company's sales: *new product development.* That's a reality in every software company, and the new product launch is important at Mary's company. If a company doesn't keep improving its products, its competitors will introduce new features and steal the old customers away.

All repurchase decisions in *any* market are driven largely by the *user's experience with the product.* If you use software to do accounting every day, as Mary's customers do, you are likely to form a strong opinion about that software. You will find the software irritating because it won't let you do X. Or you'll think that the software is great because it automates Y, which used to take a week to do by hand. The software will either be easy or hard to use, and the user's manuals and customer support service will either be helpful or unhelpful. The many hours of contact between the user and the product are the third key to sales success or failure for Mary's company.

The shift from a budget focus to an influence point focus

Mary's marketing budget doesn't have line items for sales, product development, and customer support. Those activities are handled by different departments — departments that probably have much bigger budgets than hers. So Mary's hands are tied by the departmental structure of her firm. Her budget, whatever it looks like, will only affect the secondary activities that support these three keys to marketing success. As Marketing Director, she has a ringside seat — but she isn't in the ring. That means her budget is not a good basis for planning the marketing program — any more than your marketing department's budget is.

Who *is* in the marketing ring? Well, certainly the people who develop new products. Don't forget the sales force, the people who write the user's manuals, the people who provide telephone and on-site customer support, and perhaps those executives who do all that entertaining. You may also have to include the programmers who crawl out of their shells a few times a year to go to computer industry trade shows. All these are potential points of contact with current or prospective customers. Each is, therefore, a potential *influence point* (defined as a point of potential contact with customers that can be used to communicate and persuade).

Ads in trade magazines are also influence points, as are those gifts handed out to customers. But some influence points are more important than others, so any marketing program needs to focus on the key, or *primary,* influence points and guide their usage throughout the year. If that means coordinating with other departments, then *coordination must be included as a key element of the program.*

Performing an Influence Points Analysis

I recommend using what I call an *Influence Points Analysis* as a start to any effort to develop or modify a marketing program. An Influence Points Analysis is, very simply put, a listing of all the ways in which the customer and company interact. You need this list to design a program, because the program's purpose is to use all these points of contact in a coordinated, strategic manner to get and retain customers. The list will help you see the full marketing process (it's always a bigger picture than we expect!) and thereby avoid the pitfalls into which Mary and her associates have fallen. The analysis ensures that you understand what your marketing program really does — and does not — consist of, down on the ground where it touches customers. Following are instructions for constructing an Influence Points Analysis.

The influence points worksheet

Fill in this worksheet for each type of customer you have.

(Yes, I do mean that you should fill out a separate worksheet for each customer type, or grouping. For example, if you sell toys to retail toy stores, and through them to children and parents, then you need a list for the stores, and a second one for the end customers. You also need a separate marketing program for each as well.) First write two lists, as follows:

Primary Influence Points

(List the two to five key points of contact with customers)

1. _____
2. _____
3. _____
4. _____
5. _____

Secondary Influence Points

(List all the other, less important types of contact or exposure be-tween customer and company. For example, while a monthly bill is not a major point of contact, it *is* a point of contact. List it here.)

1. _____
2. _____
3. _____
4. _____
5. _____
6. _____
7. _____
8. _____
9. _____
10. _____

(or more)

Second, add two columns on the right-hand side of your page, the first labeled "Control" and the second labeled "Estimated Budget."

Who controls each influence point?

In the Control column, write in the name of the person or department who controls each of the points of contact. If dual control exists, then enter both names. Doing so allows you to see how important coordination is going to be to any program. If control of key contact points is beyond your own department, then you need to get involvement from other departments in the initial stages of program development — not just in haggling over budgets. And if considerable coordination is required, you better budget appropriate time and money to generating cooperation. You need to plan some meetings or team development activities, plus consider networking your computers with those of other departments. And plenty of travel is a must if geographic barriers exist.

You may need months, not weeks, and you may spend a great deal in travel, meeting time, presentations, and persuasion to convince various managers to support your plan. Coordination is usually a vital marketing function, but most marketing departments fail to plan or budget for it.

How much is spent — by everyone — on each influence point?

In the Estimated Budget column, enter the total costs associated with each influence point over the last year. This task is not easy, because budgets and expense reports are not organized in the same way. You will have to guesstimate how much of which line items really applies to a point of contact. But when you have done so, you can finally step back and look at the reality of your firm's previous marketing program. You will be able to see roughly where you invested in those influence points where marketing has a chance to sway purchase decisions.

Going back to Mary's case, say that she filled in the first line with the Primary Influence Point: "Sales calls on prospects (accountants who might buy our software)." Under Control, she listed Sales Manager, because the marketing department has very little control over this point of contact.

To fill in the Estimated Budget column, Mary had to study the Sales Force's records. She decided that about one fifth of all sales calls were on prospects — the rest were made on existing customers. So she broke out one fifth of the direct costs of the sales force to put in this column. To that she added a portion of the marketing department's expenditures on product literature, brochures, and premium items. She also learned that executives rarely entertain prospects — they usually get to know client-company executives after the sales force makes an initial sale. So she didn't put any of the executive entertainment budget in this category. Nor did she put anything from the trade show budget here, because she learned that the software people run the booths, and rarely send any leads to the sales force. However, she *did* include a small portion of the advertising budget here, because some of the ads generated customer inquiries, which the sales force used to set up appointments.

When she added everything up, she had the following items in the Estimated Budget column for *sales calls on prospects:*

- ✔ Sales force expense: $115,000

- ✔ Literature and brochures: $3,000

- ✔ Premium items (gifts): $1,000

- ✔ Print ads generating sales leads: $8,000

- ✔ Total: $127,000

This breaks down to be about 17 percent of the entire program.

That is a fair estimate of the past year's expenditures on getting in front of accountants at companies and trying to convince them to make a first-time purchase. Note that Mary could not have understood this key aspect of her company's marketing program without performing the influence points analysis. Her department's budgets and records fail to reveal the true characteristics of the existing marketing program — and so do yours, so please don't rely on them alone!

Asking questions about your marketing program

Armed with this information and similar insights into what the company actually does, *from a customer's point of view,* Mary is in a far better position to think about next year's marketing program. She can ask intelligent questions about her program — and you can, too:

- ✔ Does my company emphasize acquiring new customers to the extent that it should, or is 17 percent of our program budget too little?

- ✔ Does my company emphasize keeping old customers to the extent we should? (Mary can also calculate the spending on this point by using the same sort of analysis.)

- ✔ Does my company coordinate its activities at each key influence point, or do some conflict with others?

- ✔ Does my company waste time and money on noncritical activities and secondary influence points?

- ✔ Do the messages communicated at different Influence Points add up to a coordinated overall message to my company's customers?

- ✔ Is my company more effective or efficient at handling some Influence Points than others?

- ✔ Are my company's competitors handling Influence Points differently? (Are competitors using clearer, different, or louder messages?)

- ✔ What message is my company communicating to the customer through these Influence Points — and are these the messages that we want and need to communicate?

- ✔ Does my company touch the right customers and prospects, at the right times, and often enough?

✔ Is my company overlooking some potential Influence Points it could start to use?

✔ Do uncontrolled influence points exist (like negative word of mouth or the misrepresentations of competing salespeople)? If so, how can my company increase its control over them?

These powerful questions are highly likely to generate insights that will improve the practice of marketing. But asking questions is not enough. You also need to come up with good answers! That takes a bit more work — in fact, the entire rest of this book addresses ways of answering these questions. You need to think about who you target, what they want and need, and lots of other things that are covered in upcoming chapters. However, if you don't start out with intelligent questions, you certainly will not have an intelligent marketing program. So the cornerstone of any marketing decision must be an assessment of current Influence Points. Know what they are. Know what your firm does at each of these points. Try to find out how customers react to what you do at these points, and why. Put some hard thought into answering these questions.

Good Marketing Turns Your Company Inside Out

If you read the preceding sections, you may have wondered whether you'd fallen into the book *Accounting For Dummies* (IDG Books Worldwide, Inc.) by accident. Yes, you *are* playing around with budget numbers, and you are putting them in a big table. You can even use a spreadsheet program for this analysis. But this work is definitely *not* accounting. Any accountant worth his or her salt would cringe at the mere sight of an Influence Points Worksheet. This worksheet is filled with guesstimates and it tears a company's neat cost categories and department structures apart.

You have to tear things apart because you are turning your company inside out. The customer sees the company from the outside in, but all your management information, including last year's marketing budget, portrays the company from the inside out. And you can't even *think* about thinking about marketing until you can see your firm from the customer's perspective.

Marketing is . . .

Peter Drucker, one of few justly famous management gurus, has defined marketing as *the whole firm, taken from the customer's point of view*. This definition is powerful, because it reminds you that your view from the inside is likely to be very different from the customer's view. And who cares what you see? The success of any business comes down to what customers do, and they can only act based on what *they* see. That's why some people in marketing and advertising say, "Perception is everything." However the *customer* perceives your brand name and product, what it is, and what they will make it. If they see a product as better and cheaper, it's a winner. If not, the product's not — regardless of what those reports from Engineering tell you.

How do you see through the customer's eyes? The standard answers involve massive surveys, large piles of computerized analysis, and crashingly dull debriefings featuring dozens of almost-identical pie charts. You *may* want to do some survey work — but not now. Not until you've turned your firm inside out with the simple exercise detailed in the preceding sections. This exercise is the first and best step to understanding the customer's point of view.

To the customer, the only things that matter are the Influence Points. These are the times when the customer interacts in some way with your people, your product, or information about your people and product. So these Influence Points are the one and only way you can affect customer perception and action. Everything in marketing boils down to these simple interactions. And how the customer experiences these interactions *is* the customer's point of view.

What marketing does

Marketing's purpose is *to reach customers and compel them to purchase, use, and repurchase your product.* This task is difficult, because customers usually couldn't care less about you and your company. All they care about is their own needs and wants — the selfish brutes! — and somehow you have to convince them that buying, using, and repurchasing your product is in *their* best interest. You won't convince significant numbers of customers that these facts are true of your product or service, unless they really are.

What marketing can't do

At best, marketing can convince people of an obvious truth. At worst, it often fails to even accomplish this feat. Marketing certainly does not have the power to make lies come true.

Purchase behaviors are difficult to influence, even when you have a well-designed marketing program, one that uses powerful Influence Points and uses them well. You need to enter into any marketing project or decision with a proper sense of humility. Consumers have their own priorities and opinions. In general, they are deeply suspicious of the marketer's intentions. They know that marketers want to make the sale and that the sale may not be in the *customers'* best interests. Even if your company sells a good, service, or other product that is truly the best thing since sliced bread, so many other charlatans are out there muddying the water that getting a nibble will still be tough.

Don't expect to solve your company's problems through your marketing program. If the product is flawed from the customer's perspective, then the best thing you can do as a marketer is to present the evidence and encourage your company to improve the product. Marketing can't make a dog win a horse race, so don't let others in your company try to tell you otherwise.

The Principles of Real-World Marketing

Because of our inside-out viewpoint, marketers are different from everyone else in an organization. Marketers have to be different or else their companies would fail miserably in its efforts to develop and market anything of value to customers.

To do good marketing, you need to adopt the marketer's unique perspective on business. Marketers march to a different drummer — the customer. Keeping the beat isn't hard, as long as you recognize certain essential truths. I hesitate to call these the principles of marketing, because that term means something different in the marketing classroom. Suffice it to say that the following sections detail the principles of *real-world* marketing.

Principle 1: Your customers aren't listening to you

Remember, you are far more eager to make sales than most customers are to make purchases. Most of the time, customers couldn't care less about you and your products. The customer is usually a disinterested participant in your marketing program. You must communicate with and motivate people who are very busy thinking about anything *but* your message. That's why marketing is so complicated. That's why this book has so many chapters on things like point-of-purchase sales, special events, and electronic relationships — things you'd rather not have to worry about but are a necessary evil when you have to get a point across to someone who isn't paying any attention.

The few exceptions to this rule involve situations in which the customer is an eager buyer with an urgent problem that needs solving. In this case, it's a lucky day for the marketer! All you have to do is get your message in front of the eager customer and the message will be lapped right up. For example, letting prospects know about an appealing job offer is pretty easy, because customers will go to great pains to search for your advertisement. (As a result, job ads are extremely efficient and cost-effective compared to other sorts of advertising.) But alas, the exceptions are few and far between. In general, you can assume the customer is an unwilling participant in your marketing program.

Principle 2: Everybody else is shouting at your customers, too

The other communication problem you have is that many marketers are competing for those inattentive customers' eyes, ears, and hearts. The average consumer is exposed to thousands of marketing messages every day (including 1,500 ads alone on average through TV, radio, outdoor, and print media). The consumer fails even to notice most of them. Of the messages he or she notices, most are forgotten right away, and only a few manage to scratch the surface of consciousness.

All these ads create a great deal of background noise. To communicate, you have to overcome this noise, which means that you have to be louder (by spending more money), or more appealing (by communicating better), or more clever (by finding novel communication strategies and channels).

The problem of noise combines with the lack of attention on the part of the customer to make marketing communications more difficult than any other form of communication, except perhaps efforts to communicate with other species. In fact, I think I'd *rather* have the job of teaching a chimpanzee to use sign language than the job of convincing millions of consumers to switch their laundry detergent.

Principle 3: The rest of your organization thinks that you're crazy

Remember, your entire firm (if you work in one) is organized and focused in the opposite direction from your customers, and you are the only person on the payroll who can possibly see things from the customers' perspective. (Even you will have difficulty.) You are always working against the grain. Be patient, but be persistent. You have to champion the customer viewpoint and build coalitions of customer-oriented fellow employees in order to get the organization to back and implement a good marketing program.

Principle 4: You can't execute your program without the rest of your organization

As a marketer, you don't control most of the Influence Points where customer behavior can be swayed in your favor. You need to build bridges to other functions and departments within your own firm, and often to other firms as well. But because others often fail to grasp the marketing perspective, they may resist your initial efforts at outreach (see Principle 3). Be persistent — you can't do it without them! Too many marketers take the Lone Ranger path, only to find it's a dead end. Outreach needs to be a constant part of your work. Marketers cannot succeed unless they are expert networkers and coalition-builders.

Principle 5: If you don't succeed, you're dead meat (but so is the rest of your organization)

In spite of these insoluble problems, your entire firm is depending on you to produce a banner year! Without customers, no business can last longer than it takes to padlock the doors. Your coworkers may think that you're crazy. They may block your access to key information and vital resources. They may insist that you cut the budget by 20 percent. They may put your department in the old wing (too bad the air conditioning doesn't work). Still, your coworkers expect you to generate enough sales to cover their salaries *and* their end-of-year bonuses. The only bright spot is that they do wonder whether some vague relationship may exist between the success of your marketing program and the likelihood of their paycheck bouncing. It's not much, but you can build on it. Good luck.

Principle 6: The more you give, the more you get

If your customers don't care and your fellow employees think that you're weird, why should you be nice? Because being nice is the only way to succeed in marketing. Bob Carkhuff, president of HRD Press, explains it this way: "In marketing, you want to give away as much as possible without cutting your throat." You're walking a fine line sometimes, but the strategy works.

HRD Press publishes specialized training materials for employee training. This firm is innovating with software-based products because the software offers more flexibility for customers than books do. While some competitors charge for demo disks in the industry, HRD Press gives theirs away. In fact, they put as much of the program's function on the disk as they can without actually giving the entire program away. The idea is to allow potential customers to start using the product easily and for free. Without this generosity, the customers may not bother to look at the software.

Similarly, some small businesses have discovered the power of generous coupon offers to attract first-time customers. Myrna O'Reilly, president of Coupon Cash Saver, Inc. (which helps small businesses run coupon programs), explains that, "Local coupons go out to the neighborhood, so everyone who receives it knows the business and is very willing to try it if they get a coupon." If, that is, the offer is generous enough to get customers' attention. A common marketing error is to use coupons that are worth too little (I show you how to handle coupons correctly in Chapter 13). If you really need to cut the price in order to encourage customers to try your product, then make sure that your discount appears generous, not stingy. Even better — *give* the product away!

Principle 7: Being good is not enough — you have to be better

Marketing is a highly competitive field. You compete for shelf space, for customer attention, and for customer sales and loyalty. You struggle to achieve and maintain leadership by introducing new products, slashing prices, or adopting new technologies. You innovate in how you produce and distribute your product in order to make the product better and more convenient for your customers. You do all these things — even though they are difficult and costly — because your competitors will eat you for dinner if you don't. It's not that marketers want to keep reinventing their markets; they have no choice. That's competition.

Keep in mind that anything you did last year isn't good enough for this year or next. Your competitors are a moving target, and you had better move faster than they do. At the risk of mixing metaphors, I'm reminded of Will Rogers' famous comment that, "Even if you're on the right track, you'll get run over if you just sit there!" As a practical matter, that means marketers should be innovators at heart, constantly pushing their organizations toward new and better approaches. You may not like wearing this hat — and your associates in other functional areas definitely don't want you to wear it. But *somebody* has to make sure that employees get their bonus next year!

Principle 8: Marketing should be the most creative part of your business (but it probably isn't)

When has your marketing really succeeded — when has it managed to hit home runs? If you think back, you will discover a little-appreciated fact: Marketing is most successful when it is most creative. Nobody invents a new product, writes a captivating advertisement, or designs a clever event by following instructions or crunching numbers. Sure, this book is full of instructions and numbers, and they may be helpful to you. But they simply provide a starting point for your imagination. You have to come up with something unique and creative, and I can't do that for you.

If you don't believe me, think about this: In marketing (unlike any other business discipline), *everything you do has to be unique.* You can't run the same ad over and over, sell the same product year after year, or even use the same sales pitch on every client. The work marketing departments produce is constantly changing. Marketing is more art than science.

Okay, you accept that creativity is essential to marketing. But face it, the rest of the world has not quite caught up to you on this one. Most organizations try to run marketing as if marketers are just another bunch of bean counters. Most marketers received no formal training in creativity before taking on marketing positions. Marketers have to swim against the stream in order to do good, creative marketing. That's why I include a full chapter on how to be creative in marketing (see Chapter 4). This chapter could well be the most important one in the book.

Principle 9: Marketing should be the most logical part of your business (but it probably isn't)

I hate to be this way, but the truth is you can't succeed *just* by being creative in marketing. Great marketers are part artist and part scientist. While singing in the shower, they suddenly come up with a brilliant insight into what their customers need, and scrawl it in lipstick on the bathroom mirror in order to remember. Then they don a sober business suit, slip in the back door of the office building, and set to work to test their insights through customer surveys, test markets, sales projections, measurements of price sensitivity, and the like. And so must you. You must learn to alternate between being a wild-eyed visionary and a pig-headed number-cruncher. You have to become a marketing Minotaur: with the head of a scientist on top of the body of an artist. You may look a little funny, but at least you'll be fabulously successful.

Principle 10: Everything is marketing

I'm not empire building, I'm just stating a simple fact. Everything your company does is marketing, in the sense that everything has the potential to influence customers and either increase or hurt sales. Yet the marketing department or function is often one of the smallest in a company. And when entrepreneurs balance multiple roles, the marketing hat is often worn the least. That means most companies underutilize their marketing resources. They don't see many opportunities to touch their customers. And so you, as a marketer, can make great gains just by putting unused levers to work.

Here's a very simple (but cheap and powerful) example of how to take advantage of the principle that everything is marketing. If you send out bills or statements by mail, they probably fall into the finance function, not marketing. Yet you can put them to work for marketing, too. First, make sure that the collection policies of your company are customer-friendly. Yes, you don't want to do business with deadbeats. But many companies make the mistake of treating all customers, even long-term loyal ones, like deadbeats the first time they miss a payment. This just chases them away. Second, think of ways of building loyalty or increasing sales through bill stuffers. A mini-catalog, a special offer, a contest or other sales promotion. All can be distributed in the regular mailings of your bills. See, everything *is* marketing, at least if you have the imagination to make it so!

What next for Eskimo Pies?

The Eskimo Pie brand name is one of the best known in the frozen novelties market, as the experts call it. This product once held a dominant market share and produced a delicious profit for its marketers at the Eskimo Pie Corporation and their satisfied shareholders.

However, Eskimo Pie made what many investors consider a series of marketing blunders, and the company is now struggling to regain its momentum. It decided to widen its product line by acquiring a soft-serve frozen yogurt company. It also added lowfat versions of its ice cream bars (the original, in case you don't know, is vanilla ice cream with a chocolate coating). Many of the company's faithful customers switched to competing high-fat, real-sugar bars when they couldn't find the traditional Eskimo Pies in the store any more. Apparently, many customers view ice cream bars as special treats, and they don't want to skimp on the fat and sugar for a special treat.

Add to this fact the problems that Eskimo Pie had with its packages and labels — oh, I didn't tell you about that! You see, somebody thought printing lots of packages (to get a cheaper price) was a clever idea, but then the labeling laws changed, and the company had to throw its inventory of packages away. . . .

You can be sure that the marketers at The Eskimo Pie Corporation are hard at work on a new marketing program.

Chapter 2

Basic Marketing Strategy: Find a Need and Fill It

*S*trategy is, to put it very simply, knowing *why*.

In marketing, becoming preoccupied with the "whats" is easy to do. So many "whats" exist. Should we offer coupons? Run print ads in magazines? Use free-standing inserts in the Sunday papers? Try a radio campaign? Maybe even TV? What about publicity? Or a point-of-purchase display? Maybe we should hire more salespeople or reps to call on wholesale accounts. Or lower our prices. Or raise our prices. Or change our image. Or add new products. Or trim the fat from our product line. Or acquire a competitor with a complementary product line. Or redesign our logo. And so it goes on and on. A truly endless variety of choices exist for the real-world marketer.

This embarrassment of riches can be confusing to say the least. When you have so many options, knowing where to focus your effort seems impossible. Unless you have a *strategy,* an organized idea for how to accomplish your goals.

With a strategy, everything becomes clear. Your program begins to fall into place naturally, almost on its own. Knowing how to use those many potential points of influence becomes increasingly obvious.

For example, your strategy may be to reposition your fast-food chain in the minds of teenagers and young adults to make it seem less child-oriented and more appropriate to adults. With this clear objective in mind, you will soon be redesigning your products to suit the target customer's taste. And you'll be developing a television ad campaign to run along with programs the target market watches — with ads that project a more sophisticated image to them. (Sound familiar? That's the strategy behind McDonald's introduction of the Arch Deluxe hamburger in 1996.)

And so this chapter and the next are musts. *You really do need a strategy —* and it probably isn't last year's strategy. Take some time now to think about your strategy. The payoff is clarity rather than chaos when you get to all those pesky little details of your marketing program!

Assessing Customer Needs

Do your customers need you? I mean *really* need you? Find you indispensable? Value their relationship with you so highly that leaving would be like losing a friend? Do they view your product as so wonderful that they can't wait to tell their friends about it? Do your customers dream about you at night?

I doubt it.

The truth is, most marketers cannot count on a high degree of customer loyalty. Most customers keep us marketers at arm's length. They know we can be replaced with another. They are fickle. They feel no obligation. In many cases, our target customer ignores us, refusing to buy at all, or even worse, choosing our competitors over us! How *could* they?

That's okay, there are plenty more customers where they came from. You just need to go find another one. Not! Far better is to build customer loyalty by making yourself more important to customers (this should be your first marketing strategy, regardless of what other strategies you adopt).

The fact is, for many businesses, finding a new customer costs more than keeping an old one. That's what S. Todd Burns, owner of six Time-It Lube stores in Shreveport, Louisiana, decided. (This business provides oil/lube/filter replacement services for automobiles.) And so he cut way back on advertising for new customers, and shifted his marketing program to things like a frequent user card with a $5 discount after four visits and the use of reminder notices mailed to past customers. Oh, and high-quality service, of course, so that doing business with Time-It Lube is a positive experience.

Customer retention is now at 90 percent, and his loyal customers also bring him new ones through positive word of mouth. (This story and others like it are covered in an excellent article called "Building Your Customer Portfolio" in the Dec. '96 *Nation's Business;* call the United States Chamber of Commerce at 202-463-5650 if you want to get a reprint.)

If you want your customers to love you, you have to take the first move — like Todd Burns did. You have to create a product so valuable to customers that you can make good money supplying them with that product. And if you want to grow your business, you have to find new customers who have a need you can satisfy. Or you have to dream up some great new product that customers will love.

It's all up to you, not the customer, because you have a bigger stake in the whole thing than they do. Your future success depends upon how well you can understand and meet customer needs. The customers' future success does not depend (usually) on whether or not they use your product.

So your first and most important strategic task is to think hard about what customers may need and want. Because if you can meet their needs and wants, and do it so well that they are pleasantly surprised and your competitors are disgusted, then your marketing story will be a happy one. If not, well, I hope you have some experience in another profession.

Understanding needs and wants

Someone once said that our wants are many, but our needs are few. And that saying contains considerable wisdom. You can probably count the basic needs of a human being on the fingers of both hands: food, shelter, love, achievement, respect, fun, and so forth. We have many and varied wants, but they can all be thought of as different ways of satisfying basic needs. I may want a good piece of pizza for lunch, whereas I wanted a sandwich yesterday. But both are expressions of my underlying needs for food and pleasure.

And while I do want a good piece of pizza, I don't have to have it. Pizza is not a fundamental need. I won't die without it. If I can't find pizza, I'll try something else. Customers are flexible about how they satisfy their wants — as long as they manage to take care of those basic underlying needs.

And so you, as a marketer, must think about your product offering on both levels. What basic needs does your product compete to satisfy — and how well does it satisfy them? Also, what specific want does your product satisfy, and how well does it compete with alternative ways of satisfying that want?

The nice thing about wants, as opposed to needs, is that they are so many and varied. You may say that our wants are unlimited. That gives marketers plenty of room for creativity. You can — and should — always think of new wants. Can you offer me a novel kind of lunch food — something other than the sandwiches, pizzas, salads, and take-out pasta dishes offered by the restaurants near my office? I am getting a bit sick of these old standbys, so something new and different may be nice. What's that? A rich bowl of stew with a fresh-baked roll? Or a sandwich on a croissant? Or how about the traditional Japanese worker's "box lunch," or some of those Jamaican meat pies in flaky pastries, or fish and chips in newspaper, like they serve in London take-out shops? Your imagination is the only limit when it comes to creating or modifying customer wants.

Another way to get creative about wants is to rethink the underlying needs that a product addresses. That sounds complicated, so I'll give you an example. Say the restaurants providing business lunches in my neighborhood all focus on two basic needs: the need for food and the need for pleasure. Thus, they all compete to produce good-tasting food that is pleasurable to eat. Now, I can compete on these two basic needs, just by finding a novel want that addresses them (see my brainstorming list above). However, I can also realign my product to address another basic need — say, the need for respect and social stimulation. Find a product that satisfies the need for respect and social stimulation at the same time that it satisfies the need for food, and you have a novel competitor in the local market. Have you thought of an alternative? I have — a lunch club. None are near my office, but perhaps one could be a success if it opened in the neighborhood. Or maybe we could combine the need for achievement, too, by featuring an educational speaker during the lunch hour. Or perhaps. . . .

The point is, you need to be both perceptive and creative when thinking about needs and wants (see Chapter 4 for more information on creativity's role in marketing). These are the basic building blocks of any successful marketing strategy. Unless you meet needs better, your current customer will defect and potential customers will pass you by.

Market Expansion Strategies

Market expansion is the most common strategy in marketing (that's just my opinion, but nobody's around to argue with me). And so I cover it first. The idea is disarmingly simple. Just pick some new territory and head out into it. Oh, and don't come back until you've struck gold.

The pioneering spirit may take you into a new geographic region — for example, Ben & Jerry's Ice Cream expanded from its Vermont roots into a national U.S. brand. It may take you from one industry to another — for example, Motorola is currently expanding into the personal computer market by creating a line of Macintosh-compatible computers that use

Apple's operating system. Or that pioneering spirit may take you into new countries — Motorola is emphasizing China and other Asian markets with its new line of Macintosh compatibles. The latter is perhaps the single most common expansion strategy today. If your company is not going global (or global already), then you will soon find that foreign competitors are bringing the global market to *you*. You may as well join the stampede.

Evaluating risk

When considering any market expansion, keep in mind that it entails *higher risk* than your current market. Why? Because you are an outsider, and because you lack the experience and knowledge of new markets that you have gained in your old markets. Also, you may get involved in new products as well as new markets in your expansion efforts — Motorola is learning how to make and market a new line of PCs at the same time it is learning how to operate in China.

Risk increases when you enter a *new market* — defined as new kinds of customers at any stage of your distribution channel. And so you should discount your first year's sales projections for a new market by some factor to reflect the degree of risk. How much? Nobody knows for sure. But a general rule is to cut back the sales projection by 20 to 50 percent, depending upon your judgment of *how* new the market is to you and your people.

Risk also increases when you experiment with *new products* — defined as anything you are not accustomed to making and marketing. You should also discount those sales projections by 20 to 50 percent if you are introducing a new product.

What if you are introducing a new product into a new market? You are running risks of two kinds, and your sales projections need to be cut back even further to reflect this risk. If you simply add up your two estimates of risk and then use their sum to discount your sales projection, you are at least recognizing the risks in some manner. And yes, I know that 50 percent plus 50 percent is 100 percent, leaving 0 percent of your sales projection. Sometimes a market expansion strategy is so risky that you really should not count on *any* revenues in the first year! Better to be conservative and live long enough to learn how to correctly handle the marketing than to overpromise and have the program killed before it can succeed.

Avoiding international complications

Bata Shoe Company markets products around the world. And its logo, a stylized drawing of three bells, provides a recognizable and appealing identity for its product wherever it's sold. Well, not quite wherever. You see, some Muslims think the logo looks a bit like the Arabic characters for Allah.

Fundamentalist Muslim demonstrators in Bangladesh took to the streets to voice their anger over this blasphemy when the logo appeared on imported sandals from Bata Shoe Company; fifty people were wounded during the protests. All because of a simple marketing oversight.

The sort of accident that Bata ran into could happen to anyone. It is common enough when operating across national and cultural boundaries, to be sure. Remember the publicity over the Nova, a Chevrolet sedan that had to be renamed in order to sell in Mexico because in Spanish *no va* means "no go"? But these sorts of problems are avoidable — with proper research and planning. All you need to do is assemble some discussion groups run by expert moderators (termed *focus groups in marketing research)* to evaluate your product — and ask the participants to think of all the negatives they can (and may as well collect positives, too, as these will come in handy for local advertising). You can find ad agencies and other experts in almost any local market you may choose to enter. Maybe your big New York- or London-based agency tells you they can handle Bangladesh from their offices in a nearby country. But the wise strategist still insists on using a local group, if only to test the product and its promotions for local acceptability!

Market Share Decisions

In this section, I show you how to think strategically about market share — and why doing so is very important. (I discuss *why* this is important soon, but here's a very brief synopsis: The bigger you are relative to competitors and the lower your costs are, the more impact you have on customer attitudes, and the more coverage you can achieve in your distribution.)

Market share is, very simply, your sales as a percentage of total sales for your product category. If you sell $2 million worth of shark teeth and the world market totals $20 million per year, then your share of the shark tooth market is 10 percent. It's that simple. Or is it?

Choosing a unit

What unit should you measure sales in? Good question. I don't care. Dollars, units, pesos, containers, or grams are fine, as long as you *use the same unit throughout.* (In other words, you can calculate your share of the North American market for fine hardwoods in board feet sold, so long as you measure both your sales and industry sales in board feet sold, and don't mix dollar sales or tons into the equation by mistake.) Just pick whatever seems to make sense for your product (read: how customers see it) and whatever you can get the data for most easily. If the government reports sales of your product by the bushel, then calculate your share in bushels.

Defining the "total market"

What is your product category? This may be the most important strategic question you'll ever ask or answer. If you sell Pop's Special Butter-n-Sugar Popcorn Kernels, then your category is obviously popcorn. But does the category include all forms of popcorn? Should you include only other brands of ready-to-pop kernels in jars? Or perhaps add Jiffypop-style products in which the packaging is also a pan for cooking the corn? What about microwaveable popcorn in a pouch? And what about prepopped popcorn in a bag, or sold fresh from a stand? Maybe you should even include popcorn-based candy. And how about rice cakes, because some of them now come in a popcorn flavor? In this market, as in many others, knowing where to draw the line is tough. And if you define your market more broadly, total market sales are, of course, higher, which makes your market share lower. So Pop's Popcorn may have a leading 25 percent market share by one calculation, but a sickly 1 percent share by another. Which is right?

Ask your customers. Are they choosing among all the popcorn options listed previously, or just some of them? What matters is *customer perception*: how the customer *sees* the category. So ask them what their purchase options are (see Chapter 6 if you want to conduct a formal study). Get a feel for how they view their choices. Then include all the likely or *close* choices in your definition of the market. For Pop's Popcorn, the choices probably include all the uncooked forms of the product, including microwaveable forms. But it does not include already-cooked products, many of which compete in consumers' minds more closely with other prepared snacks such as potato chips. In contrast, uncooked popcorn products are viewed as an activity, not just a snack. Drawing the line around them is safe when defining the total market for Pop's.

Wow. Bet you never imagined measuring market share was so complicated. But it is — even though the math is blindingly simple — because your judgment makes a big difference to the outcome, and the outcome makes a big difference to your marketing program.

Finding market size/growth data

To calculate market share, you need to estimate the total sales in your market. Doing so requires some research on your part. (Sorry — you can't avoid the research!) While you are at it, why not try to get some historical data — the sales in your market for the past five or ten years, for example? This information allows you to look at the growth rate of your market — which is an indicator of its future potential for you and your competitors.

Such data is most easily obtained from industry trade associations or from marketing research firms, many of which track sales by year in different product categories. Other sources of data on market size and trends are available from your friendly research librarian, who (at any major city or college library) will be able to direct you to sources such as *Standard and Poor's Industry Surveys*, *Directory of US and Canadian Marketing Surveys and Services*, and the trade magazines for the industry of your choice (which generally cover industry size and trends at least once a year). Trade magazines are often the best source for the business-to-business marketer. If you compete against public companies, also ask the librarian to dig up annual reports, which often break out sales into useful categories.

Such data is now increasingly available on the World Wide Web, too. For keyword searches, enter the name of your product combined with "sales figures" or "market size" and see what you can find.

I also recommend *Sales & Marketing Management* highly, especially for consumer-products marketers (Bill Communications is the publisher — call 800-821-6897 or, from outside the U.S., 609-786-9085). For a modest subscription or single-issue price, you can get more data than you care to crunch on what is called *Merchandise Line Sales* for all of the U.S., and also by individual metropolitan areas (along with a ranking of metro areas by size).

Merchandise lines are just groupings of closely related products, and your product fits into one of them. So, for example, a men's clothing company operating in the New England area can divide its sales by the total sales (in that region) of all Men's & Boy's Clothing to find out what its market share is regionally. If you decide the magazine's categories are too broad, then you may have to do your own research. Ask your distributors or retailers what their total sales are for your product category — some are happy to help out. Or if you must, hire a marketing research firm to survey customers in order to find out what percentage of their purchases are of your brand versus competitors. Larger companies generally do their own annual surveys in order to get market share data in a consistent and reliable form.

Using the napkin method for estimating market share

Does my advice in the preceding section sound too complicated? Here is a simpler method of estimating market size and share that can be done on the back of a napkin if you haven't the time or money for fancier approaches:

1. **Estimate the number of customers in your market (how many people in your country are likely to buy toothpaste, how many businesses in your city buy consulting services).**

2. **Estimate how much each buys a year, on average (six tubes, fifteen hours).**

   You can check your sales records, or ask some people what they do, to improve this estimate.

3. **Now, just multiply the two figures together to get the total size of the annual market, and then divide your sales into it to get your share.**

Setting market share goals

Market share gives you a simple way of seeing how you are doing relative to your competitors from period to period. If your share drops, you are losing. If your share grows, you are winning. It's that simple. And so most marketing programs are based at least partly on a *strategic market share goal,* such as "increase share from 5 percent to 7 percent by introducing a product upgrade and increasing our use of trial-stimulating special offers." And the *post mortem* on last year's program should always be based on an examination of what market share change accompanied it. (If you don't already do routine post mortems, or careful analyses of what happened and why it differed from your plans, you should!) If the past period's program doubled your market share, seriously consider replicating it! But if share stayed the same or fell, you're ready for something new.

Should you invest in growing your share?

In addition to its use as a benchmark, market share may also give you insights into the meaning of life. Well, at least into the future profitability of your product. Some people believe that market share is a good long-term predictor of profitability, arguing that market share leaders are more profitable and successful than other competitors. This belief is taken so seriously in some companies that low-share brands are dropped so as to focus spending on those brands with a chance at category leadership.

If this theory is correct, then you need to build market share aggressively. You should always work toward a portfolio of products that includes mostly share leaders. So should you run out and cut low-share products? Acquire high-share products? Boost quality and double ad spending on mid-share products to raise them to a high-share position? Such strategies sacrifice short-term profits in the hope of bigger long-term returns. But they are risky — and they depend to some degree on the validity of the market share theories. So look at the evidence before making a decision.

First, some good studies are showing that high-share businesses have higher returns on investment on average. The Strategic Planning Institute (a consulting firm in Cambridge, Massachusetts) has extensive data on market share and financial returns in its PIMS (Profit Impact of Marketing Study) database. I like their database because it looks at *business units* (divisions or subsidiaries in a single market) rather than whole companies, so it is more marketing oriented. And those business units with higher market shares have higher pretax ROIs (or *returns on investment;* the percentage yield or the amount earned as a percent of the amount invested). The relationship is roughly as shown in Table 2-1.

Table 2-1	Profiting from Market Share
Market Share (percent)	*ROI (percent)*
Less than 7	10
7+ to 15	16
15+ to 23	21
23+ to 38	23
38+ or more	33

Also impressive is some PIMS data suggesting that a gain in market share seems to lead to a corresponding gain in ROI (although the ROI gain is a half to a quarter as large on a percentage basis).

Oh, by the way, the reverse is also true — loss of share leads to loss of ROI. So a good strategy for many plans is *defend existing market share.* You can accomplish this by keeping your brand's image well polished (see Chapter 4), by innovating to keep your product fresh (see Chapter 14), and by designing good marketing programs (see Chapter 1 and — although I hate to make work for you — the entire rest of this book!).

Why these strong relationships between financial returns and market share? Higher-share businesses achieve some economies of scale, in everything from production to marketing. They may also have more knowledge and expertise than smaller competitors. They have greater bargaining power with suppliers, distributors, even with lenders. And, I think equally important, higher-share businesses often have greater visibility in the marketplace because of the larger scale of their marketing efforts. This point matters because of the *noise problem.* The noise problem is caused by all the noise we marketers make. The constant din of marketing messages creates background noise and you have to be pretty loud to cut through it.

Also, consumers are simply more likely to recognize and trust their brands just because they encounter marketing information about them more often. Frequent exposure strengthens attitudes toward your brand, and it's easier to accomplish when you are big relative to competitors.

And so, on the strength of all this information, I generally advise marketers to defend leading shares, and to try to grow their shares into leading positions. For example, if you are a strong third-place finisher in the share race, you should probably consider investing in a growth effort in order to leapfrog the #2 player and get within striking distance on the #1 slot.

But, *but,* I have to warn you that not all studies say the same thing about market share. A lively debate is currently going on in the academic journals on this topic. Professors sling statistics like overripe tomatoes, and occasionally marketers get hit in the crossfire. A recent (and well-done) study by Cathy Anterasian of consulting firm McKinsey and Co. in collaboration with John Graham of the University of California at Irvine concludes that "smaller businesses emphasizing stable operations and sacrificing market share during [an economic] boom tended to be more profitable over the multiyear cycle than businesses that maintained or gained market share."

In other words, if you are a small business, don't get so excited about market share that you allow its pursuit to destabilize your operations. Like all strategic goals, the pursuit of market share must be undertaken with caution, and with an eye to possible interactions with other goals. Don't do anything crazy, okay?

Chapter 3

Advanced Strategy: Define Your Message

· ·

In This Chapter

▶ Diagnosing your market's life cycle stage

▶ Selecting an appropriate strategy for your stage

▶ Defining your target market

▶ Writing the all-important positioning statement

▶ Answering the Four Questions of strategy selection

▶ Applying the Common Sense Test to your strategy

· ·

*T*he basic strategic question is "why?" That's the question I discuss in Chapter 2. Asking why leads you to define the customer needs your product addresses and to set some expansion and market share goals for your marketing effort.

But you still may not be ready to go on to the *whats* . . . all those important details of a well-developed marketing program. Asking one more strategic question first is often wise. That question is "How?" More specifically: "How is our company going to communicate our wonderful benefits to customers so that they will agree that we have the ultimate solution to their needs?"

By asking this question, you take your strategic thinking further toward the practical realities of a marketing program. And the answers do a great deal to help you to clearly *focus* your program.

The focus comes in large measure from knowing whom you are talking to — what your target market is and what motivates it. Focus is also improved by thinking about how you will generate the next sale. Will that sale come from spreading the good word about your product to customers who have yet to try it? From competing to steal customers from other companies? Or perhaps just reducing your *churn,* the rate at which old customers desert you, by building customer loyalty? I explore all three of these strategic alternatives in the following pages.

Finally, you must, absolutely *must,* summarize your strategic thinking in a positioning statement. A *positioning statement* is a clear description of who your customer is and how you want him or her to see your product. After all, strategy means nothing until real, live customers understand and appreciate it. And so the final step in turning strategy to action is to transfer all this good thinking from the marketer's head to the customer's. Your positioning statement tells you how to do that, and with it, you are ready to go forth and market.

Strategies Over the Life of the Product Category

Every *product category* — the general grouping of competitive products to which your product belongs (be it good, service, idea, or person), has a limited life. At least in theory — and usually in all-to-real reality — some new type of product comes along to displace the old. Once horse-drawn wagons handled inner-city transportation, and it was a wonderful thing to build and market wagons. But then some clever people dug canals, and barges displaced wagons. Then railroads displaced both. And then highways permitted trucks to displace railroads. Now air transport is taking some business from both railroads and trucking.

The result is a never-ending cycle of birth, growth, and decline, fueled by the endless inventiveness of competing businesses. And it produces product life cycles, in which categories of products arise, spread through the marketplace, then decline as replacements arise and begin their own life cycles.

The *product life cycle* is part of the academic canon. Every marketing student struggles through test questions on the product life cycle, and some even claim this knowledge helps them later on in their work. But many fail to grasp the practical implications of the product life cycle. I am, therefore, going to show you a more practical version of it than most marketing students have encountered on campus. Master my version, and I promise you will be able to choose between three powerful marketing strategies — which is a lot more valuable than just being ready for a multiple choice test!

The central idea in this model is that products can and do go through a *life cycle,* from birth — or *introduction* — all the way to eventual decline and withdrawal from the market. This cycle is the result of marketers' constant efforts to innovate and improve. Your company, like its competitors, introduces new products periodically. And eventually even the finest product tends to be replaced by something new and better.

Now, when I say "product" I don't mean your specific brand. Sales of your company's particular entrant in a product category have little effect on that product category's life cycle.

On the contrary, the product life cycle has a great deal to do with driving your particular brand's sales. So to use the life cycle model in the real world, you have to think big — to look at the *overall market,* as indicated by the sales of your brand and all its major competitors. For example, if you are in the inline roller-skate business, you need to plot the sales of your own brand of products, *plus* those of Bauer, Rollerblade (who introduced the product in the mid-80s), First Team Sports, and other competitors.

Interpreting and predicting market growth

Over a long period of time, sales (in dollars, units, or as a share of the potential market) will (a) follow a sigmoid growth curve (like a stretched-out, right-leaning S, or sigma, in shape), (b) level off to grow at the rate that the customer base grows, and then (c) fall off when a replacement product enters the market. Having trouble visualizing that? See the bottom half of Figure 3-1 for a picture of this life cycle curve. Because of this characteristic pattern, products generally go through a series of four life cycle stages.

As Figure 3-1 shows, when a market becomes saturated, more sales come from past users than new users. This trend slows sales growth. It also shifts the focus of advertising and other marketing initiatives.

The introduction phase

A plot of the inline roller-skate product's sales reveals a typical life cycle, with gradual increases during the early 1980s, accelerating to a steep growth rate in the late '80s and early '90s, followed by slower growth in the late '90s. Why? Because a new product concept like that one takes some time to gain momentum and catch on. That makes the introductory phase of the life cycle a tough one for marketers. You have to educate consumers about the advantages of the new product. And the more unfamiliar the product is, the more change the product demands from users, the longer this introductory phase takes.

The growth phase

After a while — often after 10 to 20 percent of the potential market is reached — the idea gains momentum. The life cycle enters its growth stage. Consumers accept the product, and begin to adopt it in greater numbers. Growth rates shoot upward. Unfortunately, the obvious success of the new product attracts more competitors — the number of competing products always grows during the growth phase, so the market leaders generally lose market share. But still, the rapid growth usually enriches all viable competitors and everybody is happy.

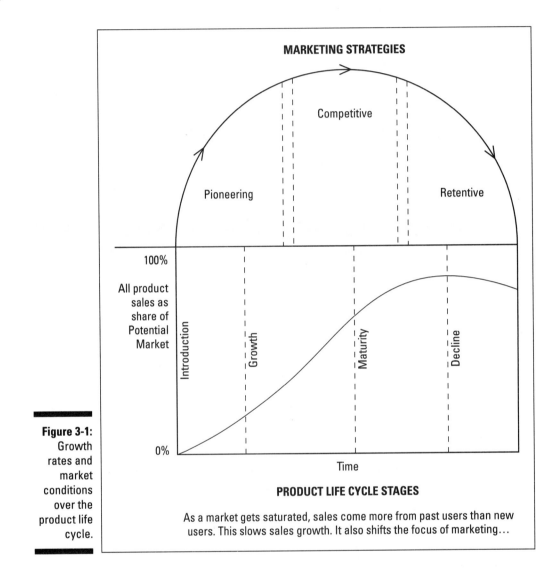

Figure 3-1:
Growth
rates and
market
conditions
over the
product life
cycle.

The maturity phase

A sad thing happens to end the growth-stage party: Marketers begin to run
out of market. Once most able-bodied people who like to skate have bought
their first pair of inline rollerskates, for example, the nature of the market
has to change. Now you cannot get rich just by spreading the good news

about this new product. You have to wait until people are ready to replace their old skates, and then you have to fight tooth-and-nail with competitors to make the sale. At best, you keep most of your old customers and pick up a share of the new people who have thoughtfully managed to be born and grow up with a proclivity for roller skating. The days of heady growth are over because your market is becoming *saturated,* meaning that most potential customers have already learned about and started using the product. When a market is saturated, you can no longer grow just by finding new customers. Your ambitions are limited by the rate at which customers replace the product and your ability to steal customers from your competitors.

Now, some markets are more prone to this problem than others. Once most households in a country have a refrigerator, for example, the market is pretty darn saturated. Consumers don't need a new one until they feel that replacing the old one is necessary. On the other hand, the market for T-shirts probably never gets saturated. Why? Because people who are *heavy users* of T-shirts — who buy the majority of them — do not make replacement purchases. They just keep on buying, whenever they see a design they like.

I happen to have done some marketing plans in the T-shirt industry, and my research amazed me by revealing that the average college student in the U.S. owns about 25 T-shirts — compared to an overall population average of only about a half a shirt per person! And even though these heavy users own fifty times more than the average American, they still say they expect to purchase at least one more in the next month. Here, then, is a product category whose sales are not limited by the life cycle model — only by the imagination of the product developers!

. . . And then you die

Finally, the product life cycle model says, people stop replacing their old products with similar new ones because something even better has come along. Who buys new LP records now that the same music is available on CDs? And so many products eventually enter a decline stage in which sales fall, profits evaporate, and most of the competitors exit. Sometimes you can make good money by hanging on to serve the die-hard loyals, but often this stage is a waste of time. Best to make hay while the sun shines and then switch your product line into some hot new growth markets.

. . . Or do you?

Some marketers — perhaps those who believe in reincarnation — refuse to give up. They think a dose of imagination and some clever marketing can revive a dying product. And sometimes they are right! Take the case of baking soda, a simple compound used by the pinch to make muffins, cakes, and other homemade delectables that the modern consumer hasn't time to bake.

Arm & Hammer, which has the largest baking soda market share in North America, watched its sales decline for years. Then some creative marketers at the company discovered something strange: Some customers — not many, but at least a few — bought huge amounts of the stuff. Boxes and boxes. What for? Further research revealed that some people used baking soda for things other than baking. Brushing their teeth. Cleaning their rugs. Deodorizing their refrigerators and kitty litter boxes. Dabbing on their underarms in place of deodorant. Amazing what people will do with the stuff.

And so Arm & Hammer went back to an introduction-phase marketing strategy. They started educating the rest of us about all these neat uses for baking soda. And the product rose from its deathbed to record-growing sales again. Voilá! Life after death.

What does the product life cycle mean for you?

In the upper half of Figure 3-1 is a *second* life cycle model, this one part of the canon in the field of advertising. I have redrawn it slightly (usually the model looks like a half of a wagon wheel) to make it tie into the product life cycle drawing. Put the two together, and you have that finest of combinations: theory plus practice! The advertising life cycle model says that products go through three stages, each requiring a different marketing strategy: *Pioneering* (use when the majority of prospects are unfamiliar with the product), *Competitive* (use when the majority of prospects have tried at least one competitor's product), and *Retentive* (use when finding new customers costs more than keeping old customers). And by tying these to the life cycle model, you can choose the right one based on the current growth rate trend in your market. Table 3-1 shows the strategic objectives of each of these stages.

Table 3-1	What to Do in Each Product Stage	
Pioneering	*Competitive*	*Retentive*
Educate consumers	Build brand equity	Retain customers
Encourage trial usage	Position against competitors	Build relationships with customers
Build the distribution channel	Capture a leading market share	Improve quality
Segment market to better serve specific needs	Improve service	Upgrade product

Everything about your marketing program follows from these simple strategies. And you can tell when you need them by looking at where you are in your product's life cycle. That makes your strategic thinking fairly simple.

For example, if you are marketing a radical new product that has just begun to experience accelerating sales, then you know you are moving from the Introduction to the Growth stages of the Product Life Cycle. Figure 3-1 indicates that a Pioneering advertising strategy should apply. And the table tells you that this strategy means you need to educate consumers about the new product, encourage them to try it, and make sure that the product is widely distributed. Now you have a clear strategic mandate as you move on to define your marketing program (using the components in Part III of this book).

For example, how should you price the product — high or low? Well, price should be low enough to keep from discouraging new customers, so the high end of the price range may be a mistake. On the other hand, no mandate exists to compete head-to-head on price (that would be appropriate to the Competitive strategy later on). So the best time to use low prices is probably in special offers to stimulate trial. In fact, perhaps free samples are appropriate now, especially if coupled with a moderately high list price. (In Chapter 13, I show you how to specify an exact price.)

And your advertising? It certainly needs to be informative, teaching or showing potential consumers how to benefit from the product. Similarly, you know you need to encourage distributors to stock and push the product, so special offers to the trade and a strong sales effort (through your own salespeople or through reps or distributors) should get a fair share of your marketing budget.

All these conclusions are fairly obvious — *if* you stay focused on the strategic guidelines in the model. And that is the beauty of strategy — it makes the details of your tactics so much clearer and simpler.

Putting Strategies into Action

In Figures 3-2, 3-3, and 3-4, I provide three concept drawings for advertisements. The first is for an imaginary product I've called Heggs. Heggs is a healthy egg mixer, sold in a carton for use in cooking. The product is formulated to offer the same taste and performance as a whole egg, but without the high cholesterol that puts you at risk of heart problems. What is the right strategy for this new product? A pioneering ad geared toward the introductory market works best.

There *are* some competing products — Egg Beaters dominate the category right now in the U.S., for example. But they generally target older consumers who have been given strict orders by their doctors. The middle-aged consumer who is health-conscious currently favors whole and natural foods, not chemical-sounding formulas. And so they avoid Egg Beaters. But Heggs targets them with its all natural claim: It's "The Healthy Egg That's All Natural, Part Egg." And so the task is to educate a new group of consumers about the advantage of an egg mixer. Thus, the listing of *facts* on the package and in the ad. And, thus, the exhortation to "Try Heggs today!" I'd also recommend giving away free samples along with a recipe booklet at grocery stores where the target consumers shop in big numbers.

An egg's an egg to many consumers, and they simply buy by price or availability. But a growing number of consumers are aware of quality differences, and they look for what they perceive as healthier eggs. Figure 3-3 shows a competitive ad geared toward the growth stage. The product in Figure 3-3, Free Eggs, targets these quality-conscious consumers by introducing an innovation: the benefit of a healthy egg from a happier chicken. "Free range chickens lay better eggs" is the claim, and the slogan teaches consumers to recognize the difference between this product and competing egg products that cannot make a similar claim. This ad also creates a

Figure 3-2:
A pioneering ad for the introduction stage.

distinctive brand identity with the humorous and memorable image of an egg with wings and a head — and with the prominent *Free Eggs* trademark that plays off this image. Distinctive difference, plus memorable brand identity, equals a successful competitive marketing strategy. This strategy will help the new brand gain a share of the competitive, mature egg market. Hopefully, consumers *will* look for this unique brand in spite of the heavy competition.

What if you are simply selling an established local brand of egg, one that has a solid base in your regional market but little else to differentiate it? Fresh eggs in cartons — a mature category if I've ever seen one. And so the ad in Figure 3-4 uses a reminder strategy to hold onto a loyal customer base in a mature market.

Unlike the Free Eggs brand, Daisy's Dairy has no significant point of difference upon which to compete. Daisy's advantage is that it is a local producer, which means it has a cost advantage in its area and also a solid base of customers who recognize the Daisy Dairy name and have bought eggs from them for years. But with the rush to store brands, Daisy's finds itself competing against the very grocery stores that it counts on for its distribution.

Figure 3-3:
A competitive ad for the growth stage.

And so the dairy needs a reminder campaign, such as the concept sketch in Figure 3-4 suggests. I'd run some print ads based on this concept and also try to get the grocery stores to give me space for signs at point of purchase. Finally, I'd use sponsorship of the local public radio station and various special events in the community to get the Daisy's Dairy name out in front of consumers on a regular basis. The key to keeping the Daisy's brand alive is making sure that consumers don't forget it!

Use POP for reminder marketing!

As the preceding Daisy's Dairy example suggests, *point of purchase* (POP) is often an effective way to implement the reminder strategy. Point-of-purchase marketing simply means doing whatever advertising is necessary to sway the consumer your way at the time and place of their purchase.

Figure 3-4:
A reminder
ad for the
maturity
stage.

Precise International (of Orangeberg, New York) uses this strategy to market its Wenger Swiss Army Knife product line in jewelry and knife stores. Working with Phoenix Display and Packaging Corp. (of Wilmington, Delaware), Precise International creates a variety of countertop and floor display cases that feature giant models of the distinctive red pocket knife with its white cross logo. Although the pocket knife market has been mature for decades, if not centuries, Wenger has a strong brand identity that allows it to maintain a large and profitable share of the market simply by reminding consumers of its product. Often consumers walking past one of these POP displays realize that a Swiss Army Knife is the perfect gift — for someone else or for themselves!

Positioning Strategies

The final strategic decision you must, absolutely *must,* make is how to *position* your product. The position I'm talking about is *the position your product holds in the customer's mind.* This decision is a three-step process.

1: Select your target group of customers

The first step in deciding how to position your product is to select your *target market segment.* An example is McDonald's decision to go after young adults who are heavy users of fast-food restaurants. A target market segment comes from first recognizing that different groups, or segments, of the market have different needs and wants. Kids versus adults. And heavy users of fast food versus light users. Each of these distinctions cuts up the population into groups. Add the two distinctions together and you have a two-dimensional segmentation of your market. You can illustrate this segmentation by making age categories into columns and usage level categories into rows. The result is a big table, each cell of which shows one of the market segments. McDonald's already dominates some of these segments, but it wants to expand its market (back to that most popular of strategies again!). And so it is marketing to a new segment, a new cell in that big table.

I don't care how you segment your market. Cut it up by age, by where people live, by how they like to shop, or by whether they like jazz or hate it. In fact, I encourage you to try wild and crazy ways of grouping customers. If the wild ways work, they lead to innovative marketing programs, and that's the sort of stuff that heroes are made of. But in order to work, your method must do one thing well: It must bring together people who share a common perspective on the product and the need that product fills. The advantage of cutting your market into smaller segments is that you can then meet the needs of these segments better than if you mass marketed to everyone. And that won't be true unless the people within a segment are more alike with respect to the product than those beyond the segment. (I go into the gory details of how to research market segments in Chapter 6 if you're interested.)

After you decide on a way of dividing the total market into smaller groups with more uniform needs, you have to decide which groups you want to target. Maybe you can target them all. But usually not. I urge you to pick one (or a few, at most) segment as the target of your marketing. And furthermore, I must warn you that, to do marketing right, you really need a unique strategy and marketing plan for each segment you target. After all, they *are* different, so your marketing must be, too.

2: Design your positioning strategy

Now that you know who your target customers are (if you read the preceding section), you are ready to design your positioning strategy. You have some obvious options:

- ✔ You may position against a competitor. "Our interest rates are lower than Citibank's." (This tactic is a natural in a mature product, where the compete strategy applies.)

- ✔ You may emphasize a distinctive benefit. "The only peanut butter with no harmful saturated fats." (This tactic is often best if you are using a pioneering strategy, in the beginning of a product's life cycle.)

- ✔ You can affiliate yourself with something the customer values. "The toothpaste most often recommended by dentists." (Doing so allows some of the virtues of this other thing to rub off on your brand.) A celebrity endorser, an image of a happy family playing on the beach, a richly appointed manor house set in beautiful gardens, a friendly giant. All have been used to position products favorably in consumers' minds.

For example, Merrill Lynch, the global retail brokerage company, decided to position itself as similar to Leonardo da Vinci. Yes, I know it's a stretch, but they worked the analogy as best they could (as this copy from a print ad shows): "Just as Leonardo used his intellect and imagination to help people make sense of the world during the Renaissance, our company is guided by a similar commitment today. With unmatched global presence, our understanding of the forces shaping the world enables people everywhere to react in more creative, fruitful ways. Like Leonardo, we believe using our intelligence to enrich people's lives makes a difference."

You must write down your positioning strategy in big print and post it above your desk to make sure that you actually stay focused on its execution. Handing out copies of your positioning statement to your ad agency, distributor, publicist, and anyone else who works on your marketing program also pays off.

Writing a positioning statement is easy. First you must decide:

- ✔ What type of customer you target
- ✔ What you do for that customer
- ✔ How you do it
- ✔ Why you do it better than competitors

Next, you should fill in the following with your own words:

Our product offers the following benefit:

_____

_____

To the following customers (describe target segment):

_____

_____

Our product is better than competitors in the following manner:

_____

_____

We can prove we are the best because of (evidence/differences):

_____

_____

When you go to the trouble of thinking through your positioning statement, you have — a positioning statement! So what? You can't use it to sell products. But you can use it to design all your marketing communications. Everything you do in your marketing program, from the product or service's packaging to its advertising and publicity, should work to convince customers of the points your positioning statement contains. So put the statement up over your desk and refer to it whenever you do marketing for that product.

3: Capture that position through your marketing program

A positioning statement makes clear what you need to communicate about the product, and to who (or whom, if you are picky about grammar). The positioning statement puts this strategy into a form so simple and clear that it probably won't get lost in the shuffle. Think of the positioning statement as a marketing plan so compact that you can put it on a scrap of paper and keep it in your wallet.

Everything you do in your marketing program — each time your program touches customers at any influence point — you need to make sure that you are reaching the *right* customers, with the *right* message. And your positioning statement reminds you who to target and what message to communicate to them.

This plan sounds so simple and obvious. I often wonder why most marketing programs waste customers' time and marketers' money on so many messages that are *inconsistent with the positioning statement.* Any marketing message that fails to explain what the product or company does that is special, and to give sufficient evidence to prove this point, is failing to position the product properly.

Every marketing program should reflect one (and only one) clearly stated positioning strategy. And doing so becomes especially important when your marketing objectives are competitive — see the discussion of the product life cycle earlier in this chapter. A positioning strategy simply states how you want customers to perceive your product, relative to their needs and wants. It then compares competing ways of meeting those needs and wants.

For example, McDonald's currently wants to position itself as a great place for adults to get good hamburgers in a hurry. Why? Because the brand is currently perceived by adults as kid-oriented. And that's natural, because McDonald's has been positioning itself as a fun place for children through its in-restaurant playgrounds, Happy Meal specials (which include a toy), and its long-time use of a clown in television advertising. And that's a good positioning strategy — children account for a big portion of the fast-food market in North America. However, research shows the "heavy user" of fast food restaurants is an adult, and McDonald's has a smaller share of this heavy-user segment than it wants. Thus, a new positioning strategy, designed to court the teenagers and young adults who eat the most hamburgers by convincing them that McDonald's offers food and an image they like, seemed to be in order. To execute that positioning strategy, McDonald's developed the Arch Deluxe product and hired ad agency Fallon McElligott (of Minneapolis, Minnesota) to create more sophisticated television ads designed to attract the attention of adults, not kids.

Testing Your Strategy in the Real World of Marketing

No strategy will succeed unless it has the ring of common sense to it. Why? Because ultimately, *you* do not implement your strategies. You depend on *others* — your salespeople, distributors, ad agencies, retailers, and so forth —

to implement a program based on your strategy. These representatives may get the program wrong unless that strategy is simple and compelling.

Do your customers "get it?"

Another, even more important reason exists to make sure that your strategy has the ring of common sense to it: *Your customers have to get it, too!* Think about Colgate's effort to introduce a special product called Colgate Junior that appeals to kids by tasting better than adult toothpastes. For Colgate Junior's strategy to work, kids and parents have to learn about the product, and realize that that product can solve a problem they have. And I can tell you that most people, whether adults or kids, are not waiting with baited breath for the latest news on toothpaste research and development. They make routine purchases, or they shop by price to take advantage of coupons and store specials. They probably don't even know what's in their toothpaste (can you list the ingredients in the brand you use?). Therefore, any new toothpaste formula had better be presented in a simple, clear, compelling manner.

How to make sure they "get it"

Does your strategy pass these two tests — is the strategy clear enough for the people who must implement it, and will customers get it? Before you try the strategy in your market, you can test its common-sense appeal by seeing how easily you can explain the strategy to others — and how long after you've explained it to them that they still remember that strategy. Try telling people who do not work with you about your strategies (just make sure that they don't work for the competition!). If your children, or boyfriend, or hairdresser, or racquetball partner can understand your strategy, and if they find that strategy interesting enough that they still remember it when you ask them about it a few days later — then you probably have a common-sense strategy — one that will stand up to the abuse of a marketing program.

What if they fall asleep or keep changing the subject or asking stupid questions? Then your strategy is not ready for prime time. Go back to square one. Here are three things you can do to refine a strategy:

✔ **Rethink the *underlying need* you address.** Is this need clear and real — and is it stated in the kind of words and thoughts that appeal naturally to customers? This problem seems like an easy thing, but often the marketer must bring real insight and imagination into the definition of customer needs. For example, a great many parents have fought with their children over tooth-brushing, and been frustrated that the kids resisted this basic hygiene behavior. Yet nobody thought to define the problem as poor-tasting toothpaste until Tom's of Maine, Colgate, and a few other companies adopted this problem definition in the last decade or so. Somebody had to have a bright idea — one that, once told to others, seems perfectly natural and obvious. This kind of insight into customer need is how marketing fortunes are made!

- ✔ **Rethink your *target market*.** Does the grouping you have created hang together in real-world marketing? I can easily visualize kids who hate brushing their teeth — I've raised several myself. And so Colgate's segmentation strategy — to divide the toothpaste market by age and by whether people like the taste of conventional toothpastes or not — has that ring of common sense. Crafting a package design or shooting a television commercial that targets youths who hate to brush won't be hard. The marketers will have a clear focus. And many kids will get the strategy — they will identify with these marketing communications right away. (Yes, I know — kids don't buy toothpaste, but their parents sure do!) But when a target market is poorly defined, the marketing program tends to lack definition, too. And this causes customers to have a hard time understanding the point of marketing communications; they are not sure whether the product is for them. Don't let your strategy fall into this trap.

- ✔ **Rewrite your *positioning statement*.** If your strategies don't seem to be commonsensical enough for everybody who hears them to "get it," then it's high-time to rewrite. Perhaps you are positioning your product in nonintuitive ways. Marketers often fall prey to the *company-think view* of their products — that what the experts who design the product say makes it special. If your positioning statement is full of technicalities, recast these in real-world benefits, using your customers' language. And make sure that you position your product against customers' *basic needs* (see Chapter 2) as well as their specific wants.

In Chapter 6, I show you how to use marketing research to identify customers' evaluative criteria — which are the things they think about when shopping in your market.

But you don't have do formal research to follow this rule of common-sense marketing strategy. For example, to the customer who is shopping for a car, what may matter is how firmly the tires grip the road when she turns in bad conditions. The designer of an automobile doesn't talk this way — he talks about center of gravity and torque and how much tire surface area is touching the pavement and lots of other technicalities. Let him talk — but not to your customers!

Keep in mind that you should always evoke customers' criteria for purchase decisions, in their own words, or words that are so natural they *become* the customer's words. If you do, you probably have a winning marketing strategy. If you don't, I guarantee failure for your marketing program. And you can take that to the bank — with your final paycheck.

Chapter 4

Let's Get Creative

*B*usinesses are idea limited. The one thing they have the least of is not money, not knowledge, not technology or skilled employees or customers — what they lack is a stream of fresh new ideas. The truth of this assertion is most obvious in marketing, where progress is the direct result of creativity.

No company can succeed without a creative approach to marketing, because in marketing, everything must change on a regular basis. You can't run the same old ads and promotions; you have to keep using new ones. You can't offer the same old products; you have to improve them because your competitors will if you don't. You can't make the same sales pitch you did last year or your customers will throw you out on your ear. You can't use the same booth at this year's trade show as you did at last year's. You can't keep pricing your product the same from season to season and year to year, because your costs, your competitors' prices, and your pricing objectives all change regularly. In fact, nothing in marketing can be kept exactly the same. If you aren't changing, you're failing. To succeed, you have to do more than just follow the trends. You have to set them!

And so creativity is incredibly important in marketing. But the funny thing is, you can't find a chapter on creativity in most marketing texts (rarely even a paragraph, for that matter!). And most managers and marketers don't think of themselves as particularly creative. They prefer to present a staid, businesslike image to the rest of their company. Creativity and business are like oil and water — they just don't seem to mix.

But then again, good marketing is like a good salad dressing — it needs to combine the incompatible, to mix hard-headed analysis with bold, crazy creativity. All great marketers are closet creators, their heads full of wild ideas upon which to draw as needed. In this chapter, I show you how to boost your and your associates' creativity in order to have a deep well of fresh new ideas for your marketing initiatives.

What Is Creativity?

You can answer the question, "What is creativity?" in two ways. First, you can do so with a formal definition — and here is my stab at one: *Creativity is making nonobvious connections between things or ideas.*

Second, you can define creativity by example. Doing so is a valuable exercise. Because if you look around you at the tangible evidence of your own and others' marketing efforts, you find that remarkably few of those efforts really stand out as great examples of creativity. Most of what passes off as creative work is fairly humdrum. The connections made are sufficiently obvious that they don't bowl you over when you see them. And as a result, you *don't* necessarily see them!

The scarcity of great creative work in marketing tells us something about creativity: It is hard to do well. You need real insight and great effort to achieve the sort of inspiration that I'm talking about.

Good examples exist — and I urge you to start collecting them, because these are inspirations to all marketers to raise our standards. For example, take the award-winning design that Drissi Advertising (Los Angeles, California) did for a point-of-purchase cardboard display that promoted the release of *The Indian in the Cupboard* in video stores in 1996. This story is a children's movie, based on a book about a boy who has a magic cupboard that has the power to bring toy characters — including a plastic Native American — to life. Drissi Advertising could have chosen many exciting scenes from the movie to illustrate in their point-of-purchase display. Instead, they decided to communicate the wonder of the magical cupboard itself. But how to show the power this cupboard possesses? The obvious would have been to show the cupboard's exterior, much as it may appear from the outside to anyone seeing it for the first time.

Here is where Drissi Advertising got really creative. They turned the image around and put the viewer in the box, looking out, past a startled Indian, through a gigantic keyhole and into the eye of an enormous child who is peeking through that keyhole! The cardboard display folds to help create the illusion that the viewer is inside the box. And the whole thing is printed on such a large scale that the viewer feels small compared to the big keyhole and giant boy looking in. The display's visual image is so powerful that it needs little copy to work — simply a banner headline across the top that says "UNLOCK THE SECRET" and the name of the movie at the bottom.

In another example of creativity in marketing, entrepreneur Ralph Rubio of San Diego, California decided to start a restaurant. This restaurant would have Mexican-style food, something quick and delicious. But what? Here is where he scored big on his first creative idea — to feature the traditional fish taco, a dish few Americans had heard of — a battered and fried fish filet in a soft tortilla with a special sauce, some cabbage, and a squeeze of lime. I've never eaten one, but now that Rubio's restaurants dot the Southern California landscape, lots of other people have — and they say this nonobvious menu item is absolutely delicious! Then Rubio added a second creative idea — a fishy cartoon character called Pesky Peskado who wears a yellow tortilla vest and appears on T-shirts, in local advertising, and even on a huge inflatable balloon. Pesky gave the fish taco an identity and visibility that helped teach the residents of San Diego about this new food option. A new fast-food menu, with a distinctively fishy brand identity to market it — that's a good example of creativity at work.

The rest of the story is just good, consistent marketing — from bumper stickers and antenna balls to sponsoring local sports teams to fliers for local businesses, plus running regular ads with coupons in the newspapers in order to encourage people to try his fish tacos. It's a success story, a local entrepreneur who doubled his revenues each of his first five years until he had built an important regional chain of restaurants. Good, careful marketing, taking advantage of as many influence points as possible. But at its heart (making it special) was a creative idea for a new kind of product, and a creative identity to bring the product to life in the minds of his customers.

The creative work behind the preceding two examples is special. The work stands out, catches the eye, and pleases the soul. It is a gift to your customers and the general public, a little bit of theater or poetry that takes its place in society because of its own special merits. Remember the principle of real world marketing (Chapter 1) that the more you give your customers, the more you get back from them. Great creative work is one thing you can give your customers that is good for you as well as them. It's a win-win equation. Nobody's throat has to get cut. Creative marketing makes your product or business stand head and shoulders above the rest, but you can't do this kind of marketing unless you have great ideas!

Generating Ideas

Okay, time to be creative. Ready, set, GO!

Come up with any good ideas yet?

No?

How about now? No?

If you can't be creative at will, don't be alarmed. Most people face this problem, whether in or out of the marketing field. Artists practice creativity every day, but people in business generally don't. As a result, most people have remarkably few creative ideas in a day, or even in a year. (How many creative ideas did you come up with and propose on the job over the last year?)

So when you need to be creative in marketing, many people find that they require some help. How do you act creative? What's involved in generating unusually creative ideas?

A student wrote the Young & Rubicam ad agency with this very question some time ago, and the question was answered in what has become a classic of the industry by Mary O'Meara, a creative director at the agency at that time. Her letter is reproduced in *The Young & Rubicam Traveling Creative Workshop* (a recommended resource — Prentice Hall, 1990), and I'm going to reproduce it here, too:

> There is the sponge *part: when you soak up all the information you can discover (and a lot of misinformation).*
>
> There is the shake *part: when you shake out the facts and question the problem itself and start to imagine all sorts of things.*
>
> There is the squeeze *part: when you wring out the sponge and scribble down the most promising splashes and driblets.*
>
> There is the bounce *part: when you and another concerned with the problem toss embryonic ideas back and forth until only the fittest survive.*
>
> There is the scratch *part: like the above, but now you scratch brain against brain hoping to spark a new notion.*
>
> There is the once-again-please *part: when you examine the survivors in the cold light of reason, abandon most, and incubate a few in the warm darkness of imagination.*
>
> There is the dry *part: when you quit thinking about the [!#*!] problem and turn your mind to pleasure or routine. (You only think you've stopped thinking.)*

There is the yahoo *part: when things connect and an idea pops into your head that turns out to be the key to the solution. Often this happens when you least expect it and aren't even thinking about the problem.*

There is the do *part: when you use your particular talents and learned skills and those of others concerned to shape and form the raw idea into a proper solution.*

Then there is the itch *part: which maybe should come first instead of last. The drive to solve problems creatively — with a new and original solution — stems from some chronic itch; dissatisfaction with all existing solutions. Even when the latest may be your own.*

I reproduce this reply because it is the richest, most honest description of creative behavior I've come across. I hate numbered lists of steps for "creative problem solving" and the like, because these lists try to make creativity a science. Creativity isn't a science, it's a habit: a loose collection of flaky behaviors. Like soaking up information, questioning the problem, tossing ideas back and forth with an associate, and then setting the whole thing aside to incubate in the back of your mind while you do something else.

Scratching the itch

Driving the creative process is that "itch" to find new and better ideas and approaches. Creative people are driven from within by their own itches. If you want to be really creative, go out and acquire an itch. You can do so quite easily in the field of marketing simply by looking at your area of concern with a critical eye. As soon as you start saying to yourself, "That's dumb, I can do better," and "How do people put up with such inefficiencies?" and "There must be a better way!" then you have the right perspective.

Because a better way *always* exists. You can invent a better product, or find a new way to distribute your product, or improve upon your advertising, or think of a better alternative to those silly coupons your firm always uses, or come up with a better design for your company's trade show booth. Whatever it is, *you* can do it better! All you need is the confidence to hang in there and do the hard work of generating creative ideas. *Lots* of ideas, because most of them will have to be rejected for practical reasons and what's left won't be very creative unless you start with a whole lot.

Group creativity

Being creative on your own is hard enough. But often in marketing, and work in general, the task is to get a group or team of people to come up with some good creative concepts. Good luck!

Most groups of people, when confined to a conference room for a morning, do little more than argue about stale old ideas. Or even worse, somebody suggests an absolutely terrible new idea, and the rest of the group jumps on it and insists the suggestion is great . . . thus eliminating the need for *them* to think. If you hope to get a group to actually be creative, you had better use structured group processes. That means you have to talk the group into going along with an activity such as brainstorming (which, while often mentioned in business, is rarely used properly). Sometimes the group resists at first, but be persistent. Ask them what they have to lose by trying your idea for a half hour. Once they try one technique, they'll see how much more productive the group is and will want to try more creativity techniques.

The following headings show what I can unconditionally say is *the best list of group creativity techniques in print*. This list is the best because I know that all of these techniques work — I've tried them often with a wide variety of groups, in marketing and in other disciplines as well. I am not including some of the really silly techniques that are likely to fail or to make everybody laugh at you. I've tried too many of those as well!

Note that these techniques generally produce a list of ideas. Hopefully a long and varied list. But still just a list. So be sure to schedule some time for analyzing the list in order to identify the most promising ideas and then develop those ideas into full-blown proposals.

Nominal group technique

The *nominal group technique* gets everyone to contribute original ideas, overcoming the natural hesitancy to participate.

1. **Start with a *clear statement of the problem* — what everyone is supposed to be thinking about.**

   For example, you may state the problem as, "Think of ideas for our new trade show booth." If necessary, someone can brief the group about the problem in order to bring everyone up to date on the relevant information.

2. **Each person writes down as many ideas as he or she can think of, working silently on individual pieces of paper.**

   I prefer to use big index cards, one per idea.

3. **The ideas are shared with the group (either have each person read his own or collect them and have one person read all the ideas).**

   Write ideas down on a board or spread the index cards out on the table.

4. **Permit questions and discussion to clarify each idea.**

5. **Conduct a vote for "the best idea."**

   Do so by show of hands or private ballot, as appropriate.

Brainstorming

Brainstorming is a great way to increase the number and variety of ideas. The goal of brainstorming is to generate a very long list of "crazy ideas," some of which may be surprisingly helpful. Brainstorming gets people to do *out of the box thinking* — in which they generate unusual ideas beyond their normal thought patterns — at least if you push them to use brainstorming this way. Don't let your group just go through the motions of brainstorming. To really get in the spirit of it, they'll have to *free associate* — to allow their minds to wander from current ideas to whatever new ideas first pop up, no matter what the association between the old and new idea may be.

You may need to encourage your group by example. For instance, if the problem is stated as "think of new ideas for our trade show booth," you can brainstorm a half-dozen to start with, just to illustrate what you're asking the group to do: a booth like a circus fun-house, a booth shaped like a giant cave, a booth in the form of one of our products, a booth decorated on the inside to look like an outdoor space complete with blue sky and white clouds overhead, a booth like the space shuttle launch pad featuring once-an-hour "launches" of a scale-model of the shuttle, a booth that revolves slowly, a booth that offers free fresh-popped popcorn and fresh-baked cookies to visitors.

These ideas are not likely to be adopted by the average company, but they do illustrate the spirit of brainstorming, which is to set aside your criticisms and have some fun generating ideas. The rules (which you must tell the group beforehand) are as follows:

- ✔ Quantity, not quality — generate as many ideas as possible
- ✔ No member of the group can criticize another member's suggestion — no idea is too wild to write down
- ✔ No ownership of ideas — everyone should build off each other's ideas

Question brainstorming

Question brainstorming is another way to generate novel questions that can provoke your group into thinking more creatively. This technique follows the same rules as brainstorming, but the group is instructed to think of questions instead of ideas.

For example, if the problem is to develop a new trade show booth that draws more prospects, then the group may think of the following kinds of questions:

- ✔ Do bigger booths draw much better than smaller ones?
- ✔ Which booths drew the most people at the last trade show?
- ✔ Are all visitors equal or do we want to draw only certain types of visitors?
- ✔ If we offer a resting place and free coffee, will this do the trick?

Wishful thinking

Wishful thinking is a technique suggested by Hanley Norins of Young & Rubicam, and one that he has used to train employees of that agency in his Traveling Creative Workshop. The technique follows the basic rules of brainstorming, but with the requirement that all statements start with the words "I wish." He explains that, "If you start with the words 'I wish . . . ' your mind may prompt such thoughts as the following: 'I wish that the moment winter starts, my family could rush to the airport and escape . . . I wish we could be snorkeling down through some crystal-clear grotto, where the fish have a thousand different colors and patterns . . . that we could sit in the sun under a beach umbrella, drinking a piña colada,' and so on." (*The Young & Rubicam Traveling Creative Workshop,* Prentice Hall, 1990.)

These sort of statements may be handy for developing an advertising campaign for a Caribbean resort hotel. If you need another focus, then all you have to do is state a topic for people to make wishes about. For example, you can say, "Imagine that the Trade Show Fairy told you that all your wishes would come true — as long as they have to do with the company's booth for the next big trade show." I know this wishing won't be quite as much fun, but some helpful ideas will still be generated!

Analogies

Analogies are a great creativity device as well. You don't think I'm serious, I know, because the idea sounds so trivial. But remember that I defined creativity as making *nonobvious combinations* of ideas? A good analogy is just that.

A famous example is provided by the chemist August von Kekule, who figured out that Benzine takes the form of six carbon atoms in a ring. He reached this important conclusion in a daydream in which he imagined chains of atoms as snakes — until one of them circled back and bit its own tail, and he had the solution!

To put analogies to work for you, ask your group to think of things that the subject or problem is similar to. At first, group members come up with conventional ideas, but they'll soon run out of these and to continue, they must create fresh analogies. For example, you may ask a group to brainstorm analogies for your product, as a source of inspiration for creating new advertisements about that product.

Advertisers for Nordic Track exercise equipment thought that a person's roll of stomach fat was like a flat tire on a car that needed changing. From this analogy sprang a winning headline, "SIMPLE INSTRUCTIONS FOR CHANGING YOUR SPARE TIRE."

Pass-along

Pass-along is a simple game that helps a group break through its barriers to free association and collaborative thinking. People used to play this game just for fun, but who plays parlor games now that we have TV rooms instead of parlors? So here are the instructions in case you've never heard of the game.

1. **One person writes something about the subject in question on the top line of a sheet of paper, and passes it to the next person, who writes a second line beneath the first.**

2. **Go around the table or group as many times as are productive.**

   This game can be done with any group from three to twenty. Fewer cycles are needed in bigger groups — in general, try to fill up a full page of lined paper. If people get into the spirit of the game, a line of thought emerges and dances on the page, each previous phrase suggesting something new until you have lots of good ideas and many ways of thinking about your problem. Players keep revealing new aspects of the subject as they build on or add new dimensions to the lines above.

For example, say a team of marketing and salespeople is meeting to generate new product concepts for the product development department of a bank. Now, that sounds like a tough assignment — what can be new under the sun in banking? But you, the savvy facilitator, pick a subject and pass the paper around:

Subject: How can we make our customers' personal finances run better?

Pass-along Ideas:

- ✔ Help them win the lottery.

- ✔ Help them save money by putting aside X percent each month.

- ✔ Help them save for their children's college tuition.

- ✔ Help them keep track of their finances.

- ✔ Give them a checkbook that balances itself.

- ✔ Notify them in advance of financial problems like bouncing checks so they can be prevented.

As this example illustrates, one idea can lead to another, so even if the first idea is not helpful, associating new ideas from the first one can produce useful thoughts. A bank is probably not going to get into the lottery ticket business (there must be a law against that!). But after the members of this group got thinking along those lines, they came up with some practical ways of increasing their customers' wealth, like plans that could help them transfer money to savings automatically each month.

Nor can a checkbook balance itself — this task has to be performed by means other than magic. But what if a computer did the work? Such a service is entirely possible if the customer is willing to a) bank over the Internet, electronically, so as to use the bank's computer, or b) use a checkbook program on her PC to track her account and generate checks and reports. Both technologies exist — why not combine one of them with a standard checking account service for those customers who like the idea of a checkbook that balances itself? As this simple example illustrates, generating novel ideas doesn't take long, even in a mature industry like banking — as long as you use creativity techniques!

By the way, did you know that you can adapt Pass-along (and other writing-based creativity processes) to your company's e-mail system or to a chat room on the Internet? Almost any networked computers permit serial contributions to a file, so you can just circulate a virtual list instead of a real one, which means the group doing the creative thinking need not be limited to people who can attend an actual meeting.

Classic questions

Classic questions are rhetorical questions that force the group to examine basic assumptions and rethink its views. Arthur Bell, author *of Business Communication and Practice* (Scott, Foresman), recommends ten such questions. They are easily customized to the topic in question (such as a product you have to design ads for) by filling in the blanks appropriately:

1. Why should we even care about _____?

2. How can _____ be divided into stages?

3. What led to _____?

4. What type of person would be interested in _____?

5. If _____ did not exist, how would that change things?

6. What aspect of _____ do I like best, or least?

7. What larger movement, field, or situation provides background for _____?

8. What are _____'s principal benefits?

9. If _____ does not succeed, what were the barriers?

10. How can _____ be explained to a ten-year-old?

Now, you may find that some of these questions fit your topic better than others. Feel free to drop the ones that are a bad match. Or write some new ones in the same spirit. For example, along with "What are the trade show booth's principal benefits?," I may ask the group "What are the trade show booth's negatives?" The advantage of such questions is that they surface aspects of the problem that the group has not considered, and so the technique is a good prelude to creative idea generation. You may consider using this technique prior to using brainstorming or the Nominal Group Technique to generate a list of ideas.

Competitive teams

Competitive teams are used frequently in ad agencies to stimulate creativity. For example, if an agency is preparing a proposal to try to win a major new account, it will often set up several creative teams, with two or more people on each team, and have its own internal contest. The teams, working competitively on a tight deadline, prepare their own proposal. Then a judge or group of judges, also from within the company, decide which proposal "wins." Finally, all the teams join forces to work together on improving and finalizing the winning concept. You can use this technique, too, for any sort of creative problem. Just break down your group or meeting into smaller teams (two or three people per team works best). Give the teams an hour to work on their own, and then reassemble the group to listen to each team's presentation and select the winner.

By the way, getting the group to switch from competitive to cooperative behavior after the contest ends can be difficult. You may want to throw away (or set aside) all the teams' work and instruct the participants to come up with a new and different approach now, working in the larger group. The only rule is that no one can insist on doing it the way his team did. This final step forces everyone to look beyond the first round of effort and try to come up with an even better approach by combining the insights and ideas of multiple groups.

Creativity in Advertising

Advertising — whether in print, TV, radio, outdoor, at point of purchase, or elsewhere — is a key area of application for creativity. If you work in the advertising industry, or use advertising and advertising agencies in your marketing, then you are dependent on creativity for your success. Why? Because if your ads just say what you want people to remember, people won't pay any attention to the ads. Too many other ads are competing for their attention. Only the most creative ones are able to cut through the clutter, attract attention, and make a permanent mark on consumer attitudes.

One way to think about the role of creativity in advertising is as a vehicle for building *relationships* between your brand and your prospects. I find this a particularly powerful way to think about advertising's role in marketing — and this role is only possible with the addition of creativity to your ads. Creativity is used to add something special and unique, to accentuate a brand's differences in order to help it stand out in the consumers' eyes.

IBM's laptops no doubt have some technical features that make them unique, more or less. But lots of other companies make good laptops, too, so how do you make IBM's stand out? One headline from a print ad for IBM laptops emphasizes its portability — but that's hardly unique — and so a special personality is added to the brand by putting the message this way:

> *It's what Shakespeare would have used on a flight to the coast.*

The ad could have shown a businessman working on a laptop, with the header "It's what the smart manager takes on a business trip," but the copywriter's creativity led to a more compelling statement and vision. (Imagine how you'd illustrate the resulting headline — have any fun ideas?) And this creative headline expresses hidden insight into the customer's need — something that goes back to the core product concept. The whole idea of a personal computer is to help the user do better work, so why not the *best* work? If Shakespeare was alive today, wouldn't he demand the best writing tools available? So should today's consumer. At least, that is the creative concept behind this successful ad.

Writing a creative brief

Advertising benefits from the use of a *creative brief,* which is an information platform on which to do your creative thinking. A creative brief lays out the basic purpose and focus of the ad, and provides some supporting information that is helpful grist for your creative mill. Sometimes people think of the creative brief as answering the journalists' basic questions: who, what, where, when, why, and how?

Here is how one leading advertising agency, Leo Burnett, designs the creative brief:

- ✔ **Objective statement:** What the advertising is supposed to accomplish. Goals or objectives should be clear and specific — and one objective is easier to accomplish than many. The objective statement also includes a brief description of whom the ad is aimed at, because this target group's actions are what determines if any objective is accomplished.

- ✔ **Support statement:** The product's promise and the supporting evidence to back that promise up. This point is where you build the underlying argument for the persuasive part of your ad. The support statement can be based on logic and fact, or on an intuitive, emotional appeal — either way a basis of solid support must be present.

✔ ***Tone or character statement:*** A distinct character, feel, or personality. You choose whether the statement should accentuate the brand's long-term identity or whether to put forth a unique tone for the ad itself that is dominant over the brand's image. The choice generally flows from your objectives. A local retailer's objective may be pulling in lots of shoppers for a special Labor Day sale. This event should be given a strong identity, so you'd want to define an appropriate tone for your ad. In contrast, a national marketer of a new health-food line of sodas should build brand identity, so her creative brief would focus on defining that brand identity in words or verbal images.

The following shows an example of a creative brief for a new coffee shop's local advertising:

Objective: To bring people who work in nearby businesses into the store to try our coffee and pastries.

Support: Features special coffees from a roasting company that is famous in other locations but has not been available in this area until now. Also offers excellent Danish pastries and croissants, baked on the premises by a French pastry chef.

Tone: A sophisticated, gourmet tone is appropriate, but also warm and inviting. This shop is where those who appreciate the finest in life prefer to go. And where they meet like-minded sophisticates who also appreciate the best the world has to offer.

Applying the creative brief

After the three sections of the creative brief are filled in to your satisfaction, you are ready to start brainstorming or using any other creativity tools you care to try. The creative brief gives you a clear focus and some good working materials as you apply your creativity to developing a great ad or other promotional piece.

The creative brief is useful for any marketing communication, for any situation in which you must design something creative to communicate and persuade.

For example, think about the task of designing a new booth for a trade show. If you write a creative brief first, you have to define what the booth should accomplish and at what sort of customers the booth will be aimed (these decisions are demanded by the Objective statement). You also have to review (and maybe do some creative thinking about) the evidence available to support your company's claims to fame. What may make you stand out among exhibitors at a trade show? If you aren't sure, then use the demands of the support statement to do some research and some creative thinking. Make sure that you have your evidence at hand so that your ideas for booth design can communicate this evidence effectively. Finally, you have to define the tone of your booth, or think about your company's overall image and how the booth can reflect that image in its tone. This step is the requirement of the Tone or Character statement.

As this example illustrates, the creative brief forces you to do some helpful foundational thinking about the booth before you actually start designing it. As a result, your designs are going to be more focused and objective-driven than otherwise.

Creativity in Product Development

New product development and the improvement of old products is covered in Chapter 14, but one thing is worthy of mention here — how you manage a product development team so that it is optimally creative and effective. The first thing to note is that you need to put together the right team. That generally means a *diverse* team, one that includes the full range of knowledge that may be relevant. Different functions, from sales and marketing to manufacturing and engineering, need to be included in the creative process. Why? Because they all have different knowledge bases that are helpful in generating good ideas. You'll need to bring them in eventually anyway, so why not now?

In midsize and larger companies, "forcing" closer interaction between research, business planning, marketing, and technical staff — as General Foods does — is essential. That company (which generates several new products every year) uses a variety of conference-type events, training, and cross-functional teams to mix up its people and help them make those nonobvious connections between their divergent knowledge bases.

Creativity and Brand Image

One of the most important things you can do in marketing is to create a strong, appealing brand image. Creativity is the key to doing just that. As you saw in addressing the creative brief, earlier in this chapter, a brand's image or personality can be an important part of what advertising communicates. Sometimes that image is the main focus of advertising — and provides a common focus for all other design decisions, too, from product design to packaging to special events and other marketing communications. A strong brand identity, or personality, can become a living entity, something that the marketer creates and gives to the world. Brand development takes creativity to its farthest extreme by creating new forms of life!

What the research shows

You should know what academic research on product development teams has to say. Convincing evidence exists (see Hiam, *The Vest-Pocket Marketer*, pp. 138-40 for details) that these teams do best when three things are in place:

- The group needs *good task-oriented management:* experienced leadership, clear plans or goals, and enough autonomy and urgency (meaning immediately important work) to make the members coalesce as a team and do good work. But that's by no means enough to ensure that the team will generate a good new product.

- The team also needs *attention to people-related issues:* sufficient trust must exist between team members, the work has to be meaningful and satisfying, and communications need to be healthy for the team members to succeed.

- The team needs full *support from the organization:* a stable workplace, sufficient resources, the involvement of upper management, and opportunities for recognition and reward once the project is over.

All three areas prove important in how well a product development team functions. If you want a team to do good, creative work, then you had better make sure that the team is well nurtured!

A caution about brand equity is sounded by the annual *Yankelovich Monitor* report, put out by a leading research firm, in which U.S. consumers are asked whether they "are buying generic brands more often." The number of yes answers goes up every year. Although that number is still well under half, it is now over one-third, which means a large chunk of consumers are learning to ignore brands and buy the increasingly similar generic and store brand substitutes.

This trend is probably due to the fact that brands don't have the quality edge they used to in many categories. Generics, store brands, and cheap imports are getting better on average, closing the quality gap between them and the brands they chase.

Weaker brands are also caused by the trend toward price competition through heavy use of discounts and other special offers. These sorts of promotional activities erode brand equity. And you take a double hit, because the more of them you do, the less money you have left to spend on brand-building advertising.

Add up these trends and you can safely predict that brands won't be as valuable in the future as they are now — on average at least. But *you* can defy this trend — if you make sure that your marketing builds brand equity instead of knocking it down, and if you keep innovating to ensure that your products are better than the competition. This is a tall order, to be sure, but you can do it — *if* you are more creative than the competition!

Part II
Technical Skills You May Need

The 5th Wave   By Rich Tennant

4 FAILED BRANDING STRATEGIES in the FAST-FOOD INDUSTRY

INTERNATIONAL HOUSE OF BROCCOLI

SQUID-ON-A-STICK

LiverLand
The Best in Balkan Cuisine

McOffals
HOME OF THE
Flame Broiled Tripe

In this part . . .

1n order to do great marketing you must be able to wear many hats. Sometimes the communications and research hats are a tight fit. Don't panic if you find yourself stuck on how to write a brochure or ad or make an important presentation. And don't worry if you are unsure of how to answer difficult questions about your customers, competitors, or marketplace.

In this part, I show you how to handle these and many more technical tasks in marketing. Communications is key to almost every aspect of marketing and so is research. I think it's fair to say that marketing demands higher levels of skill in both areas than any other aspect of business. Both communications and research skills are presented in a practical way in this part of the book so that you can pick up any skills you need with ease.

Chapter 5

Marketing Communication — Writing and Design

● ●

In This Chapter

▶ Communicating persuasively by crafting your basic appeal

▶ Giving your brand a positive personality

▶ Using Stopping Power

▶ Using Pull Power

▶ Creating great writing

▶ Creating great visuals

● ●

*S*o many things go into great marketing that I have to keep stopping myself from saying that *each* chapter is the most important. That struggle is harder than ever when it comes to communication, because communication is what good marketing is all about. At least *almost* all about. A great deal of your marketing budget goes toward communicating *what* you have to offer and *why* that product or service is so incredibly wonderful for the target customer.

If you can make these points more noticeably and persuasively than your competitors, then your marketing communications are a success. If not, then you are throwing precious marketing dollars away, and you probably will not convince many people to buy your product.

Communication goes on in many ways, at many points of influence — as I demonstrate in the first chapter of this book. You need to craft a compelling message to send out through all those influence points. But how do you do this? What *is* a compelling marketing message?

> ✔ A compelling message starts with your *positioning* of the product in your customer's minds. The right positioning strategy has to be there as a foundation — along with products that follow through on the promise. (See Chapter 3 for more information about positioning.)

✔ Next, you have to craft a *basic appeal,* some motivating message that gets that positioning across.

✔ Then you need a creative *"big idea,"* something that packages your appeal in a message so compelling that people stop in their tracks; the message should persuade them of your point or drive them to do as you bid.

That sequence, when done well, creates a compelling marketing message and communicates it persuasively. The task is a difficult but a vital one — this chapter shows you how to craft the compelling message you need for all your marketing communications.

Appealing to Customers

You want to help people see what makes your product great. You want to get them to come into a store, send an e-mail, or make a phone call to buy it. But you can't just tell them that it's great, because they won't pay any attention. They've heard that one before. What you need, to start with, is a way to make your message *appeal* to them. The message must sell itself!

The problem is this: What can you communicate that will appeal to the receiver's basic motives and desires — and do so with enough strength to move him or her toward action?

This task is not a simple one. As a parent, I have ample opportunity to put it in perspective. Every time I tell my children to do something, I get a lesson in how hard motivating someone through communication is. Like all parents, I spend a lot of time repeating myself. And my children, like most children, have developed that remarkable "selective deafness" that immunizes their ears and minds against the virus of parental instructions. It takes a special effort, and often a crafty appeal to *their* wishes and desires, to get children to do the sorts of things we adults want them to do. Why do your homework before you play? Why make your bed when you get up in the morning? Children don't see the benefits of these behaviors. (By the way, my children often complain about *parental* deafness. It works both ways. Wonder if marketers ever get deaf to what their customers are telling them? Hmmm.)

And so parents must either resort to pure force (I haven't the energy for that), or we must craft our message in a way that links our goals to *their* goals. The clever parent studies the child's motives and knows how to use intangible rewards (like praise and fun) and sometimes also tangible rewards (like allowances and trips to the mall) to make their communications more motivating. This exercise is the art and use of the *appeal,* defined as anything in a communication that evokes the receiver's motives and stirs him toward an intended action.

Unappealing appeals abound

I must warn you that most appeals are ineffective. Motivating a consumer is, in fact, more difficult than motivating a child — as marketers, we have far less access to and influence over consumers. And so you see lots of appeals in marketing communications that are weak at best.

I'll just pull a magazine off my bookshelf, open it up, and I guarantee I'll find a silly appeal. Yup. Here's an ad IBM placed in *Forbes* — a two-page spread that must have cost thousands of dollars. The appeal contains no artwork. What stands out is the huge word "Timbuktu" in 2-inch-tall blue letters (I guess they are "Big Blue" letters — cute). If you read the small print (but why would you unless you are particularly interested in this particular West African village?), you can see what their appeal is:

> *If my six-year-old can make friends on the Internet from here to Timbuktu, surely someone can get the folks in my regional offices to work as a team.*

The ad turns out to be about how to use Lotus Notes in the workplace. Lotus Notes is a fine product, I admit, but I don't see what it has to do with somebody's daughter's Internet explorations. The appeal is muddy at best. It doesn't really work because the appeal tries to cash in on a trendy topic — the Internet — rather than finding some more solid and relevant appeal.

Does Lotus Notes allow teams to do better work, faster? If so, then that's a great appeal — especially if I happen to have to work with a team of dolts. So a better appeal would be to communicate the ability of this product to *save my butt when I'm stuck with a nightmare team.* Anyone in that situation — and there must be many! — is going to find that appeal far more motivating than some prattle about somebody's daughter surfing the Internet. As this example illustrates, it is possible to design appeals that have their own substance — something to attract and hold attention — but also tie in well with the product and make a key point about it.

Great appeals strike to the core of our motives

The preceding Lotus Notes example illustrates the problem of appeals that are superficial in nature. A good appeal should cut to the quick. The art of the appeal is perhaps best stated by Bill Bernbach, who reigned as the leading creative guru of the advertising industry in the '60s (source: his American Association of Advertising Agencies speech on May 17, 1980):

> *There may be changes in our society. But learning about those changes is not the answer. For you are not appealing to society. You are appealing to individuals, each with an ego, each with the*

dignity of his or her being, each like no one else in the world, each a separate miracle. The societal appeals are merely fashionable, current, cultural appeals which make nice garments for the real motivations that stem from the unchanging instincts and emotions of people. It is the unchanging person that is the proper study of the communicator.

Relate this line of thought to the Lotus Notes example. The ad is fashionable, but it does not get to those basic, timeless personal motives very quickly or effectively. The ad's appeal is easy to ignore and hard to relate to the product. In revising the appeal (a few paragraphs back), I followed Bernbach's advice. First, I switched the target from "the folks" in some regional office to a single individual — the person who is stuck with a bad team. And the appeal to this individual is simple and compelling — Lotus Notes can solve a big problem she has at work. It can save her butt.

Now, how you *communicate* an appeal like that is a separate issue. Should you show the poor person surrounded by monkeys dressed in business suits, creating havoc in an office or conference room? That is an arresting and potentially amusing visual image, and the image ties in well with the point of the appeal.

What headline might you use to accompany this visual image? How about "Is your team monkeying around with your career?"

This statement ties in with the appeal, too, but adds a provocative twist through the play on words that relates to the visual image of monkeys in business suits. I think it would make for an ad that has real *stopping power* (the ability to grab and hold attention — more about it later) and that manages to communicate a compelling appeal for Lotus Notes effectively once the reader's attention has been grabbed.

My design may work — but hundreds of other ways to communicate the same basic appeal must exist as well. Once you have a good appeal, you still have to generate lots of creative ideas for communicating it (see Chapter 4 for tips on generating ideas). But the key point is that any ad or other communication you create for Lotus Notes — or your own product — must be *based on a compelling appeal*. If not, no amount of creative communication will turn it into an effective ad.

Appeal to Logic or Emotions?

You face a choice in any marketing communications: Should you build your appeal and communication strategy around a strong claim, backed by irrefutable evidence? Or, in contrast, should you make an emotional appeal that "feels" right to the customer, but lacks hard evidence?

The reason you have to make this choice is that we all make decisions in both ways. People usually make an emotional decision about who they want to marry, but they usually make rational decisions about what jobs to search for and which employment offers to accept. Similarly, in purchase decisions sometimes the emotions prevail and sometimes the hard, logical parts of our minds are dominant.

And, to complicate matters even further, people are inconsistent about when they use which mode. Some people make highly emotional decisions about major purchases like cars and houses. Others are carefully rational, comparing statistics and running the numbers. Which camp do you fall into? If you have ever bought an automobile, try to recall why you bought it. If you say, "Because I liked it" or "Because I felt that it was a good car" or something similar, your emotions probably dominated your purchase decision. If, however, you say things like "Because it has good gas mileage and *Consumer Reports* rated it highly on safety and maintenance," then you made a logical or rational decision.

Each person tends toward one end or the other of this range — he makes decisions more rationally or emotionally. And so you can pitch your marketing communications at the rational buyer or at the emotional buyer. You can even segment your market based on this difference, and design separate marketing programs for each! You can describe these two ways of thinking in many ways, as Table 5-1 indicates. When it comes to designing your appeal, however, you generally want to focus on one side or the other of this table.

Table 5-1	Two Styles of Thinking
Rational	*Emotional*
Logical	Intuitive
Hard	Soft
Words	Images
Fact-based	Value-based
Rule-following	Ethics-following

Volkswagen decided to reposition itself in the American market (in 1996) as a fun-to-drive car for Generation Xers who are moving into parenting and responsible work roles but still feel an urge to express themselves as individuals. Volkswagen's approach was to emphasize the fun of driving their cars — and to convince consumers that *their* customers are special because of their love of driving and zest for life. This example is a classic emotional appeal, pushing all those "soft" buttons on the right-hand side of Table 5-1. The ads emphasize images over words and have a strongly intuitive appeal that is grounded in the values of Generation Xers. You learn nothing factual about Volkswagen when you view their television ads, but you do get a strong emotional hit.

When you design your communications, I recommend you follow Volkswagen's lead and emphasize one or the other way of thinking strongly. When you waffle, trying to appeal to both sides of the brain at once, your message usually ends up weaker.

However, you should also keep in mind that the same person may make the same sort of decision *differently* on different occasions — sometimes the nature of the product itself can determine whether you're logical or emotional. The product's intended usage is also important. The wealthy executive who buys a Volvo wagon for driving his children around may have made that purchase decision based on rational considerations — the car is safe and lasts a long time, even though it is not exactly a beauty. So a rational appeal may work best. Imagine that the same executive wants to buy a fancy red sports car to drive for fun on the weekends. He is now a sitting duck for an emotional appeal, as he is now seeking emotional rewards from a car — feelings of youthfulness, fun, status, and so forth. And so any consumer may respond to either an emotional or a rational appeal, depending upon the circumstances and product. Your job, as the communicator, is to "get into the customers' heads" well enough to *sense which is the hotter button* — the emotional one or the rational one.

Let's Get Personal: Giving Products Personality

In Chapter 4, I discuss the importance of giving your brand a personal identity, as if the brand were a living thing. In fact, the best way to think about the task of building a brand's value is to imagine that you *are* bringing it to life. This tactic is especially important where an emotional appeal is appropriate, because a compelling personality always attracts emotional buyers. But even if your appeal is a logical one, I urge you to give your brand a supporting personality. While a supporting personality won't be as decisive, it will still help communicate and remind consumers of your basic appeal.

But what sort of being will you create when you bring your brand to life? A Frankenstein-like monster with its own will, beyond your control? Not if you give serious thought to its personality. Don't leave this step to chance — design the perfect personality for any new product, brand, or business right from the beginning.

You must *define your brand's personality* so that you can cultivate that personality whenever you communicate with customers and the outside world in general. A richly-scripted personality has the power to shine through all your marketing program's influence points, providing a consistent touchstone for all communications. If you "know" your brand well enough, then you can communicate that same intimacy to your customers.

Taking a page from fiction

How do you define a personality? This task is called *character development* in fiction writing, and it ain't easy. But we can learn a thing or two about character development from good fiction writers.

One device that works well in fiction or marketing is to define a character's personality by his likes and dislikes. For example, we know that Sherlock Holmes, one of the most enduring fictional characters of all time, likes to smoke strong tobacco in his pipe when thinking about a problem and also plays the violin. He has a deep interest in aspects of science that have to do with crime, and he fills notebooks with clippings about famous criminals and their doings. But he has no interest in romance and no close friends but Dr. Watson, who helps him solve his cases. He is a cold, rational problem-solver with a touch of artistic imagination (the latter inherited from Vermier, the Impressionist painter, who is a distant relative). All these facts about the man help create a characteristic image, one that publishers, game and toy makers, and movie producers have cashed in on throughout the twentieth century.

Similarly, you can draw up a list of things to associate with your brand or company name — things that add up to a distinct personality. Jaguar ads often associate fine old country houses and estates with their vehicles, so we know that if the Jaguar sedan were a man, he would enjoy spending the weekend at his country estate — and, of course, would enjoy driving there in speed and comfort!

Another device I like to borrow from fiction is to write a short event-based chapter about a character. Many authors give you a description of some actions or events in order to develop their character. This description may appear within a chapter or as a freestanding chapter in a novel, for example, and it gives you a chance to get to know a main character well. You can do the same. For example, if you are marketing Jaguar cars, you can write a brief story about how a Jaguar spends its weekend. Pretend this project is for your next novel. Have fun with it. Imagine the car as it drives through a rainstorm, winds along an old road beside a canal, and then turns up the long cobbled driveway to its grandfather's Edwardian-style farmhouse. What does the car *sound* like as it drives through that rainstorm? Does it whine? No. Does it roar? No, the sound is more subtle. Smooth but powerful. Perhaps its engine is so quiet that the sound is lost in the timpani of rain-drops on the hood and windshield — but the Jaguar can no doubt feel a faint, low humming down in its drive train somewhere.

And how does the car *feel* as it leaves the highway and winds along the old canal road? Bored? Certainly not. Worried about the conditions? No . . . our character never worries about road conditions. Probably it feels lighter, at peace, but at the same time more alive and alert. And when the car turns up the cobbled drive to its ancestral home? Is it excited? No, too strong a word for this mature, self-possessed vehicle. But certainly it feels a sense of belonging, and there must be a familiarity to each bump and bend of its path that gives the automobile a surefootedness and reassurance no other car would feel here.

With these sorts of thoughts, you can soon bang out a good description of this car's weekend trip, and as you work on this piece of fiction, you will find a personality taking shape and form, new nuances emerging on the page with each bend of the road and scratch of the pen.

The preceding exercise has another valuable benefit for you and your brand. It helps you and other marketers achieve consistency in how you present the brand to customers. Once you have developed a description of the brand's human personality, everyone can use this as a guide by asking — whenever they do sales or marketing — whether their activities fit with that personality.

Go ask your shrink

Psychologists have studied the puzzle of human personality for decades, sometimes even making a little progress. And so you can also draw insights from the field of psychology as you struggle to create and communicate a personality for your product.

In particular, I recommend the *trait perspective,* an approach used by psychologists in their research. The trait perspective seeks to understand the variation in human personalities by identifying the various traits that make up each individual personality. And you can give your brands a personality by describing their essential traits. The trait perspective is helpful because it focuses on describing, rather than explaining, human behavior. And marketers are pragmatists — we don't need to know why personalities develop, we just need to figure out what personality to give our products. That's a simple descriptive task. No need for a therapist. A sharp pencil will do.

One trick I like is to use a *personality self-assessment instrument* — a fancy word for a survey-type form in which you select things that fit you, and then key out your "type" or "profile" from the answers. Only I use these questionnaires to describe my product, instead of me! You may have used one of these yourself, because many companies use them to train, or even to screen, new employees.

One popular test is based on psychologist Carl Jung's personality types. The test uses 126 questions written by Isabel Myers and Katheryn Briggs, so it is called the Myers-Briggs test. You can order a simplified version of the test, called Observations of Type Preference, from International LearningWorks (send for their latest catalog to 1130 Main Avenue, Durango, CO 81301 or fax your inquiry to 970-259-7194). However, I prefer another product, called the Insight Inventory, because I find the personality profiles it produces are particularly useful. Order it from HRD Press (Pelham, MA) by calling 413-253-3488 or (in the U.S.) 800-822-2801. And they offer a single copy of the instrument with a six-page interpretive guide for just $6.50 — all you need for researching your brand's personality.

Until you get around to ordering the Insight Inventory, Table 5-2 gives a sampling of the personality traits the inventory describes. You can give your product a selection of desirable human personality traits in order to help communicate its identity to customers. I've picked some for this table that are generally considered favorable traits, because the goal is obviously to make your product likable. After all, these traits are (in a sense) a gift to your customers, who may choose to associate with your product if they like its personality.

Table 5-2	Personality Traits from the Insight Inventory
Trait	*Description*
Accurate	Attentive to details, correct, precise, puts a lot of effort into order and organization
Animated	Lively, playful, energetic, displays emotion, uses lots of facial expressions and gestures
Charming	Very friendly, talkative, gains attention when in groups of people, persuasive
Convincing	Compelling, good with words, outgoing, able to influence others easily
Easygoing	Relaxed, patient, tolerates frustration well, steady
Forceful	Direct, assertive, speaks candidly, vigorous, authoritative
Life of the party	Lively, expressive, meets and greets others easily, likes attention, enjoys being around lots of people
Serene	Calm, easygoing, patient, able to wait without getting frustrated, not easily upset
Strong-willed	Steadfast, not easily influenced, forceful, demanding, unwavering
Tolerant	Accepting, forgives easily, lenient, patient, doesn't anger easily

Stopping Power

STOP!

Stopping power is the ability of an advertisement or other marketing communication to stop people in their tracks, to make them sit up and take notice. Communications with stopping power generate "WHAT did you say?" or "Did you see THAT?" responses. They generate a high level of attention — unlike most marketing communications.

You can be sure that thousands of other marketing messages will barrage your customer along with your own. As the second principle of real-world marketing says (in Chapter 1), *everybody else is shouting at your customers, too.* The high level of noise in the marketing environment means that most efforts to communicate will fail. Most ads go unnoticed by most of the people they target.

Ask people to recall five ads they saw on TV last night (if they watched TV last night, they probably saw several dozen). And watch their reactions. A puzzled look usually crosses their faces, as they try desperately to remember what they know they must have seen. Then they may say, "Oh, yeah. I saw that funny ad where this guy . . ." They may come up with several ads that way, if last night's crop of advertising was fairly good. And of these, they may remember the brands of one or two — but rarely all.

And if you do the same exercise, but ask about print ads in a magazine or newspaper, you may well draw a complete blank. Many people don't recall even one ad in a magazine they read yesterday unless you actively prompt them. Or try asking about radio ads. Same problem.

This simple activity puts the importance of stopping power into perspective. Your ads need to have much more stopping power than most if you hope to get a significant number of people to remember and think about them!

Stopping power is a wonderful thing, but hard to bottle up and sprinkle on your work. What gives some ads a high degree of stopping power when most have so little of it? The following sections explain.

The seven principles of stopping power

According to Hanley Norins, who spent a lot of time training the staff at Young & Rubicam to make better ads, seven principles apply in making an ad or any marketing communication a real stopper:

1. **The ad must have *intrinsic drama* that appeals to everyone.** That means the ad is capable of attracting many people outside of the target audience. If kids like an ad aimed at adults or vice versa, that means it has intrinsic drama.

2. **The ad must demand *participation* from the audience.** That means the ad draws people into some action, whether it be calling a number, going to a store, laughing out loud, or just thinking about something. But the ad shouldn't permit the audience to play a passive role.

3. **The ad forces an *emotional* response.** This principle should hold true even if the appeal is rational in approach. Some basic human need must still be at the heart of the ad, something about which people feel passionate.

4. **The ad must stimulate . . . what? *Curiosity.*** The audience should want to know more. This desire gets them to stop and study the ad — and follow up with further information searches afterward.

5. **HEY! The ad should *surprise* its audience.** A startling headline, an unexpected visual image, an unusual opening gambit in a sales presentation, a weird display window in a store — all have the power to stop people by surprising them.

6. **The ad must communicate expected information — in an *unexpected* way.** A creative twist, a fresh way of saying or looking at something — these devices make the expected unexpected. You have to get the obvious information in: what the brand is, who it benefits and how. But don't do so in an obvious way or the communication won't reach out and grab attention.

7. **The ad must *violate* the rules and personality of the product category.** This step is necessary to make the product stand out. People notice things that violate expected patterns, and patterns certainly exist in marketing. Unless your ad is distinctly different from what consumers have come to expect in your category, they won't stop for it.

These points are based on a wonderful book by Hanley Norins called *The Young & Rubicam Traveling Creative Workshop* (Prentice Hall, 1990). I recommend you get it (you'll probably have to order it through your local bookstore) if you plan to do much advertising. It shows how Norins' agency trains its copywriters to do great creative work.

As I wrote this list, one thought kept recurring to me: the hidden importance of *creativity.* To make an ad that has drama, that surprises people, that violates the pattern, that says the expected in an unexpected way — all requires creativity. And so perhaps the most essential secret to stopping power is creativity. When in doubt, then, go to Chapter 4!

Sex, anyone?

Advertising research reveals another secret of stopping power: Sex in ads is a good stopper. The header I chose for this section is intended to illustrate the stopping power of sex. Even the word catches one's eye. And so to give an ad stopping power, just give it some sex appeal.

However, there *is* a hitch. (Figures.) The same research that shows sex-based ads have stopping power also shows that these same ads are *not very effective* by other measures. Brand recall — the ability of viewers to remember what the ad was for — is typically *lower* for sex-oriented ads than other ads. So while these ads do have stopping power, they don't seem to have any other benefits. They fail to turn attention into awareness or interest. They don't change attitudes about the product. In short, they sacrifice good communication for raw stopping power.

The only exception to the rule that sexy ads are bad communicators is when sexy is *relevant to the product.* If you are selling a perfume that you claim makes women irresistible to NBA basketball stars, then showing a bunch of scantily-clad seven-foot-tall hunks flocking after a woman like moths to a flame probably makes sense. (Okay, it's a dumb example, but at least it illustrates my point.) David Ogilvy, the famous founder of Ogilvy & Mather, learned this point the hard way. "The first advertisement I ever produced," he says (in *Ogilvy on Advertising* — a wonderfully fun book from Vintage), "showed a naked woman. It was a mistake, not because it was sexy, but because it was irrelevant to the product — a cooking stove. The test is *relevance.*"

Pull Power

"Hey, YOU! Come over here!"

Pull power is the ability of a marketing communication to draw people to a place or event. National advertisers don't worry too much about pull power, as they are often building brand strength or working to change people's attitudes about a brand through repositioning (see Chapter 3 for information on doing that). However, local marketers are usually more concerned with pull power than *brand equity* (building the value of your brand) or positioning. After all, *somebody* has to actually *sell* any product at the ground level — in the local market, and customer by customer. And so at this level what matters is drawing in those customers. Pull power is everything.

Pull power is the primary goal of all local advertising. (By local advertising, I mean advertising focused on a specific city or county — which includes almost half of all advertising in the U.S. and many other countries as well.)

And pull power also includes a great deal of the publicity, personal selling, direct mail, price-based promotions, and point-of-purchase spending — probably more than half of all the money spent on all forms of marketing communications through all available influence points.

Because of this pull orientation, local marketing communications are uniquely different:

- ✔ Local communications tend to be part of a short-term effort, rather than some long-term campaign. A two-week run of a print ad in a local newspaper needs to generate immediate results in local advertising — or it is deemed a failure. Similarly, this month's store windows and point-of-purchase displays (covered in Chapter 16) ought to be taken down early if they don't pull enough people into the store and close enough sales.

- ✔ Local communications tend to be done on shoestring budgets that are far smaller than the millions spent by national or multinational advertisers. This fact helps the marketer keep her impact in perspective — and quantify the returns. A one month effort to publicize the offices of a brokerage house in a city ought to generate enough sales leads to more than pay for the marketing cost. If it doesn't, the marketer should be able to find out quickly. The calculations are simple because of the short time frame and relatively small numbers.

- ✔ Local communications ought to generate customers in the store, or make the phone ring, or bring more folks to your Web site, or accomplish some other pull-oriented tactical goal. Contrast this objective with the goals of national advertising, which often aim to build brand identity and strengthen or alter a brand's position. However, other marketing goals are common to both local and national advertising: increasing awareness, boosting market share, and reminding past customers to repeat their purchases. The elements of good marketing are the same whether they are practiced locally or globally, but the order of priority is often different.

- ✔ Local communications need to make more creative use of media than national communications because of the local focus and relatively small budgets. In fact, some of the best pull-oriented local marketing communications are virtually free.

Think *pull*. Communications aren't working if they don't generate store traffic, stuff your mailbox, or light up your switchboard! Make sure that every local communication gives people a strong reason to act. Tell consumers that you are in the market and that you have what they need. And keep telling them, always in new and creative ways, so consumers never forget you.

Great Writing

What, one may well ask, constitutes great writing in marketing communications, and how can it be achieved? More to the point, how might one go about the writing task — might there not be some secret or secrets that increase the probability of success? To be good, writing would have to communicate its point succinctly and simply enough to avoid losing the audience. And it would need to capture and hold attention sufficiently to ensure that . . .

And that, in case you didn't notice, is *bad writing*!

And yet much of the writing in marketing communications is even worse:

- ✔ It fails to come to the point.

- ✔ It uses passive sentences (where you can't tell *who* is doing *what*).

- ✔ It employs sophisticated vocabulary without proper cause — I mean it uses big words needlessly.

- ✔ It uses difficult verb tenses instead of the present tense ("writing would have to communicate" instead of "writing communicates" for example).

- ✔ And as a result, this writing bores or confuses its readers.

Now I know what not to do. So I can rewrite that terrible introductory paragraph. And rewrite. And rewrite. Until the whole thing really sparkles! How about:

> **Need great writing? Keep the writing direct. Keep the writing simple. Make it reach out and grab the reader.**

Notice that my first draft of this paragraph uses 75 words, and the paragraph is not even complete. The new, improved version uses 19 words. That's a 75 percent reduction. And the comma count went from 4 to 0, which illustrates a key point about great writing: It's succinct.

Great writing should also be *clear* — and my rewrite is certainly a lot clearer than my first try.

If you can find a novel way to make your point, do. Remember the need for originality and surprise if you want your writing to have stopping power. But above all else, make sure your writing is simple and clear.

You can only get to the essence of a communication through many rewrites. Keep reworking, keep rethinking, keep boiling your words down until you have something that penetrates to your point with startling clarity.

And then, once you make your point, shut up.

Great Visuals

Imagine the following: A kid is playing tennis against a backboard when a dog runs up and steals the ball. The ball, bright yellow and fuzzy, overflows the dog's mouth as the camera zooms in to show the ball and mouth, filling the TV screen.

This visual image is simple. But it communicates a lot. Like how much fun kids, and dogs, have when playing with tennis balls. And the image offers drama — how does the kid feel when the dog takes his ball? How does the *dog* feel when he gets the ball? Most of all, the image reminds us that tennis is good fun for everyone, regardless of skill level, age, or even species!

This visual image is at the heart of a television spot from the U.S. Tennis Association to promote the sport of tennis. This spot illustrates the power of a good visual image or sequence of images to capture attention, tell an interesting story, and communicate a point.

And the spot also illustrates a key to successful visuals — that they *focus on one strong, relevant image*. In this case, that image is the tennis ball, proudly framed in the dog's jaws. In your case, well, the image can be anything — as long as that thing is visually compelling, easily recognizable, and relevant to your appeal.

Importance of visual design

Let me first warn you that I cannot show you how to be a good designer or artist in the few paragraphs I'm devoting to the topic. You will need to work with artists unless you are one yourself. Gaining the technical skills and design sense to do something as simple as an illustrated brochure takes a long time, let alone more complex tasks like a four-color print ad, a package design, or a television spot. But still, you may find yourself having to take on some of the smaller design tasks in your marketing department or business. A catalog sheet, brochure, store window display, or other visual design may have to be done right now, without the budget for a creative agency or graphic designer. And the modern computer can put considerable design power into the amateur's hands.

For example, if you have a Macintosh with clip art files, running Quark Express and Photoshop software, with a high-quality scanner to bring in photographs of a product, you can "play" designer pretty effectively. I do this often when a project is too small to justify bringing in the pros.

But, I must warn you that most of the homemade designing I see coming off of people's desktop computers and laser printers stinks. The results are a waste of the paper they're printed on, an insult to the customer, and an embarrassment to the profession of marketing. Doing the design work yourself is now technically easy, but if you don't know much about design, you can get in more trouble, more quickly, with the new technologies. (You can find more information about this subject in *Desktop Publishing and Design For Dummies,* published by IDG Books Worldwide, Inc.)

Good design integrates words and images

Ultimately, you have to accept the reality that people first encounter your marketing communication *as design*. We "look at" ads, displays, packaging, and other visual communications. And if they appeal to us on a design level, we may choose to become more involved. To actually read or listen to the ads.

But the words are wasted unless the design draws the audience to them.

And so you must learn to think of the words in your message as a designer does, which is very different from the writer's perspective. How do the words look on the page? Do the words have enough contrast and visual interest to draw the reader to them? Do the words work with the other design elements to form appealing patterns and to draw the viewer into a focal point? The designer views print as just one more element on the design palate. And that makes the design perspective the "final word" on any marketing communication. If the ad doesn't work from a visual perspective (or a musical perspective for radio ads), then the words are wasted.

Chapter 6

Marketing Research: Customers, Competitors, and Industries

● ●

In This Chapter

▶ Understanding the four secrets of successful research

▶ Gaining insights into a market through existing information sources

▶ Making better questionnaires

▶ Finding specialized research firms

▶ Measuring customer satisfaction

● ●

*M*arketing research generally focuses on clarifying customer behavior or attitudes, and on exploring the structure of industries and the positions of competitors. But this quick definition does the marketing research field injustice. Marketers need to know so much, and so little of that information is readily available, that marketing depends very heavily on a wide variety of research efforts. The more research marketers can do, the better their work.

One of the most striking differences between the leading marketers and the rest of the crowd is that the leading consumer products companies and their global ad agencies do an incredible amount of research. They think nothing of surveying a few thousand customers just to find out whether attitudes toward dandruff are changing. And they routinely examine their ads to find out what percent of viewers remember each of dozens of ad elements. The big firms bring in top statisticians to crunch all this data, and they generate a horrifyingly large number of graphs and charts to interpret it.

The big investment in research seen at companies like Procter & Gamble (P&G) gives these large corporations an advantage over smaller competitors. Bigger companies often spot a trend or identify a customer segment early. But even these behemoths make mistakes because of the difficulty of conducting and interpreting marketing research. And just because the conglomerates outspend their smaller competitors doesn't mean that the small fry can't tap into the power of marketing research, too. You can conduct research on a small scale in many economical ways, some of which I'll cover in this chapter. Whatever you decide to do, however, please be sure you know — and take full advantage of — my four "secrets" of marketing research, covered in the main text of this chapter.

Are You Marketing Blind?

Most marketers underutilize research. These marketers are like drivers with no windshield wipers racing down a freeway while wearing dark glasses on a rainy night. As long as the road keeps going straight and no competitors switch into their lane, their occasional glimpse of the road is enough to keep them in the race (winning is another matter). But when anything changes, their lack of a clear market view can be fatal.

The remedies for this problem are many and varied. I cover a wide variety of methods and strategies in this chapter, and I also refer you to a host of specialized research services in case you need to go even further. But even if you don't read a word more of this chapter today, I hope you will do one thing: Draw a big question mark on a piece of paper and tape it to the wall in sight of your desk. Whenever you glance up from your work, let your eyes rest on that question mark so that you will always remember to *ask questions*.

This inquisitive spirit is at the heart of marketing research. And it is free — you don't have to have P&G's research budget to take advantage of it! Ask yourself why customers do what they do; what caused a change in your market; or where those customers you lose end up going. Almost any question works as a starting point. The first — and most important — step in any research effort is to ask a penetrating question! It's that simple. So no excuses, okay? Get out there and do some research!

Secret #1: You Have to Work Backward

I know your instinct is to first gather lots of information and *then* think about what you should do. Research first, analyze later. But that turns out to be a terrible waste of your time and your company's money. You won't be any closer to doing the "right" thing just because you immersed yourself in data. You'll only be shorter on time.

To profit from marketing research, you have to start with *a careful analysis of the decisions you must make*. For example, say you are in charge of a two-year-old software product that is used by small businesses to develop their marketing plans. As the product manager, what key decisions should you be making? The following are the most likely:

- Should we launch an upgrade or keep selling the current version?
- Is our current marketing program sufficiently effective or should we redesign it?
- Is the product positioned properly or do we need to change its image?

So before you do any research, you need to *think hard* about those decisions. Specifically, you need to

- Decide what your realistic options are for each decision.
- Assess your level of uncertainty and risk for each decision.

Then, for any uncertain or risky decisions you need to

- Pose questions whose answers should help you reduce the risk and uncertainty of the decision.
- And *now*, with these questions in hand, you are ready to begin your research!

When you work through this thinking process, you often find that research is unnecessary. For example, maybe your boss has already decided to invest in an upgrade of the software product you manage, so researching the decision is pointless. Wrong or right, you can't realistically change that decision. But some questions make it through the screening process and turn out to be good candidates for research. For these, you need to pose a series of questions that have the potential to reduce your decision-making uncertainty or to reveal new and exciting options for you as a decision-maker.

For example, take the question, "Is the product positioned properly or do we need to change its image?" To find out whether repositioning your product makes sense, you might ask how people currently perceive the product's quality and performance, how they view the product compared to the leading competitors, and what the product's personality is (see Chapter 5 for information about product personality). If you know the answers to all these questions, you should be far better able to make a good decision.

That's why you must start by defining your marketing decisions very carefully. Until you know what decisions you must make, marketing research has little point. (See Figure 6-1 for a flowchart of the research process.)

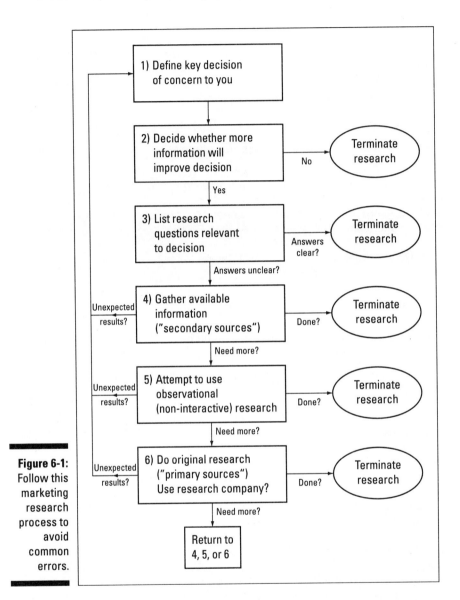

Figure 6-1:
Follow this marketing research process to avoid common errors.

Secret #2: You Can Always Find Free Data

The world is overflowing with data, and some of it is just what you need to get started on your research project. So before you buy a report or hire a research firm, dig around for some free (or at least cheap) stuff.

Of course, you generally get what you pay for when it comes to free data. For example, I visited the U.S. Census Bureau's home page on the World Wide Web (at `http://www.census.gov/`) to see if I could get detailed census data on households in several Massachusetts counties. Yes, you can buy their data at modest price, on paper or computer disk, but you have to play phone tag for a day and then wait endlessly for delivery. Or you can go to one of many private vendors that analyze and update the census data and are happy to sell you customized reports, but for much more money. However, getting the data yourself, and cheap, is very appealing. But for the record, I was stymied by the Census Bureau's software, which froze up on me in the middle of my search and crashed my poor computer. Ah, well, perhaps I will have to spend a little money after all.

Even if you get the data free, it may be old or lacking in detail. So you may well need to spend some money before your research questions are fully answered. But at least the free stuff can get you started by narrowing down your focus and helping you form some good hypothetical answers to test later on. And sometimes, if you are lucky, the free data is all you need!

Free data generally falls into a category known as *secondary data* — meaning already collected or published by someone else — and so you are getting it second-hand. Some secondary data is available for free; other secondary data is sold by publishers and research firms. But whether for free or for sale, secondary data is (almost) always cheaper than *primary data,* or data collected specifically for your current needs.

Primary data may be collected through surveys of all sorts, by observation, and in other ways — I cover survey methods and primary and secondary data research later in this chapter.

Never underestimate the value of secondary research. The resourceful researcher can learn a great deal by poking through other people's data. And the cost savings of using a combination of free and for-sale secondary data is pretty high. A secondary-only research project may cost you a few hundred to a few thousand dollars. A primary research project involving one or more surveys typically costs anywhere from $10,000 to a great deal more.

Secret #3: You Can Research ANYTHING!

One of the puzzling things about the marketing research profession is that it is really dozens of different, specialized professions. No one version of marketing research exists. What you need depends on lots of things — mostly on your realizing that, whatever the decision or problem, a specialized form of research is available to help you out.

Let your questions be your guide

Please remember that you, the marketing researcher, need to pose well-defined questions before you collect data.

Yet too often, marketers go off half-cocked with a research goal such as "We need to find out all about the cookie market." Great. Pretty soon you'll have a yard-high pile of tables and articles. But you still won't know how to make any money in that market! You can only learn from research by posing focused questions, such as "Who eats cookies?" and "Who eats the *most* cookies?" and "What types of cookies do these heavy users like the most?" and

"What media reach these heavy users most effectively?" and "What brands do they prefer right now?" (Substitute your product to adapt such questions to suit your needs.)

If you have trouble thinking up appropriate research questions, go back to your starting point, which is your definition of the decision or decisions you want the research to affect (refer to Figure 6-1). Think about what questions you need to answer in order to make that decision more intelligently, and then go out and do the minimum research needed to answer those questions.

You can hire a firm to audit retail stores in order to see if your point-of-purchase displays (covered in Chapter 16) are properly displayed. Or you can have a firm interview shoppers to see what they think of the displays. Or you can hire a firm to create an artificial store in order to see how a selection of shoppers responds to your new packaging concept. In order to help you increase an accounting firm's market share, you can do research to find out how companies perceive the accounting services available to them. Perhaps you have what you think is a great print ad — but you want to test it to be certain before you run the ad. Maybe you want to find out what new products or marketing plans your competitors are developing so that you can shape your response ahead of time. Or perhaps you'd like to find out how your products or services would fly in Asian markets and how to find distributors to handle them in that region.

I could go on. In fact, I *do* go on. My point is that if you are unable to do the proper research, researchers are ready and eager to support you in any marketing task, and when better information can improve your decisions, then hiring a research firm to do some primary research is generally profitable. Table 6-1 identifies 29 different types of marketing research and gives examples of firms that claim to be expert in each. Twenty-nine types of research! Have a look. I bet at least a few apply to your work right now.

Table 6-1	Specialized Research and Providers
Specialized Research Areas	*Examples of Research Provider*
Ad Copy Evaluation	Research International, New York NY, 212-679-2500
Advertising Effectiveness	Audits & Surveys Worldwide, New York NY, 212-627-9700
	NFO Research, Inc., Greenwich CT, 203-629-8888
Asian Markets	MRD Co., El Cerrito CA, 510-525-9675
Brand Evaluation	Brand Consulting Group, Southfield MI, 810-559-2100
	The Landis Group, West Palm Beach FL, 407-684-3636
	Burke Customer Satisfaction Associates Headquarters: Cincinnati OH, 800-264-9970
Business-to-Business Marketing	Beta Research Corp., La Miranda CA, 714-994-1206
	Industrial Market Research Co., Whittier CA, 310-698-2341
	Burke Customer Satisfaction Associates Headquarters: Cincinnati OH, 800-264-9970
Competitor Intelligence	The Becker Research Co., Rocky Hill NJ, 609-951-8570
Consumer Products	The BASES Group, Covington KY, 606-655-6000
	Research International, New York NY, 212-679-2500
Controlled Store Testing	Capstone Research, Inc., Lyndhurst NJ, 201-939-0600
Copy Testing	NFO Research, Inc., Greenwich CT, 203-629-8888
Corporate Image Research	I.D. ENTITY, Brea CA, 800-355-9817
Customer Satisfaction	The Blackstone Group, Chicago IL, 312-419-0400
	Polaris Marketing Research, Atlanta GA, 404-816-0353
	Burke Customer Satisfaction Associates Headquarters: Cincinnati OH, 800-264-9970

(continued)

Table 6-1 *(continued)*

Specialized Research Areas	Examples of Research Provider
Data Collection and Processing	Data Recognition Corp., Minnetonka MN, 612-935-5900
Demographic Analysis	Data Mapping Services, Akron OH, 216-929-1353
Ethnic Markets	Hispanic Market Connections (HMC), Los Altos CA, 415-965-3859
Eye Tracking	Perception Research Services, Fort Lee NJ, 201-346-1600
	Toronto Focus, Toronto, Ontario, Canada, 416-250-3611
Focus Groups	Roanoke Focus Group Centre, Roanoke VA, 703-342-5364
	Manhattan Opinion Center, New York NY, 212-557-3085
Food & Beverages	GFK/Sofema International, 10 Rue Lionel Terray, Rueil Malmaison Cedex 92500, France, 3-31-47-14-44-00
	Creative & Response Research Services, Chicago IL, 312-828-9200
In-Store Interviewing	Audits & Surveys Worldwide, New York NY, 212-627-9700
Mail Surveys	Questar Service Quality Research, Eagan MN, 612-688-0089
Market Segmentation/Structure	SERS, Chicago IL, 312-828-0702
Media Studies	The Arbitron Company, New York NY, 212-887-1300
	BAI, Tarrytown NY, 914-332-5300
Mystery Shopping	Capstone Research, Fairfield NJ, 201-939-0600
Name Testing	NameQuest, Carefree AZ, 602-488-9660
New Product Research	The BASES Group, Covington KY, 606-655-6000
	SERS, Chicago IL, 312-828-0702
Package Design	Perception Research Services, Fort Lee NJ, 201-346-1600

Specialized Research Areas	Examples of Research Provider
Simulated Test Markets	The BASES Group, Covington KY, 606-655-6000
Store Audits	O'Connor Survey Service, Knoxville TN, 615-525-9989
Survey Processessing	Scantron Corp., Tustin CA, 714-259-8887
Test Marketing	Maritz Marketing Research, Fenton MO, 314-827-1610

Using secondary research

Secondary data, defined earlier as data gathered previously that may be of use to you if you can get ahold of it, is generally cheaper and, thus, marketers should look for it *before* they do primary research. Yes, I know that telling you to do secondary research before primary sounds contradictory, but I didn't make up the names.

Where do you find secondary data? First, a word on the best source of free or almost-free data: your national government. Almost all governments collect copious data on economic activity, population size, and trends within their borders. In the U.S., the Census Bureau is the best general source of data on how many of what sorts of people and households live where (look on the Internet at `http://www.census.gov/`). And the Department of Commerce has endless data on what sorts of businesses do how much of what sorts of business.

Demographics!

I have to add that exclamation point to the word "demographics" or nobody will pay any attention to it. *Demographics* — statistics about a population — seem kind of boring to most people. Yet trends in the ethnic makeup of your market, its average age, or its educational levels, are very good clues as to how your marketing ought to change. For example, the populations of the U.S., Canada, most European countries, and Japan are aging. What does that mean to marketers?

Nothing at first glance. So what if the average person is a year or two older today than a decade ago? You can still target products to people of different ages and ignore the long-term demographic trend.

Or, you can take a closer look at this trend and see all kinds of opportunities. Many consumer products marketers are working with Charles Schewe, an Amherst, Massachusetts-based consultant who studies the aging population, to redesign their products and services for this growing segment. Older Americans share a common set of values and attitudes that makes targeting them with marketing messages easier. They have common needs — for example, they need easier-to-read packaging and easier-to-use controls. And they have a great deal of disposable income, because the majority of the wealth in most societies is held by elders. And as the population ages, this already-attractive marketing segment is growing faster than others.

This sort of opportunity is easy to find when you pay close attention to demographic data and other secondary sources of information. Yet many marketers ignore these inexpensive sources of data and overlook important changes in their markets as a result.

Your sales data!

Another easily-overlooked gold mine of secondary data (hence the exclamation mark). Which types of customers defect? When and why? Who are your biggest or most profitable customers? Which regions are you gaining or losing in? Such questions and many like them are best answered by digging into your company's sales records. And if those records aren't sufficiently detailed, try reading sales reports or interviewing your salespeople or distributors. Somebody who works for your company probably knows a great deal more about your customers and competitors than you do. Go find them!

In bigger companies, where hiring goes on constantly, a few new employees come from competitors or other players in your industry. Stop by the Human Resources department and ask them to send these people around to your office for a quick debriefing in their first week or two on the job. (Be sure to avoid pressuring them to answer anything that may violate trade secrecy laws — check with your HR department to see if this problem could be an issue in your industry.) Marketers rarely take advantage of the competitor intelligence these employees carry with them.

Conducting primary research

Primary research gathers data from people in answers to questions. In general, this type of research gathers data by observing people to see how they behave or by asking them for verbal or written answers to questions.

Following, I give you a very quick overview of the various approaches.

Observing your customers

Years ago, managers from the Boston Aquarium wanted to find out which attractions were most popular. They hired a researcher to develop a survey, but the researcher told them not to bother. Instead, his solution was to examine the floors for wear and for tracks on wet days. The evidence pointed clearly to certain attractions as most popular. The floors in front of those attractions had the most wear. And damp paths led clearly to the attractions that visitors preferred to go to first.

Observation and Sherlock Holmes

Marketers need not be Sherlock Holmes, but they can benefit from the method of detection in which he carefully observes all the details before forming any theory. Holmes' powers of observation often surprised his associate, Dr. Watson, but they always seemed so obvious when explained. Yet Holmes' approach to observation is a particularly precise and inquisitive one, as exemplified by this brief explanation of it in the story, *A Scandal in Bohemia:*

"You see, but you do not observe," Holmes says to Watson. "The distinction is clear. For example, you have frequently seen the steps which lead up from the hall to this room."

"Frequently."

"How often?"

"Well, some hundreds of times."

"Then how many are there?"

"How many? I don't know."

"Quite so! You have not observed. And yet you have seen. That is just my point. Now, I know that there are seventeen steps, because I have both seen and observed."

To count every set of steps you climb would be crazy, but *sometimes* doing so is necessary. And sometimes, marketing researchers need to switch gears from *seeing* to *observing* when gathering data toward a question.

Consumers are all around us — shopping for, buying, and using products. Observing consumers and learning something new of value is not hard. And even *business-to-business marketers* (who sell to other businesses instead of end-consumers) can find plenty of evidence about their customers at a glance. The number and direction of a company's trucks on various roads can tell you where their business is heaviest and lightest, for example. Observing a great many things of value in marketing research is not difficult, and yet most marketers are as guilty as Dr. Watson was of Sherlock Holmes' accusation that "you have not observed, and yet you have seen." (See the sidebar "Observation and Sherlock Holmes" for more on Holmes' method of detection.) Observation is the most underrated of all research methods.

I hate to make a generalization like the preceding one and then leave you to translate the statement into particulars. So let me help. Here is what I want you to do: Find a way to *observe one of your customers as he or she uses one of your products.* I want you to observe, not just watch. Bring along a pad and pencil, and take care to notice the little things. What does the customer do, in what order, and how long does he spend doing it? What does he say, if anything? Does he look happy? Frustrated? Disinterested? Does anything go wrong? Does anything go right — as in surprising him with how well the product performs? Take detailed notes, and then think about them. I *guarantee* that you will end up gaining at least one insight into how to improve your product, regardless of what that insight is.

One observation of one customer interaction with one product does not a research project make. But if you can gain insight from doing that project once, what might you learn if a half-dozen researchers spend time watching fifty different customers as they use one of your products? Okay, you get my point.

And now for another generalization. Whenever you consider doing primary research, first give yourself a few days to think up clever ways of using observational techniques. You may actually need that long, because people generally just *see* things much more often than they truly *observe* them. Observational research can usually be conducted in some creative way, and I don't want you to overlook any possibilities.

Asking people questions

Survey research methods of various sorts are the bread and butter of the marketing research industry, and for a good reason. You can often learn something of value just by asking people what they think. The biggest shortcomings of survey methods are that customers don't always know what they think or how they'll behave, and that even when they do, getting them to tell you can be quite costly. Nonetheless, every marketer finds good uses for survey research on occasion, as the following discussion shows.

Improving a questionnaire

One of the things I'm asked to do most often is to look at someone's survey and offer suggestions for improving it. I think this request comes because marketers realize that a little extra care and editing up front makes all the difference in the value and validity of the results. And I recommend you adopt the practice of having people review your questionnaires, too.

If big money is at stake, then you or your research firm should do a formal pretest of your survey by trying it out on a small sample of respondents, and then checking to see if they seemed to understand the questions and if their answers seem to make sense.

But in many cases, the stakes aren't high enough for a formal review. You can get just as good feedback by asking an assortment of friends, marketing people (who hopefully have some expertise in research!), and a few customers to have a look at the questionnaire. And don't forget to put on your own editor's hat and review the questionnaire with a critical eye.

Here are seven questions to ask when reviewing a survey:

1. **Is the survey *appealing* to respondents?**

    The survey should be interesting or rewarding for them to do. A good topic, well-written instructions, easy, quick questions, and perhaps the inclusion of a sales promotion (coupon, entry form for a contest, and so on) can make the respondents' experience more pleasurable — and ensure a reasonably high response rate. Too many surveys are confusing and lengthy. Cull everything but the vital questions and make those questions easy and interesting! (And make sure that your *list* — the people you contact and ask to participate in the survey — is good; prequalify respondents if possible. No survey is appealing to the wrong respondent.)

2. Do any questions *combine* more than one concept?

If so, break them apart. For example, I recommend breaking the following question from an employee survey by a garden and gift store into multiple separate items: "How do you rank the variety of our plant and gift selections? 1 2 3 4 (1 = meager, 4 = complete)." The simplest fix is just to offer two questions, one for plants and one for gifts. An even better way to handle it, because a number of major plant categories exist, is to break the question out like this:

How do you rank the variety of our plant selections?			
Herbs	1	2	3	4
Annuals	1	2	3	4
Hanging Baskets	1	2	3	4
Perennials	1	2	3	4
Bulbs	1	2	3	4
Christmas Trees	1	2	3	4
	meager		excellent

In fact, Annie's Garden & Gift Store in Amherst, Massachusetts used this very question in a customer survey, and the results helped store management decide which product lines they needed to extend. A more general form of the question would not have given them the specific feedback needed to make their next year's buying decisions.

3. Do scales permit a *full range* of answers?

Sometimes the author's assumptions limit the respondent's options. Expand the possibilities and also use "Other: _____" whenever possible.

If you are using numerical scales, such as the 1 to 4 scale in Question 2, ask yourself what the pros and cons of a longer or shorter scale would be. For example, would a 5-point scale have any advantages over the 4-point scale? One obvious difference is that the 5-point scale permits respondents to give a neutral answer. This difference is important when you have an agree/disagree scale, as some people will want to fence-sit. Although *you* may not want neutral answers, you may want to permit them if respondents are determined to give them.

By the way, survey research firms generally use a 5-point or 7-point scale, and I recommend you do the same unless you have a good reason not to. More choices don't really slow down respondents. Once they understand a scale, they can use it pretty quickly — as long as the scale doesn't change from question to question! And the longer 1 to 7 scale should give you a finer measure of respondent opinions, because it breaks out the range into more categories.

4. Are any questions *leading* or *misleading*?

Check that questions are as clear and neutral as possible in their wording.

For example, the question "Do you agree that our customer service is excellent? Yes__No__" isn't worth the ink needed to print it. First, the question is biased toward positive answers because of its use of the words "agree" and "excellent" within the question itself. (People tend to tell you what you ask them to tell you in questionnaires, so make sure that you don't give them obvious hints!) Second, respondents may be confused about where to put their check marks. Is a "No" answer indicated with a check before or after the No? Here is a rewrite of the question that solves these two problems:

Please evaluate customer service:						
Terrible						Excellent
1	2	3	4	5	6	7

(Also see the section on measuring customer service at the end of this chapter.)

5. Are any questions *irrelevant* to your actions?

Cut questions unless they help improve an important decision or process.

Most questionnaires are at least 75 percent waste questions. Really! Here's how I know. Actions do not result from most of the questions after managers examine the results. And if the result doesn't produce action, then the question was an obvious waste of everybody's time. For example, Annie's Garden and Gift store has no need to ask the following questions on its questionnaire:

---

1. Are you: __male __female

2. Do you visit Annie's

__ on your own

__ with a partner

__ with children

__ with friends

3. Would you come back to Annie's to shop again? __yes __no

- The first question is probably included for the sake of tradition. Don't all surveys gather demographic data on respondents? But the tradition comes from large-scale, random-sample surveys in which researchers expect that men and women, or people of different ages, or companies in different industries, will give significantly different answers. Researchers use such questions when they anticipate a need to segment their respondents and analyze each group separately. They will cross-tabulate all the other questions by these demographic variables and look for statistically significant differences. And then they will customize marketing to each segment.

  But Annie's — and, in all likelihood, you — won't. Small sample sizes and informal sampling methods (like handing out a survey at the counter) make that sort of statistical analysis impossible — even if the results would mean anything, which I doubt they would.

- The third question seems much more useful. After all, return business is very important, so why not ask customers if they intend to come back to the store? But this particular survey's instructions say "Complete and return by the end of the month and get $5 off your next purchase of $20 or more!" Therefore, we can assume many respondents will take this survey home in their shopping bags and return the survey only if they, too, return. Most "no" answers will never make it back to the store to be analyzed.

6. Are any questions better determined through observation?

The other category of unnecessary questions asks questions whose answers you do need — but could more easily obtain through observation.

Assume for a moment that Annie's *does* have an important need for data on the gender of its customers, with whom they shop, and whether and how often they return. All of this information is easier to obtain through simple observation of who comes into the store (and in what groups), and through use of secondary sources such as the store's credit card records. An employee can fill in an observation form to record information about the people who come into the store. And an evening with the old credit card records can tell you what percentage of customers who paid by credit card were repeat customers in a given period, and how often they returned. Of course, this source leaves out all check and cash customers, so you may want to start collecting customer names at the register. Many stores do already, either through a computerized cash register system or through a sign-up to receive a newsletter or the like.

An observer can measure another important aspect of customer behavior better than a survey can: How many customers come into the store, look around, but don't find what they want? Every retail store has some of these — and they are often the biggest percentage of shoppers. A survey given out at the register misses these consumers. If the survey was given out at the door, most would still be missed because dissatisfied customers rarely volunteer to fill in surveys. Yet observation can tell you a great deal about these lost customers at low cost. An employee can count them in a random selection of fifteen-minute periods, allowing you to estimate the number of them per day or week. (To learn more, you could also have an employee intercept some of them and ask them what they were looking for and why they are leaving.)

I strongly recommend collecting observational data on both the *rate of repeat business* and the *number of lost customers*. Both statistics are manageable, meaning that once you measure them regularly you can experiment with changes and then see if the measures move in a favorable direction. And both are typically best measured through observations rather than questionnaires.

7. **Does your questionnaire allow respondents to *tell you something you don't know*?**

This question, the last of my recommended ones, is the most subtle. Many questionnaires are well constructed and get useful information — yet fail to reveal a critical fact, because the author didn't know to ask about it.

For example, what if customers like to visit Annie's Gift Store during their lunch hours and wish they could bring or buy a sandwich and eat it in the garden during good weather? Annie's included a number of open-ended questions and a blank page to give respondents a chance to tell them something like that. My favorite of the open-ended questions in their survey is "If you had a garden store, what would you do differently?" This question is designed to get the respondent's imagination going and is likely to generate the sort of creative suggestions that more structured questions cannot.

Secret #4: The Greatest Insights Are Unplanned

I started this chapter with the admonishment that you have to define your marketing decisions before performing your research. And I stand by that advice. A methodical, decision-oriented approach is the only way to go. You have to have a plan.

However, I have to warn you that the research process is sometimes perverse. On occasion, research turns up something so startling and unexpected that the only smart thing to do is to throw away your initial definition of the decision and make up something new on the spot.

For example, look back to my opening example in this chapter, in which the manager of a software product is trying to decide whether to reposition the product or not. I said that in order to find out whether repositioning your product makes sense, you might ask how people currently perceive its quality and performance, how they view the product compared to the leading competitors, and what the product's personality is.

Say you set out to research these three questions by hiring a research firm to compose a telephone survey and call potential users of your product. Now imagine that when this firm calls potential users and tries to ask them what they think of your product, *78 percent of respondents say they've never heard of your product.*

Surprise! Turns out you were working on a false assumption — that the marketplace was sufficiently aware of your product for it to hold a definite position in the first place. But here is clear evidence that the market is unaware of your product. Serendipity has just thrown a valuable insight in your lap.

The right thing to do now is to toss that survey in the trash — because it deals with positioning rather than awareness — and to go back to the question drawing board (refer to Figure 6-1). This is no time to fiddle around with your product's positioning. What you probably need is a massive awareness-building campaign to inform the market that your product exists. Scrap those other decisions and focus on the decision of how best to boost awareness of your product.

When good assumptions backfire

I have to add a stern warning here. In my varied experience as a marketing manager and consultant, I have seen many research projects backfire when a common assumption was proven wrong. And most of the time, people responded by going into deep denial. I'm talking head-in-sand denial. For some reason, admitting your initial assumptions were dead wrong is terribly hard and so is adopting a new approach.

What most people will do when confronted with the survey results that prove a given assumption wrong is to throw out the responses from people who are unaware of the product, and only analyze the minority that were able to answer the questions "correctly." That saves researchers' egos by allowing them to retain their initial decision focus. But doing so produces bad marketing, because a valuable insight is overlooked.

So please, *please,* resist the temptation to assume the research is wrong and you are right. Whenever you get a strange result, *think about it* — and nothing else — until you understand *why* the result is so different from your initial assumption. Maybe the sample was poor or the question misleading. But often, the research is right, and you are wrong. Then you have the chance to discover a surprising and valuable insight into your product and market. And that's when marketing research yields the greatest returns.

Are Your Customers Satisfied?

In a sense, marketing is very simple. If customers are happy, they'll come back. If not, *adios.* And because recruiting new customers costs anywhere from four to twenty times as much as retaining old ones (depending upon your industry), you can't afford to lose customers. Which means you can't afford to dissatisfy them. That's why *every marketer needs to measure and set goals for customer satisfaction.*

Yet I don't see marketers giving this issue the attention it deserves, in spite of a major two decade-long effort on the part of so-called "experts" like me to put this issue on the agenda. So far, the majority of marketers don't really walk the talk when it comes to customer satisfaction.

I'm not just griping. Well, actually, I am griping, but everyone else is, too. For several years now the University of Michigan and the American Society of Quality Control have collaborated on a survey of 28,000 consumers that measures customer satisfaction in a wide range of U.S. industries. And the latest data available to me as I write — 1996 vs. 1995 results — demonstrate a remarkable lack of progress. The typical consumer is furious about the service received from restaurants, airlines, and the media. And overall, businesses were rated 2 percent *less friendly* than they were a year ago. Of 206 companies analyzed, only a third improved, and only 7 percent of companies made significant (4 percent or greater) improvements.

If you work for the two-thirds majority of businesses that don't increase their customers' satisfaction each year, you need to get cracking. And the best whip to crack is a customer satisfaction measure that portrays your company or product in a realistic light. Once this measure gets reported to everyone on a regular basis, your company will have to look hard at customer satisfaction.

Many such measures fluff up customer satisfaction to conceal problems. This tactic is like evaluating the comfort of a mattress by spreading a soft comforter over it and then seeing if it looks level. The best measures put some weight on the mattress. The more stress you induce, the more meaningful the response!

For example, any measure based on a survey that asks customers to "rate your overall satisfaction with our company on a 1-to-10 scale" isn't much use. What does an average score of 8.76 mean? Sure, that's pretty high. But are customers satisfied? You didn't really ask them. And even worse, you didn't ask them if they were *more* satisfied with you than they used to be. Or if they were *less* satisfied with competitors than you.

Customer satisfaction is a dynamic thing. It changes with each new interaction between customer and product. It's a never-ending race, and you need to make sure that you are measuring where you stand relative to those shifting customer expectations and competitor performances.

Your customer satisfaction has to be high, relative to both customer expectations and competitors' ratings, before it has much of an effect on customer retention rates. Make sure that you ask tough questions to find out whether you are below or above customers' current standards. For example, the following questions are going to be very revealing:

---

1. Which company (or product) is the *best* right now?

(Give a long list with instructions to circle one, and give a write-in blank labeled Other as the final choice.)

2. Rate [your product] compared to its competitors:

Far Worse			Same		Far Better	
1	2	3	4	5	6	7

3. Rate [your product] compared to your expectations for it:

Far Worse			Same		Far Better	
1	2	3	4	5	6	7

Breaking down customer satisfaction into what you think are its *contributing elements* is also helpful. (Focus groups or informal chats with customers can help you come up with your list of contributing elements.) For example, you could ask the following questions about an overnight letter carrier:

---

1. **Rate Flash Deliveries compared to its competitors on speed of delivery.**

2. **Rate Flash Deliveries compared to its competitors on reliability.**

3. **Rate Flash Deliveries compared to its competitors on ease of use.**

4. **Rate Flash Deliveries compared to its competitors on friendliness.**

Ending this chapter with assessments of customer satisfaction is especially appropriate because customer satisfaction is the ultimate goal of your marketing activities. When doing research, it's easy to lose sight of this end-of-process goal. Sure, you may need to find out about lots of other issues in order to design your marketing program or diagnose a problem. But none of what you find out matters unless it boils down to increased customer satisfaction in the long run. Whatever else you decide to research, make sure you keep one eye on customer satisfaction. It's the ultimate reality test of any marketing program!

Part III
Using the
Components of a
Marketing Program

The 5th Wave   By Rich Tennant

"By the way, who's the genius that decided we use an acronym?"

In this part . . .

All the analysis and stategizing in the world doesn't mean a thing until you get out there and start delivering marketing messages and goods or services to your customers. In this part of the book I show you exactly how to use the many possible elements of a marketing program to recruit new customeers and keep old customers coming back for more. And more. And more.

Your choices are many and varied — thank goodness, because your task is a difficult one! Use this part to develop or refine your product offerings, to price them, to get them to where customers need and want to buy them, and to figure out how to spread the good word about them.

Remember that you can communicate with and persuade customers in an incredible variety of ways. The Internet. A direct mail campaign. Personal selling. Advertising in magazines, newspapers, catalogs, billboards, and signs — or on TV, radio, even on the sides of busses, trains, and trucks. You name it; the information you need is here.

The same goes with special events, trade shows, contests, gifts, special offers, and premiums. Do whatever it takes to make the sale and keep the customer happy. And you won't find a bigger menu of options anywhere, so read on!

Chapter 7

Marketing on the Web

• •

In This Chapter

▶ Putting the World Wide Web to work in your marketing program

▶ Designing Web pages and banners

▶ Interactive advertising comes of age

▶ Direct marketing on the Internet

▶ Publishing on the Internet

• •

*H*ow do you market on the Internet? I've been asked that question more often in the months I took to write this book than any other. And so I'm breaking with marketing tradition and addressing electronic marketing right now, in detail, and before I go on to the more traditional elements of a marketing program. You asked for it, you got it.

The Internet and the World Wide Web combine to create a wonderfully versatile — and often misused — new medium for direct marketing. Most people in marketing have already dabbled with electronic media — Web pages are springing up like mushrooms. But I rarely encounter anyone who is making a significant amount of money on the Web. It's not that you can't. The Internet, like any mass medium, has the potential to be of great value to marketers (the Internet will someday be a major retail force, for example). But most people do even sillier things than usual when they try to market in a new medium. So I've devoted considerable thought and research, and a fistful of pages, to helping you avoid being a fly caught in the Web.

Unfortunately, I'm afraid that this chapter will age more rapidly than the rest of the book. Electronic media are evolving so rapidly that major news breaks every week and creative new marketing practices emerge every month. So I'll give you a tip for how to keep up with the fast-changing field of Net marketing. I think you ought to subscribe to . . . *Net Marketing! Advertising Age* has just introduced this new publication as *Marketing For Dummies* goes to print, and I'm impressed by the first issue. Contact *Advertising Age* (write for information at 220 E. 42nd Street, New York, NY 10017; or fax your request to 212-210-0111) to find out how to subscribe to it. And for now, *Net Marketing* is going to be free to *Advertising Age* and *Business Marketing* subscribers, although if it succeeds, it no doubt will switch to a subscription basis.

It's Gonna Be BIG!

If you add up the money spent around the world on online advertising (on Web sites, e-mail, and online and offline services) for 1996 — the best data available as I write — you get about $275 million in ad spending. That's an impressive figure for a new medium, but it is dwarfed by the billions spent in other media worldwide.

However, if you look at the year quarter by quarter, you discover a startling fact. Spending on online advertising starts small, at just $30 million in the first three months of the year. It jumps about 40 percent in the second quarter and about 30 percent in both the third and fourth quarters. In 1997, the growth rate dipped for a while, but seems to be settling down at about 10 percent a quarter. That's still phenomenal. You are looking at the birth of a major new advertising medium, one that I predict will reach spending levels of several billion dollars a year by the end of the century!

Entrepreneurship on the Web

Say that you have a great product, but no access to conventional distribution channels. Then direct marketing is a great way to bypass them and find your own consumers. But what if you don't have the cash or know-how to do a big mailing or run *direct-action ads* (ads designed to generate direct inquiries or sales) supported by a *call center* (an office set up to handle incoming phone orders)? Then the Internet may be your low-cost solution. You can create a Web page and start attracting customers for almost nothing. And *sometimes* doing so even works.

The first big success story to catch the world's eye is the case of novelist Nan McCarthy, who self-published a book called *Chat* and sold it direct, via the World Wide Web. The book is about Web-heads — people who devote a great deal of their lives to surfing the Internet. It tells the story of an e-mail romance, so perhaps the book has special appeal to Web users.

The book came to the Web community's attention when Ms. McCarthy wrote a funny letter to humorist Dave Barry. Mr. Barry actually replied, and then the Internet community somehow learned about the letters and several news groups asked for permission to post them.

From there, so the story goes, fame and fortune — and a contract for a second edition with a "real" publisher — quickly followed. And when McCarthy introduced her second novel with a mailing to all those who had visited her Web site, 70 percent responded with orders. Not bad!

However, this popular Web fable, told in innumerable newspaper and magazine stories, needs to be put into perspective. McCarthy reports that she sold more than 2,000 copies of her first novel on the Net. While that's far better than having the books sit in a box, the number doesn't come close to what major publishers can do through conventional channels — bookstores, book clubs, and direct mail.

So yes, the Internet can give entrepreneurs cheap access to customers. But no, it is not yet big enough to take the place of a full-blown marketing program that uses multiple media and distribution channels.

One reason online advertising took off in 1996 is that standards began to emerge for advertisers. Standards help. They make buying and selling advertising space and time easy in this medium, just like in any other. For example, general agreement has been reached on eight standard banner sizes for online ads, which should simplify the design and production of them considerably (if the standards hold — stay tuned!). If you get involved in designing Web pages or other online advertising, you will find that following these standards is helpful and maybe even necessary. That way you'll be in sync with the rest of the Web world, and your ads will fit their spaces. And it's not hard — just request ad requirements from anyone selling ad space on the Net. As standards take hold, you will find these requirements becoming less individualized, meaning that an ad designed for one Web page or service will be suitable for others without modification. A nice convenience.

To find out what's going on in the world of online marketing, you need to keep in regular touch with experts and practitioners. The Web is a fast-moving target — part of what makes it such an exciting new medium. You can learn a lot just by browsing the Web regularly (I often type in keyword searches on advertising or marketing just to see what's up). For example, a detailed study called *Research Program on Marketing in Computer-Mediated Environments* is published (and periodically updated) on the Web by two professors from Vanderbilt University. You can check it out at http://www2000.ogsm.vanderbilt.edu/. And if you feel like traveling, you should contact Interactive Conferences, Inc., in Minneapolis, Minnesota (phone at 800-323-0310 or fax at 612-922-2320), which puts on Marketing on the Internet conferences that collect leading practitioners on the topic.

Outreach via the Web

Perhaps the simplest way to take advantage of the World Wide Web is to use it to find prospects through direct-action advertising.

Direct-action, or *direct-response,* advertising is what you are doing whenever you take it upon yourself as a marketer to create and manage customer transactions at a distance through one or more media. In other words, it's when you reach out through media to find individual customers. I'll treat print advertising, mail, and telephone media later on in this section, but you need to know what direct marketing is now because the Internet is emerging as a useful tool for direct marketing.

Direct-action advertising's goal is to get prospective customers to contact you so that you can get them into your direct marketing database and start building a business relationship with them. And the Web is an increasingly good medium for this task. In fact, I think that Web ads and pages are going to be the cheapest media for direct-action ads, as measured on a cost-per-response basis.

Why? Two factors (aside from the obvious growth in the number of people cruising the Web) tell the tale:

> ✔ **The cost structure of Web space is different from other media.**
>
> You can create a *home page* (the Net equivalent of an information booth about you), or distribute a *virtual publication* (an electronic version of a newsletter or magazine), on the Web. To the extent that your stuff is interesting to prospective customers, you will attract traffic. And the economics of doing so are fundamentally different than in any other medium because your Web space costs you mostly in what accountants call *fixed costs,* or *up-front expenses* that do not vary with usage. You have to spend some money on hiring the designers or techies to help create your page or on hiring a writer to design a virtual newsletter for the Web. And you have to spend something each month for Internet access — probably by renting it from a commercial company with an appropriate server. But these are fixed costs. They won't go up appreciably as readership goes up. So as you attract more visitors, your cost per visitor goes down significantly!
>
> Compare this cost structure to other media, where the *variable costs* are typically much more important than the fixed costs. You have to pay for every reader in a magazine's circulation, every name on a direct mail list, and so forth. The cost of producing a mailing or ad is a fixed investment, to be sure. But then you have to make a significant variable investment on top of it. So your costs don't go down as rapidly as

volume goes up. Only on the Web can you escape your costs through scale so effectively (because as you reach more customers, you don't have to incur more costs!). And that means the Web is going to become the most cost-effective medium for outreach via direct advertising. This cost advantage has nothing to do with the allure of high technology. All media choices come down to cost and quality of an exposure. The advantage of the Web is an economic one — if you are savvy enough to see and exploit it.

✔ **There is more Web ad space than needed.**

The cost structure advantage described in the first bullet applies to those who want to design (or have someone else design) their own Web pages. But much can be said for buying ad space on other people's sites. The main advantage of this strategy is that you can tap into the traffic already visiting these sites. Just like advertising in other media, where you buy access to the viewers, listeners, or readers. And, just like in other media, Internet ads are priced to reflect the number of exposures they will likely receive. So you'll pay plenty for a banner on a main screen from America Online because of the high viewership.

The trend is toward per-thousand pricing on the Internet, making its ad price structure comparable with other media. Banners now cost between $10-40 thousand for 500,000 exposures according to a recent *Wall Street Journal* analysis (Feb. 24, 1997, p. B9). Cost-per-thousand or CPM is the standard pricing method for ads in other media, and it tells you how much you will pay to put an ad before one thousand of the users/subscribers/viewers/listeners/readers of the medium. Who they are and how they view (or listen to) an ad differs from medium to medium, but the CPM figure helps give advertisers a standardized measure of the cost-effectiveness of any potential purchase of ad space or time.

I'm convinced that the rapid expansion in Web sites means that a great deal more advertising space will be for sale than the number of advertising buyers for the next few years at least. So the smart buyer should be able to find extremely good deals in Web advertising!

If you don't do much ad buying on the Web, you may want to go to a specialist for help in finding good deals. Any ad agency or media buying shop with Web/Internet experience should be helpful. I am excited to see a new generation of specialized firms emerging to help with Web media buying. For example, WebConnect can hook you up with ad space, and it also offers Web-specific services like tracking software, selected site groupings based on the similarities of their users, and access to more than a thousand *managed sites* — sites they handle for clients. (The advantages of managed sites include more consistent quality and more information about users.)

WebConnect is at http://www.webconnect.net, or you can reach them by phone at 800-331-8102 (within the U.S.) or fax at 561-241-3599 — they are located in Boca Raton, Florida.

I also recommend an interesting new company called FlyCast Communications Corp., based in San Francisco that auctions unsold advertising space on the Internet. They can provide more systematic access to discounted Web ad space because they are building relationships with the advertisers. You can reach their Web site at http://www.flycast.com/.

Designing Banner Ads and Web Pages

The *banner* ad (brightly colored rectangles at the top of a Web page) is the Web's answer to display advertising in a print medium or outdoor advertising on a billboard. Viewers won't want to read as much copy as they might in a print ad, so use banners the same way you use a billboard — to get across a very simple, clear, and engaging message. A single, brief headline, perhaps supported by a logo and a couple lines of body copy. Or maybe a brand name and an illustration. In either case, the ad must be simple and bold — able to attract the viewer's attention from desired information elsewhere on the screen for long enough to make a simple point. Don't expect too much from a banner ad!

If you decide to use the Web for direct-action advertising, be sure to include a clear call to action in the ad. Typical Web banner ads don't give enough information about the product to stimulate an urge for immediate action. Nor do they make taking action easy. They are simply awareness-builders at best.

How to design a Web page: An interview with Arthur Torres

There is a world of difference between good and bad Web sites. And, of course, you want yours to be good, not bad. But what *is* the difference, anyway? Since this is such a new medium, I decided to interview an experienced Web site designer to find out what his advice is on the topic. Here then are some dos and don'ts from Arthur Torres. If you want to know more (or ask someone to evaluate or design your page for you), call him up at 413-259-1618

in Shutesburry, Massachusetts. In any event, make sure you follow this advice:

✔ **Don't do it yourself — unless you are fairly knowledgeable.** Your ad or page is out there for the whole world to see, so you want to create something that makes you look good. You probably wouldn't design and shoot your own TV commercial, but lots of people try to do their own Web sites.

✔ **Do offer tangible, interesting information.** Visits to your Web site need to be fruitful. I'm a designer first and a Web page designer second, and the technical aspects are less interesting to me than what goes into it — the images and information. While the site needs to be technically accurate to work, that's not enough to make it a success. Make sure the content is good and presented through good design.

✔ **Don't imitate successful sites.** What works for one site won't necessarily for another. Image and content decisions depend on whose site it is. A rock band's site should include some of their songs. Songs are a very specific sort of information, which is good. But other marketers need other sorts of information. An aspiring actor's site should have clips of performances, for example. And a lumberyard should include price lists for various clients — keyed to a customer code since different customers get different discounts. And any retailers should include bargain bins to liquidate their closeout items.

✔ **Do include an e-mail link so they can get in touch with you.** I don't see the Web as one big marketplace. It's used more often to gather information — so while it can be an electronic mall, many visitors will prefer to do their research online, then call or visit you to make their purchases. Make sure it is easy for them to get from your site to you or you'll lose a lot of business.

✔ **Do include *metatags*.** Metatags are strands of keywords that you put in the actual software codes. You can use hundreds of them, and when your site is uploaded to a server, its search robots will pick up your metatags and find your site through keyword searches.

✔ **Do limit your links to other sites.** Some sites are all links, but from a marketing perspective, you want to limit the number of exits to the most pertinent and necessary options. And you should put the exits near the end so you don't lose visitors before they see your information. You wouldn't design a retail store with dozens of exits, but that's just how many Web sites are designed. You need to manage the flow of traffic through your site.

The Web-page banner is simply a very high-tech display ad, so the rules of good print design apply — or ought to! See Chapter 5 for applicable rules and guidelines. If you're running what's supposed to be a direct-action ad (see Chapter 18), make sure that you include multiple options for prospects to contact you (see Chapter 18 for ideas). Give your Web address, and also a button or click-on option of some sort for direct linkage to your Web page. Even if you don't have a regularly-updated Web site, you should establish an *automated form* (an electronic fill-in-the-blanks contact sheet for people to give you their contact information and request follow-ups or place orders). Finally, be sure to include standard contact options for those who may prefer the postal mail, a fax, or a telephone call.

Don't forget to *try* to make a sale. Even if your product is complex and expensive, some people may prefer to place an order immediately rather than waiting for follow-up from you. Give consumers this option! Too many Web ads act as barriers to the eager customer. What an easily avoided mistake!

Interactive advertising on your Web page

Interactive advertising is advertising that engages its audience in entertaining, creative, or learning experiences. This type of advertising is pretty rare — most ads are made to be seen or heard, not used like a toy. Yet creating interactive advertising is a reality on the Web, because viewers are already sitting in front of a computer with a mouse and keyboard at hand. Internet advertising has an opportunity to develop advertising into an active communication with the customers instead of a passive one.

Color me rich

The easiest way to get you excited about interactive advertising on the Web is to share an example of a successful interactive Web ad for Crayola brand crayons (it appeared on their Web page at http://www.crayola.com./). The ad targeted households with young children, and it did so in a novel way — through a coloring contest in which parents entered their work and kids were the judges. In fact, a contest was held for the judges, too — with kids filling out a written application. The winner of this Big Kid Challenge, as the contest was called, received $25,000 worth of gold and silver. Not bad for a crayon drawing!

And because the contest was such a big draw, Crayola had lots of traffic throughout its page. Other options on the site include a section on how crayons are made and, for the practical parent, advice on how to remove stains. (The site was designed by Black Box, a Web developer in Allentown, Pennsylvania.)

I recommend visiting this site, not to see the promotion described above but to see what they are doing now. You can be sure it will be different. Because one of the advantages of Web-based promotions is that you can change them as often as you like. The development time and cost is low compared to other sorts of events (see Chapter 12).

Checking your page

Okay, you have a great-looking Web page (thanks to your own Web savvy or that of a designer). But does the page work, and is anyone visiting your site? Do the graphics take so long to download that people give up? You need this kind of data in order to evaluate and improve a site.

One way to find out whether your Web page needs improvement or will work well is to use the free testing service offered at `http://www2.imagiware.com/RxHTML`. This company's software is designed to test Web pages, and they are happy to have you demo the software on your page. One of the best features in my mind is *link verification* — making sure that the stuff you *don't* see also looks good. I better tell you what that term means now, as you'll need to know about links when you start marketing on the Web. Link verification checks out your links to other sites — links being software linkages that help interested Web users find their way to your site (which makes them pretty important!). The software will catch simple spelling and syntax errors as well. And an image analysis test will tell you how long the typical user must wait to download your material.

What the statistics of a testing site don't tell you is whether your page is too aggressive or sneaky in how it obtains information from users. This determination is a judgment call in many cases, because the FTC has yet to issue any clear guidelines and industry groups are still debating what is and isn't proper. For now, keep an eye on the headlines to make sure that you find out about any new regulations, and try to do things that wouldn't upset you if *you* were the customer. A classic ethics test is to ask yourself if you'd be embarrassed if a story about your activities were published in your local hometown newspaper.

Be especially careful if your site attracts kids. Don't blur the distinction between editorial and advertising content — you don't want to be accused of deceiving children. And don't use children as your spies to collect information about their households that their parents wouldn't want you to know. This practice has garnered some negative headlines already, and is one of the reasons the Council of Better Business Bureau's Children's Advertising Review Unit (CARU) is developing standards for kid-oriented Web advertising. The standards aren't available at the time of this writing, but you can contact the Council for more information at 703-276-0100.

Getting to know your visitors

Each time someone visits your Web site, he is exhibiting interest in you and your products (or he's lost — unfortunately always an option!). And when someone exhibits interest, that makes him interesting to you. So whatever you do, however you go about setting up a site, make sure that information about your visitors is captured in a useful form and sent to you regularly.

An agency or service bureau should have the capability to get information about visitors to your site for you. Ask. Or you can purchase specialized software or services to track visitors on your own site. For example, VISITrac Tracking Solutions Provider (or VISITrack TSP) specializes in tracking, measuring, and reporting on Web site activities. It is located in The New York Information Technology Center (55 Broad Street, New York, NY 10004) at 212-482-0851.

Publishing on the Web: A Hot Opportunity

When I poke my head into the World Wide Web, I am usually terribly disappointed in the content I find there. Publishing on the Web is at a ridiculously primitive state. But why should you, as a marketer, care? Because publishing on the Web — the creation of useful or entertaining materials others will want to read — is essential to building the value of the Web for advertisers. The publishing side of the Web delivers attractive content, and that attracts Web users, and once you can attract Web users you can then deliver marketing messages to them. Just like in the magazine industry, where everybody knows your circulation depends upon good editorial content. But so far, many of the Web pioneers are marketers — which is good; I like to see us wear the leadership hat. But the trouble is, we aren't always as focused on developing compelling content as we are on making or selling ad space.

Most Web sites are really just huge, interactive advertisements or sales promotions. After a while, even the most cleverly designed ad gets boring. To increase the length of time users spend with your materials, and to ensure high involvement and return visits, you need to think like a publisher, not just an advertiser. Create and deliver fascinating content and refresh it regularly. Even consider going so far as to distribute your content (like a virtual magazine) so that you don't have to wait for Web users to find you. Build a distribution list of e-mail addresses and put your content (plus ads) in their virtual mailboxes. Publishing is an unfamiliar hat to many marketers, but it's one that fits them well when it comes to marketing on the Internet.

Playing publisher to extend your Web

Think about a world in which publishing a book and getting it into a bookstore was so easy that anybody who felt like publishing did so. What would happen to the quality of content? Well, that's what happens on the Web! And that's why most users screen out a great deal of the content that's posted to the Web — including many marketing messages we wish they wouldn't overlook.

And therein lies the hidden problem of the World Wide Web — the barriers to entry are so low that publishing on the Web is easy, and subsequently, much of the content is of very poor quality.

Whenever you have a hidden problem with a medium, you should have clever ways to turn that problem into an *opportunity.* That's what Michael Dortch advocates. He is publishing a high-quality, electronic column and is building up a readership base the old-fashioned way — by finding and retaining interested readers! He writes about the topics he likes to consult in so that the contacts his newsletter creates may someday turn into paying business for him. And you can build meaningful customer contacts through a Web newsletter, too — it's a surefire formula for attracting repeat visitors and building those fabled electronic relationships that everybody wants but so rarely achieves.

Dortch is an old hand in the computer industry, having worked and consulted for most of the leading companies at one time or another. Now he provides consulting services for developing communications/marketing strategies for the Web. And he is also an experienced book author and journalist, so when he writes a column or Web page, it's engaging and informative. And, surprise, when you put out good content like that on the Web, it really stands out. *High-quality material attracts repeat readers.*

Eventually, the rest of the world will get over its puppy love with the Internet and realize that the same rule applies in this medium as in any other:

> ***You have to have killer content to win the attention war and attract readers to your site!***

Cutting-edge technology and cool graphics can attract readers to your site, but content is what keeps them there. Nobody puts amateurish videos on TV and hopes to hold an audience. But for now, most companies and individuals who try to promote themselves on the Web don't seem to realize the need for good, fresh (which means constantly changing!) content. So opportunity does exist for you. Do like Dortch: Research, write, and deliver good content, in a simple, user-friendly format, and magically, you *will* attract users!

But how do you replicate Dortch's strategy? First, note that your content must *change*. Most of what you can put on the Web loses its news value just like yesterday's newspaper articles. You are in essence a publisher, producing a periodical. Never mind that the publication is on the Web — the medium is *not* the message! The message must stand on its own — in any medium. You wouldn't send the same catalog to a mailing list over and over, so don't leave the same old stuff on your Web site either.

Here is Dortch's further advice on how to develop a column, newsletter, or such that really works to attract and hold Web readers, in his own words (I just downloaded this from the Web with his permission):

1. **Topic and Content:** You might search and browse the Web to see what's already out there on the topic or topics of most interest to you. Or, you can just ask your closest friends what they find interesting in print and online. (If there's enough other stuff, you might have fun just producing a regular annotated summary of other people's stuff!)

2. **Layout and Format:** If your plan is to distribute your publication exclusively via e-mail, it's hard to go wrong with *plain old text*. However, it would help greatly to make sure it's pithy, grammatically correct, well-spelled and otherwise generally readable — and that's separate from it being entertaining.

3. **Distribution:** If you're a subscriber to an online service, search the member directory for folks you know of who'd be interested. Check the author credits in every article you read for an e-mail address, and send copies of what you write about each article to the person who wrote the source material itself. (A well-written personal cover note wouldn't hurt, either.) When source material comes from other publications, online or otherwise, offer to trade subscriptions.

4. **Follow-up:** Write your first few recipients and ask for honest, detailed feedback. Reassure everyone about the proprietary nature of your distribution list. (You can't do this too often.) Also, check and double-check your e-mail addresses with each distribution, to make sure the wrong folks aren't receiving your work and that the right people are, at the address they prefer. (***Bonus Tip:*** Folks seem to prefer receiving e-mail from a human's address over receiving it from a list server.)

5. Everything After: Be ready to respond to requests for addition to your distribution list, removal from same, permission to re-distribute and/or post your writings online, angry letters from readers and prospective work. Preparation most likely includes development of standard letters, a biography, a capabilities statement, references and other documents (which PR/marketing-communications types call "collateral"). And whatever you do, DON'T EVER just stop publishing and "disappear" without explaining and/or apologizing profusely.

If you're interested in engaging help in carrying out any of the above steps, by all means, get in touch!

— *Michael Dortch*

You can reach Dortch via America Online at MEDortch; on CompuServe at 76711,1500; on the Internet at: medortch@aol.com; or by fax at 415-386-9854. He is based in San Francisco, California.

Putting Real People in Your Web Ads

One more thing — some late-breaking news. I've just learned that Lucent Technologies (http://www.lucent.com/internet) is developing a call center that you can contract to service visitors to your Web site. The idea is that your customers can, with the click of a button, reach a human operator who will interact with them over the computer to answer questions and take orders. This could turn out to be a very useful tool for you, the virtual marketer, and for your customers.

I cover the important topic of how to set up and run call centers in Chapter 18, but the Web may very well someday antiquate the roughly 60,000 telephone call centers that now operate throughout North America.

Chapter 8

Print Advertising

*P*rint advertising (any paid-for marketing message in printed form) is big, very big. Most marketers budget more for print advertising than any other type — the exception is the major national or multinational brands that are marketed largely on television. But for most local and regional advertising, print is likely to be the most flexible and effective all-around advertising medium.

If you are marketing services or products to other businesses (called *business-to-business marketing*), the thousands of specialized trade magazines and newsletters that target professionals and tradespeople are almost always the best first choice for advertising. Furthermore, you will find that many direct mail campaigns build their mailing lists from subscriber lists provided by magazines. You can easily integrate a print ad and a direct mail campaign so as to target them to the same people. (I cover list acquisition and management in Chapter 18, by the way.)

Print advertising also integrates well with many other marketing media. Written brochures and other sales support materials (which I consider a form of print advertising) can be used to support personal selling (see Chapter 17) or telemarketing (see Chapter 18). Similarly, a print ad in a magazine can generate leads for direct marketing (again, see Chapter 18). Print ads work well to announce sales promotions or distribute coupons (covered in Chapter 13). Finally, I often recommend that clients develop their print ads first and then adapt their appeal (see Chapter 5) to ads in other media, like radio, TV, or direct mail. Print is usually the best choice for your primary medium in local marketing and in business-to-business marketing (national consumer marketers use TV as their primary medium). In cases where print should be the cornerstone of your program, designing your ad first is especially important. After the ad is designed, other forms of advertising can be integrated into your print campaign.

Many marketers start with their print advertising campaign, design a series of good ads for different magazines or newspapers, and then work outward from there to incorporate the appeal and design concepts from their print ads into other forms of advertising.

Brochures, *tear sheets* (one-page, catalog-style descriptions of products), posters for outdoor advertising, direct mail letters, or catalogs all use the basic elements of print advertising, too — good copy and visuals, plus eye-catching headlines. Therefore, mastery of print advertising is an essential part of all good marketers' knowledge base. This chapter covers the essentials.

The Anatomy of a Print Ad

Before I can talk about how to create great print ads, I have to *dissect* one and identify its parts. Fortunately, you won't find anything gross or disgusting inside most print ads. Just parts. And each part has a special name. Here they are:

- **Headline:** The large-print words that first attract the eye, usually at the top of the page.

- **Subhead:** The optional addition to the headline to provide more detail, also in large (but not quite as large) print.

- **Copy or body copy:** The main text, set in a readable size such as might be used in the main text of a book or magazine.

- **Visual:** An illustration that makes a visual statement. May be the main focus of the ad (especially where the point is to show readers your product), or may be secondary to the copy. Also optional. After all, most classified ads use no visuals at all, yet are generally more effective than display ads for the simple reason that people *look for* classified ads!

- **Caption:** Copy attached to the visual to explain or discuss it. Usually placed beneath the visual, but may be on any side or even within or on the visual.

- ✔ **Trademark:** A unique design that represents the brand or company (like Nike's swoosh) ought to be registered — see Chapter 14.

- ✔ **Signature:** The company's trademarked version of its name. Often advertisers have a logo design that features a brand name in a distinctive font and style. The signature is a written equivalent to the trademark's visual identity.

- ✔ **Slogan:** An optional element consisting of a (hopefully) short phrase evoking the spirit or personality of the brand. For example, Timberland used a series of print ads in which the slogan *Boots, shoes, clothing, wind, water, earth and sky* appeared in the bottom left corner, just beneath the company's distinctive signature and logo — which are displayed on a rectangular patch of leather such as may appear on one of their products.

Figure 8-1 shows each of these print ad elements in a rough design. Instead of writing a headline, though, I just wrote "headline," and so forth with all the other parts so that you can easily see all the elements in action. This fairly simple palette of the print ad design permits endless variation and creativity. You can say or show anything, and you can do so in many different ways. I'm going to explore some of these choices with you.

Putting the Parts Together: Design and Layout

Design refers to the look, feel, and style of the ad. Design is an aesthetic concept and, thus, hard to put into precise terms. But design is vitally important: It must take the basic appeal and make that appeal work visually on paper (see Chapter 5 for details of how to develop appeal). Specifically, the design needs to overcome the marketer's constant problem: Nobody cares about your advertising. So the design must somehow *reach out* to readers, grab their attention, and hold it long enough to communicate the appeal and attach it to the brand name in the readers' memory.

Jay Schulberg, the chief creative officer at ad agency Bozell Worldwide, sees ad design as a creative task whose goal is to find *"an imaginative way to grab people by their eyeballs."* Many designers start with the idea that they will make the ad attractive, or efficient at conveying information, or some other boring notion. Sorry. Great advertising has to rise off the page, reach out, and grab you by the eyeballs. In the cluttered world of modern print advertising, this design goal is the only one that really works!

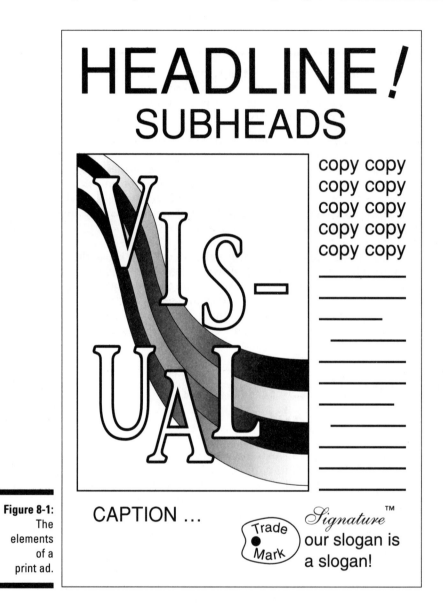

Figure 8-1:
The
elements
of a
print ad.

Nike achieves this concept in a print ad for a shoe called Air Max by using a design that looks for all the world like a rough, hand-made collage instead of a polished advertisement. The four-color print ad is actually mostly black on white — or, to be more accurate, on photocopier gray to give the white space a rough, homemade feel. The transparent tape used to hold words and pictures onto the page is clearly visible in this ad, further evidence of a rough-and-ready style.

REAL WORLD

Shoes for sharks

Nike's Air Max design uses a novel layout. *Layout* is the arrangement of the format elements of the ad I just reviewed, from the headline and illustration to the body copy and slogan. In the Air Max ad's layout, the entry point for the viewer's eye is on the right, near the bottom. That's right — the *opposite* of how we naturally read. The design turns everything about print advertising on its head. The entry point consists of the word *LOOK:* in bold red capitals — the only red type on the page, located in the bottom right of the ad. The viewer must then turn 90 degrees to read *THIS IS:*, which finally leads to the product name in the top right corner: "AIR MAX." The shoe is shown — upside down — on the right side of the page. Its caption: "THIS IS NOT A SOUVENIR."

Rough, hand-done pasteup. Text flowing from bottom right instead of top left. Product shown upside down. This design has an attitude! And that's just what the designer wants to convey about the product. The product's appeal is that it is anti-authority, a fighter, a rebel. When you finally get to the body copy in the ad (and most readers will because this ad has them by the eyeballs), the first line you read says "If we made fishing poles, you'd see us at shark-fishing tournaments." The copy ends with the statement, "But we make athletic shoes, so we associate ourselves with world-class athletes. And anyone else who loves a good fight." This product has an attitude that the design effectively conveys.

Designing a Brochure

I want to show you how to lay out a good printed brochure, because in my experience, this form of advertising is the most popular for do-it-yourselfers. Your word-processing or graphics software, a good laser printer, and the help of your local photocopy or print shop (which will also have folding machines) allows you to design and produce brochures quite easily.

But I must first admit to a personal bias on the topic. I believe most brochures are a foolish waste of money. They don't accomplish any specific marketing goals, they just look pretty at best — some of them look pretty ugly. Before you start, make sure that you know who will read the brochure, how they will get it, and what they should learn from it.

Marketers often order up a brochure without a clear idea of what purpose the brochure should serve. They just think a brochure is a good idea. "Oh, we need them to, *you* know, like, put in the envelope along with a letter, or, um, for our salespeople to keep in the trunks of their cars like they do the other brochures. Or maybe we'll send some out to our mailing list. Or give them away at the next trade show."

And maybe you won't. With this many possibilities, the brochure will not be suited to any single use. The brochure will be a dull, descriptive thing that just talks about the company or product, but doesn't hit readers over the head with any particular appeal or impetus to action.

To avoid this widespread plague of brochure-itis, start by defining up to three specific uses for the brochure. No more than three, though, because your design won't be able to accomplish more than three purposes effectively. The most common and appropriate uses for a brochure are:

✔ To act as a reference on the product or technical details for prospects

✔ To support a personal selling effort by lending credibility and helping overcome objections (sales are covered in Chapter 17)

✔ To generate leads through a direct-mail campaign (covered in Chapter 18)

Say you want to design a brochure that will do all three of these tasks well. Start by designing the contents. What product and technical information must be included? Write the information down, or collect necessary illustrations, so that you have the *fact base* of the brochure in front of you.

Next, list the most *common sales objections* — the reasons prospects give for why they don't want to buy your product. Organize your fact base according to the objections, as if you were listening to their concerns and answering each with an appropriate response. You can write subheads like "Our Product Doesn't Need Service" or whatever so that salespeople or prospects can easily see how your facts (in copy and/or illustrations) overcome each specific objection.

Finally, you need to add some basic appeal (see Chapter 5), communicated in a punchy headline and a few dozen words of copy, along with an appropriate and eye-catching illustration, if possible. This appeal has to be included to help the brochure stand on its own as a marketing tool when the brochure is sent out to leads through the mail or passed on from a prospect or customer to one of his or her professional contacts.

Notice that you have to include copy (and perhaps illustrations) designed specifically for *each* of those three purposes above. The appeal, with its enticing headline and compelling copy and visual, go on the front of the brochure — or the outside when it is folded for mailing. The objections are picked up in the subheads that structure the main copy, on the inside pages. And the fact base, needed for reference use, is organized in the copy and illustrations beneath these subheads. If you don't know what each part of your brochure is doing, then you have not designed a good brochure. You've just wasted your money and time on something that won't do any single marketing task well.

Figure 8-2 shows how such a brochure might be laid out, along with dimensions for text blocks or illustrations. Although a brochure can be laid out in many ways, I often prefer this format. It is simple and inexpensive, because the brochure is printed on a single sheet of legal-sized paper that is then folded three times. The brochure fits in a standard #10 or #12 envelope or can be taped and mailed on its own. This layout allows for some detail, but not enough to get you into any real trouble. Larger formats and multi-page pieces tend to fill up with the worst, wordiest copy, and nobody ever reads them.

The design shown in Figure 8-2 is useful for direct mailings to generate sales leads, and can also be handed out or used for reference in direct selling situations. You can produce this brochure by using any popular desk-top publishing software, and it can even be printed and folded at the local photocopy shop if you don't need the thousands of copies that are required to make off-set printing cost-effective. To convert this design to an even simpler, cheaper format, use $8^1/_2$-x-11-inch paper and eliminate the return mailer (the left-hand page on the front, the right-hand on the back). If you do so, however, be sure to include follow-up instructions and contact information on one of the inside pages!

Stages in design

Designers often experiment with numerous layouts for their print ads before selecting one for formal development. I strongly recommend that you do the same — or insist that your designer or agency do the same. The more layouts you look at, the more likely you are to get an "out of the box" idea that has eyeball-grabbing power. The rough sketches designers use to describe layout concepts are called *thumbnails*. They are usually small, quick sketches in pen or pencil — or, more recently, in design programs like Quark or PageMaker.

Thumbnails with promise are developed into *roughs,* full-size sketches with headlines and subheads drawn carefully enough to give the feel of a particular font and *style* (the appearance of the printed letters), and with sketches for the illustrations. Body copy is suggested by lines (or nonsense characters if the rough is done in a computer program).

Are you using an ad agency or design firm to develop your print ads? Sometimes clients of ad agencies insist on seeing designs in the rough stage, in order to avoid the expense of having them developed more fully before presentation. I recommend that you do, too, even if your agency is hesitant to show you its work in unfinished form. Once the agency realizes that you appreciate the design process and won't criticize the roughs simply because they are rough, you will be able to give the agency more guidance and help during the design process.

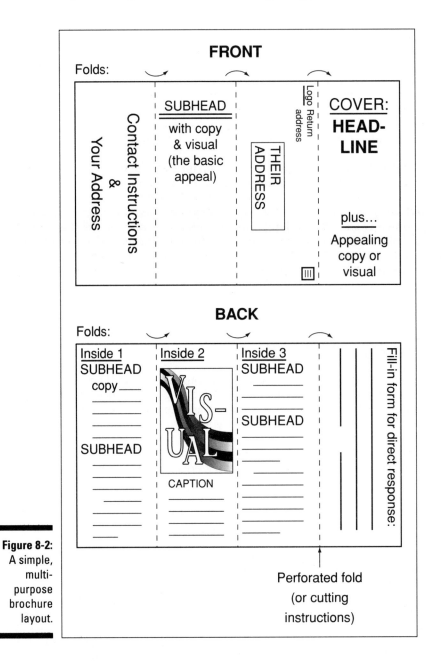

Figure 8-2:
A simple, multi-purpose brochure layout.

A rough that passes muster is developed into a *comp,* which is short for *comprehensive layout.* A comp should look pretty much like a final version of the ad, although it is produced on a one-time basis, so the comp may use paste-ups of photos or color photocopies for the illustrations, and paste-ups of typeset copy and headlines. Comps used to be assembled by hand, but now many designers and agencies do them on their computers, because a high-end PC and color printer can produce something that looks almost like the final printed version of a four-color ad. A computer-made comp is often referred to as a *full-color proof.*

A *dummy* is a form of comp that simulates the *feel* of the final ad, not just the look. (Every ad should have a feel or personality of its own, just as products should have a personality — and often the best personality for an ad is the product's personality — and consistency helps.) Dummies are especially important for brochures or special inserts to magazines, where the designer often specifies special paper and folds. By doing the comp as a dummy, you can evaluate the feel of the ad in addition to its appearance.

Designs may be sent to the printer in two different ways:

✔ The modern, and more popular, way is to send the design on disk in a desktop publishing program that the printer accepts. Even the color separations for four-color work can be done on your PC and included in the disk. (Ask the printer for instructions to make sure that you submit the design in a format that the printer's system can use.) The printer then makes *plates* for printing the ad straight from the disk (plates are metal or plastic sheets with your design on them — they apply the ink to the paper when the printing press does its thing).

✔ The traditional way to submit an ad is to generate what printers call *camera-ready art,* a version of the ad suitable for the printer to photo-graph with a large-scale production camera in order to generate *color keys* (to convert colors to specific inks) and *films* — one film for each layer of color to be printed. The designer usually produces this camera-ready art by making a *mechanical* or *pasteup,* in which typeset copy, visuals, and all the other elements of the ad are pasted onto a foam-core board by using a hot wax machine.

A hot wax machine heats wax and spreads it on a roller so that the designer can roll a thin layer of warm wax onto the back of each element. The wax sticks each piece neatly to the board, but also permits it to be peeled off easily in case repositioning is in order.

Charrette, the art supply company, makes a cheap hand-held version of a hot wax machine called the Hand Waxer for people like me who only use this traditional method occasionally and don't want to spend the money on more sophisticated equipment. Ask your local art supply store to order the Hand Waxer for you if you need one. (I sometimes use my Hand Waxer to do quick roughs by using materials from multiple sources, thus avoiding the need to get everything scanned and into the computer until I'm sure of what I want to use.)

Clear sheets of acetate are often taped to the top of the pasteup, each with a layer of color for the design, or with instructions to the printer about which elements to include in that layer and its color. Making a pasteup for a complex layout is quite a lot of work, which is why designers are rushing to computerized alternatives as fast as they can!

Finding your font

A *font* is a particular design and its accompanying attributes for the letters, numbers, and symbols (the *characters*) used in printing your ad. Normal people call this the *print,* but in marketing, you must call it the font or other marketers will think you don't know what you're talking about.

Typeface refers only to the distinctive design of the letters (Times Roman). *Font,* on the other hand, actually refers to one particular size and style of a typeface design (such as 10 point, bold, Times Roman).

The right font for any job is the one that is most *readable* and that *harmonizes* with the overall design most effectively. For a headline, the font also needs to **grab the reader's attention**. The body copy need not grab attention in the same way — in fact, if it does, it is often at the expense of readability. For example, a reverse font (white on dark) may be just the thing for a bold headline, but if you use the reverse font in the body copy, too, nobody will read your copy.

Choosing a typeface

What sort of typeface do you want? You have an amazing number of choices, because designers have been developing typefaces for as long as printing presses have existed.

A clean, sparse ad design, with lots of white space on the page and stark contrasts in the artwork, deserves the clean lines of a *sans serif typeface* — meaning one that is without any decorative *serifs,* those little bars or flourishes at the ends of the main lines in a character. The most popular body-copy fonts *without* serifs are Helvetica, Univers, Optima, and Avante Garde. Figure 8-3 shows some fonts with and without serifs.

Figure 8-3:
Fonts with and without serifs.

But a richly decorative, old-fashioned sort of ad needs a more decorative and traditional *serif typeface* such as Century or Times Roman. The most popular body-copy fonts *with* serifs are Garamond, Melior, Century, Times Roman, and Caledonia.

Table 8-1 shows an assortment of typeface choices, in which you can compare the clean lines of Helvetica, Avant Garde, and Optima with the more decorative designs of Century, Garamond, and Times Roman.

Table 8-1	Popular Fonts for Ads
Sans Serif	*Serif*
Helvetica	Century
Univers	Garamond
Optima	Melior
Avant Garde	Times Roman

In tests, Helvetica and Century generally top the lists as *most readable*, so a very simple design rule is to start with one of these for your body copy; only change the font if it doesn't seem to work well. Furthermore, research shows that people read lowercase letters about 13 percent faster than uppercase letters, so avoid long stretches of copy set all in caps. We also read most easily when letters are dark and contrast strongly with their background. Thus, black 14 point Helvetica on white is probably the most readable font specification for the body copy of an ad, even if the combination does seem dull to a sophisticated designer.

Generalizing about which headline typeface is best is no easy task, because designers play around with headlines to a greater extent than they do with body copy. But if you want a general rule, you can try using Helvetica for the headline when you use Century for the body, and vice versa. Or you can just use a bolder, larger version of the body copy font for your headline. Or you can reverse a larger, bold version of your type onto a black background for the headline. Anything to make the headline grab the reader's attention, stand out from the body copy, and ultimately lead vision and curiosity into the body copy.

Sometimes the designer combines body copy of a decorative typeface, one with serifs such as Times Roman, with headers of a sans serif typeface like Helvetica. The contrast between the clean lines of the large-sized header and the more decorative characters of the smaller body copy is pleasing to the eye and tends to draw the reader from header to body copy. This book uses that technique. Compare the sans serif bold characters of this chapter's title with the more delicate and decorative characters in which the text is set for a good example of this design concept in action.

Style choices within the typeface

Any typeface gives the user many choices, and so selecting the typeface is just the beginning of the project when it comes to designing the print in your ad. How big should the characters be? And do you want to use the standard version of the typeface, a lighter version, a bold (or darker) version, or an italic version — one that *leans* to the right? Wow — what a hassle!

The process is really easier than it sounds. The thing to do is to look at samples of some standard point sizes (12 and 14 point text for the body copy, for example, and 24, 36, and 48 point for the headlines). Many designers make their choice by eye, looking for an easy-to-read size that is not so large as to cause the words and sentences to break up into too many fragments across the page — but not so small as to give the reader an intimidatingly large number of words per line. Readability is the goal to keep in mind.

Figure 8-4 shows a variety of size and style choices for the Helvetica font. As you can see, a wonderful range of options is available even within this one popular font.

Figure 8-4:
These are some of the many choices that the Helvetica font offers ad designers.

Helvetica Light 14 point

Helvetica Italic 14 point

Helvetica Bold 14 point

Helvetica Regular 14 point

Helvetica Regular 24 point

Helvetica Regular Condensed 14 point

Helvetica Bold Outline 24 point

Keep in mind that you can change just about any aspect of type. You can alter the distance between lines — called the *leading* — or you can squeeze characters together or stretch them apart to make a word fit a space. Assume that anything is possible, and ask your printer or consult the manual of your desktop publishing software to find out how to make a desired change.

Now, having said that anything is possible, I want to warn you that *the eye is quite conservative* when it comes to reading type. Although most of us know little about the design of typefaces, we find traditional fonts instinctively appealing. The spacing of characters and lines, the balance and flow of individual characters — all this pleases the eye and makes our reading easy and pleasurable. And so, while you should know that you *can* change anything and everything, you should also know that *too many changes may reduce your ad's readability*. Figure 8-5 shows the same ad laid out twice — once in an eye-pleasing way and once in a disastrous way.

WHEN LIFE GIVES YOU LEMONS...

What should you do? Juggle them? Make lemonade? Open a farm stand? Or give up and go home to Mamma?

WHO KNOWS? It's often hard to come to grips with pressing personal or career problems. Sometimes it's hardest to see your *own* problems clearly. Fortunately, JEN KNOWS. Jen Fredrics has twenty years of counseling experience, a master's in social work, and a busy practice in personal problem solving. Call her today to find out how to turn your problems into opportunities.

And next time, when life gives you lemons, you'll know just what to make. An appointment.

WHEN LIFE GIVES YOU LEMONS...

What should you do? Juggle them? Make lemonade? Open a farm stand? Or give up and go home to Mamma?

WHO KNOWS? It's often hard to come to grips with pressing personal or career problems. Sometimes it's hardest to see your own problems clearly. Fortunately, JEN KNOWS. Jen Fredrics has twenty years of counseling experience, a master's in social work, and a busy practice in personal problem solving. Call her today to find out how to turn your problems into opportunities.

And next time, when life gives you lemons, you'll know just what to make. An appointment.

Figure 8-5: Which copy would you rather read?

Don't just *play* with type for the sake of playing (as the designer did in the left-hand version of the classified ad in Figure 8-5). Stick with popular fonts, in popular sizes, except where you have to solve a problem or you want to make a special point. The advent of desktop publishing has lead to a horrifying generation of advertisements in which dozens of fonts dance across the page, bolds and italics fight each other for attention, and the design of the words becomes a barrier to reading instead of an aid.

Picking a point size

When designers and printers talk about *font sizes,* they are referring to a traditional measure of the height of the letters (based on the highest and lowest parts of the biggest letters). One *point* equals about $1/72$ of an inch, so a 10 point type is about $10/72$ of an inch high at the most.

Personally, I don't really care — I've never measured a character with a ruler. I just know that if the letters seem too small for easy reading, then I need to bump the typeface up a couple of points. Ten point type is in fact too small for most body copy, but it can be best if you have to squeeze several words into a small space. (But why do that? You're usually better off to make your body copy shorter and then bump up the font size to make the copy more readable!) I also know that my eye cannot distinguish easily between fonts that are only one or two sizes apart, so I generally specify a larger jump than that to distinguish between body copy and subhead or subhead and headline.

Placing Your Print Ad

Say that you want to advertise a mail-order food business's product line. (Many new businesses exist in this market — mail-order food buying is currently one of the fastest-growing markets in the U.S.) The brand name is Healthy Holidays, and the company sells a healthy line of holiday cakes and cookies, which you want to advertise to health-conscious, female baby-boomers in the months of November and December. Your expectation is that these women will serve them at their holiday celebrations and also send them as gifts to friends and relatives.

You decide to advertise in *Health*, a Time Inc. magazine specializing in your target market and experiencing rapid growth in readership right now. You call the magazine, ask for someone who handles ad sales in your area, and explain what you want. She offers to send you information, and a package arrives in the mail a few days later. The package includes all the standard information that magazines and newspapers make available to their pro-spective advertisers:

> ✔ **Publisher's Statement:** This statement gives data on the circulation, or readership, of the publication. *Health's* average paid circulation (the average of all issues audited) is 947,682 — a number high enough to generate all the business you could handle if the ad works well. Further-more, you notice as you read the details of this statement that most of the subscriptions are for a full 12 months, and that most subscriptions are ordered without a premium. These two statistics suggest that readers are selecting *Health* at the regular subscription price and sticking with their subscriptions — good signs that the magazine has strong appeal to your target market and that its readers really do read it!

✔ **Audited data in the Publisher's Statement:** The audit bureau that gathers data on circulation should be referenced on the first page of the publisher's statement. Some smaller publications may not employ an auditor, in which case you should question their data. *Health*'s data is provided by a major supplier of audit services, the Audit Bureau of Circulations in Schaumberg, Illinois (847-605-0909).

✔ **Data on your target market as percentage of readership:** The circulation audit often breaks down readership into basic demographic categories (gender, age, education level, income, and so forth). For example, 70 percent of *Health* readers are women 35 or older — placing them in Healthy Holidays' target market.

You can supplement this data by learning something about readers' purchases of various consumer products. Look up *Health* in *Simmons Study of Media and Markets* (available in print form or on disk). Simmons will tell you, for example, whether *Health* readers buy more or less cookies for their households than the average American household buys — the answer is that they *are* heavy cookie consumers and, thus, a ripe market for Healthy Holidays! (Call Simmons Market Research Bureau in New York at 212-373-8900 for details.)

✔ **Issue and Closing Dates:** Each publication provides a schedule to advertisers, and you better make their dates if you want your ad included! Say you pick the following two issues in *Health*'s schedule:

Issue	1998 Closing Date, National Ads	On Sale Date
October	8/1/98	9/24/98
Nov/Dec	8/30/98	11/5/98

✔ **Rates:** What's the bottom line? The cost of running your ad depends upon the size you choose and whether you want to print the ad in black & white (cheapest), two-color (also fairly cheap), or four-color (more expensive, but probably necessary to illustrate a food product properly).

Rates also vary with the circulation, and the audit bureau provides what is termed a *rate base,* a round number representing the circulation figure they are confident each issue will achieve.

Finally, rates also vary depending on the number of issues you buy space in. Publications generally reward advertisers for buying more ads. *Health* offers a discount of 5 percent on three or more purchases, 8 percent on six or more, and 12 percent on twelve or more.

As a marketer for Healthy Holidays, you are enticed by that 3x discount and change your plan to include three insertions of your ad — in the September issue, the October issue, and the November/December issue. That means you can deduct 5 percent from the 1x base rates for four-color ads:

Size	1x Rate	3x Rate (5 percent discount)
1 Page	$36,290	$34,475
2/3 Page	27,580	26,200
1/2 Page	22,860	21,715
1/3 Page	16,330	15,515

Selecting ad size

What size ad should you buy? The answer depends in part on the design of your ad. Does the ad have a strong, simple visual or headline that will catch the eye, even if it is only a third of a page in size? Or does the ad need to be displayed in a larger format to work well?

In addition to your (or your designer's) judgment about the specifics of your ad, you can also take into account some general statistics on what percentage of readers *notice* an ad based on its size. As you may expect, the rate goes up — bigger ads get more notice, all other things being equal, according to a study by Cahners Publishing Co. (see Table 8-2):

Table 8-2	Selecting the Right Size
Size of Ad	*Percent of Readers Noting Ad (Median)*
Fractional (part-of-page) Ads	24%
One-Page Ads	40%
Two-Page Spreads	55%

Thus, the bigger the ad, the bigger the impact. But also consider the fact that the percentage of readers noticing your ad does *not* go up *in proportion to the increase in size*. A doubling of your ad's size will give you something like a quarter more viewers, but not twice as many. That's partly why the rate for a full-page ad is not twice the rate for a half-page ad. But the difference may not be reflected fully in the rates.

For example, a full page four-color ad in *Health* costs 59 percent more than a 1/2 page four-color ad. But my best guess is that the same ad, run at full versus half size, would attract at most about a third more notices by readers, meaning your cost per reader exposed to the ad is higher for that full-page ad than the half-page ad.

Many advertisers would not care that a bigger ad costs more per exposure, because they may have other objectives in mind. A major national advertiser may consider a fractional ad inconsistent with its big-company image or too small for its copy. And the ad may have a *reach goal* — in other words, it may have to reach more of *Health*'s readers than a fractional ad would.

But an entrepreneurial advertiser like our hypothetical Healthy Holidays company wants the best buy, as measured in *cost per thousand exposures to the target market*. (Advertisers generally convert their cost data to a per thousand basis in order to be able to work with convenient numbers.)

Comparing cost per thousand exposures

In this case (and the logic applies to any case), the cost per thousand is estimated as follows:

1. **Convert cost from rate base basis to target market basis.**

   Because 70 percent of *Health*'s readers are the target market of Healthy Holidays (women 35+), you can calculate that of the 900,000 guaranteed readers of this magazine, .7 x 900,000 or 630,000 women over 35 will read an issue in which you place your ad.

2. **Discount the target market circulation based on expected notice.**

   You know that many of those 35+ women reading *Health* will overlook your ad. So don't include them in your cost per thousand estimate. Using the Cahners data as a benchmark, I estimate that Healthy Holidays can expect a well-designed 1/2 page ad to attract 30 percent of *Health* readers' notice. For a one-page ad, I'll go with the Cahners figure of 40 percent. When I take these percentages of the target-market readership, I get estimates of how many 35+ women will notice my half- or full-page ad. With a one-page ad, about 252,000 women in my target market will notice the ad; with a 1/2 page ad, approximately 189,000 readers in my target market will notice the ad.

   What happened to that 900,000 circulation! Some aren't in the target market, and some won't even notice the ad, so you can't count them as useful exposures. In media buying, you have to read between the lines.

3. **Finally, figure out what it will cost per thousand to expose these 35+ women to one ad in *Health*.**

   The cost of the one-page ad is $36,290. Divide the estimate of the number of people in your target market who'll see the ad into this cost to get a per-person cost of exposure of about 14 cents. Multiply this number by a thousand, and you get a cost of *$144.01 per thousand* for the full-page ad.

   Doing the same calculations for the half-page ad, you get a cost of *$120.95 per thousand*.

Will your ad pay off?

I want to show you how Healthy Holidays' marketers can calculate the return on their advertising. Marketers must always think about returns, not just expenses.

To calculate the return on this direct-response ad in *Health* magazine, I have to estimate the *response rate,* which is the percentage of viewers who will respond to the ad as instructed. In this case, the response I need to forecast is calling Healthy Holidays' 800 number to ask a question or place an order. Because Healthy Holidays is new, I don't have any historical data to rely on, so I'm going to pick a conservative 1.5 percent response rate for my forecast. Furthermore, I'm going to assume the response rate only applies to the targeted readers — those 35+ women — because they are the ones my ad is crafted to address.

I know a single ½ page ad should be seen by about 189,000 35+ women readers of *Health*. I'll just bump that up to 300,000 for the three-ad run I'm planning, because I know the same 30 percent of readers won't note my ad each time. (I'm not quite sure how much overlap will occur, but my guess is reasonable.)

If 1.5 percent of these 300,000 women respond, that means I'll log 4,500 calls as a result of these ads. How much will I pay to generate these calls? The price of the ad campaign, three ½ page ads for a total of $65,145, plus some production costs to create the ad (I'll assume $10,000). That's about $75,000 in costs, or $16.67 per telephone call generated.

Is this a profitable proposition? The answer depends on how much profit I make from each caller on average. If 80 percent of callers place an order for this holiday season, and the average order is $70, and my profit margin is approximately 30 percent, then I make .8 (.3 x $70) or $16.80 per call according to these projections. In other words, I'm just above the break-even point. I'll clear about $0.13 per call when the dust settles, not including my operating costs for answering those telephones (hope that's built into the "shipping and handling"!). Multiply this number by the expected number of orders (80 percent of 4,500 callers) and I net a whopping $468 from this ad. Whoopie!

As an entrepreneur, I'd go for it, because I would expect to build long-term customer relationships with many of those callers, and, thus, profit more substantially from them in future holiday seasons. Having a print ad pay for itself and generate a customer base for future use isn't too bad. But if I wanted to make a quick killing this year, I don't think I'd bother. Throwing my money away on a few lottery tickets is so much simpler — which just goes to show that making easy money in business sure is hard!

For the penny-pinching entrepreneurs at Healthy Holidays, the half-page ad is the best choice. Three insertions of a four-color, half-page ad in the September, October, and November/December issues should give them about 3 x 189,000 or 567,000 exposures to their target market. (The cost per exposure is actually lower than what was calculated in the preceding steps, because with *three* insertions, the marketers get a 5 percent discount, which brings the cost down to $114.89 per thousand or around 11 cents per exposure — an excellent price!)

Many of these exposures will be repeats, because the circulation data tells us that *Health* has regular subscribers and readers. While guessing *exactly* what will happen is difficult, you can assume that the use of three insertions will catch the eye of at least half of *Health*'s readers and that you will also manage to hit most of the readers more than once — a good strategy when you are trying to motivate them to dial your 800 number and place a holiday order. Some readers may need a "reminder" exposure before they act anyway, because people generally procrastinate when it comes to holiday shopping!

Testing and Improving Your Print Ad

Is anybody actually reading your ad? A *direct response* ad, one that asks readers to take a clear, measurable action, gives you a clear indication of its effectiveness within days of its first appearance.

Going back to the fictional Healthy Holidays ad campaign in *Health* magazine, for example, I expect to receive lots of inquiries and orders over the telephone during the week the issue with my ad goes on sale. If I don't, I know I have a problem. Now what?

I may need to supplement my ad campaign with some last-minute *media buys* — purchases of additional advertising space or time. For example, perhaps I should call up public radio stations in key regional markets and purchase sponsorship of programs for Healthy Holidays, along with mention of its 800 number. And while redesigning the ad in *Health* is obviously out of the question (because its next two issues closed back in August), I may be able to use a last-minute direct mailing to a selection of names from *Health*'s subscriber list to add strength to the ad's message. And whatever I decide to do in the marketing arena to help overcome the lack of responses to my ad, I should also consider scaling back my sales projections so as to avoid getting stuck with a lot of perishable inventory!

What if you want to know more about why that direct response ad didn't get the desired level of response? Or what if you want to study an *indirect response ad* — one that creates or strengthens an image or position in order to encourage sales? Much brand advertising is indirect, leaving it to the retailer or local office to close the sale. No phones ring, whether the ad is good or bad, so how do you know whether the ad worked?

To get this sort of information, you need to go to a marketing research firm and have your ad tested for effectiveness. In fact, if you plan to spend more than, say, $200,000 on print ads, the $20,000 or so needed to hire a research firm to pretest the ad is probably money well spent. *Pretesting* means exposing people to the ad in a controlled setting and measuring their reactions to it. (Of course, if you hire a big ad agency, they'll offer research services, along with design and media buying — but you should still know enough to supervise and direct their decisions!)

You should also know that you can tap into the large-scale studies of ad readership done routinely by some research firms. All you have to do is subscribe to the study and the firm will feed you detailed data about how well each ad you publish works (see Chapter 6 and next paragraph for names of research firms).

A number of commercial research services can give you additional information about how and to what extent people read your ad. Roper Starch Worldwide (212-599-0700) may be the best known of these services. If you sign up for its Starch Readership Service, the service will ask consumers whether they noticed your ads. Starch surveys 75,000 consumers each year, asking them about specific ads in order to find out to what extent an ad is noticed and read, and to measure the level of interest the ad generated.

Specifically, Starch identifies three categories of readers of your ad. The categories are

- ✔ **Read Most:** Referring to the people who read half or more of the copy in your ad
- ✔ **Associated Reader:** Those who noticed the advertisement and also read enough to note the brand name
- ✔ **Noted Reader:** People who noticed the ad but did not necessarily read it

What you want is people who "Read Most" of your ad, and what you don't want is people who "Noted" the ad but did not go on to gain any useful information from it — or even worse, lots of readers who failed even to notice the darn thing at all.

You also get data from Starch that compares readership of your ad to readership of similar size ads in the same publication. So you can find out if readership of your ad is lower or higher than that of the average comparable ad. If higher, then your cost per thousand is lower than average, and your return on that advertising investment is high!

Say that the Starch data shows that readership of your ad is a little lower than average, and that while many people note the ad, few read enough to get the point or even the brand name. Should you kill this ad and start over?

The answer depends on what's wrong with the ad. And again, Starch data (or data from similar services) can help you find out, because the Starch survey looks at individual elements of the ad as well as the overall ad. You can find out how many people read the headline (or even the first versus second line of a two-line headline). Then you can see how many went on to the first paragraph of the body copy, or to the photograph, or to the logo and signature.

REAL WORLD

A breath of fresh air from Altoids

Marketers generally assume that they have to work in four colors to make their ads highly noticeable. Statistically, they are right. But don't discount the power of imaginative design. Sometimes a two-color ad outpulls four-color ads. Take a half-page ad for Altoids, "the curiously strong mints" that come in a distinctive white metal tin with red trim around its edges. A vertical half-page ad appears in some news weeklies that is printed only in black and red, yet I bet the ad is noted by more than 90 percent of readers.

Its full 12 inches of height is filled with the figure of a person clad in a shiny silver suit and helmet such as might be worn by a moon walker or a welder repairing a containment vessel at a nuclear power plant. The face and head are entirely concealed behind a dark-tinted glass visor and full helmet. In the figure's

heavily gloved hands is . . . a box of Altoids, which it is opening as if to reach in and pop one into its mouth (don't ask me how).

The copy is strikingly simple. Across the bottom appears, in bright red, large, 3-D, outlined capitals, the product's name. Beneath it is only the trademarked slogan (in white, outlined in black): "The curiously strong mints." This is all the copy except for an Internet address (it's http://www.word.com/altoids in case you want to see what they do with readers who follow up on this ad). Two colors. Five words. A guy in some kind of weird suit. This very simple, inexpensive ad is highly effective at building brand awareness and creating a quirky personality for the brand. Great print advertising doesn't have to be expensive, it just has to be *clever.*

Sometimes you find a problem that can be fixed without starting from scratch. For example, maybe your headline and photo get high Starch scores, but the body copy flunks. In this case, you can try rewriting and shortening the copy, and you may also try changing the layout or your choice of fonts. Perhaps the body copy is in reverse (light letters on dark background), which is hard to read. Often switching the text to dark letters on white raises the Starch score, without any other changes!

Or, perhaps, you need to switch from a black-and-white or two-color visual to a four-color one. Sure, it costs more, but if the Starch scores go up enough, the result may be an ad that yields a better return despite its higher price. Cahners Publishing also reports from its studies that black-and-white ads and two-color ads attract the notice of about a third of readers, while four-color ads attract almost half of readers — 46 percent to be precise. So as with size, more is better when it comes to colors. However, you need to run the numbers to see how the extra costs and extra readers will affect your cost per thousand figure. As with all print ad decisions, you should be able to reduce the options to reasonable estimates of costs and returns and then pick the highest-yielding option.

Chapter 9
Radio and Television Advertising

• •

In This Chapter

▶ Thinking about the media selection decision

▶ Designing ads for TV

▶ Using the emotional power of TV

▶ Buying TV ad time

▶ Designing ads for radio

▶ Writing radio scripts that catch and hold attention

• •

First . . . a Word on Media Selection

"Early to bed, early to rise, work like hell, and advertise." So goes the personal motto of Gertrude Boyle, the feisty chairman of Columbia Sportswear. Good idea. But how? If only she'd make clear whether to advertise in magazines, newspapers, TV, radio, or some other medium.

Most campaigns emphasize one medium. But which? Well, I'm here to tell you that the best medium is . . . whatever works! Sometimes you can make your point more effectively or cheaply in radio or outdoor display ads than you can in print. And sometimes the movement and realism of TV is just what you need to make the maximum impact. So you need to be ready to master whatever medium your program demands. (You find a more formal set of criteria for selecting media based on your marketing goals in Chapter 19.)

While most companies and programs emphasize a single medium as their primary one, exceptions to that focus rule exist. Sometimes spreading your advertising across several media equally (more or less) makes more sense. I recommend trying a multichannel approach more often.

Basically, you want to use multiple media whenever *maximizing the number and variety of exposures* is essential. When you have to hit the target over the head with your message, then a multichannel "POW!" approach may be just the thing.

This approach gives you more points of influence, and it varies your message to avoid losing the target's interest. Perhaps you could lead with print ads, but pulse with a strong radio campaign — and reinforce the whole thing with broad-exposure outdoor advertising to make sure that everybody is familiar with your brand name and its positioning.

And how about adding an active Web site and a telephone call center to increase your one-on-one interactions with customers and prospects? Programs like this one deliver high impact and can accomplish multiple marketing goals. But you have to become versatile — able to work well in multiple media.

Radio, TV, posters, billboards, transit buses, subway signs, T-shirts, flags, calendars, even boat sails are used to communicate marketing messages. When I lived in San Francisco, I often saw a tall sailboat on the Bay with "Esprit" emblazoned across its sails. And I see that small billboards are now on display as you ride the chair lifts at many ski resorts. (Would you advertise ski beverages on these, or would disability insurance be more realistic?) The point is, the options are many and growing, and your creativity can lead you to media that are fresher and less cluttered than the traditional ones. *Anything* may go, if you can find a way to make the medium work.

I discuss how to use print media in Chapter 8; this chapter focuses on TV and radio. Print, TV, and radio are the media that receive the bulk of advertisers' dollars, and even if your company goes with the flow and makes print, TV, or radio its primary medium, you still need to consider supporting your advertising with through-the-mail or electronic communications, telemarketing, point-of-purchase, and other options.

Most of the many media alternatives are really variations on print advertising. An outdoor poster or sign, a banner, a silk-screened mug, or T-shirt giveaway all use the elements of good print advertising — copy and art — adapted to the size and viewing time constraints of the medium in question. (Think about how long the average person views an ad in each medium — shortest for print ads, longer for radio, even longer for TV, and so on.) The principles of good print design from Chapter 8 apply to these media (and to Web pages and electronic display ads, as well as to direct mail letters and catalogs — see Chapter 11 for more information on these).

But two of your media choices — TV and radio — are substantially different, each with its own design requirements.

Designing Ads for TV

TV is theater. It combines visual and verbal channels in real-time action, making television a remarkably rich medium. Yes, the writing must be as tight and compelling as good print copy, but the words must also *sound* good and must *flow with the visuals* to create drama or comedy.

TV ads must be *great* theater: comedy or drama condensed to a few seconds of memorable action. Think of a really powerful, moving, and memorable scene from a movie. How about (for you Bogart fans) the scene from *To Have and to Have Not* in which Lauren Bacall says to Humphrey Bogart, "You know you don't have to act with me, Steve. You don't have to say anything, and you don't have to do anything. Not a thing. Oh, maybe just whistle. You *do* know how to whistle, don't you, Steve? You just put your lips together and blow." as she slinks out of his hotel room.

These few seconds of drama seem to etch themselves into the memory of anyone who watches that film. Why? I don't know for sure. Great theater is hard to reduce to a formula. A good script with just the right touch of just the right emotion. Great acting. Good camera work and a good set (remember the moody, shadowed lighting of that black-and-white film?). The suspense of a developing relationship between two interesting characters. You don't need to achieve this level of artistry to make a good TV ad, but you certainly need to achieve a higher than average level to stand out. And if you *can* create truly great TV, your ad will pay off in gold.

TV looks simple when you see it, but it's not. Hire an experienced production company to help you do the ad, or (what many marketers do) hire a big ad agency at big ad agency dollars to design and supervise the production of your ad. This choice is costly, but at least you get quality work.

Video follies

I'm not going to go into too much technical detail about design for television for the simple reason that most readers shouldn't be doing much design for this medium. While television commercials and other sorts of videos are common and important in marketing, their production is expensive and technically difficult. I decided to produce a videotape for the employee training market recently, and I'm sorry that I did. The crew spent an entire morning just getting the lighting right before they would let me say my thirty seconds of introductory copy. I nearly lost my mind, and my wallet, waiting for them to get everything right! Some small businesses do succeed in making their own videos or commercials, so it is certainly possible. But it's hard. You'll need to make a much bigger commitment to it than I was able to.

Bringing design, production, and even media buying in-house is far easier for any other medium than for TV. However, you do need to have a good grasp of how to use this unique medium well in order to get the most out of your production company or agency. *You* ultimately decide whether the script has that star potential or is just another forgettable ad. Don't let the production company shoot until they've got something as memorable as an old Bogart film (or at least close), okay?

If you work for a smaller business and are used to shoestring marketing budgets, then you may be shaking your head at my advice. You think you can do it yourself. Yes, I know you *can* go to a local cable station and shoot your own talking-head ads in their studio at little cost. But boy, do those ads look cheap! Why embarrass yourself in your own local market, and why waste even a little money on ads that don't work? If you're going to do TV, do it right. Either become expert yourself or hire an expert. Without high quality production, even the best design won't work. Why? Because in most countries, people watch so much TV that they know the difference between good and bad ads — and don't bother to watch anything but the best. As one authoritative reference book on advertising puts it, "Every viewer is a TV advertising expert" (*Kleppner's Advertising Procedure*, 13th Edition, Prentice Hall 1996, p. 588). That's a sobering thought.

Here's a bit of contrarian advice to balance the above warning. If you are on a shoestring budget, consider doing a self-made spoof ad. Make fun of one of the silly TV ad genres, like the one where an overenthusiastic salesman does a frantic 30-second sell. Because the whole point is to make a campy spoof, you don't want high production value. This strategy is actually the easiest to do on your own, but you'll still need help from someone with experience in setting up shots and handling camera and lights.

Let's get emotional

TV differs from other media in the obvious way — by combining action, audio, and video — but these features make TV different in less obvious ways as well. For example, TV is great for evoking *emotions,* just like traditional theater is. When you plan to use TV as your marketing tool, always think about what emotion you want to evoke.

Select an emotional state that is most compatible with your appeal and the creative concept behind your ad. Then use the power of imagery to evoke that emotion.

This strategy works whether your appeal is emotional *or* rational. Always use the emotional power of TV to *prepare* your audience to receive that appeal. Surprise. Excitement. Empathy. Anxiety. Skepticism. Thirst. Hunger. The protective instincts of the parent. You can create all these emotional states and more with a few seconds of TV. A good ad generates the right emotion to prime viewers for the appeal. The classic Prudential "own a piece of the rock" commercial, for example, is a strictly emotional appeal, designed to give us a feeling of permanence and dependability about the investment products it pitches.

Some marketers measure their TV ads based on *warmth*. Warmth is generally defined by research firms as the good feelings generated from thinking about love, family, or friendship. The commercially-available tests of warmth in TV ads include the TRACE method from Market Facts, Inc. and BBDO Worldwide's Emotional Measurement System. You may want to use one of these products to measure the warmth of your TV ad or other advertisements.

While you may not need to go into the details of measuring warmth, noting *why* people measure warmth is helpful. The reason is simple — emotions, especially positive ones, make TV ad messages far more memorable. This effect is stronger than many marketers realize, because it is not picked up in the standard measures of ad recall. In day-after recall tests, emotional-appeal TV ads are usually about as easily recalled as rational-appeal ads. But in-depth studies of their effectiveness tend to show that *the more emotionally charged ads do a better job of etching the message and brand identity in viewers' minds.*

So when you think TV advertising, think emotion. That's what TV can do — better than any other medium — and emotion makes for highly effective advertising.

Look, Ma . . .

Be sure to take full advantage of TV's other great strength: its ability to *show*. You can demonstrate a product feature, show a product in use, and do a thousand other things just with your visuals.

Actually, in *any* ad medium, you want to show as well as tell. (Even in radio, you can create mental images to show as well as tell. I explain how later in this chapter.) The visual and verbal modes reinforce each other. And some people in your audience think visually while others favor a verbal message, so you have to cover both bases by using words and images in advertising. But in TV, this rule should be adapted: The TV ad should SHOW and tell (note the emphasis on showing). Compare this with radio, where you should show and TELL. Or print, where the two modes are generally more balanced, so the rule is simply to show and tell.

This emphasis on showing is why TV ad designers rough out their ideas in a visually oriented script, using quick sketches to indicate how the ad will look. You — or preferably the competent agency or script writer you've hired — need to prepare rough *storyboards* as you think through and discuss various ad concepts. The storyboard is an easy way to show the key visual images in sequence. The sketches run down the center in most standard storyboard layouts. On the left appear notes about how to shoot each image, how to use music and sound effects, and whether to superimpose text on the screen. On the right appears the rough version of the *script*: the words to be said by actors in the scenes or in a voice-over for each scene. See Figure 9-1 for an example storyboard.

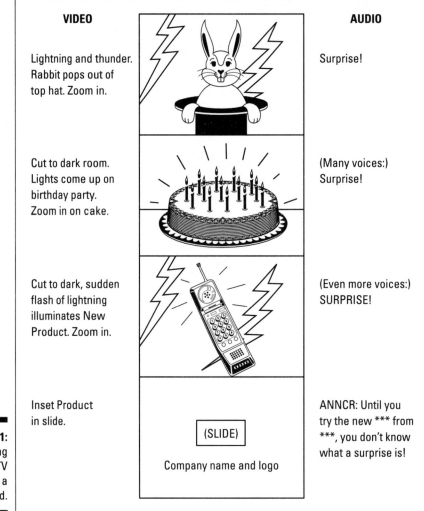

Figure 9-1:
Roughing
out a TV
ad on a
storyboard.

A question of style

You can use a great variety of *styles* in TV advertising. A celebrity can endorse the product. Claymation fruit can sing and dance about it. Animated animals can chase a user through the jungle in a fanciful exaggeration of a real-life situation. Imagination and videotape know no limits, especially with the recent growing availability of high-quality computerized animation and special effects at a reasonable cost. But some of the common styles are better — on average — than others in tests of ad effectiveness. Table 9-1 shows styles that are more and less effective.

Table 9-1	It Don't Mean a Thing if It Ain't Got that Swing
More Effective Styles	*Less Effective Styles*
Humorous commercials	Candid-camera style testimonials
Celebrity spokespeople	Expert endorsements
Commercials with children	Song/dance and musical themes
Real-life scenarios	Product demonstrations
Brand comparisons	

Again on average, *humor* and *celebrity endorsement* styles seem to work best in most studies. So try to find ways to use these styles to communicate your message. On the other hand, making ads that are the exception to the rule is possible, so don't give up hope on other styles. Just make sure that your ad is well above average if you don't want the rule of averages to apply to it.

A word on buying ad time on TV

Which television venues work best for your ad? For example, should you advertise on a network or cable station? Should the ad run in prime time, evening, or late night time slots? What programs provide the best audience for your ad?

As in other media, buyers rely on demographic studies to find out what audience size and characteristics are. The ubiquitous Simmons Market Research Bureau and Mediamark Research both provide useful data in publications and by subscription (see their coverage in connection with print advertising in Chapter 8). And *SRDS's TV & Cable Source* is also an excellent source of data — and the only one I've seen that combines data on Asia, Europe, and Latin America with U.S. listings.

But the key data in North American television markets is that provided by research firm A.C. Nielsen. Its Nielsen Television Index rates programs based on *sweeps* or four-times-a-year surveys of viewership in major media markets. The surveys are performed by having participants keep logs of what they watch. And now a high-tech improvement over this approach is coming online: in-home boxes called *people meters* that record what a household is watching and relay it to Nielsen (or to Arbitron, Nielsen's main competitor in this business). The resulting ratings are supposed to tell you how many television sets are tuned in to any particular program in any geographic market. However, advertisers and the television industry argue about their accuracy constantly, because slight differences in ratings make a big difference in the cost of advertising!

Rating surveys provide the following statistics by geographic area:

- ✔ How many TV sets are in the market in all (= *television households* or *TVHH*)
- ✔ How many TV sets are turned on (= *households using TV* or *HUT*)
- ✔ What percentage of the HUTs are tuned to a specific program (= *audience share*)
- ✔ What percentage of the TVHHs are tuned to a specific program (= *rating*)

For example, say a city has 800,000 TVHHs. If 25 percent of these are tuned to a particular program, then that program gets a rating of 25. If only half of all televisions are on, then HUT equals 400,000, and that program's share of market is 50 percent.

In the television industry, *market* means households with their TVs on. But market may mean something very different to advertisers, who define their market as those people who they hope will buy their product. And so, in general, advertisers pay more attention to ratings than to share of market data.

A *gross rating point* (GRP) is the total rating points achieved by your media schedule. (Your *media schedule* is all the times you run an ad over a specific period.) When media buyers purchase a series of time blocks on TV for your ad, they will add up all the ratings from each of the times/places where your ad runs, and give you the total — your campaign's GRPs. The number will be big, but it won't tell you very much.

Part of the problem is that the number does not distinguish between new exposures (*reach*) and repeat exposures (*frequency*). Maybe your ad reached ten million television households, but were they the same one million households, ten times over — or did you reach ten million households one time each? The answer probably lies somewhere in between — but what is it exactly? Obtaining reach and frequency estimates for any TV ad schedule is important to help you interpret the GRP figure. In some campaigns, you may want ten or twenty repetitions. In others, one or two may be your goal. Let your agency or media buyer know.

A helpful general rule is that more repetitions increase the certainty and usability of the attitudes your ad forms in the viewer's mind. So plan on more repetitions if you think these aspects of attitude need work. But one or a few repetitions are generally enough to form the initial attitude, so you don't need many repetitions when you think the viewer will quickly agree with your ad's message and have no trouble remembering it in purchase situations.

One further refinement should be added to audience data. The data is broken down into demographic and other categories to help marketers figure out what percentage of all those households tuned into a program are actually the right people, the group the ad targets. And I recommend always converting overall ratings into a number that represents *your own target market* — that number is bound to be smaller, of course, because your target will only be a portion of all those viewing any particular program. And that means the cost per thousand viewers will be higher than it looks if you go by the book and use the CPM figures provided by the rating services.

In fact, the key variable in determining whether the ad is a good buy or not is often how rich in target viewers any television audience is. Rating points emphasize the size of the program's audience, not the match between the audience and your target market. So be sure to convert — or *ask your agency to convert* — ratings into figures that represent reach into your target market and exclude those who you don't need to advertise to. When you look at the TV buying decision this way, you often end up advertising on different channels and programs than if you went by straight rating points.

Designing Ads for Radio

Like TV, radio is also a form of theater, and, therefore, has more in common with TV than with any other medium. Most marketers overlook this point because they assume the lack of visuals limits radio severely. Not true!

My twelve-year-old son got a set of tapes of old radio shows featuring that amateur sleuth known as The Shadow, and so we've been listening to these classic radio dramas in our household lately. Why are the old radio dramas so engaging? Because you can *see* the action so clearly as it unfolds. The script and sound effects (*SF* or *SFX* in radio lingo) create a string of powerful visual images in your mind as the story unfolds (note that the script tells you what the sound effects are to make sure you "see" them).

"Oh no, the giant black cat is coming toward us! My God, its eyes are glowing! *(SF: Meeeowww. Snarl, snarl.)* "Help, it's backing me toward the edge of the roof of this ten-story building!" *(SF: Snarl, spit, snarl.)* "Look out Margo, you'll fall off!" *(SF: Sound of falling, with a woman's scream fading into distance.)*

You can see what's happening, can't you?

Conventional wisdom says you have only three elements to work with when you design for radio: words, sound effects, and music. And that's true in a literal sense, but you won't create a great radio ad unless you remember that the object is often to use those elements to generate *mental images* for the listener. And that means you can often perform the same basic plot on radio as on TV. Radio is not really as limited as people think. We just rarely use radio to full advantage now that society's love affair with radio has been eclipsed by its love of TV and movies.

Here are some tips for designing great radio ads, which I've adapted from an old checklist developed by marketing professor and well-known textbook author Courtland Bovèe (Hiam, *The Vest-Pocket Marketer*, Prentice Hall, 1991):

- ✔ Engage the listener's imagination by evoking pictures with your words and sound effects.

- ✔ Find and use truly memorable sounds — a cool sound effect, interesting voice, or catchy musical phrase. Not all sounds are created equal!

- ✔ Stick to one strong idea. Radio ads fight the audience's tendency to treat radio as background sound, so your ad has to have incredible focus in order to penetrate to mental engagement. (In many countries, people spend more time with radio than any other medium — but they are not necessarily paying attention during most of that listening time!)

- ✔ Flag down your targeted listeners right away. The beginning of any great radio ad needs to help listeners self-select so that the right people pay attention.

    For example, if the ad targets people who need a haircut but are frustrated with their current salon's service or quality, then start by reaching out to these people. Your ad could start with the sound of breaking glass (a mirror shattering?), followed by a narrator's voice saying, "Not another *bad hair* day!" Now listeners who feel their hair needs work are all ears, ready to listen to your marketing message.

- ✔ Favor direct over indirect action goals. Sure, sometimes you will want to use radio just to create brand awareness (that's *indirect action* advertising). Dialog Design, a leading ad design firm based in Leverett, Massachusetts (at 413-548-8198), sponsors public radio arts programming simply to create name recognition for itself — an indirect advertising goal. And I always figure you can learn from how ad agencies market themselves! But Bovèe points out that in general, the most effective radio ads call for *direct* action.

Come into one of our convenient stores. Call our toll-free number. Participate in our contest — entry forms available at stores today. Buy tickets to our upcoming event. Tune in to our television special, tonight at 7:00. All these are appropriate direct-action goals for radio advertising, and if you think about it, radio audiences do often take action in response to instructions from their radios. They often call into a talk show, or phone in a request for a song, or call to buy a ticket to something. Heavy listeners — the core of the radio market — are action-oriented. So don't be afraid to add your instructions, too!

✔ Mention your brand name and its key benefit early and often. Research shows that more listeners remember the brand name when it appears early than late. And repetition helps too — remember that you must often communicate to someone who is treating the radio as background sound while they drive or work. Also, I believe that all radio ads can accomplish the indirect-action goal of building brand awareness. Even ads that have a direct action goal should be designed to accomplish this indirect goal, too.

Put that brand name in early and often, regardless of the script. If you fail to generate the desired direct action, at least you will build awareness and interest for the brand, which supports other points of contact in your marketing program. Radio is a great support medium for other media, and not enough marketers use it that way. You may as well fill the vacuum with *your* marketing message!

Sound effects hazard ahead

I also want to add a simple rule that can keep you out of trouble by helping you avoid confusion. Be sure that your script *identifies all sound effects.* Sound effects are wonderful and evocative, but in truth, many sound just about alike. Without context, rain on the roof could be bacon sizzling in a pan, a blowtorch cutting through the metal door of a bank vault, or even an alien spaceship starting up. So the script must identify what that sound is, either through direct reference ("Oh boy, I think that alien spaceship's motor is starting") or through the context.

You can provide context by the script, the plot, or simply by other sound effects. The sounds of eggs cracking and hitting a hot pan, coffee percolating, and someone yawning all help to identify that sizzle as the breakfast bacon, rather than rain on the roof or the kryptonite drive mechanism of an alien spaceship.

A word about buying radio time

I often find myself urging marketers to try radio in lieu of their standard media choices. Why? Because, while radio is frequently used for local pull-oriented advertising by retailers, most other marketers overlook it. They don't realize how powerful radio can be — and they may not be aware of its incredible reach either. For example, in the U.S., 96 percent of people listen to radio at least occasionally, and 81 percent are listening on any given day. That's a lot of people. I bet your target audience is in there somewhere!

In fact, radio reach is higher than that of other media in the U.S. (and many other nations as well). Table 9-2 shows the daily reach figures for U.S. radio, TV, and newspapers.

Table 9-2	Reach Out and Touch Someone
Medium	*Daily Reach (percentage of U.S. population 18 years old and up)*
Radio	81%
Television	76%
Newspapers	69%

Theoretically, radio can deliver a larger audience for your ads than print or TV can. Radio is definitely a good medium for broad reach goals.

Furthermore, you can target radio advertising quite narrowly — both by type of audience and by geographic area. This fact helps make radio a very good buy. So does the general lack of appreciation for this medium, which keeps ad prices artificially low in my opinion. Table 9-3 looks at some statistics on the average *CPM,* or cost of reaching one thousand people (over the age of 14), with a radio ad compared with other media:

Table 9-3	The Cost of Doing Business			
Country	*Radio*	*TV*	*Newspapers*	*Magazines*
U.S.	$1.53	$6.66	$11.26	$4.91
Germany	$2.20	$13.31	$7.41	$6.91
Italy	$3.24	$11.62	$5.80	$4.89

Radio ads are 77 percent cheaper than television ads and 86 percent cheaper than newspaper ads in the U.S. — an amazing difference (according to these statistics, which come from a recent academic study). And radio is generally cheaper in other countries, too. This difference is partly because of the problem, discussed previously, that people may not be paying any attention to the radio they have on in the background. But a well-designed ad can often capture their attention for a few seconds. And this problem is not unique to radio. I'm not at all sure that the households tuned to TV programs according to those ratings are actually paying any attention either. And when people read the newspaper, they usually do pay attention — but perhaps only to the stories that catch their eye, so *your* ad may easily be overlooked. For my money, radio is an awfully good buy, regardless of its differences from other media. (I talk about why outdoor advertising is also an incredibly good buy in Chapter 10.)

Targeted advertising via radio

I like the fact that radio stations make a real effort to target specific audiences — which is after all what most advertisers are trying to do as well. You can get good audience data — both demographic and lifestyle or attitude-oriented information is available on radio audiences. And you can often find radio stations that reach a well-defined audience that is rich in those people you wish to target, making radio an even better buy.

Details of audience characteristics for all U.S. radio stations are available from SRDS in Des Plaines, Illinois (847-375-5000; Web site: `http://www.srds.com`). A monthly SRDS publication, *Radio Advertising Source,* gives you enough information to plan most radio campaigns or handle the buying. The publication also offers details of how to buy radio time on the state, regional, or national levels for major campaigns. A one-year subscription costs $405, so this book is for people who really need it, but if you work with radio, that's you. And I imagine SRDS can provide information in other formats and at other price points if you need it.

And here's another option for radio advertising that I bet you haven't considered. How about running ads over the internal broadcasting systems used in many stores? This is another great way to target a particular audience — for example, advertise your brand of tires at an automotive store. This kind of ad is called *in-store audio advertising.* It is an entirely different medium from a buying perspective, because the programming is developed and controlled by the store or a specialized service provider. As a result, most marketers don't know how to use in-store audio programming. But an ad agency may be able to help you gain access, and some specialized media buying firms handle this kind of advertising, too. For example, 3M Media can book in-store audio advertising for you in a hundred different U.S. markets according to SRDS's *Out-of-Home Advertising Source.* (You can reach SRDS at 800-851-7737 or 847-375-5000 if you need help finding media buyers for your radio or in-store audio ads.)

And now for my parting shot on this topic, just to make sure that you get the point: *Don't overlook radio!* It can give you better reach, better focus on your target market, and a lower cost per thousand exposures than any other medium. Like TV, radio can *show* as well as tell — you just have to use the listener's imagination to create visual images. And if you manage to create a really good script, I guarantee you will catch and *hold* audience attention.

Chapter 10

Outdoor Advertising: Billboards, Banners, Signs, and More

*O*utdoor advertising refers to a variety of large to very large signs and posters, including roadside billboards. This medium is also called *out of home* by some marketers. Signs, flags, and banners are not conventionally included in this medium — but I don't know why not. (Except that these are usually designed and displayed by the marketer rather than through the services of the advertising industry, so the powers that be don't control them.)

To my mind, any poster-type display of a marketing message in a public or semi-public space, whether indoors or outdoors, belongs in the outdoor category, whether you're talking about a huge billboard beside the freeway or a tiny window sticker on somebody's car.

Why? Because all these methods are attempts to *communicate your message through public display* of a poster, sign, or something of similar design requirements. That's why I incorporate signs, flags and banners, bumper stickers, transit advertising, and even T-shirts in this chapter, along with the traditional billboard formats. These media are more powerful than many marketers realize — some businesses succeed by using no other advertising, after all! In this chapter, I show you how to design for and use outdoor advertising and review many of the varied options so that *you* won't overlook this important medium in your marketing program.

Outdoor Design Requirements

Here's a simple exercise to help you understand the design requirements. Draw a rectangular box on a sheet of blank paper, using a ruler as your guide. Make the box $2^1/_4$ inches wide and 1 inch high. That's the proportion of a standard outdoor *poster* (a large, printed advertisement posted on a signboard or building). While the poster will be much larger, from a distance it may well *look* as small as that box on your sheet, held at arm's length. (See Figure 10-1.) Now hold your paper (or Figure 10-1) at arm's length and think about what copy and artwork could both fit in this space and be easily read at this distance. Not much, right? Be careful to limit your message to a few, bold words and images or it will be unintelligible.

Figure 10-1:
From a distance, a large roadside poster will look no bigger than this.

CAN YOU READ THIS
CAN YOU READ THIS
CAN YOU READ THIS
CAN YOU READ THIS
CAN YOU READ THIS

That's the problem with outdoor advertising in general — it must be readable, in a hurry, and often from a considerable distance. That means the ad has to be simple. Yet the same ad will probably be viewed over and over by people who travel the same road or sidewalk (or take the same elevator or ride the same bus route) daily. So it has to combine lasting interest with great simplicity. That's tough!

Outdoor advertising is like print advertising, except that outdoor advertising must use far fewer words and far simpler images to make its point more economically and clearly — but, hopefully, with an entertaining hook or device to hold attention. With all these constraints, designing effective outdoor ads is difficult.

Billboard formats for outdoor

You have several standard choices regarding the size of your outdoor ad and its distance from the average viewer.

✔ You can choose a huge *spectacular,* a custom-made, often building-sized display such as those that grace Times Square in New York. These cost a bundle and are generally treated as long-term, image-building investments.

If you want to show your new pest control spray killing a giant cockroach, perhaps you should consider a giant can of the stuff on top of a building, timed to emit a puff of harmless spray once a minute in the face of a huge cockroach that is crawling up the outside of the building. Pretty? No. Attention-getting? Yes. Few rules apply to spectaculars — aside from the rules of gravity and engineering — so you can have some real fun with this unusual form of outdoor advertising.

✔ You can choose a standard *30-sheet poster* (although with modern printing they no longer have to use thirty separate sheets!). This billboard-sized ad measures 21'7" wide x 9'7" high.

✔ You can use a *bulletin,* a huge version of the poster that measures 48' wide x 14' high. And bulletins can be extended with extra panels on the bottom, side, or top (see Figure 10-2 for details). A bulletin is four times as big as a 30-sheet poster, giving it incredible impact close up. Bulletins also make the text readable from a greater distance, so these are a good choice along high-speed roads where the viewer is not near your ad for long enough to read anything requiring close-up attention.

✔ You can also scale down for sidewalk-level viewing to the standard 11' x 5' *eight-sheet poster,* also called a *junior poster* in the industry. This poster is about a sixth the size of the standard 30-sheet poster, but when placed closer to viewers is sometimes even more effective. Anyway, advertisers seem to think so; the format is growing in popularity.

Figure 10-2 shows the proportions and relative sizes of the standard outdoor formats.

You can also explore the growing number of variations on these standards. Want your message displayed on the floor of a building lobby, on a kiosk at a mall, or alongside the notice boards at health and fitness centers? Or how about on signs surrounding the arenas and courts of athletic events? All these options and more are available, both directly from the businesses that control such spaces, and through a host of ad agencies and media-buying firms that can give you larger-scale access.

Maximizing the returns on outdoor advertising

The costs of outdoor advertising are highly varied, but to give you some idea of what's involved, a bulletin along an expressway in the midsized city of Denver, Colorado, costs $2,250 per month to rent. If you rent a similar bulletin in the smaller, nearby city of Colorado Springs, where traffic along the freeway is less, then the cost is $1,685 per month.

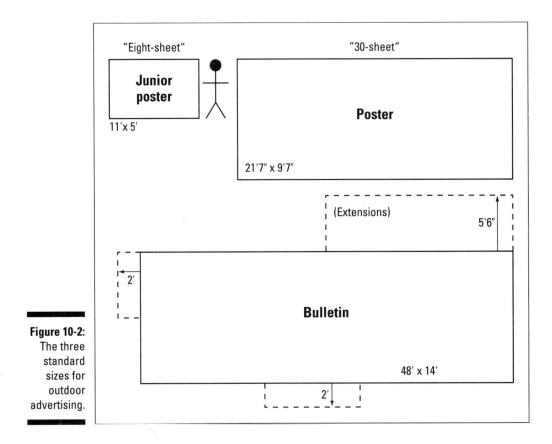

Figure 10-2:
The three
standard
sizes for
outdoor
advertising.

Given the high traffic rates on many expressways, that's a pretty good buy on a cost per thousand (CPM) viewers basis. For example, a Denver bulletin delivers about 31,200 exposures (*reach* — number of viewers — versus *frequency* — how many times viewers see it — is unknown, but assume plenty of repeat exposures from commuters). That works out to a price of $2,250÷31,200 or $0.07 per thousand exposures. While prices vary — and I picked an especially cheap price to illustrate my point — outdoor is generally cheap on a CPM basis.

A study from Simmons Market Research Bureau estimates the CPM for reaching adults 18 years and older at $1.43 per thousand for the average U.S. 30-sheet poster. While that's a far higher number than my quick estimate for that Denver billboard, it is still far cheaper than most other media. (It's about half of radio's cost and a small fraction of TV and print costs!)

My statistics on those Colorado billboards come from *Out-of-Home Advertising Source,* published by SRDS in Des Plaines, Illinois (at 847-375-5000 or 800-851-7737). This annual publication covers the U.S. outdoor market for a reasonable $149 — a bargain compared to information on other media.

Of course, the CPM figures I calculated and the average figure from Simmons are just the beginning point for a serious marketing planner. You need to factor in your estimate of the percent of exposures that reach *your target market* — perhaps small, given the mass nature of the medium, in which case the divisor in that CPM equation goes down and the price goes up. (Simmons estimates, for example, that the average CPM for reaching female baby boomers aged 25-49 with a 30-sheet poster is $6.11 — more than four times as costly as when you don't care what sort of adults your poster reaches.)

You need to consider the likelihood that those exposures lose value after the commuter has seen your billboard many days in a row. Is the tenth view of the same billboard anywhere near as effective as the first or second? Will anyone even bother looking at the same billboard multiple times? Often not. In outdoor advertising, marketers talk about *reexamination rates,* the average number of times viewers bother to read the same outdoor ad. The best billboards have higher reexamination rates because people find them interesting enough to look at again and again.

You also need to keep the limited message potential of outdoor advertising in mind, which means what you can communicate for that cheap price is pretty minimal, too.

Still, at those prices, outdoor advertising is a good buy. If you want cheap exposure for your brand name or to make consumers aware of a local product or service in a hurry, outdoor advertising is generally the cheapest way to do so. And in most urban markets, you can readily purchase enough outdoor advertising to (theoretically, at least) cover the entire market. This practice is called a *100 showing* in the out-of-home advertising industry, meaning that your billboards are sufficient in number and location to make it possible that 100 percent of the people in that market will be exposed to your message. (Similarly, a *50 showing* gives you a maximum of 50 percent coverage.)

As in print advertising in general, the costs vary based on ad size as well as audience size. A bulletin costs about four times as much as the standard poster ad — reflecting the fact that it is about four times as big. A junior poster costs about a quarter of a poster ad, and is about a sixth as large.

However, *effectiveness* does not vary with size as much as it does in standard print advertising for two reasons, each of them exploitable by savvy marketers.

✔ First, when you read a magazine, your eye is equidistant to all ads, regardless of their size. But in outdoor ads, the smaller format ads are generally placed closer to a flow of traffic than the larger ones are. That means a junior poster may be *effectively* as large and readable as a poster, in spite of its smaller size, because it is placed down low and close to the road. Even if the junior poster is not quite as impressive, it is still much more than a quarter as impressive — so it is truly a bargain by comparison.

✔ Second, outdoor differs from print ads in magazines and newspapers in that the speed of the viewer or reader is not constant. You can assume that people flip through the pages of a magazine at the same rate, regardless of whether you buy a quarter-page or full-page spread. That's why the full-page spread catches the reader's eye more effectively — it stands out much better in that split second in which her eye scans the page before turning it.

Outdoor ad rates are based on a similar premise. They assume all traffic is equal because they are often based on *traffic counts* (number of vehicles per day — or day and night if poster is illuminated — times the average occupancy of a vehicle). But a big difference exists between someone viewing a poster at 65 miles per hour on a freeway, someone viewing a poster at 45 miles per hour on a local road, and someone sitting next to a poster for ten minutes in the traffic jam leading to a toll booth or bridge. If you or your media buyer care enough to shop around (and possibly wait your turn) for locations with high and low-speed traffic, you can get a billboard that will be read more slowly and carefully by a higher percentage of the people who pass by!

In sum, not all outdoor advertising is equal. Location makes a huge difference to the effectiveness of your ad. And a smart shopper can find good locations that give a bigger bang for the buck than the average outdoor ad by far. That's why some outdoor advertisers hoard good spaces, even committing to rent them for years at a time just to hold onto them.

Eight-sheets to win!

The junior poster (or eight-sheet poster) is growing in popularity. Introduced fairly recently in the U.S. to make outdoor advertising more affordable for small businesses, junior posters are now catching on with all advertisers and spreading across the globe. Part of the reason for this spread is the fact that a junior poster can be placed nearer the flow of traffic — especially traffic on slower-moving local roads.

The rest of the eight-sheet story has to do with the emergence of a standard size 11' x 5' poster in 12' x 6' frame. The Eight-Sheet

Outdoor Advertising Association, Inc. is responsible for this helpful advance, which has made producing and placing these smaller posters as easy as working in the old 30-sheet standards (which, by the way, are distributed in the U.S. by the Institute of Outdoor Advertising).

Overall, the eight-sheet format is estimated to be about *three times as cost-effective* as the traditional 30-sheet poster. The eight-sheet format is almost equally visible in comparative studies, and readership and recall measures are generally the same according to the Eight-Sheet Outdoor Advertising Association's data. This is also helpful in calculating the number of exposures to a poster — multiply these percents by the traffic data for a location to get total exposures in a day as shown in the nearby table.

So if the eight-sheet format is available where you need outdoor advertising, I recommend you give it a try!

	8-Sheet	**30-Sheet**
Visibility	30%	37%
Readership	29%	29%
Re-Examination	1.3	1.5

When *not* to use outdoor

A quarter of all U.S. outdoor ad spending is dedicated to alcohol and cigarette advertising (far less in countries that don't limit cigarette and alcohol advertising on TV). As a result, most U.S. marketers think of examples of these billboards when they think about outdoor advertising. Unfortunately, they end up with the wrong idea about outdoor advertising, because these ads generally misuse the medium.

Outdoor advertising is not appropriate to alcohol and tobacco products because it is demographically a *mass medium* (although geographically, a highly targeted one). And alcohol and tobacco advertising should not use a mass medium (I show you why in a second). In addition, the mass exposure of outdoor advertising is inappropriate for these products because accidental exposures to segments of the population who should not be exposed to the ads is high.

Outdoor advertising is *geographically specific* — because you can choose signs by city or commute route. That's great for a local advertiser with a product having broad-based appeal in the local area. For example, if you market auto body services in five cities, then you can assume just about everyone who owns and drives a car in those cities will drive by your outdoor ads at some point. However, just about anybody may be in those cars that drive by your ad. This is why you should generally treat outdoor advertising as a mass medium.

You can't be sure whether people who drink alcohol regularly will drive by, versus those who don't, for example. Drivers are a pretty diverse bunch. Only 55 percent of adults of drinking age in the U.S. say they've consumed an alcoholic beverage in the last six months (*American Demographics,* Jan. 1997, p. 4) — a surprisingly low figure to most people. When you take into consideration the many who are underage and can't legally drink, this means that far less than half the population are appropriate targets for an alcohol product's marketing program. Yet outdoor ads guarantee equal exposure to that majority who aren't in the target market. Similarly, only about 20 percent of adults smoke cigarettes, yet the large majority of nonsmokers is exposed to outdoor tobacco ads, too. That's a terrible waste of advertising money.

The point I'm driving home (heh, heh) here is that using outdoor advertising just doesn't make sense unless the exposure you get will be rich in your intended audience. Otherwise, you are exposing lots of people to messages that don't concern or benefit them — and you're doing so on a truly colossal scale!

Exercising moderation

Outdoor ads are often rather intrusive. Many people get angry when their view is obstructed by gigantic advertisements! You need to keep this in mind as you think about how and when to use the medium.

A new wave of bans on some forms of outdoor may be gaining momentum — a landmark is the city of Baltimore's recent ban on most forms of alcohol and tobacco outdoor ads. While the legal battles stemming from this ban are not yet over, the ban may bring in a more hostile climate toward outdoor in U.S. markets.

But regardless of whether your product is viewed as harmful or not, using outdoor just doesn't make sense unless exposure will be rich in your intended audience.

If marketers want to continue enjoying the freedom to run ads virtually at will, they must try not to take the disrespectful, in-your-face attitude that seems to characterize much of modern advertising.

And please, don't run outdoor advertising that may offend some viewers. Trust me, souring communities to this medium and fueling the drive toward out-and-out bans is simply not worth the risk. Far more targeted media are available for such messages. I'm sure that you can find a magazine, radio station, or mailing list that delivers your target without any chance of offending nontargeted people.

Back to Basics: The Essential Sign

Here's a strange thing I discovered while writing this book: *Signs* (small, informational outdoor ads or notices) don't show up in the index or table of contents of most books on marketing. *Signs.* You know, those things with brand or company names on them — and sometimes a short marketing message or useful information for the customer, too?

Signs are all over — if you're in an office right now, step to the nearest window and you will probably be able to see a handful with ease. And signs are undeniably important. Even if they serve only to locate a store or office, they do a job that marketers need done. If your customers can't find you, you're out of business. (I soon show you other ways to use signs.) So why do marketers — or at least those marketing experts who write the books — tend to ignore signs so completely?

You won't find a national or international set of standards for signs. Neither will you find a major association to promote standards and champion best practices. I can't send you to "the experts" as easily when it comes to signs as I can with radio, TV, print, or other outdoor media. You will probably end up working with a local sign manufacturer, and you and your designer will have to specify size, materials, copy, and art.

A sign for the times

Many signs have a public purpose — to keep you from running down pedestrians in the crosswalk, for example. These don't seem to have anything to do with marketing. Yet they do have the same *basic goal* — to alter someone's behavior, usually in the immediate term, and usually by affecting where they go or don't go.

Those street signs offer clues to the design of all signs. Notice how simple and clear they are. Signs have to be simple because of their small size, combined with the viewing conditions: *People look at signs from a distance and in a hurry.* The same constraints hold for commercial signs, so be sure to design them with this fact in mind. The ability of signs to communicate is fairly limited. After all, if the typical sign could convey a marketing message with adequate visibility and force, then billboards would never have been invented!

But still, you can't count signs out of the picture when looking for those all-important points of influence over your customers and prospects. Outdoor and public-space signs play a vital role in attracting customers to locations. And indoor signs are gaining importance in the point-of-purchase advertising arena (see Chapter 16). Taking signs for granted is too easy — don't forget about them when designing a marketing program!

Many towns and cities regulate the display of signs in public places (restrictions are usually available from local zoning boards). And if you rent retail or office space, your landlord may also have put some restrictions or a *right of review* into your lease. You better research these possible constraints before spending any money on design and construction of signs! If restrictions seem likely to cause trouble, you will probably need to hire a lawyer to clarify your options or advocate for an exception before you start the design process.

When it comes to having a sign made, consult your local or regional business telephone listings. You should find several options. You may want to talk to a good design firm or experienced designer for a personal reference.

Also consider hiring a cabinet-maker, stained glass artist, oil painter, or other art or craft professional to make your sign. Most signs are obvious examples of commercial art — with little real art about them. So when a business hires an artist to carve its name and logo into a big piece of mahogany, the result is something truly special! Unusual and beautiful signs tell the world that your company is special, too. In fact, a really special sign, well displayed in a high-traffic area, has more power to build an image or pull in prospects than any other form of local advertising.

What your sign can do

Signs are limited in terms of what marketing goals they can accomplish — but perhaps not as limited as you think. Marketing consultant Robert Bly, author of the *Advertising Manager's Handbook* (published by Prentice Hall), writes that signs can perform these communication functions:

✔ **Signs can direct people to your business location:** Bly explains the concept very nicely when he says that *"signs index the environment."* Many marketers understand this need to the extent that they use outdoor advertising on freeways to tell travelers to visit their store. But then the marketers fail to post directional signs for those travelers after they leave the freeway. Don't underestimate the average customer's ability to get lost. Make sure that your signs really do index the environment well enough that you lose no customers along the way!

Using signs like indexes can help you play the location game better by giving you a presence near competitors' locations. You know the old saying about the three rules of successful retailing — that they are location, location, and location? Well, you can use signs to create a broader visual footprint for your location. For example, if you put signs for a store throughout a mall, more customers will come to your store and fewer will be lost to competitors' locations!

✔ **Signs can provide street advertising:** Signs are, after all, the original and most basic form of outdoor advertising. They are smaller, more local, and more intimate than the huge billboard-sized posters used in modern outdoor advertising. But they can be even more effective than billboards. They announce your presence; they can and should communicate a great deal about your *personality,* too (see Chapter 5 for how to choose and use a personality in marketing). Signs should be designed to make your location as visible as possible to anyone walking or driving on your street. And they should do so in a manner that is consistent with your *business image* — that personality you want to project to your customers and prospects.

✔ **Signs can build image:** The quality of a sign says a lot about the quality of the products or services a customer can expect. I urge you to *outspend all your competitors on signs* in order to project a higher-quality image. In marketing, perception is reality, and for many businesses, the signs have a big effect on customer perception!

✔ **Signs can provide helpful information:** What products or services do you provide? How and when should customers do business with you? What makes you different from other options? What kind of business or customers are you looking for? Too often, customers cannot answer such questions by looking at a business from the outside. The details just aren't available. But those details can be included on signs. And when signs answer all these questions, customer and noncustomer confusion is minimized. You attract more of the sort of business you want and little or none of the business that you don't want. Take a critical look at your signs — do they really provide enough information for customers, prospects, and the merely curious? Make sure that your signs communicate who you are, what you do, whom you do it for, when, where, and how!

Copy for signs

Writing for signs is a strange art, but one the marketer needs to master. Too often, the language on signs is ambiguous. The sign just doesn't say anything with enough precision to make its point clear. Before you approve any design, review the copy to make sure that it is the model of clarity in writing! *Try* misinterpreting the wording. Can the sign be read to mean something you don't intend to say? And try thinking of "stupid" questions that the sign doesn't answer. For example, some people have a terrible sense of direction, so a sign on the side of a store will leave them confused about how to enter that store unless it has an arrow and the instructions "Enter from Front" clearly displayed on it!

Some signs are designed to convey substantial information — directions, for example, or details of a store's merchandise mix. Informational signs are often too brief *and* too lengthy. The copy and design ought to be divided into two sections, each with a separate purpose.

- ✔ The first section is like *the header* in a print ad, and its purpose is to catch attention from afar and draw people to the sign. Given this purpose, brevity is key — and large, catchy type and/or visuals are also essential.

- ✔ The second section of the sign needs to communicate *the essential information* accurately and in full. If the first section does its job, viewers will walk right up to the sign to read the informational part, so that type need not be as large and catchy. Instead, the wording and type needs to be easy to read and interpret, and it needs to be sufficiently complete that it answers all likely viewer questions.

Most signs do not have these two distinct sections, and as a result, they fail to accomplish either purpose very well. They neither draw people very strongly nor inform them fully. Unfortunately, most sign makers have a strong urge to make all the copy the same size. When pressed, the sign makers sometimes make the header twice as big as the rest of the copy. But to go farther than that seems to upset them. Well, to get a good sign, you may have to upset some people. As in many aspects of marketing, if you want above-average performance, you're going to have to swim against the current.

Another problem with the copy on most signs is that it is written in the most dumb-obvious manner. Tradition says that a sign, unlike any other marketing communication, must simply state the facts in a direct, unimaginative manner. The dictionary ought to give "creative signs" as an example when it defines "oxymoron," because "creative" and "signs" tend to mix like oil and water.

One reason you don't see much creativity in signs is that most marketers assume people *read* signs. That's the conventional wisdom — that your customers and prospects will automatically find and read your signs.

The average downtown street in the average city has more than a hundred signs per block. Try walking such a block and then listing all the signs you remember seeing. Some will stand out ("DON'T WALK," for example), but most go unseen. And I bet you can't recreate the text of very many of those your eye bothered to linger on long enough to read.

I hate to be the bearer of bad news, but the idea that everyone reads signs is a marketing myth, and a dangerous one at that. In truth, only the best-designed signs capture and hold attention at a high level. This medium probably contains more clutter than any other. You really need to apply the principles of good design and writing (from Chapter 5) to your signs. And, even more important, you need to break with tradition and try some creative approaches to making your signs stand out and attract viewers (see Chapter 4 for more about generating great creative concepts).

That's the bad news — that our faith in signs is sadly misplaced. The good news is that whenever you find other marketers making dumb mistakes, you can turn their errors into your opportunities. And signs permit innovation in two interesting areas. You can innovate in the copy and artwork, just as you can in any print medium — from a magazine ad to a roadside billboard. But you can also innovate in the form of the sign itself. Experiment with materials, shapes, lighting, and ways of displaying signs to come up with some novel ideas that give your sign drawing power. Signs should be creative and fun! (For that matter, so should all of marketing.)

Here are some of the many variations in form that you can take advantage of when designing a creative sign:

- ✔ Vinyl graphics and lettering (quick and inexpensive but accurate to your design)

- ✔ Hand-painted (personal look and feel)

- ✔ Wood (traditional look; routing or hand carving enhances the appeal)

- ✔ Metal (advantages are durability and accurate screening of art and copy; but not very pretty)

- ✔ Window lettering (hand-painted or with vinyl letters/graphics)

- ✔ Lighted boxes (in which lettering is backlit; highly visible at night)

- ✔ Neon signs (Wow!)

- ✔ Magnetic signs (for your vehicles or to sabotage the competitors' computer files)

- ✔ Electronic displays (also known as *electronic message repeaters;* movement and longer messages, plus a high-tech feel, make these appropriate in some situations)

T-shirts, umbrellas, and bumper stickers, anyone?

In addition, don't forget that you can sometimes induce people to display your signs on their vehicles or bodies. I cover T-shirts in Chapter 11 when I discuss premiums (which offer many other mostly in-home ways of displaying your message, too). Your customers may think of a nice T-shirt as a premium item or gift for them, but you may see it as a body billboard! Isn't it nice that people are willing to go around with your advertising messages on their clothes? Don't overlook this concept as a form of outdoor advertising.

Similarly, umbrellas (also available from premium companies — see Chapter 11) can broadcast your logo and name and a short slogan or headline — although only in especially wet or overly sunny weather.

And don't overlook bumper stickers and car-window stickers. If they are clever or unique enough, people will eagerly seek them out in order to deface their nice new cars with them. Don't ask me why. But because they do, and because the cost of producing bumper stickers is cheap, why not come up with a clever design and make stickers available in target markets as giveaways on store counters, as bill stuffers, or whatever?

You can even include a nice sticker in a direct mail piece, where it can do double duty — acting as an incentive to get people to retain and read the mailing, and then as outdoor advertising for you when they display the sticker on their vehicles. (Contact local print shops, sign makers, or T-shirt silk-screeners; any of these types of businesses sometimes produce bumper stickers, too.)

It's in the bag

While I'm on the topic of ads your customers will display for you, what about shopping bags? The big department stores believe in their importance as an advertising medium (see my discussion of them in Chapter 15). But most other businesses fail to take advantage of the fact that shoppers carry bags around busy shopping malls and downtown areas, and also on subways, trains, and buses, thus giving high exposure to any messages on the bags.

To use bags effectively, you need to make them far easier to read and far more interesting than the average brown paper or white plastic shopping bag. Remember, you're not just designing a bag, you're designing a form of outdoor advertising. So apply the same design principles. Come up with a hook: a striking image or attention-getting word or phrase that will get everyone looking at that bag. And try alternative colors or shapes. (By the way, most suppliers are also able to customize their bags — check with suppliers in your local area. If not, contact printers and silk-screeners. They can always handle bag orders for you, too.)

If you offer the biggest, strongest bag in a shopping area, then you can be sure that shoppers will stuff everyone else's bags into yours, giving your advertising message the maximum exposure. Sure, bigger, stronger bags cost more, which is why most stores offer wimpy bags that hurt your hands or rip open and spill their contents in the mud. But if you have an ad message to get across, the cost of a better bag is pretty cheap compared to other media, so why not go for it?

If you aren't in the retail business, you may think that this idea doesn't apply to you. Wrong! Plenty of store managers view bags as an irritating expense, rather than a marketing medium. Offer to supply them with better bags for free, in exchange for the right to print your message on the bags. Voilá! A new marketing medium for your program.

Don't yawn when it comes to awnings

Another variation on the sign needs to be mentioned. Don't forget about awnings and canopies (providers are listed under that heading in most telephone directories). For retailers, awnings and canopies are often the boldest and most attractive form of roadside sign, and they can also be valuable for office sites as well.

Awnings combine structural value with marketing value by shading the interior or, even more important, extending the floor space of the store by capturing some of the sidewalk as transition space. An awning can perform all of the functions a sign can, and more, and do so in a way that is highly visible but not intrusive. Yards and yards of awnings don't look as crass and commercial as huge signs, even though that's what they are. Our eye accepts them as a structural part of the building.

Why Don't Marketers Take Flags and Banners Seriously?

While I'm on the topic of creativity and fun, let me take a quick look at flags and banners. They provide some creative alternatives to signs and other forms of outdoor advertising.

The Metropolitan Museum of Art in New York City uses huge, brightly colored cloth banners to promote special shows. They make a wonderfully decorative contrast to the old gray stone of the building's facade, and they attract considerable attention from passersby on the business street and sidewalks below.

A number of companies specialize in making custom-designed flags and banners. Of course, you see tacky paper banners — often produced by the local photocopy store — hanging in the windows of retail shops on occasion. But I'm not talking about those. I mean a huge, beautiful cloth flag flapping in the breeze. Or a bold 3' x 5' screen-printed flag suspended like a banner on an office or trade-show wall. Or a nylon table banner that turns the front and sides of a table into space for your marketing message. Or a street-wide banner, suspended from a wire cable, complete with air vents, tie-downs, and even sand pockets to keep the message readable in any weather.

Consider using a flag or banner as a sign for your store or business. This use is perhaps my favorite because so few marketers take advantage of it. A flag or banner is less static and dull than the typical metal or wood sign. Cloth is *much* more exciting. Cloth moves, and even when it isn't moving, we know it has the potential for movement. Also, something about flags or banners is decorative and festive. We associate flags and banners with special events, because they are traditionally used in that context rather than for permanent display. If you are one of the first to break with that tradition, you can take advantage of a higher interest level than fixed signs command.

The smaller size and decorative nature of most flags and banners makes them less offensive than other forms of outdoor advertising, especially those big billboards along freeways and in downtown areas. In the U.S., many communities and several states have created partial or full bans on billboards, but none have banned flags and banners. (However, zoning laws may require approval of your design. Check with your local town hall.) Thus, where public acceptance of a large billboard message is at issue, try a more low-key, decorative approach by using multiple flags and banners instead. You will need to find lower, nearer locations to display them because they are smaller, but a local realty firm should be able to line up building owners willing to fly your flags. Anyway, it's worth a try!

All these options and more are available from flag companies, which are accustomed to sewing and screening large pieces of fabric, and can also supply cables, poles, and other hardware needed to display flags and banners. In recent years, silk-screening technology and strong synthetic fibers have made flags and banners brighter and more permanent, expanding their uses in marketing. Check it out!

For example, a full line of stock and custom products is available from the Arista Flag Corp. (Saugerties, New York, at 914-246-7700 or toll-free within the U.S. at 800-382-4776). Ask for their custom flag and banner price list, which includes lots of design ideas and specs, and also some photos of effective banners from clients as diverse as Xerox, *The New Yorker,* the YMCA Summer Camp, and the Coca-Cola Concert Series. (Consider combining a producer like Arista with a good design firm like Dialog Design, referenced earlier in this chapter, in order to get a flag or banner that is truly compelling.)

Figure 10-3 illustrates the most common standard options and terminology of the flag and banner industry.

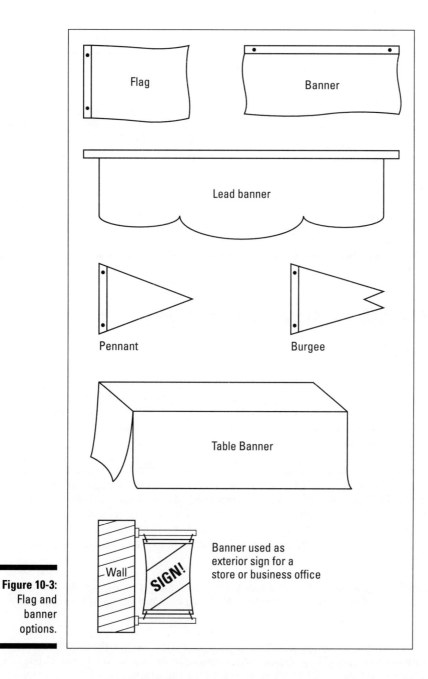

Figure 10-3:
Flag and
banner
options.

REAL WORLD

Y-M-C-A

The YMCA Summer Camp banner is a great example of how to use this medium well. The banner is illustrated in the Arista catalog if you want to see it, but I'll give you verbal description. The top two thirds of this wider-than-tall banner is taken up by a series of silhouettes of kids playing — basketball, jump rope, baseball, swimming, and gymnastics are all illustrated clearly by these simple visuals.

The bottom third contains the only copy, in big, clear capital letters: YMCA and its logo on one line, and SUMMER CAMP just below it. With this minimal design, the banner conveys the brand name and tells us a lot about what is offered to whom. And because the message is on a shiny cloth banner, viewers also get the idea that the message must be something special and exciting.

Transit Advertising: Messages on the Move!

Transit advertising is any advertising in or on public transportation systems. These may include buses, taxis, commuter trains, and subway systems, along with advertising in airport, bus, train, and ferry terminals. Who knows? Maybe NASA will start renting ad space on the outside of the space shuttle some day.

Transit advertising is classified by the advertising industry as a form of outdoor advertising. This classification is misleading, because some transit ads are indoors: ads at an airport terminal, ads displayed within subway cars, and so forth. Such confusion surrounding the term *outdoor* led to the development of the alternative term *out-of-home.* Out-of-home fits transit advertising better because the aim is at people in transit rather than in their homes.

Standard options — the ones most easily available through media buying firms and ad agencies — include shelter panels, and bus and taxi exterior signs.

Shelter panels are 46" x 67" posters (in some cities — in others, different standards apply). They appear at bus-stop shelters. I prefer to see them mounted behind a Lucite sheet to minimize the graffiti problem. In many cities, some of the shelter panels are backlit for nighttime display as well. A one-month showing typically costs anywhere from $400 to $1,000, depending upon the city. You may need as many as one hundred to three hundred panels to achieve enough exposures to reach a 100-percent showing in a city, depending upon the city's size.

Bus signs come with well-accepted standards in North America — although some local bus services now offer full-bus painting as an option as well. Following are the bus standards:

- **Large bus poster:** A 30" x 144" poster in a frame mounted on the side of the bus. This poster can be displayed on either the street side or curb side (in the U.S. the street side is generally the right-hand side). Sometimes called a *king size ad.*

- **Medium bus poster:** A 30" x 88" poster, especially suited for the curb side of a bus. If you want to make sure that bus passengers and other pedestrians on the route and near bus stops see your poster, then the curb side is for you! Sometimes called a *queen size ad.*

- **Small bus poster:** A 21" x 44" poster on the side of a bus, sometimes called a *traveling display.* If you have a simple message and a tight budget, this format may be big enough to give you the visibility you need.

- **Front and rear bus displays:** These measure 21" x 70" and give high visibility to drivers near the bus. A rear-end poster (or *tail-light ad*) gives great exposure to people in cars behind the bus. But if the bus exhaust is messy, your ad may not look so great after a few days, so check it out before buying.

- **Combinations:** Sometimes advertisers combine a front-end bus ad (or *headlighter*) with a curbside ad to maximize impact on pedestrians as they watch the bus go by. Add a shelter poster to the mix and you have incredibly good coverage! Such combinations can be effective, especially if you think your ad may be challenging to read or if you want to display two or three complementary ads to the same viewer.

If you are advertising in a European or other country, these North American standards may not apply. Outdoor ads in general, and especially transit ads, are not fully standardized in all countries. So check with the bus line, billboard owner, or whoever controls the ad space first, before you design your ad.

One advantage of transit advertising is that it typically delivers *high frequency* in a short period of time. Public transit vehicles generally travel the same routes over and over, and so an ad on them will eventually be seen multiple times by almost everyone who has their eyes open along the route.

Keep this high frequency in mind when designing transit ads — you want to make sure that your ad does not become tedious or irritating upon repeated exposures. To do so, avoid cheap humor and overly simplistic gimmicks.

Consider breaking the rule of outdoor advertising that says you have to make your design clear and simple. In transit advertising, you may be better off to layer the design so that you provide a clear, large-scale, simple message for first-time viewers — but also a more detailed design and message for repeat viewers to find within the poster. You could hide a Waldo-like character in your ads for people to find. Or include a riddle or puzzle for viewers to solve. The idea is that viewers can go deeper into the design over time, as they see it repeatedly, and that this attraction will keep the ad fresh and build viewer's interest in the ad and its message. I'll leave it to your imagination to figure out how to accomplish this goal in your particular case. But I urge you to try, because should you succeed, you will have an unusually effective transit ad.

This idea is considerably more obvious — but still overlooked by many marketers. Does your company have its own vehicles on the road? If so, are you using them for outdoor advertising? Most marketers say either "no" or "sort of" when I ask them this question. Small, cheap, magnetic signs on the doors don't count. Nor does just a painted name on the door or side panel of a truck. If you were *paying* for as much display space as even a standard-sized van offers, you would probably hire a designer or agency and put great care into your message. And, in fact, you *are* paying for the exterior space on your vehicles; the cost just doesn't show up in the marketing budget. So why not cash in on this investment more fully by treating it as a serious advertising medium? Mount frames for bus-sized posters and display a rotating set of professionally-designed ads. Or hire a competent airbrush painter to do a custom job on each vehicle.

When I said your own vehicles offer free advertising space, I lied. You *should* spend money on one thing — make sure that you *clean* the vehicles often enough to keep the ads looking good.

Chapter 11

Publicity, Premiums, and Word of Mouth

*Y*ou may be wondering how publicity and premiums ended up in the same chapter. Maybe it's because both are underutilized marketing media. Certainly most marketers are not very good at getting the news media to help them out with their marketing objectives, yet doing so is a very effective strategy. Similarly, while lots of companies use premiums and incentives, the typical approach is pretty lame. Please don't show me a cheap pen with your company's name on it, or I'll be tempted to take your copy of *Marketing For Dummies* away from you.

In this chapter, I show you how to make effective use of these two under-rated media, and I also discuss an even more misunderstood medium—customer word of mouth.

Word of mouth is the single most powerful form of marketing communication, because it has more sway over purchase decisions than advertising or any other form of marketing promotion. Yet most marketers simply ignore word of mouth on the assumption that they can't affect what customers say. Bull. Word of mouth ought to be an integral part of any marketing program. You need to track word of mouth and at least make an attempt to influence it in your favor.

So read on for ideas about how to give these three orphan media good homes in your marketing programs.

No News is Bad News: Using Publicity to Your Advantage

Publicity is coverage of your product or business in the editorial portion of any news medium. If, for example, *Consumer Reports* runs an article praising your product as best in a category, that's publicity. Good publicity. If, in contrast, the evening television news programs run a story saying that your product is suspected of causing numerous accidents, that's publicity, too. Bad publicity.

These two examples illustrate two common reasons for journalists to cover a product as a story — either because the product is better or worse than expected. In both cases, *product quality is the key to the publicity.* Keep this fact in mind.

The best way to initiate positive publicity is to design and make a truly superior product. The best way to generate negative publicity is to make something bad. So the quality of your product development and production/ delivery processes is an important factor in your use of publicity. Good publicity starts with a pursuit of quality throughout your firm's management processes!

Here's a simple rule: When your organization and products are not getting covered at all, that's your fault as a marketer. Marketers need to be proactive and generate some positive publicity. But when your product is getting bad coverage in the press, that's generally management's fault. Of course, you still have to take the rap and cope with the negative exposure, but because the problem most likely originates with management errors, you should involve senior management right away.

Public relations (PR) is the active pursuit of publicity for marketing purposes. PR is what you do to generate good publicity and try to minimize bad publicity. Generally, marketers are responsible for generating good publicity. If they create good stories and communicate them to the media effectively, the stories will be picked up and turned into news or entertainment content. Good publicity.

Marketers or general managers also wear the PR hat in smaller organizations, but large companies generally have a PR person or department whose sole job is to generate positive publicity. Also, many businesses hire *publicists* or *PR firms* — experts who do PR on a freelance or consulting basis.

There is also such a thing as *bad publicity.* Any negative news needs to be countered and the root causes eliminated if at all possible. Handling bad publicity is also an important marketing issue.

Marketers don't go looking for bad publicity. Bad publicity is usually the result of poor overall management (which produces bad financial results or poor quality products), or it is the result of specific management errors (like approving an unsafe design in order to get a product out quickly). And sometimes bad publicity is the result of plain bad luck — in which case, you'll need to present an honest, concerned face to the media until the storm blows over.

When something goes really wrong and the media are having a field day reporting it, then you have a *PR crisis*. The first step in solving a PR crisis is to get a top executive alone in a room and force him or her to tell you what really happened; once the media starts digging, the truth will eventually come out anyway. The next step is to try to get the executive to agree to come clean with the media by making a truthful statement about what went wrong and how the company plans to try to fix the problem. If you can't get management to do so, forget it. You won't be able to stem the tide of negative PR. The crisis will keep growing. In that case, your best fallback is to polish your resume and find a better job. (Only kidding!)

Crisis management is a gloomy topic, and hopefully you won't ever have to do it. In contrast, generating positive PR should be a daily or at least weekly marketing activity. The following sections show you how to do so.

How do I sniff out good stories?

To a journalist, a *good story* is anything that has enough public interest to attract readers, viewers, or listeners and hold their attention. More specifically, a good story for a journalist covering the plastics industry must be sufficient to hold the attention of people in that industry. And I'm sorry to say that most of what you want to communicate to your market is pretty far from a good story.

Journalists and editors do *not* want stories about

- ✔ Your new product or service and how it differs from competitors or your previous models (unless that's their coverage specialty)

- ✔ Why you or your company's senior executive think your products are really great

- ✔ Your version of an *old story* — one that they've covered in the same way before

- ✔ Anything that seems boring or self-serving to anyone who doesn't work for your firm

Yet those are the kinds of stories reporters often get, because the people handling PR generally aren't skilled journalists, and aren't even trying to *think like* skilled journalists. That's what you must do. You have to sniff out a story, put together sufficient information to back up the story, and script a version of the story that is virtually ready to be run in your target media. To be good at generating positive publicity, all you have to do is . . .

. . . think like a journalist!

What's the hook?

If you don't know how to think like a journalist, here's a simple exercise to help you get the idea. Scan today's newspaper (whichever one you like to read) and rank the top five stories based on their interest to you. Now analyze each one in turn to identify the one thing that made that story interesting enough to hold your attention. The *hooks,* the things that made each story interesting to you, will differ. But each story will have hooks. And even though they differ, these hooks have certain elements in common:

- ✔ Hooks are often based on new information (information you didn't know or weren't sure of).
- ✔ Hooks make that new information relevant to your activities or interests.
- ✔ Hooks catch your attention, often by surprising you with something you hadn't expected.
- ✔ Hooks promise some benefit to you — although the benefit may be indirect — by helping you understand your world better, avoid something undesirable, or simply enjoy yourself as you read the paper.

If you performed the preceding exercise, I think you could write the next paragraph as well as I can:

The logical conclusion is that you need to design hooks to make your marketing message into appealing stories for journalists to use. And your hooks need to be just like the ones that attracted your attention to those newspaper stories, with one exception: They must, somehow, be tied to your marketing information. At least a thin line has to exist from the hook to your brand identity, the news that you've just introduced a new product, or whatever else you want the public to know. That way, when journalists use your hook in their own work, they will end up including some of your marketing information in their stories as an almost accidental side effect.

Journalists don't want to help you communicate with your target market. They couldn't care less about your target market. But journalists are happy to use any good stories that you're willing to write for them, and if your product gets mentioned or your marketing manager gets quoted as a result, that's not a problem. So the secret, the key, the essence, of good publicity is to develop stories with effective hooks and give them away to overworked journalists who are eager for a little help from volunteers like you.

How do I communicate a story to the media?

When teaching PR most people start here — with the form, not the content. In my experience, content is 90 percent of the battle, form 10 percent, so I've reversed the traditional emphasis. But form does matter, too. You need to put your story into an appropriate and professional format so that journalists know what the story is and find it easy to work with.

The most important and basic format for communicating a story is the *press release* or *news release,* a short, written document with a clear headline at the top, sufficient facts and quotes to support a short news story, brief supporting background on the company/product involved, a date, and contact information for journalists who want to follow up with a phone call to get more information or to arrange an interview.

Yes, I know that's a lengthy definition, much longer than the ones in the textbooks on public relations. But when I define press release that way, I don't have to tell you much more about it for you to be able to write one yourself. Just make sure that you include all the elements that are in the definition — and that you have good content, a hook, to start with — and you will write an effective press release.

Figure 11-1 includes all the essential elements of format and style. You can use the release shown in the figure as a template for your own press releases.

The odds of your release getting picked up by media and receiving any coverage at all are terribly low. Sorry to disappoint you. Journalists and editors throw away more than 90 percent of the releases they receive. So your goal (as in direct marketing, discussed in Chapter 18) is to beat the odds by writing a release that stands out from the junk in a journalist's in box.

March 31, 1997

FOR IMMEDIATE RELEASE

For more information, contact:
Alexander Hiam (413) 253-3658

CRAZY AUTHOR WRITES BOOK FOR DUMMIES

FIRST MARKETING TITLE TO ADDRESS REAL-WORLD NEEDS

AMHERST, Mass. — He's nearly done now. Just a section on public relations. Then the manuscript is off to production and — perhaps — history will be made. This title isn't just another book about business. This book is a redefinition of the marketing field that finally brings it up to speed with the harsh realities of business. And the book is, appropriately, by an author who straddles the boundaries between the ivory tower of business schools and the trenches of marketing management.

"What we teach about marketing on campus is pure fiction," complains Alexander Hiam, author of *Marketing For Dummies* (IDG Books Worldwide, Inc., 1997). "It's based on academic research, not on real-world practices and problems." Hiam threw out all his textbooks and visited past clients and other marketing practitioners before designing his new book. As a result, it . . .

Figure 11-1:
Writing a
killer press
release.

To beat the odds, pay attention to content (to make sure you have a good story — see preceding). And avoid these errors that journalists complain about in press releases:

✔ **Don't send inappropriate or late releases.** Target the right media and contacts. The food critic doesn't need a release about a new robotics manufacturing facility. And the business correspondent doesn't either, if the facility opened two months ago.

You need to build up an accurate database of media contacts, and to mail your press release first class on occasion to validate it (with first class mail, you get envelopes back if addresses don't work). Faxing or e-mailing your release is often sensible because journalists work on tight deadlines, so include fields for fax and e-mail numbers in your database. But I recommend developing a list by identifying authors of stories you like and think are similar to your own stories. That way you get a smaller list, but one that is a much tighter match with your content and target audience. Commercial lists and directories of journalists are readily available from mailing list vendors.

✔ **Don't make any errors.** At all. Typos throw the facts into question. And don't include any inaccurate facts. You want the journalist to trust you to do his or her research, which is a big leap of faith. Prove that you are worthy.

✔ **Don't give incomplete contact information.** Be sure that you include names, addresses, and phone numbers that work. Brief the contacts as to when to be available and what to say so that they will be cooperative. Also, brief the switchboard or give journalists instructions for how to navigate through the computerized voice mail system. You don't want gatekeeping to prevent a reporter from making that interview!

✔ **Don't ignore the journalists' research needs.** The more support you give them, the easier they can cover your story. You can include photos of the expert you've quoted in a mailed release (date, name of person, and information about the supplier of the photo to be included on the back or the margin). Also consider offering plant tours, interview times, sample products, or whatever else may help journalists cover your story.

✔ **Don't bug the reporters.** Journalists don't want to send you clippings of the articles they write, so don't bother asking. Nor do they care to discuss with you why they didn't run a story, or why they cut off part of that quote when they did run a story. They are busy with the next story. Forget about it. You should focus on the next story, too.

✔ **Don't forget that journalists work on a faster clock than you do.** When a journalist calls about your release, return the call (or make sure that somebody returns it) in hours, not days. If you handle their requests slowly, they will have found another source or written another story by the time you get back to them.

Should I consider video and electronic releases?

You can get a story out to the media in other ways, too. You can generate a video release, with useful footage that a television producer may decide to run as is or as part of a news story. You can also put a written press release on the PR Newswire or other such services that distribute hard copy or electronic releases to their media clients — for a fee to the source of the release, of course. You can also pitch your stories to the Associated Press and other newswires. I'm not going to cover these options, because they are not that important to many marketers, and because if you want to pursue them you will most likely need to hire a publicist or PR firm anyway. Just know that the options exist, and ask your publicist for details if these options seem appropriate to your story.

Premiums: The Most Abused and Misused Medium of All!

A *premium* is any product with a marketing message on it that you give away. (Okay, maybe you don't *always* give them away, but the idea is that you make getting them easy so as to spread your message as widely as possible.) Classic premiums include T-shirts with your company name or logo on them, coffee mugs with the same, pens, wall calendars, and baseball caps. But you don't have to confine yourself to these choices — nor should you, because they are often the *wrong* choices.

The problem is, *you've seen it all before*. How many pens with some company's name on them have made their way into your possession over the last five years? If the answer is too many to count, then one more won't create the slightest change in your consumption behavior.

Designing the premium — using an "impact scenario"

As in any marketing initiative, the object of a premium is to *change someone's behavior*. And that's a hard thing to do with a cheap pen or mug. What you have to do in order to make a premium work is build an *impact scenario*. An impact scenario is a realistic story about the premium and its user in which the premium somehow affects that user's purchase behavior.

For example, say that you are marketing a new set of banking services for small businesses, and you want to spread the word about these services to business owners who currently have checking accounts with your bank. Specifically, you want to let them know that a variety of new services is available that they might find helpful, and you want the business owners to call or visit their branch office to learn more about these services.

This wish list of what the target customer should learn and do is the start of an impact scenario. You finish the scenario by thinking of ways that premium items might accomplish your wish list goals.

What if you have the bank's name and the slogan *servicing small businesses better* printed on pens, which you then distribute in the next mailing of checking account statements? This marketing tactic is easy and cheap. But try to imagine the scenario. Small business owner opens bank statement.

Pen falls out. He grabs the pen and eagerly reads the slogan. Then, curious about what the slogan means, he immediately dials his local branch and waits patiently on hold for a couple of minutes. When he finally gets someone on the phone, he says, "Hey, I got your pen! Please tell me all about your services for small businesses!"

I dunno. What do you think? Somehow this scenario doesn't seem plausible. In fact, I think that most people would just toss the pen into a drawer or even into the trash can without reading the message or thinking about what the slogan means. Yet if you really look at most premiums, they are a part of equally unlikely scenarios. Sure, they often cost little, and so marketers often fall for them. But they usually work poorly, too.

But don't give up hope. You must be able to find some impact scenario that works — some way to use a premium so that people will actually get the message about those new small-business banking services and, as a result, take some action.

Perhaps a coffee mug would work better, because it has enough room on it to print more information about the services. The mug could be printed with a "DID YOU KNOW?" headline, followed by short, bulleted facts about the problems the bank can solve for a small business owner: "Miser National Bank offers automatic bill paying," and so forth. A customer, drinking coffee from that mug at the office, is a little more likely to be curious enough about one of the services listed to ask for details next time he goes to the bank.

Or how about this for an out-of-the-box idea? Call up American Slide Chart Corp. (in Wheaton, Illinois, at 630-665-3333) to obtain a slide-chart, wheel-chart, or pop-up (it unfolds when opened to a three-dimensional object) to include in that next mailing of checking account statements. I like the idea of a slide or wheel chart because the chart is novel and interactive. The chart can easily be designed to solve a problem or give access to selected information for the user. For example, the chart may say "HOW TO SOLVE THE FIVE MOST COMMON FINANCIAL PROBLEMS OF SMALL BUSINESS" on the outside, along with a listing of those five problems. An inner sheet is then printed with black dots next to those handy solutions (each solution, of course, involving the use of one of your bank's new services).

To use the chart, the customer selects one of those five options by sliding the inner sheet until a black dot appears in a hole through the outer sheet next to a selected problem. Doing so aligns the appropriate solution in a window on the bottom of the outer sheet. If you like, you can add other pages to the chart, such as a tear-off mailer to sign up for service or request information.

Here's the impact scenario for this slide chart: The customer pulls an odd object out of the envelope, glances at it (unfamiliarity generates curiosity), sees that the object claims to solve financial problems for small businesses, and — at least sometimes — starts fooling around with the chart. Soon the customer has selected one of those five financial problems — presumably the most relevant one — and is now reading in the display window about how one of your new services will solve the problem in a jiffy. Perhaps the customer even picks up a pen (not noticing that it is imprinted with the name of a competing bank), fills in the tear-off postcard, and tosses it in the out box for mailing.

Will this premium work? Maybe — at least the scenario is reasonably plausible. You would have to run the numbers to be sure, of course. For example, if you estimate that one in twenty customers receiving the slide chart will end up trying one of your new services, will this number give you a big enough return to justify the cost of producing and mailing those slide charts?

At least you are barking up the right tree because you have a scenario that appeals to common sense. Unlike most marketers, your premium is not just wasted marketing money. Your premium at least has a chance of affecting consumer behavior according to a predesigned plan.

Considering the premium options

As you think about ways of using premiums, you should consider a wide range of choices (see Table 11-1). If I hadn't run across a clever slide chart recently, I would not have known about the American Slide Chart Corp. and what it can do for marketers.

Table 11-1	Finding the Premium Options
Old Classics	*New Classics*
Pens, pencils	Clocks, watches
Calendars	Mouse pads
Key chains	Imprinted computer disks
Note pads	Pocket knives
Rulers	Flashlights
Mugs	Calculators
Caps	Stress-ease balls (The Drawing Board has 'em: 800-210-4431)
T-shirts	Frisbees
Thermometers	Leather pad holders and portfolios
Coasters	Children's toys
Balloons	Canvas or nylon tote bags
Umbrellas	Magnetic calendars

Old Classics	New Classics
Golf balls (call Spalding Sports Worldwide at 413-536-1200)	Packaged snacks (popcorn, candy)
Lapel pins	Sports/water bottles
	Books with customized covers
	Globe paperweights (a neat design in Lucite is offered by Best Impressions, 800-635-2378)
	Kaleidoscopes (call Van Cort Instruments at 413-586-9800 or 800-432-2678)

The premium industry offers such a wide variety of choices to advertisers that thinking of premiums as *many* specialized media is more accurate than thinking of them as a single medium.

Using the quality strategy

Most marketers think about the *message* (the copy and/or artwork) that they put on the premium. But this focus can lead you to forget that *the premium itself communicates a strong message*. The premium is a gift from you to your customer. Therefore, the premium tells your customers a great deal about you and what you think of them. A cheap, tacky gift may look good when you run the numbers, but it won't look good to the customer who receives it. Yet most premiums are of low or medium quality. Few are as good as, or better than, what we'd buy for ourselves.

You can make your premium stand out simply by selecting something of higher-than-usual quality. A better gift is more memorable, creates a stronger and more positive image of the marketer, and is more likely to be kept and used for a lengthy period of time. Of course, a better gift usually costs more. But you can justify this cost by selecting a gift that will make a greater impact — and reduce the cost by distributing the gift to a better-quality, more selective list.

Let me show you an example:

Premium A (Cheap gift with direct mail solicitation)

Cost of Premium A = $5 or $5,000 for a distribution of 1,000.

Response Rate (Customer orders within 1 month) = 1.5 percent or 15 per thousand.

If profit from each order is $1,000, then *premium gross* = $15,000.

Return = gross of $15,000/thousand – cost of $5,000/thousand = $10,000 per thousand.

Premium B (Expensive gift with direct mail solicitation)

Cost of Premium B = $25 or $25,000 for a distribution of 1,000.

Response Rate (Customer orders within 1 month) = 12 percent or 120 per thousand.

If profit from each order is $1,000, then *premium gross* = $120,000.

Return = gross of $120,000/thousand – cost of $25,000/thousand = $95,000 per thousand.

And if the higher quality of the $25 gift item is significant, you can expect a more positive impact on your customers — and higher response rates in any direct response program. Thus, the return is often considerably higher on a high-quality premium — provided you target the premium to the right customers (ones who are likely to respond according to your scenario) and don't just blast it out to a poor quality list.

Most marketers have difficulty bringing themselves to give away an expensive gift. They waver, lose their nerve, and go for a $5 item over a $25 item. Don't assume the cheaper one will be better! Run the numbers first. Very often, the quality strategy wins, giving you much higher returns as well as the far more favorable intangible benefit of improved brand image and customer loyalty. (If you aren't sure about response rates, you can experiment on a small scale before making your final decision.)

I gave a contact for each of the more unusual premium items listed in Table 11-1. For example, the kaleidoscopes and other unusual items made by Van Cort Instruments are both unusual and unusually high in quality. Odds are your customers will never have received premium items such as the ones this company makes! The more common items are available from many sources (including the companies mentioned in Table 11-1), and I encourage you to shop around for the best service, prices, and quality.

For a quality take on some classic premiums, plus a broad assortment of high-quality clothing and luggage options, try Land's End Corporate Sales (call 800-338-2000 to get their catalog or fax them at 800-965-3329 or 608-935-9341). They offer everything from aprons to sweaters, canvas bags to beach towels, and they embroider your logo and message neatly. The result is a high-quality gift, one that stands out from the average premium item. If you think a high-quality polo shirt with attractive embroidery is more in keeping with your image than a cheaper silk-screened T-shirt, then by all means call Land's End.

REAL WORLD

Premiums as profit centers

Speedo, the bathing suit/sports equipment marketer, uses T-shirts very effectively to promote its brand identity. It hires excellent designers to develop truly unique and attractive T-shirts that incorporate the Speedo name and logo within their artwork. And people love these shirts. So much so that quite a few of the shirts retail through sporting goods stores.

Get that? The quality of this premium item is so high that wholesale and retail customers will *pay* for it. Speedo doesn't have to give its shirts away to get people to wear them. People pay for the privilege of advertising the Speedo brand name on their bodies.

Similarly, some companies find their brand names so appealing that they can *license* the name and logo to clothing, bag, and other manufacturers. These manufacturers are willing to pay a percent of their revenues for the name and logo because they find it helps sell products.

Any popular sports team can make good money from its licensing operations — in essence, getting paid to advertise instead of having to pay for the exposure! And well-known brand names like Coke and Caterpillar also generate millions of dollars in licensing revenues.

If you build the strength of your brand, you, too, will find that other marketers want to cash in on its good name — and that you can use their products to advertise on, just as if they were premium items!

Singing the praise of T-shirts

On the other hand, sometimes a cheap T-shirt is just the thing. My dresser has a drawer stuffed full of them, and many have artwork that promotes a company or brand name. At times, T-shirts are just the right thing to wear, and if a T-shirt is appropriate to your brand, then by all means use T-shirts as a premium item! Check out the nearby sidebar, "More Ts, please," to help you decide whether this is a good option for your company.

Even a good-quality T-shirt is pretty cheap, so implementing the quality premium strategy in T-shirts is not hard. Quality is achieved through a heavy, all-cotton fabric, plus a compelling design developed by a real designer (if you really don't have one, call the firm I send my clients to: Dialog Design, 413-548-8198).

Oh, and one other thing. You need to use an experienced, quality-conscious silk-screener to put that fine design on those good T-shirts.

More Ts, please

Why do I go into T-shirts at such great length? Because I have recently done some research into T-shirt buying and usage habits that convinces me this is an underestimated market. What I found is that people do not treat T-shirts like other sorts of clothing. Young adults (through college age) own at least a dozen, and heavy users own more than 50. Adults (up through baby-boomers — but not older Americans) often own five or more, and those who are physically active tend to own more than

20. We are talking big numbers of T-shirts here!

Furthermore, when you ask people how many Ts they've bought in the last month, or intend to buy in the next month, you find that those with the most Ts also buy the most. That means the market for T-shirts doesn't become saturated. People who like T-shirts are always eager to add to their collections.

Many T-shirt owners and buyers are frustrated with the selection of shirts available to them through stores and other sources. What holds these customers back is a lack of exciting new designs, not their lack of drawer space. So all you need to do to get children, young adults, or middle-aged adults to want your T-shirt is put a cool design on it. Here is one premium item that consumers can't get enough of — provided your design is fresh and good. No, I don't really want another cheap pen with some company's name on it. But I'm happy to have another good T-shirt. Heck, I may even pay *you* for it.

To find companies that provide customized T-shirts, try your local Yellow Pages for listings of silk-screening shops near you. (Although silk-screening shops screen onto many different materials and products, they are generally listed under T-shirts in telephone directories.)

The bigger silk-screening shops and many of the smaller ones claim that they offer design services, too, but few have the truly skilled graphic designers you want to make your T-shirt more desirable than the average. Because most silk-screeners don't do great design, I'd still call a specialist to do the design work. You'll spend a little more, but doing so ensures a shirt that everyone wants and wears, which is the key to making this premium item work as a marketing medium.

Some smaller companies create some good designs, too. For example, a small but sophisticated screen shop called Howlingbird Studio generates some very unusual and appealing designs for its corporate clients. They are in Falmouth, Massachusetts, at 508-540-3787.

Word of Mouth

If you survey customers to identify the source of positive attitudes toward new products, you generally find that answers like "my friend told me about it" outnumber answers like "I saw an ad" by ten to one. It's not that word-of-mouth communications about your product actually outnumber advertising messages; but when customers talk, other customers listen.

Word of mouth (WOM) is the most credible source of information about products, aside from actual personal experience with those products. What consumers tell each other about your products has a huge impact on your efforts to recruit new customers. Word of mouth also has a secondary, but still significant, impact on your efforts to retain old customers.

How can you control what people say about your product? Encouraging customers to say nice things and preventing them from slamming your product is hard — many marketers assume that doing so is impossible. But you can influence word of mouth, and you must try to do so. Following are some ideas for how to manage word-of-mouth communications about your product:

- ✔ **Make your product special.** A product that surprises people because of its unexpectedly good quality or service is special enough to talk about.

- ✔ **Do something noteworthy in the name of your product or company.** If no aspect of the product itself is incredibly wonderful and surprising, do something cool and associate that with the product. Support a neat not-for-profit organization in your neighborhood (see Chapter 12). Stage a fun event for kids. Let your employees take short sabbaticals to volunteer in community services. All of these strategies have worked well in the past to generate positive publicity and word of mouth. Get creative. You can think of something worthwhile, some way of helping improve your world, that will make people surprised and happy about the good you're doing in the name of your product.

Honesty pays

A week after I bought my last new car, I received a surprise in the mail — a note from the saleswoman apologizing for a computational error and a check for a small amount of money to refund the difference.

The amount involved was a tiny fraction of a ridiculously large purchase price. But the refund is what I remember, because I was so surprised that the dealership voluntarily found the error and fixed it. This action violated my basic mistrust of car dealerships and salespeople.

I've told many people this story, and eventually some of them will go to that dealership to buy a car.

✔ **Use exciting sales promotions and premiums, not boring ones.** A 24-cent coupon isn't worth talking about. But a sweepstakes contest in which the winners get to spend a day with the celebrity of their choice is noteworthy. It will generate positive PR and lots of WOM. Similarly, if you give away note pads and pens with your company name on them, nobody will mention it to their friends and relations. But if you think of something really unusual to give them, this will become a talking point. Especially if the premium is something they wear or display prominently in their home or office, because people will ask them about it.

✔ **Identify and cultivate decision influencers.** In many markets, some people's opinions matter a lot more than others. These are *decision influencers,* and if you could diagram the flow of opinions, you would find that many of them originate with these people. In business-to-business marketing, the decision influencers are often obvious. A handful of prominent executives, a few editors working for trade magazines, and some of the staff at trade associations probably exert a strong influence over everybody else's opinions. Identifiable decision influencers can be found in consumer markets as well. For example, in the market for soccer equipment, youth coaches, league managers, and the owners of independent sporting goods stores are important decision influencers.

To take advantage of decision influencers, develop a list of who they are and then a plan for cultivating them. Match them with appropriate managers or salespeople who can take them to events or out to lunch, just for fun. The idea is simply to make sure that your people are in the personal networks of these decision influencers. Consider developing a series of giveaways and informational mailings to send to them. I'd send free samples of a new soccer cleat to youth coaches if I wanted to sell the shoe to youth players. When you know who is talking and who is listening, then you can easily focus your efforts on influencing the talkers.

Chapter 12

Special Events and Trade Shows

● ●

In This Chapter

▶ Using events in your marketing program

▶ Sponsoring an event

▶ Creating your own events

▶ Considering trade shows — the ultimate event for business-to-business sales

▶ Conducting demonstrations — how not to mess them up

● ●

*T*he crack product development team assembles in a conference room; your marketing people and engineers mingle with the teams from your supplier companies and major customers. The talk is serious and hushed as small groups huddle to plan the day's events. First, a team-building activity, followed by a recreational break and lunch. After lunch, a briefing from the project manager, followed by more team-building work and dinner. Early the next morning, leaders of the break-out teams will receive special leadership training. After breakfast, those leaders will break out with the teams to begin the design process.

Oh, by the way, did I mention that the first team-building exercise is a paint ball survival game and the second a canoe trip on the River Wye; the leadership training consists of a one-hour helicopter flying lesson; and the recreational options include rally driving and a clay pigeon shoot at Baskerville Hall? All because this event is taking place on an estate in The Marches, that beautiful countryside on the border of England and Wales, courtesy of Escapade, which provides these novel recreational options along with "event management, conferences, and confidence building courses" (they are in Kington, Herefordshire, England HR5 34B; phone 44 01544 230033). The combination of the environment, amenities, and activities will make this event special — probably the most memorable thing any of the attendees will ever do in the name of work.

Special events, the subject of this chapter, serve many purposes in business and marketing. But the common theme to all is that they make an experience special. In this chapter, I show you how to bottle up the special event magic and put it to work in your marketing program.

The Marketing Power of Special Events

A *special event* is anything that attracts attention to your product and message by drawing attention to itself first. In other words, the event has to have considerable drawing power of its own. A special event is *theater* — a performance of some sort that entertains or stimulates people in a satisfying way.

Special events are a great example of the real-world marketing principle that you should give away as much as you can. In the competition for consumers' attention, you often have to give them an interesting performance and win their attention in return. That's what TNN did by creating a weekly series of car races (see the nearby sidebar, "Off to the races"). And that's what you can do, too. But how? Should it be a party? A musical performance? A weekend at a golf resort for your top customers, along with prizes for the wining golfers — and everyone else too? A fundraising dinner for an important charity? A community event like a fair or children's workshop? A major trade show for people in your industry? A performance by a leading modern dance company? Or perhaps a mud-wrestling event? The possibilities are endless and varied. What they all have in common is that they attract people and hold their attention. That attention is what you need in order to communicate and persuade as a marketer.

Do it yourself or piggyback on other events?

You have a great deal of choice — not only over the type of event, but also over the level and nature of your participation. You may put on the event, like TNN did. That's a costly and difficult process, but sometimes it is the best solution — especially if you want to have enough control to keep any

---

Off to the races

TNN stands for The Nashville Network, a Tennessee-based cable company owned by Gaylord Entertainment Company. Like many cable television competitors, TNN is fighting for its audience with the three major U.S. television networks plus a growing number of cable options. TNN's marketing has been remarkably successful in this tough industry, as evidenced by double-digit growth in advertising revenues and subscriber revenues (the two main sources of revenue for a cable company).

What's its secret? According to Brian Hughes, vice president of programming for TNN, the company's strategy uses events to build an awareness of the network. For example, TNN knows that its target viewers like auto racing. And so the network ran 69 auto races in 1996 in order to be able to provide live coverage of racing to its audience! Now that's a serious commitment to special events!

other marketers from using the audience attention that the event generates. But you may also just pick an event that others are organizing and sign on as a sponsor. That's easier and often cheaper but may be less powerful in terms of marketing impact.

Consumer audience or business audience?

You also have to choose whether you want to use consumer-oriented events, like TNN did, or whether you want an event that focuses on a business audience.

Trade shows are great because they draw people who are wearing their business hats, ready to make purchase decisions for their companies. You can also put on special events for your own customers or employees. (In fact, employee events often provide that extra motivating power that you need to get your people fully behind your marketing plan.)

Whatever the business-oriented event, remember, you're still trying to *attract and hold the attention of people*. Not businesses. People. It is the people in any business who make the purchase decisions. Corporations only have legal lives. They are dead as doornails when it comes to marketing. So above all, make sure that your business-oriented events are interesting to the people involved.

Getting stuffy and businesslike is very easy, but do people *really* want to sit through two days of lectures on the impact of new technologies in their industry? You're better off to offer them optional, one-hour panel discussions on the topic, with a backbone of outdoor sports and recreation events that are great fun, and, by the way, also help a bit with team building.

The need for originality

The fact that you need to be creative and original is a general rule of real-world marketing, but it applies *even more* in the area of special events. So pay close attention while I tell you the one thing you must never forget about event-based marketing:

> *It's never as good as the first time!*

Got that? Good. Now be sure to apply this principle when you work with special events. Don't sponsor the same event twice, just because it worked well last year. Don't do the same sort of demo, in the same booth, at three different trade shows in the same year. Always look for something new, different, and fun. Avoid stale reruns. Give people something new and exciting.

I bet you're saying, "But that's obvious!" I know, I know. No performer worth his salt tells the same joke or sings the same song twice in a row. Once the audience laughs or applauds, everyone knows that it's time to move on to something new. All of us, that is, except young children. When my children first learned to tell jokes, I remember they were so pleased by the resulting laughter that they kept telling the same joke over and over. And giving them a sincere-sounding laugh got harder and harder. It was a blessing when they get through that stage, and fortunately it only took a month or two.

But some companies never learn. Many — and yours may be one — repeat the same basic events as if they are religious rituals. The worst for employees are those awards dinners, or holiday gift-giving rituals, or executive motivational speeches, because the employees themselves have to put up with the dull repetition. But think how often you do the same thing to your customers.

If your company, like most, uses the same basic booth staffed by the same brochure-waving salespeople at every trade show, then it may as well be telling the same joke over and over.

Similarly, if your company gives to the same charities every year, the repetition has probably long since dulled the impact of those sponsorships.

The local bank down the street from my office does only one public event each year — the United Way campaign. Every fall, someone drags out the same six-foot-tall board, with the same faded painting of a thermometer on it, to track the donations as if they were rising mercury. Each year, the thermometer seems to take a little longer to heat up. And each year, I get a little closer to an act of vandalism. Now, maybe a United Way fund drive is just the right event for this bank (and maybe not — I doubt they've thought about it). But even if it is, *they should never do their fund drive the same way twice without a very good reason.* They should try a fundraising party, or a one-day blitz, or a youth soccer sponsorship campaign in which each donation is made in the name of a player. Or they should bring a trained horse to town and have it count out the total raised by tapping its hoof on a drum.

I don't care *what* you do — as long as the activity is something new and different that actually has some entertainment value. If a special event is a gift to your customers, then why keep giving the same old gift, year after year?

Special note: When should you repeat a sponsorship? Sometimes you want to break the something-new rule, but be sure you have a good reason. The best reason I know is that a particular sponsorship has all the right attributes for you, and has lasting entertainment value. Like an annual tennis or golf tournament. Once a year isn't really too much for a truly interesting event, and a long-term sponsorship can have a huge impact by identifying your brand name permanently with the event. But note that this doesn't apply to any event that fails the long-term interest test — including a United Way campaign. If you truly want to keep sponsoring the United Way, then you better think of some creative approaches to the campaign in order to maintain public interest.

Sponsoring an Event

Some people assume that special events are only useful in special circumstances, when a major effort and expense is justified. Not so. Staging small-scale events or (as I review here) riding on the coattails of somebody else's event is possible, too.

Why create your own event when so many wonderful events already exist? That, at least, is the thinking of the many companies that sponsor events as a way to expose their names to desirable audiences.

For example, take Verite, a not-for-profit organization that works to end child labor and sweatshop conditions in the production of imported consumer products for the U.S. and European markets. Verite put on a fundraising event, offering dinner along with jazz music by noted vocalist Montenia, at Hampshire College in Amherst, Massachusetts. And many for-profits sponsored the event in exchange for the exposure. The food was donated by local restaurants, musicians donated their time, the college offered its facilities, and many other businesses made cash donations in exchange for being listed on the program. All received visibility as sponsors, and the positive public image of Verite and its cause "rubbed off" a bit on each of them. The hundreds of supporters of the cause who attended the event or viewed the fliers, letters, and publicity about it hopefully formed a positive impression of the sponsors. The sponsors had to do very little work and spend very little of their hard-earned cash in exchange for these benefits.

You can find local organizations through local chambers of commerce or by following the events notices in local papers and on local radio stations. You will also find that nonprofits can refer you to other nonprofits. For example, Verite keeps track of and works with a great many other organizations in the child labor and human rights areas, so they may be a good contact for sponsorship ideas anywhere in the world. (You can call Verite at 413-253-9227.)

Cause-related events

The Verite event described earlier is a good example of *cause-related event sponsorship,* one of your many options as an event sponsor. Businesses in North America alone spend an unbelievable $485 million on cause sponsorship per year, and the total is growing at an amazing 15 percent per year. The goodwill generated by cause sponsorship is extremely valuable — at least if the cause and event are appropriate to your target market.

However, too much of this money is thrown away on events that are appealing to somebody at the sponsoring company, but *don't appeal to its customers*. Be careful to pick causes that appeal not only to you and your associates, but also to your target customers. Maybe your CEO really gets excited about those United Way campaigns. But have you checked with your customers to see what charities *they* are excited about? Many auto dealerships sponsor sports events that appeal to their male executives, forgetting that the majority of their customers are female. (Yes, the majority of car buyers in the U.S., and in some European countries, are women. How about sponsoring a breast cancer awareness program instead of the local football team?)

Also, customers are easily offended — and that means cause-related sponsorship can *backfire* big-time. For example, don't sponsor a pro-life rally outside an abortion clinic, because surveys show that the majority of U.S. consumers take a dim view of the cause and its headline-grabbing tactics. Plenty of causes exist that all your customers *will* find appealing. (Who could possibly be in favor of child labor, for example?) But many other causes — and events, in general — exist that some people will oppose or feel are sexist, racist, or classist. The best defense is to ask a selection of customers what they think.

Similarly, donations to political campaigns are likely to offend about as many people as they please in the U.S., because most political races divide voters fairly evenly. In European countries and others where multiple parties compete, political sponsorships usually offend *more* voters than they please, because no single candidate is likely to take a majority of votes. From a marketing perspective, then, you are crazy to throw money into political races. Pick a cause or organization with 90 percent or higher support — which automatically rules out all politicians.

A simple way to find out whether a cause has high support is to circulate a pro/con survey to your employees (if you have lots of employees). If most employees favor the cause, then odds are it is broadly popular. Causes having to do with health, children, preventing diseases and drug abuse, helping animals, and conserving the natural world generally pass this test — unless the particular organization takes a controversial approach.

Another clever way to test public attitudes about a cause without spending money to do it is to post a request for opinions on your company's Web page. Describe (without using specific names) a selection of causes you might sponsor, and ask people to give you their votes and comments. Then avoid anything that generates angry comments. Avoid it like the plague.

Running the numbers on an event

Be careful to pick a cause-related event or other event that *reaches* your target customers efficiently. Like any marketing communication, an event sponsorship needs to deliver reach at a reasonable cost. So ask yourself how many people will come to the event or hear of your sponsorship of it. Then ask yourself what percentage of this total is likely to be in your target market. That's your *reach*. Divide your cost by this figure, multiply it by 1,000, and you have the cost of your reach per thousand. You can compare this cost with cost figures for other kinds of reach, such as a direct mailing or a print or radio ad.

If you think the event sponsorship is more credible and convincing than an ad, because of its affiliation with an appealing cause, you can adjust your cost figure to compensate. Doing so is called *weighting the exposure*. For example, say you decide one exposure to your company or brand through a cause sponsorship is twice as powerful as exposure to one of your ads. Then multiply the number of people the event reaches by 2 before calculating the cost. That way, you will be comparing the cost of reaching 2,000 people through the sponsorship to the cost of reaching 1,000 people through advertising, which adjusts for the greater value you attach to the cause-related exposure.

In my experience, the *right* special event is often many times more effective than an advertisement. But the event has to be appropriate or it is worthless — so keep reading.

Evaluating the options for sponsorship

If you are considering event sponsorship, you are in good company. World-wide spending is over $12 billion a year for this type of marketing alone, according to the International Events Group, or IEG (Chicago, Illinois, 312-944-1727). This organization provides consulting and information-packed publications to event sponsors globally. The *IEG Sponsorship Report* shows that North American sponsorship spending is highest for sports events, and that entertainment, tours, and attractions (as shown in Table 12-1) is the next biggest category.

Table 12-1 Sponsorship Spending in North America by Type of Event		
Type	*Percent of Total*	*Spending in U.S. Dollars*
Sports	66 percent	$3.54 billion
Entertainment, tours, and attractions	10 percent	$566 million

(continued)

Table 12-1 *(continued)*

Type	Percent of Total	Spending in U.S. Dollars
Festivals, fairs, and annual events	9 percent	$512 million
Causes	9 percent	$485 million
The Arts	6 percent	$323 million
Total		$5.4 billion

(Source: *IEG Sponsorship Report,* Chicago, 1996)

If you take these numbers at face value, they say that sports events are the best place to spend your money, followed by entertainment. And they say that the arts are the worst place to spend your money. That *may* be true — but I seriously doubt it. Why? Because most event sponsorship decisions are not made systematically. They reflect gut instinct or habit more than careful planning. To avoid this trap, use my sure-fire three-step selection process.

By the way, as I go on to examine other forms of events, you will find that the same three-step process is useful. That's because you need to design all events through careful examination of options, by running the numbers, and by screening for relevance.

Step 1: Explore the options

Some businesses are deluged with requests for sponsorships, and so they have plenty of options just sitting in their in baskets. For example, Storybook Vineyards, a small specialty producer of fine California zinfandel wines, receives on average one request every day for donations of wine to special events (it sponsored the Verite fundraiser described earlier in this chapter). But even if you have as many requests as they do, you may overlook some kinds of events. Most countries have millions of events a year. The more of them you know about, the better.

IEG publishes a sourcebook listing many of the options, including just about every large-scale event (call 312-944-1727 and ask for the *IEG Sponsorship Sourcebook*). Also, contact chambers of commerce in towns and cities where you want to target your sponsorship dollars. They offer lists of local events that may be the biggest thing in town, even though you've never heard of them. Also, call organizations that seem like a good match with your product and customer to see if they know about or put on appropriate events. For example, if you market sports equipment, educational games, or other products for kids, you may want to call the National Basketball Association to see if you can participate in one of their many events (perhaps a Stay in School event featuring popular musicians and basketball stars?).

And don't overlook schools and colleges. They usually have a strong base of support in their communities, and some add a broader reach through their alumni, sports teams, prominent faculty, and the like. So try calling their public relations offices to see what kinds of events they have that may benefit from your sponsorship.

Here's an easy way to find out about unusual events in need of sponsors: Read the SponsorQuest column that appears regularly in *Advertising Age,* a newsweekly published by Crain Communications Inc. and whose subscription department is in Detroit; from the U.S., the toll-free number is 800-678-9595; or you can access the electronic version through the LEXIS-NEXIS Internet site (http://www.lexis-nexis.com). This column features events as interesting and varied as:

- **Sports Day.** A Stamford, Connecticut, multisport activity day that offers "on-site presence and product promotion with extensive pre-event multimedia publicity" for a minimum sponsorship cost of $5,000. With typical attendance of more than 15,000, this event can offer reach at a minimum cost of $333 per thousand people (depending on the extent of overlap with your target market).

- **Motivational Media Assemblies.** This Burbank, California-based company seeks sponsors for Powerplay, a multimedia educational and entertainment program that reaches approximately three million U.S. elementary through high school students through their classrooms. Options for the sponsor include in-program identification, product promotion, couponing, and sampling. The cost of sponsorship starts at $20,000, which works out to a price of just $6.76 per thousand students.

Why the huge difference in cost for two events that both target kids? You probably get a longer, more involved exposure from the local town-run event than from the nationwide multimedia programming. And one targets a particular community while the other blasts your sponsorship out across 3,600 schools in a wide range of communities — which is fine unless your customers only live in certain types of communities. One will be the better choice for the individual sponsor, but which? You need to do further analysis to be sure.

Step 2: Run the numbers

Analyze the marketing impact of each candidate for sponsorship carefully. Cut any from your list if their audiences are not a good match with your target market. Cut any that are controversial and likely to generate negative as well as positive attitudes. Cut any that do not seem to have strong positive images — no point sponsoring something unless your customers feel passionate about it! Now compare what's left by calculating your cost per thousand exposures through each one.

This process may lead you away from the most popular types of sponsorship. A big, popular event (like a World Cup Soccer match) certainly exposes you to lots of people — millions if it is televised. But how many are really in your target market? And what is the cost of reaching them this way?

If you calculate your cost according to the formula (see "Running the numbers on an event"), you may find that the cost per thousand for your target customers is really quite high. Big sports and entertainment events often charge a premium because of their popularity and size (large scale events deliver big audiences conveniently, without requiring much creativity and effort on the part of the marketer). But they aren't worth that premium if you can buy similar reach for less by sponsoring several smaller events. When you run the numbers, you often find that sponsoring a selection of smaller, more specialized events gives you better reach for your dollar than sponsoring one huge event, because the small events allow you to target your audience more accurately.

Step 3: Screen for relevance

Relevance is how closely the event relates to your product and its usage, and it is the most important, but least considered, factor. Let me give you a few examples to illustrate the importance of relevance.

In North America, the most heavily sponsored sport is car racing (38 percent of all sports sponsorship spending goes to motorsports, according to IEG). Some of this spending passes the relevance test, but much does not. If Ford sponsors a car race, perhaps this sponsorship communicates something relevant about Ford automobiles. But what about top motorsports sponsors Philip Morris and Anheuser-Busch? The relationship between car racing and cigarette smoking is pretty weak. And while a relationship between drinking beer and driving fast may exist, it is certainly not a good one! These companies should not be sponsoring motorsports according to the relevance test. (However, tradition does play a role — in some regions of the U.S., beer and cigarette makers are traditional sponsors of car races and their customers — who often smoke and drink at races — see nothing odd about the association.)

Their ad agencies disagree with me — I know that before this book even breaks into print. They no doubt argue that the viewers of a car race are, in other contexts, potential beer drinkers and cigarette smokers. And because they like car racing, why won't that favorable attitude spill over to the cigarette and beer companies that sponsor the events? Well, maybe it will. But not as much as if the event was directly relevant to the product. They could be getting more bang for their sponsorship buck.

Now let me give you an example of a highly relevant — and very successful — sponsorship. This one involves a privately owned Italian restaurant called Il Pirata in Amherst, Massachusetts. (I'm familiar with its marketing because the owner sometimes picks my brains for ideas when I go there for lunch.) The restaurant provided free food for an art gallery opening nearby. This early-evening event attracted a large number of local residents interested in the arts. People came. They looked at the pictures. And they ate the food. Then they walked over to the restaurant and stood in line to be seated because their taste test convinced them that Il Pirata was just the place to go for dinner. And many of them became regular customers.

This event sponsorship passes the relevance test with flying colors. Those who appreciate art often appreciate good food as well. By trying the food, they overcame any uncertainty they may have had about its appeal. What could be more relevant than a chance to expose potential customers to your actual product in a pleasing setting? Similarly, a safe driving clinic that an auto company like Ford sponsors by lending its cars or name to the event seems more relevant than an event in which people just watch cars speed past a big "FORD" sign on a race track. A chance to use the product, or at least to *see* the product in use, makes the event highly relevant. And the more relevant the event, the more valuable those exposures. I'd gladly pay five or ten times as much for a thousand exposures if it bought me a high degree of relevance!

Putting on a Public Event

Sometimes you have no alternative but to stage the event yourself. None of the sponsorship options fit your requirements. Or you really need the exclusivity of your own event — a forum in which no competitors' messages can interfere with your own.

For example, a large software company once hired me to be the keynote speaker at a series of conferences it put on in major cities around the U.S. I spoke about the work I was doing then in the area of total quality management, and attendees received copies of my book on the topic. Then they were fed a sumptuous lunch. Finally, after all this warm-up, the executives of the software company took the podium to share some case histories of management problems and how their software helped solve them. A few people slipped out after lunch, but many were happy for a day out of the office and stayed on to learn about the company and its products. The conferences and their advance marketing cost hundreds of thousands of dollars to put on. But a few months later, when I called the marketing director at the software firm, I learned that they had generated enough sales leads to pay back the expenses many times over in the first year alone.

Selling sponsorship rights

Another way to make your event pay for itself is to find other companies that want to sponsor the event. Not your competitors, of course. Many companies often have an interest in the same event as you do, but for different reasons, and these firms make good cosponsors. Basically, if the event is relevant, novel, and is likely to draw in their target audience, then you have a good pitch. Now you just need to go out and make sales calls on potential sponsors. (Also be sure to publicize the event well by listing it in *Advertising Age* and the trade magazines in your industry and by posting the event on the World Wide Web.) Or consider hiring an event management firm (see the following section for a listing). Some of these firms sell sponsorships as well as help to organize and run events.

VH1, the U.S. music cable channel, made good money on a special event by selling sponsorships. They put on the VH1 Fashion Awards as part of their effort to increase their ad revenue from fashion, health, and beauty advertisers. Awards at the show emphasized the links between fashion and music (who's the best-dressed musical performer?), and everybody who's anybody was there (I'm afraid I missed it). They even had a Viewers' Choice Award, based on votes from viewers in the month prior to the show. (Customer participation increases the entertainment value and relevance of an event!) And the best part for VH1: Companies like Clairol and Hanes coughed up a total of $7 million in sponsorships! If you don't ask, you won't receive. And if you do ask, you may just make a profit on your event.

Need help managing your event?

Some people specialize in managing special events; they work on a consulting basis, from conception through completion, to make sure that everyone comes and everything goes just right. Many such specialists exist, from independent experts (check your city's business-to-business Yellow Pages directory) all the way to major companies like Adrenne International Inc., which bills itself as "the full-service Event Management company" (they're based in Halifax, in the Canadian province of Nova Scotia; telephone 902-492-8000). I recommend bringing in a specialist of some sort to help you design and manage any event that involves lots of people, shows, speeches or activities, meals, conference and hotel room reservations, security, transportation, and all those sorts of details that have to be done right in order to avoid disaster.

The acid test for whether you need expert assistance is whether the event you plan is *disaster-prone*. You'd be surprised how many events are disaster-prone. Why? Because any glitch that delays, frustrates, or offends attendees is a disaster. This kind of glitch creates a strong negative impression that may override the positive aspects of the event. You must ask yourself two questions to find out if your event is disaster-prone:

    ✔ Does the event depend upon the coordination of multiple activities by multiple people from beyond your department or company? If you must depend upon hotels, limo services, a catering service, and a troop of trained monkeys, the odds are at least one will flake out. The specialist knows this fact, and baby-sits all of them to make sure that the event goes on as planned.

✔ Are attendees sensitive to minor deviations from the plan? If it rains, will your golf weekend be ruined? Certainly. Similarly, if the breakfast coffee, pastries, and fruit are not delivered before the morning session of your conference starts, will the attendees be upset? Certainly. Whenever an event has to follow its plan pretty closely in order to succeed, then a specialist should be overseeing its every detail. Plans don't unfold in an orderly manner on their own. For some events, a little deviation from the plan is okay. You can improvise, and the attendees will understand. But in other cases, they won't. Make sure that you know which category your event falls into!

Exhibiting at Trade Shows and Exhibitions

Do you need to exhibit at trade shows? If you are in a business-to-business selling situation, I assume that you do. Exhibiting is almost always necessary, even if you only do so to keep competitors from stealing your customers at the show! That's why business-to-business marketers in the U.S. devote a fifth of their marketing budgets, on average, to trade shows, and in Europe the figure is even higher — one quarter of the budget goes to trade shows (these figures are from a July 1995 study in the *Journal of Marketing*).

Other sources suggest that trade shows generate 18 percent of all sales leads on average — and thus account for a bigger proportion of sales than of budgets. That suggests that trade shows provide a higher return than other components of the marketing program — at least if sales leads are what you need. And it also suggests a way of evaluating your spending level. Why not compare percent of budget and percent of leads, adjusting the percent of budget figure until you find the spending level that yields the best return in leads?

Running the numbers on trade shows

Say you try spending 10 percent of your budget on trade shows and doing so produces 15 percent of sales leads for the year. Then you try spending 20 percent of your budget on trade shows and doing so produces so many more sales leads that they make up 75 percent of all leads. The experiment tells you that you get increasing returns from investment in trade shows, and you may be tempted to try an even higher trade show budget next year. Perhaps 25 percent of your budget? Eventually you'll find the ceiling, and then back off your spending a little. You can also estimate the actual sales revenues generated from those leads, allowing you or your accountant associates to calculate the return on investment (ROI) of different levels of trade show investments until you find the level with the highest ROI.

What trade shows can accomplish for you

Trade shows are a great place to generate leads, find new customers, and maintain or improve your current customers' perceptions of you. You can also use trade shows to introduce a new product or launch a new strategy. And they are great opportunities to introduce back-office people (like the sales support staff or even the president!) to your customers face-to-face.

Use trade shows to network in your industry. The best manufacturer's representatives and salespeople are usually found by making connections at trade shows. And if *you* are secretly hoping to find a better employer, a little mingling may yield an offer at the next big trade show. Also, be sure to talk with lots of attendees and noncompetitive exhibitors in order to find out what the newest trends are and what your competitors are doing in the market. The information a good networker gleans from a trade show is often worth more than the price of attendance. Never mind selling — get out there and *chat*.

In short, trade shows are essential to your marketing program for many reasons. Even if you think you'll lose money on the deal, a trade show may be worthwhile over the long run. And usually a well-designed exhibit produces an almost immediate return on investment.

Building the foundations for a good booth

Marketers focus on the *booth* when they think about how to handle a trade show. But the booth is really just a part of your overall marketing strategy for the show. And you don't have a show strategy until you have written something intelligent down under each of these headers:

- ✔ How do we attract the right people to the show and our booth?
- ✔ What do we want visitors to our booth to learn and do at the show and in our booth?
- ✔ How we will communicate with and motivate visitors when they get to the booth?
- ✔ How we will figure out who visitors are and how to handle them in the booth?
- ✔ How we will capture information about them, their interests, and needs?
- ✔ How we will follow up to build or maintain our relationship with them?

The strategy has to start by attracting lots of prospects and customers, and the easiest way to do so is to "go with the flow" by picking a show that potential customers are already interested in attending. Ask yourself what shows your customers are going to attend. For example, if you import gift items and your customers are the buyers from retail gift stores, then where will they go to make their purchases? Will the New York Gift Show give you full access to the market in the Eastern half of the U.S., for example, or will you need to go to regional shows like the Boston Gift Show and the Portland Gift Show? One way to decide is to ask the sponsoring organizations for data on who attended last year's show and/or who has registered for this year's show. You need to see high numbers of your target customers. Otherwise, the show is a waste of time and money for your company.

You can also ask a sampling of customers for their opinions about your booth. The simplest way to do this research is to use what researchers call *informal qualitative interviews* — and ordinary folk refer to as *conversations*. Just talk to some customers, preferably at the show because their memory of your booth will be clear then. See what they think. Or you can do some *intercept interviews* at the show. An intercept interview is when you walk up to people as they pass by your booth and ask them if they will answer a few questions, such as "Do you like the such-and-such booth?" and "How exciting is this booth's design?" See Chapter 6 for details of how to structure such questions. (I recommend making the questions closed-ended by adding a rating system.)

Attractive company seeks compatible trade show for romantic weekend

How do you find out about possible trade shows? I thought you'd never ask! If you subscribe to trade magazines, the shows in your industry find you, because the magazines sell their lists to the show sponsors. But don't go just by what comes in your junk mail, because you may overlook something important. The Trade Show Exhibitors Association (Springfield, Virginia, 703-941-3725) can provide you with information about shows in your industry. The association is also a great source of information and training for trade show booth designers and exhibitors. Its mission is to provide "knowledge to marketing and management professionals who utilize the trade show medium to promote and sell their products."

American Exhibition Services (AES) handles over 300 major shows, so you should check with them as well (call Corporate Communications at 205-323-2211). And Convention Central USA is a good source, too — it bills itself as "your link to convention centers, conference resorts, and meeting/incentive facilities," and it also compiles a calendar of events. (By phone: 619-674-6363. And try their new listing service on the World Wide Web: www.sdic.com/CCENTRALUSA/ccentral.html.) Connelly Business Exhibitions Inc. puts on many trade shows — get their schedule by calling Ottawa (Ontario, Canada) at 613-731-9850.

But you do have another source, one that I find much more reliable than any other. That is *your customers*. The whole point of exhibiting at a trade show is to reach customers, so why don't you just ask *them* where you should exhibit? Call or drop by a selection of your best customers and ask them for advice on where and when to exhibit. They'll know what's hot right now and what's not.

Designing the perfect booth

Next, you need to select a location and booth size. Near a major entrance, the food stands, bathrooms, or any other place that concentrates people is good. On the end of an aisle is good. And bigger is better, too — in general, the biggest booth you can afford is the right one for you.

But even if you end up with a miniature booth in the middle of an aisle, don't despair. Many shoppers try to walk all the aisles of a show, and these locations can work, too, provided the show draws enough of the right kind of customers for you. In fact, smart retail buyers often look at the smallest, cheapest booths in the hope of discovering something hot and new from a struggling entrepreneurial supplier.

Again, experts can be helpful in designing and building your booth and helping you manage the trade show program and handle the sales leads that result from it. The Freeman Exhibit Co. builds exhibits, manages leads, and coordinates international and domestic trade show programs (they're in Houston, Texas at 713-681-7722). Inquiry Handling Service, Inc. in San Fernando, California, specializes in lead management (818-361-7286; within the U.S., 800-847-5323). InterEx is another company which specializes in design, fabrication, and support of customer exhibits for trade shows, and also graphic design and production, point-of-purchase displays, lobby displays and permanent showrooms. In addition, they can handle contracting for show services, production timelines, and routing logistics — all things you may not have the stomach for (Amesbury, Massachusetts, 508-388-8755).

Many other firms provide booth design services, too — consult business directories at a library or cruise the Internet for leads. And many ad agencies handle trade shows as part of an overall marketing communications program. For example, Dawson & Associates (Lexington, Massachusetts, 617-861-9808) provides what they call "integrated marketing services" that include trade shows along with many other ad agency services.

Demonstrations

Seeing is believing. This old saying contains wisdom, and if you think a demonstration is applicable to your goods or services, you should definitely consider giving one. Demonstrations are often the most effective ways of introducing a new product, or even introducing an old product to new customers. You can do a demonstration at *any* event. Really. Even when you sponsor someone else's event, if you ask early on, they can often find a time and place for you to stage a demonstration (and that's a great way to increase the relevance of your exposure as well!). And when you control the event or a part of it, then you have considerable freedom to design demonstrations. Let me show you some specifics.

Store, mall, and sidewalk demos

In a retail store, mall, or other consumer-oriented location, a demonstration is often the most persuasive form of promotion. You see these lame demos used at your local grocery store on occasion: A bored woman handing out teeny-tiny bites of some sloppy new kind of bean dip from a card table at the end of the toilet paper aisle? Give me a break. A proper retail demo should be:

- ✔ **Realistic!** Show the product in a *natural use* context, and that includes normal portions of foods. (Natural use means how the customer would normally use it. If a food product is eaten for dinner, find a way to demonstrate it that way.)

- ✔ **Wonderful!** The event should be one worthy of attention, with real entertainment value that adds excitement to the product. Try a cooking demonstration with lots of action, not just a one-bite taste. Or make the demonstration a taste test in which the new bean dip wins a contest and the tasters get the prizes. Imagine you are creating a skit for a television show — that's the sort of entertainment people pay attention to.

- ✔ **A marketing priority!** Here's your chance to sell your product directly to customers. Think of a political candidate going out to shake hands (notice the candidate always wears his or her best suit and biggest smile). Yet too often poorly qualified temps are put in charge of the demos. Who do you really want out there selling your product — someone who makes the product look good or someone who you wouldn't dare talk to if you sat next to them on the subway?

When you follow these three rules, you create great demos. But note that they are more expensive than the lame demonstrations we usually encounter. That's okay, because they are more effective. Use them more sparingly, but put more into each one, and they will reward you with a surprisingly high level of customer enthusiasm.

Trade show demos

At a busy trade show, a good demonstration can overcome the anonymity problem and draw people to your booth who would never have noticed it otherwise. Mim Goldberg, an experienced planner of trade show demos, is president of Marketech Inc. (Westboro, Massachusetts), a company that helps design exhibits and train exhibition staff. She says to keep your demo under ten minutes in length, including time for a question-and-answer period. That is as long as you'll hold an audience at a trade show, and that time frame allows for periodic repetition of the demo. Her advice for a good trade show demo provided my inspiration for the following strategies:

- ✔ **Make sure that you focus on key benefits for your target audience.** Don't try to entertain or convince everyone at the show or you'll lose your focus.

- ✔ **Select a specific message for the demo and stick with it.** Also, make sure that the demo message fits into the overall message of the booth.

- ✔ **Know what you'll do with the warm bodies.** If lots of people come, you need to provide sufficient standing room, a way for traffic to flow through the booth, and perhaps even a seating area. Make sure that the booth is big enough, or get permission to spill over into the aisle from the show's management and the neighboring exhibitors.

- ✔ **Train your staff to give the demo instead of hiring an actor.** The staff's knowledge of the product and industry makes them better suited to answering questions and performing follow-up sales.

- ✔ **Rehearse and train, just like actors and other performers do.** With practice, presenters can work from a short list of points instead of reciting a dull script. And they will be better able to interact with and respond to the audience, which makes for a more effective demo.

- ✔ **Plan the before-and-after.** How will you promote and announce each demo so as to draw a large and appropriate audience? How will you capture the names and addresses of prospects who come to the demo? Remember, the objective of most trade show exhibitors is to generate sales leads. Hand out forms to fill in for more product information or to participate in a drawing for a prize. Have extra staff circulating to answer questions and handle inquiries and orders. Make follow-up requests for information easy for the audience by dropping their business cards in a collection box at the back of the crowd.

Gift Giving and Events

Premium items, as the industry calls them, are simply gifts for your customers or employees. Not bribes. Gifts. They should be given as reward for doing something — after the deed is done, not as a condition of doing it. Often gifts are a stupid waste of time and customer good will — who wants a cheap calendar with their insurance company's name on every page of it? But the right gift, given in the right way, becomes an event worthy of notice. Think of gift giving as a form of theater, as a special option among special events, and you will avoid the standard stupidities. Heck, you may even gain customer attention and goodwill! (See Chapter 11 for more information on premium items.)

Chapter 13

Pricing and Price-Based Promotions

● ●

In This Chapter

▶ Understanding the customer's perception of price and value

▶ Avoiding the Three Myths of Pricing

▶ Establishing or modifying your list price

▶ Using price-based special offers (discounts, coupons, and so on)

▶ Staying out of legal hot water (the water is *very* hot when it comes to pricing!)

● ●

"The customer's always right." "Give people what they want." "Find a need and fill it." "Customers first, last, and always."

Sentiments such as these fairly gush from marketers' mouths. They adorn the walls of marketing department corridors and offices. And sometimes they even affect the way we treat customers. But there is one big exception to the rule that customers are always right, and that's when it comes to pricing. Because price is where you get what's yours, where all those great things you do for customers are supposed to be reciprocated. When it comes to pricing, you have to make sure that your company gets what it deserves. Nobody will pay you more than what you ask for, so be careful not to underprice yourself.

Before I lurch into the many technicalities of setting prices and selling on the basis of price, I want to illustrate the unique role of pricing with a little story told by journalist John Tierney in his *New York Times Magazine* column, "The Big City." He was curious to find out just how customer-friendly the infamous New York taxi driver was. So he donned black clothing and a ski mask, tossed a bulging cloth sack with the word "BANK" printed on it over his shoulder, and tried to hail taxis from the curb in front of bank branches. In five tries, he had no trouble getting a cab. Furthermore, when he told them he had just stolen $25,000 and asked if doing so was wrong, they offered only supportive words — and even sped up when he said he was worried about being followed!

However, there *was* one limit to the cabbie's tolerance of customer requests. When he asked one driver to pull over in front of another bank and wait, he said no way, and insisted on being paid immediately.

New York taxi drivers know something about marketing the rest of us need to learn: The customers are always right, so long as they *pay*. And you will be a successful marketer if you adopt that cabbie's philosophy, too. (Well, not literally — don't condone illegal behavior — but you get the point!) The bottom line of all marketing activities is that the customer needs to pay — willingly and (hopefully) rapidly — for your products or services. To ensure that customers pay early and often, please avoid the three myths of pricing.

(Don't Fall for) The Three Myths of Pricing

Many marketers assume the following myths to be true — at their peril! Make sure that you don't fall for these appealing, but utterly incorrect, beliefs about pricing. They will only get you in trouble.

Myth #1: People buy on the basis of price

Most companies fall prey to this myth. They set their list prices lower than need be. Or when they need to boost sales, they do so by offering discounts or free units. As you will see in this chapter, if you insist on selling on the basis of price, your customers will buy on the basis of price. But alternatives almost always exist. You can build brand equity (see Chapters 3 and 14), increase quality, use prestige pricing (covered later in this chapter), or create extra value through time and place advantages (see Chapters 7 and 16). Sure, price is important, but it doesn't have to be the only thing — unless the marketer believes this myth.

Myth #2: Lower is better

Marketers are timid about price increases, and often afraid to try them. Don't be! Don't assume the customer will balk and sales will drop too low to make the increase profitable. When marketers make the added mistake of combining this fear of raising prices with the common assumption that marketing problems can be solved by a price cut, you find a general downward trend in prices over the product life cycle in many industries. This fear of price increases costs many companies in lost profits. Remember, any price increase can be taken back with a subsequent price cut. Price increases are much easier to take back if they don't work than are price decreases.

Even if a price increase cuts sales, profits may receive a boost. For example, take a product that has a 30 percent gross profit margin right now. If you raise the price 5 percent, you will break even in profit if sales fall 14 percent. Anything less than that is a gain. Similarly, a 10 percent price increase is profitable at anything less than a 25 percent drop in sales. On the other hand, a 5 percent price cut has to stimulate a 20 percent increase in sales just to keep profits the same — an unlikely scenario for most products. And a 10 percent cut breaks even at a 50 percent sales increase — also an unlikely result. So don't fall prey to the myth that lower is better. Always check the numbers to see what your profit would be. And always check with your customers to find out how they will respond! (See the following treatment of price sensitivity for details of how to gauge customer response.)

The point is that customers may not be as price sensitive as you fear. They may tolerate an *increase* better than you think, and they may not respond to a decrease in price as enthusiastically as you need them to in order for that decrease to be profitable. They may even assume that price correlates with quality — in which case they won't buy your product unless the price is *high* enough. Rather than assume a price cut is needed whenever you want to boost profits, start by experimenting with a price increase. Be a contrarian. They are usually the ones who succeed!

Price sensitivity mathematics

I'm going to get technical now, for just a minute. You can — and should — estimate the level of customer price sensitivity. In other words, you should *figure out how much sales will change for any change in price*. You can do this equation mathematically, using the economists' model of *price elasticity of demand* (which equals percentage change in quantity demanded divided by percentage change in price). If you have altered the price in the past, and have good sales data for what happened afterward, you can do the computation. Then you can use the price elasticity statistic to forecast response to another price increase.

Of course, this model assumes customers will respond the same. But you know they won't. For example, if you raise prices 5 percent and see a 1 percent decrease in sales, then according to the formula, you have a negative elasticity of .2. And that should mean that another price increase will yield a decrease of only .2, or one-fifth the magnitude. (For example, if you raise prices 20 percent, sales would fall only 4 percent.) If this is true, then I'll just keep raising prices, because doing so doesn't hurt sales very much and profits are boosted substantially. But, of course, it isn't true. Don't ever believe a formula! The problem is customers will be more sensitive to changes in price as the price gets higher, and probably as it gets lower, too. The relationship is not a simple, straight line — a complex *demand curve* (or curved line to represent the changes in demand at different price levels) has to be constructed. And so you really need lots of data, over a wide range of prices, and lots of separate calculations, in order to find out how consumers will behave.

You probably don't have extensive records of how sales responded to price increases and decreases, independent of any other factors, at multiple price levels. Even if you have access to modern scanner data, it may be inadequate — it depends upon the history of your product category. Often grocery-store scanner data *is* used for this purpose, but the process is elaborate and not always satisfactory. If you want to explore it, hire a consulting expert.

So how in the world can you estimate the price sensitivity of customers when you lack good data? The following checklist lists a series of *qualitative indicators* of price sensitivity. What you have to do is ask yourself a bunch of questions about your customer, product, and market. Then you add up all these answers and see which way they lean. This study is not scientific, but it is better than ignoring the problem altogether!

Checklist for Guesstimating Your Customer's Price Sensitivity

Instructions: Check each box that you answer with "yes."

❒ **Is the price expected?** If you are operating within an expected price range, then customers will not be very price sensitive. Outside of the expected price range, they will.

❒ **Is the product valuable at (almost) any price?** Some products are unique, and customers know that they will have a hard time finding a cheaper substitute. That fact lowers price sensitivity.

❒ **Is the product desperately needed?** I don't care how much fixing a broken arm at the emergency ward of a hospital costs — at least, I don't care if my arm is broken! And I'm not too price sensitive about roadside repair and towing services if my car is broken down on the highway at night. These products meet essential needs. But if your product is a *nonessential* (customers want it but don't have to have it right now), then they will be more price sensitive.

❒ **Are substitutes unavailable?** If the customer is purchasing in a context where substitute products are not readily available, then price sensitivity is lower. Shopping for price requires substitutes at different prices. (For example, if you are the only company offering emergency plumbing repairs on weekends in your town, then your customers will happily pay a high price for your services.)

❒ **Is the customer unaware of substitutes?** What the customer doesn't know costs him. And shopping is a complex, information-dependent behavior. I live in a small New England college town, where not many substitutes for consumer products exist. Prices are high as a result. But I keep a Manhattan Yellow Pages phone directory in my office, and often shop in New York City by phone in order to get better prices. If more of the consumers in our local market knew how easy

---

this method of shopping is, they would be more price sensitive, too — but they are unaware of the option.

☐ **Is comparing options difficult for the customer?** Even where options exist, they can be very difficult to compare in some product categories. What makes one doctor better than another? I dunno — I have no idea which doctor will be better able to treat me. The technical complexity of their work, plus the fact that you can't consume medical care until after you make the purchase decision, means comparing options is hard. And that makes health care consumers less price sensitive — and doctors richer.

☐ **Does the product *seem* inexpensive to customers**? Customers don't worry too much about price when they feel like they are getting a good value. However, if customers feel pain when they make the purchase, they will pay close attention to price. That's why we negotiate so hard when we buy a car or a house. Even products that cost far less can *seem* expensive if they are at the high end of a price range. For example, you will be more price sensitive if you shop for a fancy, high-performance laptop computer than for a simple, basic desktop unit, because the former is likely to cost 50 to 100 percent more, making the laptop expensive by comparison.

The more boxes you checked, the *less* price sensitive your customer will be. If you checked multiple boxes, you probably can raise prices without hurting sales significantly. And that's great news!

You can supplement your estimate of price sensitivity (from the preceding checklist) with actual tests — for example, if you think a 5 percent increase in prices will not affect sales, try that increase in a test market or for a short period of time, holding the rest of your marketing constant. Were you right? If so, roll out the increase nationwide (or townwide, for you small business folks). Also, you can try asking customers what they think. Of course, they don't always know how they'll behave (you shouldn't count on customers to forecast their response to prices accurately), so researchers ask them to choose between alternative combinations of price and product benefits in order to find out. This process is called *trade-off analysis*. (For details on how to do marketing research, see Chapter 6.)

Myth #3: Price is what matters

When we think about pricing, we often assume that our focus should be on the *price*. But your company's cash flows and profits are driven by many factors, not just by the list price of your products. Think back to the New York cabbie in this chapter's introduction. He was not concerned about the price he would charge a bank robber — that's set by law anyway — only about *when* he would collect the fee. If your manager tells you to figure out how to raise prices because profits are too low, don't assume she's right.

Check to see how collections are going — are vendors paying in 65 days? If so, cutting that time by 25 days may make up the needed profits without any price increase.

Your company's revenues and profits are also affected by all the discounts and allowances it offers, and so you need to look at these, too, before you assume that price is the culprit. Are customers taking advantage of quantity discounts to stock up inexpensively and then not buying between the discount periods? If so, you have a problem with your sales promotions, not your list prices. Or perhaps you are in a service business that charges a base price plus fees for special services and extras. If so, look hard at the way in which fees are assessed. Perhaps your company is failing to collect fees in some cases. Or maybe your fee structure is out-of-date and does not reflect your cost structure accurately. For example, a bank that charges a low price for standard checking accounts, plus a per-check processing fee, may well find its profits slumping as customers switch to automated checking over the bank's computers — because introductory fees for this service are often set low or waived to stimulate trial. If so, then the problem is not with the base price of a checking account, but with the nature of the fee structure.

By the way, Myth #3 applies to customers, too. Marketers assume that customer costs are captured in the price they pay. Not so. Usually other costs are involved as well, and in some cases, the customer's other costs are larger than the price itself. Here's an example. Do you own a car? If so, you probably don't remember exactly what price you paid for it. But you do know what the last service cost you, what your monthly loan payments are, perhaps even what you have to pay for car insurance. And you know what filling the gas tank costs and the amount you had to pay for your last parking ticket. When you add up all these additional costs, plus any sales tax you had to pay upon buying the car and any property taxes you pay as an owner, you may actually spend *more than twice the car's list price* over the time you own it.

The true cost of ownership is always higher than the list price — for some car owners, much, much higher. What if you get in a serious accident? You may need to purchase medical care, and you will probably have to pay something out of pocket for the repairs (insurance comes with a deductible — and premiums go up if you have an accident).

Furthermore, you may suffer pain or discomfort, and may be unable to do some things you want or need to do, because your car is broken down or you are injured. These latter are examples of *opportunity costs,* as would be the lost opportunity to spend that car money on a new house or an MBA program. And while opportunity costs are not always viewed as important by customers, sometimes they can be.

But doesn't Myth #3 at least apply to simple, lower-priced products? No. Take something really simple, like a bottle of laundry detergent. I can buy the same brand that I usually get at the grocery store for 25 percent less if I go to the nearest cost club warehouse store. But I don't, because that store is a half hour farther from my home than the grocery store. And the extra time and gas money are worth far more to me than the 25 percent discount off the list price. The only way to understand my purchase decision is to look at my total costs for the two options, not the list prices of them.

You should *always explore the customer's total costs,* both by thinking about it on your own and by asking or observing a sample of customers. Table 13-1 may also be helpful in thinking about the customer's total cost for your product. After a quick look at it, I'm sure you'll never take a price at face value again!

Table 13-1 What Is the *Real* Price for Customer and Marketer?

What Is the Real Cost to the Customer?	What Costs Reduce the Marketer's List Price?
Customer's Total Cost = Price Paid Plus:	Marketer's Actual Price = List Price:
Taxes (sales tax, property tax, and so on)	Retailers'/distributors' deviations from your list price
Special fees	Retailers' markups
Shipping costs	Distributors' markups
Purchase costs (in time, money, or frustration)	Quantity discounts
Set-up costs (in time, money, or frustration)	Cash discounts
Disposal of packaging	Trade-ins Trade discounts (that is to distributors and retailers)
Disposal of the product at end of its life	Free samples
Costs of financing the purchase	Direct costs of sales
Maintenance costs	Service and support costs
Operating costs	Warranty costs
Insurance costs	Returns
Risks of ownership	Uncollectible and late payments
Opportunity costs (what else could you have done?)	Inventory costs (is product sitting around on your nickel?)

(continued)

Table 13-1 *(continued)*	
What Is the Real Cost to the Customer?	**What Costs Reduce the Marketer's List Price?**
Any other costs you can think of	Co-op advertising expenses (paying the ad bills of retailers)
	Opportunity costs (should *your* money have been spent more wisely?)
	Disposal or rework of quality rejects
	Disposal of old, unsellable products
	Any other costs you can think of

Setting or Changing a List Price

If you need to establish a price, you are stuck with one of the toughest things anybody does in business. Surveys of managers indicate they suffer from a high degree of price anxiety. So let me take you through it logically, step-by-step. Price setting doesn't have to be a high-anxiety task if you do it right! (Figure 13-1 illustrates the process that I describe below.)

Step 1: Figure out who will set prices

This step is nonobvious. You, as the marketer, can and will set a list price. But your price may well not be what the consumer ultimately pays. You may encounter a distributor or wholesaler and a retailer, all of whom take their markups. Furthermore, the manufacturer generally does not have the legal right to dictate the ultimate selling price. That is left to the retailer. So your list price may just be a suggestion, rather than an order. If the retailer doesn't like the suggested price, the product sells for another price.

And so you need to start by determining who else will be setting prices along with you. Involve these parties in your decision-making by asking some of them what *they* think. (That's why you do this step first.) They may tell you that you have constraints to consider. Know what those constraints are before you start.

For example, if you are setting the price for a new book, you will find that the big bookstore chains in the U.S. expect a 50 percent or higher discount off the list price. Knowing that, you can set a high enough list price to give you some profit even at a 60 percent discount rate. But if you don't realize

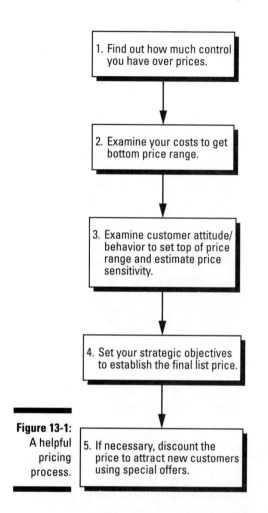

1. Find out how much control you have over prices.

2. Examine your costs to get bottom price range.

3. Examine customer attitude/ behavior to set top of price range and estimate price sensitivity.

4. Set your strategic objectives to establish the final list price.

5. If necessary, discount the price to attract new customers using special offers.

Figure 13-1:
A helpful
pricing
process.

that these chains expect much higher discounts than other bookstores, you may be blind-sided by their requirement.

Marketers who operate in or through a multilevel distribution channel (that is, they have distributors, wholesalers, rack jobbers, retailers, agents, or other sorts of intermediaries) need to establish the *trade discount structure*. Trade discounts (also called *functional discounts*) are what you give these intermediaries. That really makes them a form of cost to the marketer, so make sure that you know what the discount structure is likely to be before you move on. Usually the discount structure is stated as a series of numbers, representing what each of the intermediaries get as a discount. The trick, however, is that each discount is taken off of what's left over from the one before it, not off the list price.

Figuring discount structures

Confused? Let me show you how to compute prices and discounts in a complex distribution channel. Say you discover that, in the market where you want to introduce your product, a discount structure of 30/10/5 is typical. That means, if you start with a $100 list price, the retailer pays at a discount of 30 percent off list (.30 x $100 = $70). The retailer, therefore, pays the distributor who sells the product to them for $70, marks it up to (approximately) $100, and makes about $30 in gross profit.

Now, we also know from the discount structure figures that other intermediaries exist — one for each discount listed. There must be a distributor who sells it to the retailer, and the distributor's discount is 10 percent off the price they can sell the product to the retailer for (that's .10 x $70 = $7 of gross profit for the distributor).

From that, we also can deduce that this distributor must have paid $70 – $7 or $63 for the product to *another* intermediary (probably a manufacturer's representative or wholesaler). This intermediary is the one the marketer sells to. And the 30/10/5 formula tells us that this intermediary receives a 5 percent discount: .05 x $63 = $3.15 in profit for them.

Subtracting again, we can also determine that the marketer must sell the product to this first intermediary at $63 - $3.15 or $59.85. In all, you, as the marketer, must give away more than 40 percent of that $100 list price to intermediaries if you use this 30/10/5 discount structure. And so any profit you make from a $100 list price has to be calculated as *costs subtracted from your net* of $59.85. That's all you'll ever see of it!

Step 2: Examine your costs

Take another look at Table 13-1 (found a little earlier in this chapter), especially the second column of it. This column lists all sorts of things that may be reducing the price you get for your product. Knowing your real current price is important if the product is already on the market. (If not, try to estimate how such factors may chip away at whatever list price you select.) The trade discount calculation in the sidebar "Figuring discount structures" is helpful, but you may need to adjust the list price downward for other factors, too, before you figure out what your real net price is likely to be.

Good. Now you can find out how much it costs you to make and sell that product. Hopefully, a nice, fat margin exists between your costs and your net price. If not, back to the drawing board.

But how do you know what your costs are? That's easy — in theory. In theory, all your costs are already captured by your company's excellent cost accounting system, and some guy in a green eye shade can simply give you the figure.

In practice, the process is a great deal harder for two reasons. First, your costs vary at different levels of sales. That makes your cost estimate dependent upon your volume estimate. And how accurately can you forecast next year's sales?

Because you must work with a sales forecast, which is inherently uncertain, the clever thing to do is to calculate the product's per-unit cost at more than one sales level — for example, by using a low-sales forecast, a medium-sales forecast, and a high-sales forecast. Then you can set a price that gives you a decent profit margin at all three levels, and you won't get fired (or go broke) if things don't go exactly to plan.

The second reason cost analysis is hard is that allocating costs accurately is difficult. I once spent a few weeks sifting through old company records for a big trucking company. They needed to know which of their routes were the most and least profitable. And they were concerned that the accounting system didn't give them enough detail to be sure. They were right. When we really dug into the details, we discovered a number of factors that were not accounted for. The biggest was the discount rates off the standard list price that were offered to different customers. Some customers got higher rates than others. And some customers used some routes more than others. As a result, the money the company netted on each route had to be recalculated. And when you subtracted out all the costs of the people, trucks, and other expenses per route, some of those routes were losing the company a lot of money! The project was hellish because this company was big, with thousands of customers and hundreds of routes. But in the end, we were able to make some price adjustments that did not affect customers very much, but did ensure profitability on all the routes.

The moral is that you should and must reexamine your accountants' assumptions whenever you look at costs. Make sure that they allocate expenses and calculate net prices in a reasonable manner, one that you understand and that seems to make sense from a marketing perspective. If not, then you won't have accurate information about profits.

Once you examine your costs carefully, you should have a fairly accurate idea of what the least you can charge may be. That charge is, at a bare minimum, your actual costs. (Okay, maybe sometimes you want to give away a product for less than cost in order to introduce people to it — but don't use this ploy to take customers from competitors or you'll be sued for dumping.) More often, what you need is a price that includes the *cost plus a profit margin* — say, 20 or 30 percent. So that means you have to treat your cost as 70 or 80 percent of the price, adding in that 20 or 30 percent margin your company requires.

This cost-plus-profit figure is *the bottom of your pricing range* (see Figure 13-2). Now you need to see if customers will permit you to charge this price — or perhaps even allow you to charge a higher price!

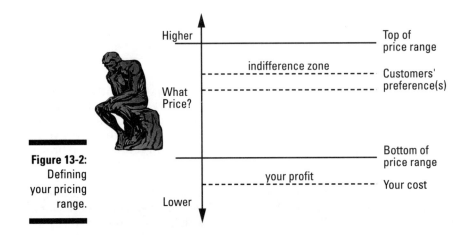

Figure 13-2:
Defining
your pricing
range.

Step 3: Evaluate customer perception of price

Your costs and profit requirements impose a lower limit on price. But your customers' perceptions impose an upper limit. You need to define both of them to know what the possible price range is. So the next step is to figure out what price customers are willing to pay.

In Figure 13-2, I show the price that customers favor as "customers' preference." Note that customer preference may not be the upper limit. If customers are not too price sensitive, then they may not notice or care if you set your price somewhat higher than their preferred price. (See the section on price sensitivity earlier in this chapter.)

Earl Naumann, a Boise, Idaho-based marketing consultant, calls the difference between the customer's desired price and a *noticeably* higher price the *zone of indifference* in his interesting book, *Creating Customer Value*. Within the indifference zone, customers are indifferent to both price increases and price decreases. However, be forewarned that the zone gets smaller (on a percent basis) as the price of a product increases. How big or small is the zone of indifference in your case? Go back to the price sensitivity checklist. The zone is small if you figure your customers are highly price sensitive, large if they aren't. Just make some assumptions that seem reasonable for now — I know doing so is partly guesswork, but still, it is better to break down the pricing decision into a series of smaller, educated guesses than to pluck a number out of thin air! If nothing else, your errors on all those little guesses may be random, in which case they'll cancel each other out. At least, that's what you can tell your boss.

You can ask customers directly for their opinion. They'll probably tell you that lower is better, of course, but if you press them, they can often say what they think a fair price would be for a particular product.

You can also do fancy marketing research to test different price levels, from trade-off survey questions all the way to *simulated test markets.* These involve the creation of a fake store (or catalog or whatever your point of purchase actually is), stocked with the typical range of choices, plus your product. (Exhibit/trade show companies and point-of-purchase display companies both make these fake stores — so check the listings in Chapters 12 and 16.) Then you have a marketing research firm recruit shoppers, who go through the fake store. Finally, you see how much of your product they buy — varying the price as the experiment progresses. Sales will drop off rapidly above some price level — that's the top of your pricing zone.

In these sorts of tests, you sometimes get surprising results. For example, sales may drop off *below* some price level if customers think price signals anything about quality. So don't be surprised to discover a bottom to the customer preference range as well as a top. Also, be warned that tests generally assume the competitors keep on with their current pricing levels. But if you suddenly introduce a competing product, they may slash prices or offer attractive discounts to keep you out. And these responses can shift the customer's preferred price downward! (Boy, marketing sure is hard.)

Another way to get at customer preference is to look at the current pricing structure in your market. What are people paying for comparable products? Does a downward trend exist in the prices of comparable products? An upward trend? Or are they stable? *Go shopping* to see what the existing price structure is; doing so gives you excellent clues as to how customers will react to different prices for your product.

Good! Through these sorts of activities, I assume you have at least back-of-the-envelope figures for what the customers' preferred price is, and how much higher you could price without their noticing. That means you have established the top of your price range.

The simplest approach to pricing is to set your price at the top of the range. As long as the price range is above the bottom limit, that is to say, as long as preferred price plus indifference zone is equal to or greater than your cost plus required profit, then you are okay.

But you can't *always* set your price at the top of the range. In the next step of the pricing process, I show you how to figure out what your final price should be.

Step 4: Examine secondary influences on price

Your costs and the customers' upper limits are the two primary considerations. They set a price range. But you need to consider many other factors. These factors may influence your decision, for example, forcing you to price in the middle or bottom of the price range instead of at the top.

Consider competitive issues. Do you need to gain market share from a close competitor? If so, adjust your price to be slightly (but noticeably) below the competitor's price. Also consider likely future price trends. Are prices trending downward in this market? Then you'll need to adjust your figures down a bit to stay in synch with your market. Similarly, currency fluctuations may affect your costs and, thus, your pricing options. If you are concerned that you may take a hit from the exchange rate, better be safe and price at the high end of the range. Finally, product line management may dictate a slightly lower or higher price. For example, you may need to price a top-of-the-line product significantly higher than others in its line.

Step 5: Set your strategic objectives

You may have objectives other than revenues and profit maximization. Many marketers price near the bottom of their price range in order to increase their market share. (They do so because a high market share later on will probably give them more profits — so it's an investment strategy. See Chapter 3 for details.)

This low-price strategy only makes sense if the customer is fairly price sensitive! If not, you are throwing away possible revenues without any real gain in market share. You should be pricing at the top of the range and using the extra revenues to invest in quality and brand-building marketing promotions in order to increase market share (again, see Chapter 3 for details on these and other strategy options).

In other cases, marketers have certain volume goals they need to reach — as when running a factory near its capacity level is essential. And so they may price in the low end of the range in order to maximize unit sales, even if doing so does not maximize net profits per unit (again, the increase in sales for a given decrease in price depends upon the level of price sensitivity).

Sometimes marketers even want to *minimize* unit volume, when introducing a new product, for example. They may not have the capacity to sell the product to a mass market and so decide to *skim the market* by selling the product at such a high price that only the very wealthy or least price sensitive customers will buy it. Then prices are lowered later on, when maximum profits have been made from the high-end customers and production capacity has been added. CD players, fax machines, and satellite dishes for receiving TV programming all entered U.S. and European markets at high prices, using the skimming strategy. (**_Warning:_** Don't use a skimming strategy unless you are sure that you are safe from competition in the short term.)

How customers perceive and remember prices

If the top of your price range for a new child's toy is $10, you probably want to drop it down to $9.99 or $9.89 for the simple reason that this price *seems* much cheaper to most consumers. Assuming they are price sensitive at all, they will buy considerably more, even though the price difference is only pennies. Why? Because people perceive prices ending in 9 as cheaper — generally 3-6 percent cheaper in their memories than even-numbered prices. It's just something about the way your customers see your price, and you can take advantage of it.

The only hook to using prices ending in 9 — which is called *odd-even pricing* — is that customers sometimes associate it with worse quality. So don't use odd-even pricing where customers are more quality-sensitive than price-sensitive. For example, odd-even pricing may cheapen the image of an original work of art for sale in an art gallery. But in general, the strategy seems to work.

You may also want to adjust your price to make it fit into your product line, or into the range of products sold by your retailers or distributors. The idea is to fit your product into a range of alternatives, giving the product a logical spot in customers' minds. This common and generally effective strategy is called *price lining*.

You may want to price relative to an important competitor or set of competitors. This practice is called *competitive pricing* for obvious reasons. If you are in a highly competitive market, you better exercise competitive pricing. Decide which competing products the customers will view as closest to yours and then make your price sufficiently higher or lower to differentiate your product. How much difference is enough depends upon the size of the customers' indifference zone — which I discuss earlier.

Should you price above or below that tough competitor? That decision depends upon whether you offer more or less benefits and quality. If less or about the same, then your price has to be significantly lower so you look like a better value. If your benefits are greater, then your price can be a little higher to signal this fact — but not too high, because you want to be sure that your product seems like a better value than the competition.

If you want to position yourself as far superior to the competition, then make sure that your prices are significantly higher. If Tiffany & Company jewelry were priced too low, the jewelry would lose its prestigious image. In fact, this is just what happened when Avon bought Tiffany — it tried to mass-market the Tiffany name by putting it on inexpensive jewelry. Millions of dollars of losses later, Avon sold out and Tiffany went back to success — at exclusively high prices again.

Sometimes you should just price exactly at the competitor's price. Doing so is a good idea if you want to differentiate the product on the basis of some subtle difference, because then customer attention is focused on the difference instead of on price.

Finally, some competitors try to convince customers that their product is better, but costs less. Nobody believes this claim — unless you present evidence. But if you do, customers will love you — we all hope to get more for less, after all! For example, a personal computer with a new, faster chip may really be better but cost less. A new antiwrinkle cream may work better but cost less if you have discovered a new formula. And a retailer may be able to sell the same brands for a cheaper price because its stores are larger and do more volume. As long as you have — and can communicate to the customer — a plausible argument, then you can undercut the competitor's price at the same time you claim superior benefits. But make sure that you back up the claim or the customer will assume your lower price means the product is worse.

Don't want to set the price? Let the customers do it!

An auction is always an option for selling your product or services — but auctions are rare outside of certain industries. Art is often auctioned, but furniture is usually sold off a list price unless it's bought through an estate sale. So if you are a furniture retailer, why not innovate by having a monthly auction? This may attract a lot of attention and allow you to turn over your inventory far more quickly. And if your inventory is nice, customers may just run up the prices higher than you could have charged normally!

I've got an even *better* idea. Why not hold an auction on the Internet? American Airlines now auctions airplane seats to vacationers on its Web site (http://www2.amrcorp.com/cgibin/aans), and other airlines are joining in. The advantage of an online auction is that the excitement of a live event is captured, and the offer is made available to customers worldwide. (To find out about other online auctions, try using "auction" for a keyword search.)

Be forewarned: It sometimes happens that, when you have a periodical "special" like an auction, your sales for the rest of the month drop off dramatically. This could actually cost your company revenue. Be sure to stay on top of your financial situation.

Playing with the Price: Discounts and Other Special Offers

Special offers are temporary inducements to make customers buy on the basis of price or price-related factors. Special offers play with the price, giving consumers (or intermediaries) a way to get the product for less — at least while the offer lasts.

Why play with the price? If you think the price should be lower, why not just cut the price permanently?

Because a price cut is easy to do, but hard to undo. A special offer allows you to temporarily discount the price while still maintaining the list price at its old level. When the offer is over, the list price is the same — nothing has been given away permanently. And that's important in many cases:

- ✔ When your reason for wanting to cut the price is a short-term one, to counter a competitor's special offer or respond to a new product introduction, for example

- ✔ When you want to experiment with the price (in order to find out about customer price sensitivity) without committing to a permanent price cut until you see the data

- ✔ When you want to stimulate consumers to try your product, and you believe that once they try it, they will like the product well enough to buy it again at full price

- ✔ When your list price needs to stay high in order to signal quality (prestige pricing) or be consistent with other prices in your product line (price lining strategy)

- ✔ When your competitors are doing it and you think you have no choice because consumers have come to expect special offers

This last reason is the worst, and it makes me mad as all get-out that so many marketers have trained their customers to expect special offers and only buy in response to them. I'm serious. Very serious. This is the biggest, dumbest mistake marketers make, and they've been making it over and over for many years. Consequently, many product categories are now purchased on the basis of price more than on the basis of quality and benefits. As a result, the rates of coupon redemptions keep climbing in the U.S. and Canada, and many European countries as well. Ultimately, special offers take up a bigger and bigger share of marketing budgets every year, and often eat unnecessarily into profits.

What happens when competitors get too focused on making and matching each other's special offers is that they flood the customers with price-based promotions. Discounts and other freebies begin to outweigh brand-building marketing messages, focusing consumer attention on price over brand and benefit considerations. Special promotions can and do increase customer sensitivity to price. They attract *price switchers,* people who are not loyal to any brand but just shop on the basis of price. And they encourage people to become price switchers, thus reducing the size of the core customer base and increasing the number of fringe customers. That means special offers have the potential to erode brand equity, reduce customer loyalty, and cut your profits. This slope is slippery, and losing your footing on it is an easy thing to do!

Procter & Gamble's marketing managers recently came to the same conclusion, and decided to stop using price-based promotions entirely. No more coupons and discounts. Period. But they couldn't make the change stick. Retailers complained. The U.S. government thought this move was tantamount to price fixing (because Procter & Gamble wanted competitors to stop, too), and that, of course, violates antitrust laws. So they are still sliding down the special offers slope, in spite of their desire to stop.

Okay, you've been warned about what General Foods executives like to call *coupon fever.* But you still may have legitimate reasons to use special offers (see the preceding bulleted list). Or you may not have the power to change practices in your market — after all, Procter & Gamble couldn't — and so you have to go with the flow. If so, if you *must* use them, the following sections explain some options available to you.

Designing coupons and other special offers

You can offer coupons, refunds, premiums (= gifts), extra products for free, free trial-sized samples, sweepstakes and other event-oriented premium plans, and any other special offer you can think up — just check with your lawyers to make sure that the promotion is legal. (Legal constraints do exist. You can't mislead consumers about what they get. And a sweepstakes or contest has to be open to all, not tied to product purchase.)

If you are promoting to *the trade,* as intermediaries like wholesalers and retailers are collectively termed, then you can also offer things like free-goods deals, buy-back allowances, display and advertising allowances, and help with their advertising costs (called *cooperative,* or *co-op, advertising*).

A large (and growing) majority of all special offers takes the form of *coupons,* and so I'll focus on them in explaining how to design special offers.

Any certificate entitling the holder to a reduced price is a coupon, which is a pretty broad definition — and that means room for creativity in this field abounds. The best way to get a good feel for the options and approaches is just to collect a bunch of recent coupons from your own and other industries.

How much to offer?

How much of a deal should you offer customers in a coupon or other special offer? The answer depends on how much attention you want. Most offers fail to motivate the vast majority of customers, so keep in mind that the typical special offer in your industry is probably not particularly effective. A good ad campaign probably reaches more customers.

But you can greatly increase the reach of your special offer simply by making the offer more generous (this fact is more true where price sensitivity is higher, of course). In consumer nondurables, whether toothpaste or canned soup, research shows that you have to offer at least fifty cents off list in order to attract much attention. Smaller offers are ignored by all but the most dedicated coupon clippers — they are attractive to less than 10 percent of consumers in surveys. But when offers get over the fifty-cent level, attractiveness grows rapidly — sometimes even reaching the 80-percent level! Within this larger percentage of interested consumers are many brand-loyal, core customers — both yours and your competitors. And these are far more attractive to you than the knee-jerk coupon clippers who make up most of those attracted to smaller offers.

So I think (and I disagree with many marketers on this point) that you do better to use fewer, bigger offers than to run endless two-bit coupons. Too much noise exists already, so why add to the clutter of messages when you can focus your efforts into fewer, more effective coupons?

Forecasting redemption rates (Good luck — you'll need it!)

Designing a coupon is not the hard part. The hard part is guessing what the *redemption rate* (or percentage of people who use the coupon) will be. And the stakes are higher for those big offers I advocate, which makes them riskier to forecast. Forecasting is getting easier in grocery store sales, because more and more stores handle redemption automatically for customers who hold store discount cards, and their databases give them the information to anticipate up front what the likely redemption rate will be. But in most cases, redemption still comes down to the question of how many customers see the coupon, clip or collect it, manage not to lose it, and then actually present it according to instructions in order to get the benefit. And if a lot more people go through this process than you expected, you just may lose your job, or even bankrupt your company! So your redemption forecast needs to be pretty accurate.

I can tell you that, on *average* in North America, a little over 3 percent of coupons are redeemed (and that the average coupon offers a bit under 40 cents off list price). So that is a good starting point for your estimate. But the range is wide — some offers are so appealing, and so easy to use, that 50 percent of coupons are redeemed. For others, the redemption rate can be close to zero. So which will yours be?

You can refine your redemption estimate by looking at your offer compared to others. Are you offering something more generous or easy to redeem than you have in the past? Than your competitors do? If so, then you can expect redemption to be significantly higher than average — maybe twice as high or higher.

Also look at your past data for excellent clues. If you have ever used coupons before, your company should have rich information about response rates. Just be sure that you examine past offers carefully to pick ones that truly match the current offer before assuming the same response rate will be repeated.

Think about price sensitivity. Again. Yes, go back to the beginning of this chapter and use the price elasticity formula in the sidebar "Price sensitivity mathematics" (if you have data) and the qualitative evaluation of price sensitivity. What your offer really does is shift the price on a temporary basis — at some cost to the customer, because of the trouble they need to go to in order to redeem the coupon. So the "real" new price is something less than the discount offered on the coupon — adjust it a little to reflect perceived costs of redemption. Now ask yourself, is this real price enough lower than the list price to alter demand? Is the price out of most customers' indifference zones or not?

Many coupons do not shift the price very far beyond the indifference zone — that's why they generally attract those fringe customers who buy on price but not the core customers of other brands. And that's why redemption rates are only a few percent on average. However, if your coupon *does* shift the price well beyond the indifference zone, then you are likely to see a much higher redemption rate than usual. That is the most common reason for people to lose their jobs over coupon deals gone wild. So always check the offer against what you know of customer perception and price sensitivity to make sure that you aren't accidentally shifting the price so far that everyone and her brother will redeem coupons.

Forecasting the cost of special offers

Okay, once you have thought about the redemption rate, say you believe that 4 percent of customers will redeem a coupon offering a 10 percent discount on your product. To estimate the cost of your coupon program, you must first decide whether this 4 percent of consumers will account for just 4 percent of your products' sales over the period in which the coupon applies. Probably not. They may stock up in order to take advantage of the special offer. And so you have to estimate *how much more than usual consumers will buy.*

If you think they will buy twice as much as usual (that's a pretty high figure but it makes for a simple illustration), then just double the average purchase size. Four percent of customers, buying twice what they usually do in a month (if that's the term of the offer), will produce how much in sales? Now, apply the discount rate to that sales figure to find out how much the special offer will cost you. Can you afford it? Is the promotion worth the money? That's for you to decide — and it's a judgment call; the math can't tell you for sure.

Some marketers have their cake and eat it too when it comes to special offers. They use what are called *self-liquidating premiums,* which don't cost them any money at all in the long run. A *premium* is any product that you give away to customers or sell at a discount as a reward for doing business with you (see Chapter 11 for lots of ideas on how to use premiums). A self-liquidating premium is one that customers end up paying for — at least they cover your costs on it. Say you run a contest in which some of the customers who open your packaging are instant winners, able to send away for a special premium by enclosing their winning ticket plus $4.95. If your direct costs for the premium you send them are $4.95, you won't be out of pocket for what may well be a fun and valuable benefit to the customer.

Staying out of Trouble with the Law

Anybody who sets prices or offers discounts off of them is running through a legal mine field, at least in the U.S. and other so-called free-market economies, because pricing practices are related to competitiveness. In the U.S., extensive (and often confusing) regulations exist to keep marketers from using prices unfairly.

By unfairly, I mean unfair in the eyes of your competitors or customers. For example, if a producer of milk cartons for school lunches sits down with its leading competitors and agrees to raise prices 10 percent, that's unfair to your customers. And it's blatantly illegal, which is why a number of executives from companies in that industry are now serving jail sentences. Similarly, if a bank charges minority applicants a higher interest rate for home mortgages than they do other people, that's unfair to customers, too, and when the dust settles, somebody is likely to end up serving time. Or what if a store puts a big sign out front saying, "Newest IBM PC for 75 percent off list!" That's fine, as long as you find the computer for sale at that price when you enter the store — but when you are told that they sold out last week, and the salesperson tries to switch you to a more expensive machine, then that is obviously unfair to the customer. Finally, what if a major grocery store chain lowers its prices in stores near local mom-and-pop grocery stores until the smaller companies are driven out of business? That is unfair to competitors and has produced some big settlements in court cases over the years.

In real world marketing, you don't have to be a legal whiz to know when pricing is illegal. Whenever a customer or competitor can make a good case for unfair or deceptive pricing, you're as good as busted. However, just to keep legal eagles happy, I'll provide a short listing of some of the more common and serious illegal pricing practices. Make sure that you read this correctly — these are things you should *not* do!

- ✔ **Price fixing:** Don't agree to (or even talk about) prices with other companies. The exception is a company you sell to, of course — but note that you cannot force them to resell your product at a specific price.

- ✔ **Price fixing in disguise:** Lots of ideas have been tried. They don't work. If your competitors want you to require the same amount of down-payment or start your negotiations from the same list prices as theirs or use a standardized contract for extending credit or form a joint venture to distribute all your products (at the same price), you better realize that these are all forms of price fixing. Just say no. And in the future, refuse even to take phone calls from them.

- ✔ **Price fixing by purchasers:** Believe it or not, even marketers should not be treated unfairly. If purchasers join together in order to dictate prices from their suppliers, this, too, is often viewed as price fixing. Have a skilled lawyer review any such plans.

- ✔ **Exchanging price information:** Look, you just can't talk to your competitors about prices. Okay? If it ever comes to light that anyone in your company gives out information and receives some in return, you are in big trouble. Even if you don't feel you acted on that information. This is serious stuff. Take it seriously. (By the way, *price signaling* — announcing a planned price increase — is sometimes viewed as an unfair exchange of price information. The problem is that sometimes competitors use such announcements to signal to others that a price increase should be made by everyone.)

- ✔ **Bid rigging:** If you are bidding for a contract, the preceding point applies. Don't share any information with anyone. Don't "compare notes" with another bidder. Don't agree to make an identical bid. Don't *split* by agreeing not to bid on one job if the competitor will not bid on another. Don't mess with the bidding process in any manner.

✔ **Parallel pricing:** In some cases, you can be charged with price fixing even if you didn't talk to competitors — just because your price structures are the same. After all, the result may be the same — to boost prices unfairly. In other cases, similar prices are considered natural. The law is complex, and this coverage is not, so I'll just say that a good-sense rule is: Don't mirror competitors' prices, unless it is blindingly obvious that you would have selected those prices on your own — *especially* if doing so involves a price increase.

✔ **Price squeezes, predatory pricing, limit pricing, and dumping:** To the average marketer, these are effectively the same (although they are tested under different U.S. regulations). They involve the use of prices to push a competitor out of business, or to push or keep them out of a particular market. For example, the classic *squeeze* involves setting wholesale prices too high for small-sized orders. Doing so drives the independent or small retailer out of the business, giving unfair advantage to the big chain buyers that can qualify for a volume discount. At the retail level, *predatory pricing* involves setting prices so low that local competitors cannot keep up. Predatory pricing is also used by chains and multinationals to drive locals out of business. If you are pricing at or below cost, you are probably doing predatory pricing. Similarly, even if you are pricing above cost, if your prices are so aggressive that they lock other competitors out of a market, then you are probably guilty of *limit pricing*. A variant is *dumping,* in which you try to buy your way into a new market by dumping lots of product into that market at artificially low prices. Don't.

So much is illegal in pricing that some people throw up their hands in despair and say, "What *can* I do?" So I'll just add that trying to influence prices in *certain* ways is okay. You *can* offer volume discounts to encourage larger purchases, so long as they don't force anybody out of the market. And while you as a marketer cannot force a retailer to charge a certain price for your product, you *can* "encourage" them to by advertising the suggested retail price and by listing it as such on your product. Also, you *can* always offer an "effective" price cut to consumers through a consumer coupon or other special offer. Retailers usually agree to honor such offers (check with an ad agency, the retailer, or a lawyer for how such contracts are formed). However, if you offer a discount to your retailers, you cannot force them to pass that discount on to your customers. They may just put the money in the bank and still charge customers full price. Hey, that's marketing.

Chapter 14

Developing, Naming, and Managing Your Products

- -

In This Chapter

▶ Designing and developing hot new products

▶ Fitting your product into product lines

▶ Finding the right name

▶ Creating strong identities under trademark law

▶ Screening out poor product concepts

▶ Knowing when to eliminate a product from the market

- -

*T*he product is the heart and soul of any marketing program. If the product is good — if the target customer is really pleased with it — then that marketing program has a decent chance of success. But if the product is no good — nothing special in the customer's eyes — then no marketing program will make that product a winner in the long run. This point is lost on many people in the field of marketing and in business in general, who underestimate their customers and overestimate the persuasive power of marketing. Something of real value has to be at the core of any marketing program. The product — whether a good, service, idea, or person — had better have some notable advantages from the consumer's perspective.

This chapter shows how such winning products are conceived and developed, how they are managed as part of a product line, and how their names are selected to amplify their natural strengths and communicate those strengths to the target customer.

Evaluating Your Product Options

Marketing texts and professors generally sing from the same hymnal when it comes to product strategies. The standard approach is to teach students that there are three options when it comes to product. You can introduce a product to the marketplace, modify the product in some manner, or withdraw it from the marketplace.

This conventional wisdom has the ring of common sense and it does define your options in a general way. Whenever you think about product strategies, you should first consider whether you should be doing one of these three things. And, because this book is for the real world, not the classroom, I am going to give you some specific criteria to help you decide when to adopt any of these three basic strategies.

But this advice is also maddeningly vague. If you are going to introduce a new product, what sort of product should it be? How do you think up brilliant new product ideas? What are the options if you are trying to improve an existing product? When and how do you terminate products? Are some approaches more profitable than others?

What practitioners desperately need is a whole additional level of detail. Following, then, are the three main product strategies, along with as many substrategies as I can find, plus some good ideas and techniques for executing them. When all is said and done, what matters may be *how* you go about one of these basic strategies, not *whether* you do. So I advise you to pay close attention to the details of execution.

When and How to Introduce a New Product

I wish I could say that you don't need to worry about new product development very often. But if your markets are like most, innovations are a major source of competitive advantage. A competitor's major new product introduction probably changes the face of your market — and upsets your sales projections and profit margins — at least once every few years. What that means is you can't afford to ignore new product development. Ever.

You should, therefore, introduce new products as often as you can develop them. The main limit you face is probably the level of investment your company is willing to make in new product development and introduction, because these activities are costly.

You need to budget time and funds to new product development in every quarter of every year. But *how much* to invest in this critical effort?

Many marketing experts say you should calibrate your new-product investment to your competitors and industry. If companies typically spend 5 percent of sales on new product development, then so must you if you want to keep up.

I don't agree. I want to win, not just keep up. And so my personal rule, never before revealed in public, is to *keep increasing your new-product budget* until you reach diminishing returns. Further, I recommend thinking of returns in terms of growth in new product sales as a share of total sales. The object is to keep increasing the percentage of your company's sales revenues derived from new products until you reach a natural limit. (What limits you is your customers' willingness to adopt new products.)

If you currently spend 5 percent of revenues on new products, try 10 percent. Say that next year the share of revenues from new-product sales jumps from 15 percent of sales to 23 percent and as a result, you experience a 53 percent gain. That's a big response, and it indicates you are nowhere near the limit of your customers' ability and willingness to adopt new products. Boost spending on new products again. And again. Until you no longer seem to be able to push your sales mix much farther. Then back off a little, and you will have found *the maximum level of new product development your customers will support*. Now you will set the standards, drive the competitors, become the market leader, and benefit in larger market shares and higher profit margins. (Just don't tell anyone else my secret or they may try it, too.)

Where to get great product ideas

Okay, you think you need a hot new product. But where do you get the idea? First, go back to the basic creativity skills covered in Chapter 4. That chapter offers a host of brainstorming and idea-generating techniques that you can use. If you and your fellow marketers are stale, bring in salespeople from the field, production, repair, or service call center. Try bringing in some customers for a brainstorming session. Your approach hardly matters, as long as it is new and different. *New ideas come from new thought processes, which come from new approaches to thinking.* Do something new to produce something new!

Also consider two cheap sources of new product ideas that the product development specialists at Rosenau Consulting (in Houston, Texas, and Santa Monica, California) report are of value: old ideas and other people's ideas. Oh, and don't forget to ask your customers for ideas.

In with the old

Old ideas are any new product concepts that have previously been abandoned by you or another company. Since people have been struggling to develop new product concepts for decades in most markets, a great many abandoned ideas are laying around. Often, companies fail even to keep good records, so you have to interview old-timers and poke through faded files to discover what those ideas were. But these ideas are a treasure trove because often the original objections are not as serious today as they were when the ideas were abandoned. Technical advances or changing customer taste may make yesterday's wild ideas practical today. Even if none of the old ideas can be used as is, they may lead you to fresh ways of thinking about the problem — perhaps they suggest a customer need that you hadn't thought of before.

Also note that old products in one market may be new products in another. Old-fashioned hand-cranked cash registers sell well in some countries, even though they have been replaced by electronic cash registers in others. The use of electronic cash registers depends upon the nature of the local economy and the availability and reliability of local electrical service. You may be able to turn your dead products from the U.S. or Europe into winners in other countries if you can partner with local distributors.

Stealing — er, borrowing — ideas

The second source, *other people's ideas,* is often pursued through licenses. A private inventor may have a great new product concept and a patent for it, but lack the marketing muscle and capital to introduce the product. You can provide that, and pay the inventor 5 or 10 percent of your net revenues as reward for his or her inspiration.

Many companies generate inventions that are outside of their marketing focus. These companies are often willing to license to someone specializing in the target market.

That's the official way to use other people's ideas; however, an unofficial way exists that is probably more common and certainly more important for most marketers. That is to simply *steal ideas.* Now, by steal, I don't mean to take anything that is not yours. A *patent* protects a design, a *trademark* protects a name or logo, and a *copyright* protects writing, artwork, performances, and software. You must respect these legal rights to other people's expressions of their ideas. But you must also realize that the underlying *ideas cannot be legally protected* in most countries where you are likely to do business.

If the ideas make it to your ears or eyes through a legitimate public channel of communication, then you can use them. (Just don't bug your competitor's headquarters, go through their dumpster, or get their engineers drunk — doing so may violate *trade secrecy laws* — ask your lawyer before planning any questionable research.)

While a competitor may be upset to see you knocking off or improving upon their latest idea, nothing can stop you as long as your source was public (not secret) and you don't violate a patent, trademark, or copyright. (You won't if you just take a public idea, and develop it all on your own.) In most markets, competitors steal ideas as a matter of routine. You can do even better by expanding the list of sources of other people's ideas. Look at other industries for inspirations that you can apply in yours. The good idea thief is open-minded — you never know where you'll find something worth stealing!

Picking your customers' brains

A final source of new product ideas is *the customer*. Customers are really the best source, but the problem is that they don't know it. Ask a customer to describe a brilliant new product you should provide for him or her, and you'll get a blank stare or worse. Yet lurking in the back of every customer's mind are frustrations with the existing products, and all sorts of dissatisfactions, needs, and wants that you may be able to help with.

How do you mine this treasure trove of needs, many of them latent or unrecognized? Collecting the customers' words helps you gain insight into how they think — so talk to them and take notes that use quotes or tape record their comments. Get them talking, and let them wander a bit, so that you have a chance to encounter the unexpected. Watch customers as they buy and use your product. Observation may reveal wasted time and effort, inefficiencies, or other problems the customer takes for granted — but would be happy to eliminate if you pointed them out.

Focus groups and in-depth interviews are both useful research techniques when you want to find out about customer needs. And many marketing research firms can help you use these standard techniques — see Chapter 6 for contacts. But one word of caution: Most companies fail to uncover less obvious customer needs — which are often the best ones to turn into new products — because they do not do enough research. More sessions are, therefore, better.

An interesting study of the matter showed that three or four sessions are needed to uncover 75 percent of customer needs. One or two only reveal half or less of the needs. And you may need seven or eight focus groups to uncover 90 percent of customer needs. I recommend doing more research into customer needs than is typical in your industry — you are sure to gain insights into your customers that competitors miss.

Using the "significant difference" strategy

Did I mention the downside of new product development? No? Oh, well, I guess you ought to know that *almost all new products fail*. Between 75 percent and 95 percent, depending upon the industry and how you define failure. (My definition of failure is (a) not providing a decent financial return on investment, and (b) not gaining a significant following among customers.) Given high failure rates, you need to make sure that your new products beat the odds — that they are much better than the typical new product. How?

Common sense and a large pile of research reports say that new products do better — make more money, for longer — when something about them is strikingly new to consumers. Walk down the aisle of your supermarket and notice the number of packages proclaiming something new. Without the word splashed across them, you might never have been able to tell.

To achieve real success you have to introduce something that is not only new, but that *looks new and different to the market*. The product needs a radical distinction, a clear point of difference. Innovations that consumers recognize more quickly and easily are those that provide a greater return to the marketer. Researchers who study new product success use the term *intensity* to describe this phenomenon — the more intense the difference between your new product and old products, the more likely the new product is to succeed.

When and How to Modify an Existing Product

Some products are so perfect that they are a natural fit with their customers and should be left alone. For example . . . well, I can't actually think of an example right now. Which tells you something important about product management: You'd better modify your products to improve performance, value, and quality with each new season and each new marketing plan.

You are competing on a changing playing field. Your competitors are trying hard to make their products better, and you have to do the same. Always seek insights into how to improve your product. Always look for early indicators of improvements by your competitors and be prepared to go one step farther in your response. And always go to your marketing oracle, the customer, for insights into how you might improve your product.

The following two sections are tests that a product must pass to remain viable. If your product doesn't pass, consider it a warning sign that you need to improve or alter your product.

Customers stop seeing anything special about your product

At the *point of purchase* — that place or time when customers make their actual purchase decisions — your product needs to have something special. It has to reach out to at least a portion of the market. Your product needs to be better on certain criteria because of inherent design features. Or it needs to be about as good, but a better value, because you have a sustainable cost advantage. (Do you? Cost advantages are more rare than marketers generally realize!) Or the product needs to be the best option by virtue of a lack of other options.

For example, if you sell sewing needles, your product may be about as good as most of the competition — but not noticeably better. But if you happen to be the company that a major grocery store chain uses to single-source needles for its small sewing section, then you have a distribution advantage at point of sale.

Don't assume your lack of special features means that your product isn't special. You can be special just by being there when customers need the product. Having a way of maintaining your distribution advantage is enough to justify keeping the product alive. But the point is that there must be *something* special about a product at point of sale in order to expect it to generate a good return in the future. Otherwise, it will be lost in the shuffle.

If your customers don't think your product is unique in any way, then you may need to kill it. But not too fast. First, see if you can differentiate it in some important way.

Your product lacks customer champions

Customer champions are what I call those customers who really love your product, who insist on buying it over others, and who tell their friends or associates to do so as well. But such loyal champions are rare. Does your product have champions?

The championship test is tougher than the differentiation test. Many products lack champions — even some that are reasonably profitable for their marketers. But when a product does achieve this special status — when some customers anywhere in the distribution channel really love it — then the product is assured an unusually long and profitable life. Such high customer commitment should be your constant goal as you manage the life cycle of your product.

Products with championship from customers get great word of mouth, and their sales and market shares grow because of it. Even more important, they are repurchased faithfully by their champions. And this repeat business is far more profitable and less costly than new business would be. (But you already know that if you read the principles of good marketing in Chapter 1.)

The hook is that the repeat buyer must *want* to repeat the purchase. They need to be converts, true believers — what Ken Blanchard of Blanchard Training & Development in San Diego, California, calls *raving fans.* Otherwise, you need to think of it as a new sale, and the sale will cost you almost as much as selling to someone who's never used the product before.

How do you know if you have champions instead of regular, ordinary customers? Because when you ask them about the product, they sound excited and enthusiastic. "I'd never drive anything but a Volvo. They are comfortable and safe, they don't break down, and they last longer than American cars." Some U.S. customers say just that when asked about their Volvos, so Volvo has an excellent base of repeat buyers. That is why its models do not vary as much from year to year as other cars do. The existence of customer champions gives Volvo the luxury of selling virtually the same car to people time after time, while GM and Ford are madly retooling their factories every year or two.

When to Kill a Product

Unlike people and companies, products don't die on their own. They never had a pulse anyway, and product bankruptcy just doesn't exist. Consequently, the marketer needs to have the good sense to know when an old product has no more life in it and keeping it going is just a waste of resources that ought to go to new products instead.

Yet often you see weak products hanging around. They are kept on the market despite gradually declining sales because everybody, from manufacturer to retailer, hates to face reality. Even worse, you sometimes see marketers investing treasured resources in trying to boost sales of declining brands through renewed advertising or sales promotions. If the thing has one foot in the grave anyway, those resources ought to be put into introducing a radically improved version or a replacement product.

You need to face facts: Many products would be better put out of their misery and replaced with something fresh and innovative. "But," you rightly object, "how will we know when our particular product reaches that point of no return?"

In the following sections, I discuss the warning signs that a product is due for replacement.

The market is saturated and you have a weak/falling share of it

Saturation means that you and your competitors are selling replacement products. You don't have many new customers around to convert. Growth slows, limited by the replacement rate for the product, plus whatever basic growth occurs in the size of the target market.

Saturation alone is no reason to give up on a product — many markets are saturated. An obvious one is the U.S. automobile market. You'll find very few adults who don't already own a car if they have the means to buy one and the need for one. So manufacturers and dealerships fight for replacement sales and first-time sales to young drivers, which can still be profitable for some of the competitors — but usually not all of them. If you have a product that has a share of less than, say, 75 percent of the leading product's market share, and if your share is falling relative to the leader, then you are on a long, slow, downward slide.

Better to introduce a replacement and kill the old product than to wait it out. You'll have to replace the product eventually, and the sooner you do, the less your share and reputation will suffer. Whatever else happens, you can't afford to be seen as a has-been in a saturated market!

By the way, don't forget that I use the term *product* in the marketing sense, to include whatever you're offering, whether a good, service, idea, or even a person — such as a political candidate or a star. Remember, too, that services, ideas, and even people sometimes need to be withdrawn from the market, just as goods do.

A series of improvements has failed to create momentum

Often, companies try a series of "new and improved" versions, new packages, fancy coupon schemes, contests, and point-of-purchase promotions to breathe life into products once they stop generating year-to-year sales growth. Sometimes these ploys work and growth is renewed. Sometimes they don't. My personal rule is borrowed from baseball, but it seems to work: Three strikes and you're out. Don't bother trying for a fourth time. Time for a new player to approach the plate.

Something is wrong with your product

All too often, marketers discover some flaw in a product that threatens to hurt their company's reputation or puts its customers at risk. If your engineers think that the gas tank in one of your pickup trucks can explode during accidents, should you (a) pull the model immediately and introduce a safer version, or (b) keep selling it and put the technical report in your shredder? A major auto company chose option "b." In the long run, it toasted some of its customers and had to stage an extremely unprofitable recall along with a repair-the-damage publicity campaign topped by several lawsuits.

Brand equity and profits take a licking whenever your customers do. But many marketers lack the stomach or the internal political clout to kill a bad product, even when the product may kill customers.

I don't know exactly why some marketers keep making these mistakes, but I hope that *you* won't. Pull the product if you find out it may cause cancer, give people electrical shocks, choke a baby, or even just not work as well as it is supposed to. Pull the product immediately. Ask questions later. And write a press release announcing that you are acting on behalf of your customers just in case the rumors are true. By taking this decisive step immediately, you let the market know that you have a great deal more integrity than most. And your brand equity will be stronger, not weaker. Trust me — pulling a product takes courage, but it is the best option when the dust settles. And if you've followed my advice — to always invest creative energy and funds in product development efforts — you will always have something better to offer as a replacement.

How to Kill a Product

Actually, getting rid of old products is the least of your troubles. Liquidators most likely call on your company already, like circling vultures hoping for a kill. If not, contact some of your distributors or your trade association for referrals. Someone can make good money by selling your inventory below your cost.

But a more elegant strategy — and one that avoids the negativity of customers seeing your old products offered for a tenth their normal price — is to stage some kind of sales promotion to move the old inventory to customers through your normal distribution channels. I much prefer this option, especially if it also introduces consumers to the new product. But this method only works if you get started before the old product loses its appeal, so you have to be aggressive about replacing your products. Don't wait for the market to kill your product; do the deed yourself. (See Chapters 12 and 13 for related information about how to do sales promotions and special events.) The following sections discuss more strategies that help you bow out gracefully.

The coattails strategy

The *coattails strategy* uses the old product to introduce the new. The variety of ways to put this strategy to use are limited only by your imagination. You can offer a free sample coupon for the new product to buyers of the old product. You can package the two together in a special two-for-one promotion. You can do special mailings or make personal or telephone sales calls to the old customers. If the two products are reasonably similar from a functional perspective, you can call the new product by the old product's name and try to merge it into the old identity as if you were introducing an upgrade rather than something brand new.

In other words, you can dress the new product in the old product's coat rather than just attaching it to the coattails. This stealth strategy needs to be defensible from a common-sense perspective, or you'll anger customers; if you can make the argument that customers are getting a "more and better" version of the same product, then the strategy ought to work.

The makers of personal computers employ this strategy. For example, the Macintosh PowerBook is completely different on the inside — and performs far better now than it did five years ago. But it is still identified by the PowerBook brand name, because that name has a strong position in the marketplace that Apple can't afford to put at risk.

The coattails strategy is a great promotional device for replacing an old product with a new one. Use it whenever you want to kill an old product in order to make room for a new one. *Room* can mean room in the customer's mind, room on the store shelf, room in the distributor's catalog, or room in your own product line. Products take up space, and either physical or mental space can be an important resource. But the risk — and it is a big one — is that when you make room for your new product, competing products can try to take that space instead. Why? Any customers still faithful to the old product are forced to reconsider their purchase patterns, and so may choose a competitor over your new option. Similarly, retailers, distributors, or other channel members may give your space to another product. So you need to hold onto your space, even as you eliminate your product. Do this by avoiding any gaps in availability of your products.

The product line place-holding strategy

You can use *product lines* to create clear product niches and hold them for replacement products. Pricing should be consistent with product positions in your product line as well — a practice called *price lining*.

For example, a bank may offer a selection of different savings options to its retail customers — a mix of straight savings accounts, savings with checking, mutual fund accounts, and certificates of deposit of varying lengths. If the bank organizes these options into a coherent range of named products and lists them in a single brochure in order from lowest-risk/lowest-return to highest-risk/highest-return, then it creates a clear product line with well-defined places for these products. (The bank must be sure that each product sits in a unique place on that spectrum — no overlaps, please!)

Now, when the bank wants to introduce a new product, it can substitute the new one for an old one, and consumers will accept that this new product fills the same spot in the product line. Or the bank can extend the product line in either direction or fill gaps in it with new products. Whatever the bank does, the product line can act as a place holder to ease the entry of new products. (See the following discussion of branding for more information on product lines.)

Branding and Naming Your Product

What will you call your new product? Should you launch it under an existing brand identity or give it a new one? Should you attempt to add value (and raise the price) by creating a positive brand identity, or should you save your marketing dollars and just get the product out to point of purchase? These are all tough decisions. Let me show you how to make them well.

Designing a product line

A *product line* is any logical grouping of products offered to customers. (Remember products can be goods, services, ideas, even people.) Usually product lines are identified by an umbrella brand name, plus individual brand identities.

The Compaq computer line includes many different products, but they all bear the same Compaq brand name, and they are all distinct enough that together they give the customer a wide range of choice. You can think of product lines like this one as families of products — and like families, their relationship needs to be close and clear.

You have two key issues to consider when designing your product lines:

- ✔ **First, you have the issue of *depth.*** How many alternatives should you give the customer within any single category? For example, should you make a single T-shirt design in XL and XXL as well as smaller sizes? How about offering the design in a greater variety of colors? All these options increase depth, because they give a customer more options.

    The advantage of depth is that it increases the likelihood of a good fit between an interested customer and your product. You don't want to miss a sale because somebody was too big to wear a size Large. The disadvantage of depth is that it does not lead your customer to buy more than one product — the customer can simply buy what she sees as the same product, but in a bigger size. This added choice avoids your missing some sales, but it will not create a big source of new sales.

You should increase depth whenever you are losing customers because you didn't have a product for them, even though they liked the product concept. Increased depth of choice reduces the chance of disappointing a prospective customer.

✔ **Second, you have the issue of *breadth*.** This is where you can generate new sales. For example, you should also consider offering more T-shirt designs in your product line. Add new art so that customer can buy two different designs, both in XXL. When you add anything the customer views as a separate choice, not a variant of the same choice, then you are adding breadth to the product line. A broad line of T-shirts would include dozens and dozens of different designs. A broad and deep product line would offer each of those designs in many sizes and on many different colors and forms of T-shirts.

You should increase breadth whenever you can think of a new product that seems to fit in the line. By *fit,* I mean that the relationship to the line is obvious to customers. Don't mix unrelated products — that's not a product line because it will never have a clear, logical identity to customers. But keep stretching a successful line as much as you can. Doing so makes sense for one simple reason: It sells new products to old customers. Of course, the line may also reach new customers, which is fine. But your old customers are an easier (read *cheaper*) sell, so you want to do more business with them in the future.

Maintaining your product line: When to change

The secret to good product management is *don't leave well enough alone.* But if you keep growing your lines, you will obviously bump into some practical limits after a while. How will you know when the pendulum is going to swing the other way, when it's time to do some spring cleaning?

You should decrease depth and/or breadth if your distribution channels cannot display the full product line to customers. Often distribution is a bottleneck, imposing practical limits on how big a product line you can bring to the customer's attention.

When I consulted to the Kellogg Brush Company some years ago, I was amazed to learn that they made many hundreds of different items. Yet the grocery and hardware stores selling their products never displayed more than a couple dozen items. Obviously their product line was far broader and deeper than their end customers ever realized. I recommended that they either develop a direct, catalog-based distribution channel in order to bring this choice to customers, or they cut the product line back to the top 20 or 30 items purchased by retailers and try to make those better and cheaper. (They chose the latter option.)

You should also cut back your product line if customers do not understand it. Procter & Gamble recently chopped its product offerings roughly in half for this very reason. Surveys showed that their customers were confused by all the variety and did not have a clear idea of what the company offered and why. Too many choices frustrate customers and lead to confusion between products. Brand identities start to overlap, and customer decisions are made harder instead of easier.

Always calibrate your product line to your distribution channels and your customers. Don't overwhelm. Don't underwhelm. Keep talking to all your customers and watching how they behave to see if you need to shrink or grow your product line.

Naming a product or product line

Naming a new product is not simple, but you can use a number of effective methods. You can choose a word or combination of words that tells people exactly what the *character* of your product is — like LongShot (see the nearby sidebar "A beer by any other name. . ."). This approach is kind of like giving a new puppy a name. You want to get a feel for its personality first, and then give it a name that fits. A stand-offish poodle can be Fifi, but a playful mutt can't be!

A beer by any other name. . .

The Boston Beer Company recently went public. Famed for its upstart products sold under the Samuel Adams brand name, the Boston-based company is an example of a local brewer that made it to the national market. But is the company in danger of losing its specialty image as it grows ever bigger? Something about drinking a beer that other people haven't tried adds to the appeal of the specialty market — and now most beer drinkers have at least heard of, if not tried, Samuel Adams.

To avoid losing the company's association with small, specialty brewing, it introduced an additional brand name: LongShot. The LongShot name is applied to the winners of a World Homebrew Contest — homebrewers make fine beers in their basements. You can find a LongShot Black Lager, a LongShot American Ale, and a LongShot Hazelnut Brown Ale — each a winner at the professionally judged contest. The event itself and the new LongShot brand name both reinforce the company's small-time roots. And the LongShot name and "1680 entries, three winners" capture the excitement of an amateur's brew making it to the big time. Somebody was wearing a marketing cap at the Boston Beer company when he or she came up with the idea for this new brand name.

The Ford Mustang, an extremely successful brand name, used this strategy. The car was simply supposed to have the personality of the small, hardy horse of the American plains from which it took its name. And the driver was presumably to be a modern-day cowboy, akin to the real cowboys who broke and used the mustangs for their work. This strategy is powerful, because many existing terms have meaning that you can apply to your product.

Another route entirely is to make up a brand new word that has no prior meaning. This approach gives you something that is easier to protect in a court of law. But it won't be as effective at communicating the character of your product. You have to invest considerable time and money in creating a meaning for the new name in consumers' minds.

But, you can end-run this problem with made-up names by making them out of *morphemes,* which are defined by NameLab Inc. as "the semantic kernels of words." For example, NameLab started with the word "accurate" (from the Latin word *accuratus*) and extracted a morpheme from it to use as a new car name: Acura. They also developed Compaq, Autozone, Lumina, and Zapmail in the same manner. Each is a new word to the language, but each communicates something about the product because of meanings we associate with its components.

This technique is called *constructional linguistics,* and it is best done by expert linguists who use elaborate databases of morphemes. Contact NameLab for details (in San Francisco, California, at 415-563-1639).

Legally Protecting Your Product's Name and Identity

You can gain legal protection for your use of a unique identifier for your product, as well as for a line of products, and even for your entire company or a division or unit of it. This protection can apply to names and short verbal descriptions, and also to visual symbols. All of these are *marks* that represent the identity of the thing to which they are applied. A tangible product's name and/or visual symbol is a *trademark.* A service name is termed a *service mark* — but it is treated similarly to a trademark under U.S. law. A business name is a *trade name* — again, with similar protection under the law.

In the U.S., you establish and protect your rights to exclusive use of any unique trademark by using it. Yes, you should register it (with the U.S. Patent and Trademark Office — contact any law firm handling "intellectual property" to learn how). But registering the trademark isn't nearly as important as using the trademark. In other countries, usage and registration also matter, but sometimes the emphasis is reversed — without registration, usage gives you no protection. So check with local authorities in each country where you plan to use a trademark.

For more information on establishing and strengthening trademarks, contact your lawyer, any experienced ad agency that does brand marketing, or a name lab. For example, Ira N. Bachrach, President, NameLab Inc., can provide marketers with helpful advice and services in this area. (NameLab is at 711 Marina Blvd., San Francisco, CA 94123, 415-563-1639.)

Registering trademarks in the U.S.

If you want to register a trademark of any kind in the U.S., call the Library of Congress in Washington D.C. for information at 703-557-INFO. They can send the appropriate form, along with an instruction booklet. You'll have to contact a lawyer who specializes in intellectual property for help registering your trademark in other countries. But doing so is certainly feasible. Most of the countries you might want to do business in subscribe to the Berne Convention (as does the U.S.), for example, which means your legal protection for a published work (including a label or ad) in one country should be honored in other countries, too.

Chapter 15

Packaging and Labeling: Dressing Products for Success

● ●

In This Chapter

▶ Helping products capture attention at point of purchase

▶ Auditing your package designs

▶ Using the VIEW model (Visibility, Information, Emotion, and Work)

▶ Trying new strategies to make packaging more effective

▶ Avoiding legal packaging time-bombs

● ●

*A*t some point in every marketing program, the product has to take over and market itself. That point is usually where the customer and product meet and the purchase decision is — or isn't — made. Customer enters grocery store, glances over the shelves, pulls a package down, and carries it to register. Customer opens catalog, flips through pages, selects an item, and dials the toll-free number. Customer uses America Online to purchase airplane tickets and make a hotel reservation. At all of these points of purchase, the marketer is out of the picture. The product must sell itself. But to do so, the product must be noticed. It must be enticing. It must appear to be better than (and a better value than) the competition.

This level of excellence is a lot to expect from your product, especially given the reality that customers cannot try most products until after they complete the purchase. In other words, nobody is able take a bite of a packaged food product in the store, or try on a pair of pants in a catalog, or test the mattress in a distant hotel room, before making a purchase decision.

To prepare your product for its solo role at this vital point-of-purchase stage, you need to give careful thought to how the product is displayed and presented. You cannot play this all-important role for your product, but you *can* select the stage and design the set and costume. The *stage* is made up of the store, catalog, or other meeting place (covered in Chapter 17), the *set* includes the shelving, signs, display, or other point-of-purchase designs (check out Chapter 16), and the *costume* is the packaging you give your product (discussed right here in this chapter).

When you carefully consider and design all these supports, the product sells itself successfully. If you neglect them, however, then the best of products end up languishing in the warehouse or on the shelf. In this chapter, I focus on the star of the show — the product and its costume. Together they make up what marketers refer to as the *packaging*.

Will Your Packaging Make the Sale?

The packaging "makes the sale" in the majority of purchase decisions (along with any additional point-of-purchase influences to draw attention to the product — but you can look at those in the next chapter). That means your packaging may well be the most important part of your marketing plan.

Yes, it is true! In spite of the vast sums of money and attention lavished elsewhere, on advertising, marketing research, and other activities, it all comes down to the package. Will the prospective customer see the package and choose it over others? Studies of the purchase process reveal that people rarely know just what they will buy before the *point of purchase* — that's the time and place at which they actually make their purchase. The majority of consumers are ready and willing to be swayed at point of purchase, as the findings in Table 15-1 (from a study by the Point-of-Purchase Advertising Institute) reveal:

Table 15-1 The Point of Purchase Decision-Making Process		
Nature of Consumer's Purchase Decision	*% of Purchases, Supermarkets*	*% of Purchases, Mass Merchandise Stores*
Unplanned	60%	53%
Substitute	4%	3%
Generally planned	6%	18%
Total = In-store decision rate of	**70%**	**74%**

As this table shows, unplanned purchases are the biggest category. Furthermore, specifically planned purchases (those not included in the table) are less than a third of all purchases — all the rest can be influenced at least partially by the package and other point-of-purchase communications. These facts make the package more important than any other element of the marketing program for most products. Wow! In fact, you may want to stop and ask yourself whether you can dispense with all other forms of marketing communication, and invest only in packaging and point-of-purchase promotions and displays. If your target customer is open to a point-of-purchase decision, then this extreme is at least a possibility (if you're not sure who your target customer is, check out Chapter 3). And by focusing 100 percent on the point of purchase, you are able to handle the point of purchase better than less focused competitors. The idea is at least worth a thought, if for no other reason than because it is so radical that your competition probably won't think of it.

What Is "The Package"?

In common language, *packaging* means anything that is used to wrap something. It can also mean the act of wrapping something. When you wrap a birthday present in bright paper and a bow, then put it in a padded cardboard box and ship it to someone, you are doing, and using, packaging. But the really interesting part of packaging from a marketing point of view is the part of this whole process that "sells" the product — "the package" in marketing-speak. While the padding and carton protect your shipment, the wrapping paper and ribbon are what make it special and memorable to the recipient. This birthday wrap is of more interest to us because it communicates something about the contents that help make them seem special to the recipient. When marketing delivers products to consumers, it is just as important to wrap the contents nicely. Think of your product as a gift to your customers. (However, remember that your package needs to reveal the identity of what it contains, not hide it as gift wrap does.)

Another curious thing about a birthday present helps us understand packaging. Until it is unwrapped, the present and its colorful paper and ribbon wrapping are often referred to as if they were one — they are "the package." "Did you get my package? Yes? Great. But remember, don't open it until your birthday!" Similarly, your product and wrapping become one in the mind of the consumer — and so the package is not only the wrapping, but the new thing you create by wrapping a product. To help you to remember this point, I suggest that you repeat the following five times: *"The package is the product, the package is the product. . . ."*

Got that? Good. It may sound like semantics, but this concept is quite important. The product does not exist on its own until it is unwrapped and used. Until then, the package is, in the consumer's mind, that new creation you form when you wrap your product. And that new creation sets the stage for the drama of consumption. It creates the first impression of the product's personality. It often introduces the product to the consumer, for, as I told you in the preceding section, the majority of purchase decisions are made at point of purchase, where the consumer is beyond the reach of marketing influences except the package. Well, actually the decision is based on the package plus any brand knowledge the customer may have picked up and whatever special point-of-purchase influences you or the retailer may have added (see Chapters 13 and 16). But the point-of-purchase promotions usually cost you extra and are rarely appropriate to use on a permanent basis, so the package itself must be your front line in the war to grab and hold consumer interest.

Every Product Has a Package!

If you work in banking or real estate, or you sell windshield gaskets to auto manufacturers, or you distribute your products by mail order instead of in a store, can you skip this chapter? Sorry, but no. Remember, the package is the product as it is first presented to the customer. Taken broadly, this definition means that every product has a package, whether it fits your traditional notion of packaging or not. And, therefore, marketers must give careful thought to package design, regardless of the product. Services, ideas, and even people are included, because they can all be products in the right context.

Okay, I assume that you accept the notion that every product has a package in principle. But how can you apply it in practice? Imagining the package for an intangible product (such as a service or idea) is difficult, but your job is to figure out what that package is so you can exercise control over the impression it makes. And when you examine such products closely, you discover a paradox: the less obvious the package, the more complex and multifaceted it is! Many elements combine to form a kind of psychological package for a professional service such as investment fund management. If you recognize all these components and use them well, you can create a very compelling package that helps sell your product and also makes the user's experience more positive. If, however, you remain blind to these package elements, as many marketers do, you will fail to control the vital first impression the customer gets of your product and its personality. So make sure that package is an important section of your plans and budgets, even if you don't market a so-called packaged good. Refer to Table 15-2 for some general guidelines to help you identify the package components of products that don't seem packaged at first glance.

Table 15-2	Finding the Hidden Package
Product Type	*Package Components*
Professional services	
	Appearance of place of delivery (if customer comes to you)
	Personal presentation of people who deliver service (if any)
	Appearance of mailings, statements, and other printed matter (this material is your wrapping paper!)
	Personality projected by telephone or computer interface with customer

Product Type	Package Components
Direct-shipped products bought via telephone or mail (These have two points of purchase — the initial decision, influenced by the "catalog package" and the first face-to-face meeting of product and consumer, influenced by the "shipping package.")	
	Cover of catalog/magazine/mailer in which product appears
	Ad which portrays product
	Appearance/image/personality of artwork showing the product
	Personality projected by telephone interface with customer
	Personality and service quality of shipper and shipping carton/materials
	Internal wrapping of product(s) within shipping container
Candidates (for political office or for a job)	
	The clothing the candidates wear
	The people they associate with (including their references)
	The places/contexts in which they are seen
	Their facial expressions (live, in photos, or on TV — expressions can be thought of as the packaging for their thoughts)
	The personality projected by their campaign materials/signs, offices, and staff (or their resumes and cover letters)
Wholesale goods for resale	
	The corporate/brand personality projected by salespeople (the point of purchase is usually in the buyer's office)
	Appearance of tear sheets, catalogs, samples, and correspondence (this material is your wrapping paper!)
	Personality and service quality of shipper and shipping carton/materials
Parts and supplies to industry	
	The corporate/brand personality projected by salespeople
	Appearance of tear sheets, catalogs, samples, and correspondence (this material is your wrapping paper!)
	Personality and service quality of shipper and shipping carton/materials

(continued)

Table 15-2 *(continued)*

Product Type	Package Components
	Internal reports to management about your product quality and timeliness of delivery (In big companies, you only exercise indirect control over this element, but you need to focus on making it look as good as possible. Know how executives measure your product, as these measures *are* your packaging to the executives!)
Retail goods without labels or packages (shoes that are displayed as is, not in their boxes, for example)	
	The exterior of the product itself (Nike puts its swish on the shoe, just as Coke puts its wavy line on the can)
	The point-of-purchase display (the in-store display for a shoe *is* its packaging; see Chapter 16 for point-of-purchase strategies)

Evaluating a Package Design

What makes one package good and another bad? You need to answer this question whenever you evaluate a marketing program (when you do an annual marketing plan or when you consider ways of improving the marketing of a product or product line, for example).

Also, when introducing a new product, or an old or improved product in a new package, you will probably have to choose among multiple package designs presented by your ad agency or package design firm. If you are a do-it-yourselfer, then you need to know which of your concepts is the keeper. If you choose a good firm, all the designs should meet the basic requirements — they should conform to legal constraints, protect the contents in shipping, storage and use, and be consistent in appearance with your brand's character or personality. But some designs will result in much higher sales than others. How do you pick a winner from a field of good contenders?

Finally, whenever you get bored or don't have enough important work to do (never mind all those trivial requests from your boss or clients), you should take a half day to reconsider your packaging (use the package audit process shown in Figure 15-1). Is the package still working well? Can the package be improved? Have competitors changed their packaging so that yours does not stand out as much — or so that yours no longer has as strong a positive image as it used to? Because the package is the product until your consumer unwraps it, evaluating it is a great "default" option whenever you are stuck for a way to enhance your marketing program.

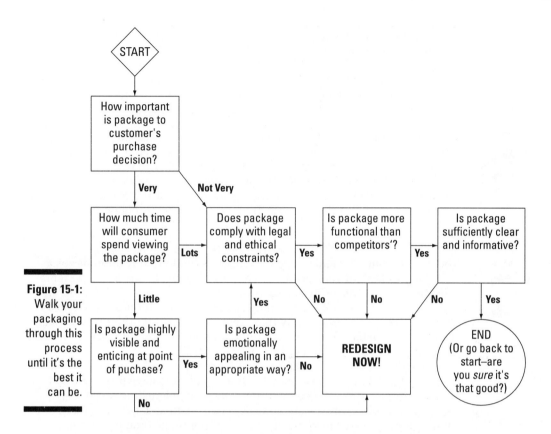

Figure 15-1:
Walk your packaging through this process until it's the best it can be.

One popular approach among experts is to evaluate designs using the *VIEW method,* which stands for visibility, information, emotional appeal, and workability. The acronym also serves to remind you of the first key function the package must perform at point of purchase — to make sure that the customer views it in the first place! In the VIEW method, you simply make sure that your product performs all four of the VIEW functions as well as possible, and better than any alternative you can think of. The functions the package needs to perform are described below, along with hints as to how best to do so. As you read about these four functions, sit where you can see one of your packages and do a quick mental audit of it. I guarantee that you'll spot some weakness or flaw that you can improve upon! (And if you can't, then my work here is done — you are a Certified Packaging Genius.)

Visibility

Visibility begs the question: "Will the package attract attention at point of purchase?" Attracting attention is harder than you think, even if you already think it is hard. Researchers report that shoppers spend an average of about ten seconds viewing products in a grocery store before selecting one. Your package must fight for this minimum of attention against all competing products and any *distracting* products — those that don't compete but that the shopper looks at accidentally. Competing and distracting packages often number in the dozens, sometimes even in the hundreds, so the average time spent looking at any single package before making a decision could well be a small fraction of a second.

It is for this reason that Nabisco modified its Oreo cookie package in 1996 (the first major change since the product was introduced in 1951). The name is now twice as large, and the white letters are thicker to remind viewers of the creme filling within the cookies. Was anything wrong with the old package? No — consumers still liked the product. But the cookie shelves are a lot busier now than they were in 1951, so visibility is a bigger issue.

Spying on your customers

You can find out how much time consumers spend viewing alternatives at point of purchase in your product category by going to several representative stores with a stopwatch to time shoppers. Then count the number of things they have to look at, including each separate alternative on display (competitive packages plus any that are likely to distract their view). Finally, divide the seconds spent viewing by the number of alternatives to obtain an average view per package for your customer and product. This figure varies dramatically depending on the product category, so collecting your own data is helpful. High-involvement, complex, and expensive products, and those with relatively little competition, have much longer average views than other product categories. Here are some estimates I developed by lurking in local stores to give you an idea of the range (and no, I wasn't arrested):

Table 15-3 Information Gathered by Spying on Shoppers . . .			
Product Category	**Length of View**	**Number of Options**	**View Time per Package/Item**
Breakfast cereals	25 seconds	65	0.38 seconds
Toothpastes	10 seconds	25	0.40 seconds
Houseplants	6 minutes	650	0.55 seconds
Catalog clothing	8 minutes	700	0.69 seconds
Air conditioners	7 minutes	8	52.50 seconds
Your product:			
_____	_____	_____	_____

Now, put your product on the other side of the room, surround it with any handy stuff to simulate the distractions of a store or catalog environment, and try to glance at it for only as long as the average view time per package based on your research. What can you see? What do you miss? Does the product stand out, call for more attention, or not? *Warning:* This simple exercise makes most package designs look bad!

Increasing Visibility

If you want to make your product more visible, consider using brighter colors, or colors that are different from the majority in your category. Also look at bold lettering and graphics. And try alternative package shapes and sizes. The key thought to hold onto here is that package visibility is a relative feature, dependent upon the other packages near it at point of purchase. If your package looks like the others, it may as well be a camouflaged moth on tree bark. So innovate — try for a unique look. A small, black, rectangular box does not stand out in general — but if it is surrounded by large, brightly colored bottles, it certainly does!

All this may sound easy — but there's a catch. Your creativity is hampered by one serious constraint, a constraint that will keep you from making all your products safety orange and putting strobe lights on them: The package must support the product's *brand identity,* its overall image and positioning. A wild day-glow wrapping would make a fine leather brief case more visible, but it would clash with the product's image. Sure, people would look at it, but then they'd look away. The trick is to maximize visibility without violating the brand identity.

One good example of this strategy is that Nabisco packaged SnackWells cookies in green, unlike competing brands. This new color was highly visible — and also consistent with the healthy "green" image of the brand.

The need for coordination between brand identity and package design sounds like a problem, but it can be turned into an opportunity. Branding (covered in Chapter 14) should be done with one eye on the visibility problem. A distinctive brand name like Snapple or a striking trademark like the Intel "Intel Inside" logo with its surrounding circular dash can become the thing that makes your package visible at point of purchase. You work hard on creating, and communicating, a brand identity. So cash in on it when trying to make your product more visible at point of purchase!

Information

Ask yourself, "Does my package communicate essential information to prospective buyers?" All packages need to make clear what the product is, and why this brand or version of the product is special or better than the competitors'. Packaging and labeling laws impose constraints on what information should be communicated and how (see that section for details). But you can include much or all of that information on the back or elsewhere, for later reading (or ignoring) after purchase. The key information to think about in evaluating the package is the information needed to get the package off the shelf and into the consumer's basket — whether that shelf and basket are literal or metaphorical. (This information should be displayed on the front of the package so as to be visible at point of purchase.)

The package must first and foremost get a simple marketing message across. The message must be simple because most packages are very small and seen very quickly at point of purchase. Imagine that you have to write someone a letter telling him why he needs to change his behavior — for example, to get a coworker to stop interrupting you during meetings. And imagine that you can't deliver it to him by mail, but instead, you have to post the message on a crowded public bulletin board in the hopes that he sees it. Finally, the piece of paper you have to work on can be no bigger than an index card. How likely are you to affect the desired behavior change? Not very! Well, that's just what the package has to do, along with other jobs. The package has to get somebody to stop and notice it, and then it has to compel her to engage in purchase behavior. It is essential to pare down the information to the absolute minimum and then figure out how to communicate it in the clearest, most high-impact way you can. The ideal is a single word or picture that encodes the key information. Think about memorable packages, like the Coke or 3M Post-It products, and you see that this difficult goal is attainable.

Package design focuses almost entirely on the point of purchase. Fair enough — it is a major challenge to marketers. But what about the point of *re*purchase? Never heard of it? Neither have I. I just made it up. But a point comes when (hopefully) the consumer says, "Hey, this thing is worn out. I better replace it." By then, your packaging has long since been discarded and cannot help you capture the repurchase. If the customer goes back to the store and finds your new package on the shelf, fine. But sometimes that doesn't happen, as when I decided to replace a favorite flannel shirt I'd bought from the WearGuard clothing catalog a few years ago. I had the new catalog, but the shirt was not in it. I couldn't remember what the design was called, so I couldn't ask the company if they had the shirt. But WearGuard has recently adopted the practice of sewing a permanent label inside its clothing with the style number and their toll-free telephone number on it. Bingo! I ordered two new shirts of the same kind, and they'll be on my doorstep by the end of the week.

The moral? Use permanent labeling on or in the product to short-circuit the normal shopping process and make reordering direct from you easy for customers. Otherwise the customer may lose essential information — and may be exposed to competitors' packaging before yours. Think of this as packaging the product for a future point of repurchase — a point where you have an advantage over competitors, should you choose to use it.

Emotion

How will the package make consumers feel, and how strongly will they feel that way? The importance of emotion varies from product to product, but it is always at least a part of the purchase decision. So you must make sure that the package evokes an appropriate feeling. To do so, first select and describe that "right" feeling. This step is easy if you've already defined it for your advertising, branding, or other positioning strategy. Just dig up those old notes and confirm that the product is supposed to have "an elegant, sophisticated feel" or whatever. If you haven't thought about the issue before, then you need to ask yourself what feeling would be most likely to lead to a purchase. If the consumer examining your package gets a sense of cheerfulness, or of excitement, or of nostalgia, or of self-confidence, or of efficiency, would this lead to a higher probability of purchase? One of these options, or another like it, is best. Remember, whatever feeling you choose to communicate in your packaging, make sure that it helps differentiate the product from competitors. You don't want to violate the visibility principle by evoking the same emotion as the three leading competitors!

Animating the package with emotion

How do you put emotion into a package design? The truth is, marketers have not really mastered this challenge. We do much better at communicating emotions in four-color print ads, radio drama-style ads, and television commercials that use actors or expressive cartoon characters. The package can be static and limiting, which seems to frustrate commercial artists. I don't get a big emotional hit from most packages. At best, the average package is subtle — it simply avoids clashing with any emotions the brand identity or past advertising may have attached to the product. But you can do better! Much better! Here is an opportunity to bring your product to life at point of purchase, to animate it with human emotion where its competitors don't. In Chapter 5, I discuss the general question of how to select and communicate an emotion, and everything there can be applied to packaging. But you should also get specific. The following sections provide some good ideas you may want to consider:

Use the human face and form

We humans are extremely good at reading emotions in facial expressions, body posture, and other nonverbal cues — and we have a natural tendency to feel the emotions we see in others. Yet people rarely appear on packaging. When they do, they usually have neutral, nonemotional expressions and postures.

Betty Crocker, the fictional face of a General Mills product line, has been redrawn many times over the decades — but never with any strong emotion. She smiles thinly, looking bored and disinterested in her own products. Yet her image has been effective at selling products, simply because it gives consumers a human face. What if General Mills decided to alter her expression and posture on different products, to express an emotion appropriate to each? For example, a chocolate cake mix might call for a celebratory, happy look — perhaps accented by the cheerful glitter of a few birthday candles. But a caring, motherly expression combined with a slightly forward-leaning posture (as if about to hug a child) might work better for a muffin mix. You get the idea.

The human face is so expressive that it has become the primary way people communicate most emotions. Why not put human faces on products to communicate emotions? Yes, I know that nobody else does it, but that makes it all the better. If consumers have to choose between looking at a bunch of boxes with words and one with a face, which will get the longest view?

And if you don't believe me, talk to the folks at JIAN, the Mountain View, California, software company that struck it rich with products like BizPlan Builder, Marketing Builder, Employee Manual Builder, and Agreement Builder. Each uses the face of a model on the front of the package and in all its advertising. These faces symbolize the products, and on an emotional level, *become* the products. For instance, the man on BizPlan Builder exudes self-confidence and competence. He is graying, but still youthful. He has a twinkle of inspiration in his eye, but his half-smile tells you that he also has a sober, careful side. He is the perfect entrepreneur, the kind of guy banks and venture capitalists throw money at. And you know when you look at the package that he will give those same emotional qualities to your business plan. Could this be why the product became a runaway best-seller in the U.S.?

Use the painter's symbols of emotion

Artists wrestle with the problem of communicating emotion, too, and often do so better than packagers. How? According to artist/teacher Nigel Holmes, the trick is to "keep the symbol simple, but let the feelings run wild." Artists use symbols to represent their emotions. Bright colors or zig zag lines can symbolize excitement, horizontal lines and neutral colors symbolize calm. Dark colors, heavy lines, and large masses symbolize strength. Light tints and thin lines symbolize delicacy. And many other emotions are triggered simply by showing things that evoke those emotions in real life. The image of a couple saying their wedding vows is loaded with emotions. And they are very different from the emotions we feel when viewing a large, ugly spider. Or an arching cathedral. Or a child running to the embrace of its mother. Or a rusty antique car, abandoned in an old field. Or the last leaf falling from an autumn tree. Images such as these can evoke powerful emotional reactions. But you rarely see this painterly approach on packaging.

What if Van Gogh designed your package? I bet it would be so full of emotion that shoppers would be unable to look at any other nearby product.

Should emotion or information dominate your design?

A final consideration is whether to make emotion, versus information, the dominant feature of your design. You can only emphasize one, not both (in theory, at least — but I'm sure that you can find *some* exception to this rule).

SnackWell's packaging emphasizes an emotional appeal to good taste and good health. It evokes the feeling of healthiness largely through the name and the fresh green color of the box. An alternative would have been to use a table, text, or a bar chart to communicate information proving that SnackWell's is a lower-fat brand than other cookies and that it is nonetheless delicious according to customer taste tests. Such an information-based package design would not work well for the brand because people generally make impulse purchases of cookies based on feelings, rather than rational analysis.

But an information-based package may be just the thing for a box of bolts on a hardware-store shelf. The consumer makes a planned purchase of this product, and usually has a range of specifications, from size to material, that need to be featured on the package.

In other product categories, either approach can work — you have to decide which is best in your particular situation. For example, some financial management and investment products are marketed and packaged based on hard information about their performance, while others are based on an emotional appeal. I'm sure that you can think of examples of each approach. Compare Fidelity's sober, information-packed brochures and statements with Merrill Lynch's "We're bullish on America" TV campaign and the use of the bull logo on all their packaging.

Workability

What jobs can the package do? Does the package perform any helpful functions for the marketers or consumers? Packaging has a functional side in most cases, and so your evaluation isn't complete until you ask yourself what work the package does. This is the last category to consider in the VIEW model.

Functions the package/label must perform

Following are the key tasks that packages generally need to perform:

- ✔ Protect the contents
- ✔ Make the contents easy for marketers to store and display
- ✔ Make the contents easy for consumers to carry and store
- ✔ Make the contents easy for consumers to use
- ✔ Make disposing of or recycling the packaging easy for consumers

No matter how standardized and well-developed packaging is in your market, I guarantee that you can find ways to improve its functionality. Room for innovation always exists. If you don't believe me, think about how packaging has changed in your market over the years. New materials, new shapes and sizes, new kinds of tops or closures, adoption of recyclable materials, drip-free bottles, new label materials and adhesives, cost-saving packaging processes and materials, and so on. If people have made it possible to improve the work packaging does so often in the past, it is possible in the future — and it is far better to be the person who introduces innovations than one of the many who must copy them.

Functions the package/label must not perform

While you are at it, give a moment's thought to what you *don't* want your packaging to do. This aspect of packaging is often overlooked by marketers, but never by consumers. Think of the last time you purchased an expensive, branded piece of fruit, only to find that the sticky label wouldn't peel off? How about the last time you bought a children's toy in a clear plastic bubble wrap, only to discover that the plastic was impervious to scissors and knives? For example, I recently cut my finger trying to open a Darda model race-car for one of my kids. And if that wasn't bad enough, my other two kids were still waiting for me to open theirs. Remind me not to buy anything in that sort of package next time I bring them presents! And then there are all those rusting cans left by the company that painted my house last summer. The town refuses to take them with my trash because they are classified as hazardous waste. I'll probably still have that packaging long after the paint has peeled off my house — and it will always remind me not to do business with that painter again.

To avoid negative consumer experiences, make sure that your packaging and labels *do not* do the following:

- ✔ Leave a residue on the product (this error is the most common; note that many temporary adhesives on labels become permanent after the product sits in a warehouse for a few months)

- ✔ Make getting at your product difficult or dangerous for consumers

- ✔ Leave consumers with waste materials that are hard to discard or recycle

- ✔ Leave consumers with waste materials that are unsafe to them or their children (choking and fire hazards included)

- ✔ Present your product identity/brand image in an unattractive way on discarded packaging materials (If your cartons are rotting in customers' garages or ending up along the nation's freeways, that's negative advertising in a big way.)

McDonald's wrestled with this problem by switching to biodegradable packaging and maintaining trash cans outside stores. Nothing is less appetizing than dirty McDonald's packages on the sidewalk!

✔ Conceal appealing aspects of your product

3M wraps Post-It Notes in a simple layer of clear cellophane with nothing but the brand name on the front, so that consumers can literally see the product they are looking for on the store shelf. If the packaging is the product, then the product can be the packaging, too.

In addition, never allow the packaging to *limit your vision of the product.* For those of you who may not have the faintest idea what I mean, let me give you an example. A couple years ago, I realized that people in business needed help in handling the radical changes sweeping through their industries and businesses. They needed to learn how to do what the experts term *change management.* As a consultant, trainer, and writer, I wanted to fill this need. But I knew I didn't have enough expertise, so I decided to assemble leading practitioners at a conference on the topic. It would be The Conference on Change Management, and I would organize and market it. But when I began looking into the details, I realized that it would be virtually impossible to assemble all the experts I wanted in one place at one time — let alone all the people in business who needed help. My plan just wasn't going to fly. Then I happened to read an article about the then-hot idea of *virtual businesses* and it suddenly struck me that a virtual conference was also possible. It just meant changing the packaging for the product! So instead of delivering the wisdom of these experts in a live conference event, I obtained written versions of their presentations and turned them into a published product called The Portable Conference on Change Management. The product is now packaged in a big red three-ring binder and distributed by a direct-mail publisher (HRD Press), but it is still the same product — just in a different package.

Keeping track of package designs

In today's business world you can easily lose control of your package designs. Dozens, even hundreds of variants may exist at any one time or accumulate over the years. And when you market across national borders, you generally have to develop new packages that meet the legal and cultural requirements of each national market that you deal with. The paper trail can be so daunting that marketers lose control over their package design. Brand identities are misrepresented on some packages or in some countries. Marketers in one office duplicate work they could have borrowed from another office. The problem is even worse when, as is so often the case today, you use a global network of subcontractors who must struggle to adhere to your company's packaging and branding regulations. Chaos is more widespread than most marketers will admit!

A software solution is now emerging, however, that takes the chaos out of packaging, and offers wonderful opportunities for synergy and collaboration as well. The new software products store digital images of packaging and make the images available everywhere via networked computers. They also provide digital

(continued)

(continued)

templates of brand identifiers for local use, records of commercials used around the world, and they can even be used for centralized review of far-flung package design decisions. The leading system is called IdentiLink, developed by The Coleman Group (in New York City at 212-421-9030). Nestle now uses IdentiLink to track the marketing of its 8,000 plus brands out of 13 offices around the world.

I think, then, it's safe to say that this software can probably handle your requirements as well.

While large-scale applications like IdentiLink are expensive, off-the-shelf networking products like Lotus Notes have sufficient capacity to do the trick for smaller firms when joined with scanners, a database of images, and lots of memory for image storage.

Similar transformations can be made in almost any product category, just by rethinking the packaging. Baking soda becomes a house-cleaning product in a bigger box, and a toothpaste when put in a tube. Books can become Internet Web sites. Tissue paper is for the face when in a rectangular box, but for the other end when in a roll. Can you think of another shape and packaging that would give it a third use? How about in a small envelope, for cleaning glasses? Or a pad, for cleaning the glass face of computer monitors? Or in a small roll within a white plastic container with a big red cross on it, for first-aid use in the bathroom? It's all the same basic paper product, but you can create new products from it just as fast as you can think of new packages.

This game is actually an important one in marketing. Witness the repackaging of food products, for example. The same food becomes a different product when it is fresh, frozen, freeze-dried, canned, or boxed. This is true in any product category — trust me! Information can be packaged and repackaged in millions of ways to create new products. So can the advice of a doctor or investment manager. The only limit is your packaging imagination.

Legal Issues in Labeling and Packaging

Whether you design the package yourself or subcontract for assistance, you need to make sure that the package complies with all relevant laws. In fact, you probably want to do more than comply — it's best to be on the "windy side of the law" as they say, where you are absolutely confident that you aren't dealing with legal or ethical time bombs. Achieving this level of assurance is not easy because, as you may have noticed if you've read other chapters, marketing law is complex and multifaceted. Everyone who can afford to hires a lawyer with appropriate expertise, and those who think they can't afford it often discover that they can't afford *not* to!

The exception to this rule, if one exists, is when you are working within safe standards of practice. Perhaps you are redesigning the label for a product that has already passed muster with experts and been on the market for some time without any legal problems. Or maybe you are introducing a package and product that are similar in most respects to many already sold in your industry. In such cases, general trade practice may be sufficient, and a full-blown legal analysis redundant. But perhaps not — you won't know until later. That's the trouble with legal issues.

In any event, whether you go to experts or rely on your own judgment, a general awareness of the main legal issues involved will help you ensure that due diligence is performed. The following sections provide a quick overview of packaging law.

U.S. Fair Packaging and Labeling Act

The purpose of this 1966 act is to make sure that consumers receive accurate information about the contents and quantity of what is inside a package (similar laws affect packaging design in many other countries as well). In theory at least, it should make simple the comparison of competing products. (Does yours?) The law applies to those who distribute goods across state lines, so it is up to the marketer, not the retail seller, to ensure that the package complies.

To comply, a package needs to include clear information about the following:

- ✔ Package size
- ✔ Sale price representations or implications (remember, the store determines the final retail price)
- ✔ A statement describing the ingredients
- ✔ How much "slackfill" or air/cushioning is in the packaging
- ✔ Package size standards

I'm not going to include details of how your packaging needs to address these requirements here because it would take dozens of pages to even begin the task. In part, this complexity is due to the fact that the general requirements of the Fair Packaging and Labeling Act have been elaborated upon for many specific situations. Your particular package may well be affected by a host of complex regulations and standards not applied to other packaging.

Who regulates your package?

You can find out more about your specific case by contacting the right regulatory body, a lawyer, or package design expert in your product category. If you are packaging foods, drugs, medical devices, or cosmetics in the U.S., the Secretary of Health and Welfare is responsible for regulating what you do (main number: 202-690-7000). If you are packaging any other form of consumer product, authority lies with the Federal Trade Commission (main number: 202-362-2222). For example, the FTC implements the Textile Fiber Products Identification Act, which must include what fibers a textile is made of, the manufacturer, and the country of origin. While the regulations issued by the FTC governing how textiles are labeled and advertised are extensive, they offer good instructions and samples of appropriate label designs to help make your job easier. So get them! If you start dialing the federal government for information of this sort now, you may have some helpful publications and guidelines in hand within a few weeks. (In Europe, be aware that both national and EC laws may apply.)

In addition, hazardous substances are regulated through special legislation, such as the Poison Prevention Packaging Act of 1970 and the Federal Hazardous Substance Act. The latter specifies a dozen separate elements of information to include on your label, ranging from whether your label should say "DANGER," "WARNING," or "CAUTION" to what kind of first aid instructions to include, if any — so you had better consult the experts on that one!

A compliance checklist for packagers

Now, in spite of the fact that simplifying the legalities of packaging and labeling is impossible without leaving something essential out, I am going to attempt to summarize the key issues that generally apply. My main source is David Hjelmfelt of the law firm Hjelmfelt & Larson, and his helpful book, *Executive's Guide to Marketing, Sales & Advertising Law* (Prentice Hall). The following list should be reviewed by the marketer of any packaged product for consumers (and, to be safe, for business-to-business sales as well). The list certainly isn't exhaustive, but on the other hand, if you haven't considered one or more of the items on this list, I guarantee that you will run into trouble! The best way to use this checklist is as a source of issues and questions to go over with an expert. But if you must do it yourself, be sure that you find out how your package is regulated, and use this list as a starting point for obtaining instructions from the relevant government agencies.

The package and its label(s) must do the following:

❏ Identify the product clearly

❏ Give the name and address of manufacturer, packer, or distributor

❏ State net quantity of contents according to FTC rules

❏ Identify the contents accurately, in the right form, and with approved terms and abbreviations

❏ Use a name and trademark that complies with legal requirements in these areas and that are not already registered to another company

❏ Comply with the FTC's various requirements concerning sales promotions (They regulate usage of terms such as "cents off," "economy size," and "introductory offer" on packaging — ask them for details)

❏ Comply with any relevant warranty rules if a warranty is made on the product

❏ Comply with any industry- or product-specific laws (Here's a partial list: Any hazardous substance, anything in the areas of cosmetics, foods, drugs, and medical devices, children's sleepwear, textiles, furs, binoculars, television sets, radios, stereo equipment, batteries, home insulations, sleeping bags, home study and vocational schools, investment services and products, and extension ladders are all subject to specific regulations)

❏ Include or come with an invoice (In which case, this must comply with approved forms — check with the FTC or your lawyer for details)

Keep good records!

Packaging laws and good sense both require that you keep clear records of your package design. Save examples of all your packages and labels, and be sure to document your research and retain records of any discussions with lawyers or other experts. In addition, keep the designs and advice of any firms you retain to develop the label and package. If you follow common practices in your industry, save some competitors' packages to make sure that you can prove you've followed common practice later on. If you've done a careful job of asking the government, your lawyers, and industry experts what to do, then, hopefully, they will bear some of the responsibility should anything turn out to be wrong later on — presuming, of course, that you can find the records needed to prove your point.

Ladies and gentlemen, start your networking!

I can't possibly list every contact in the industry (and wouldn't if I could as it would take days of typing!). Instead, I'm going to offer you a different set of contacts, each one a potential entry point into your own research and telephone networking. From any of the following sources, you should be able to find your way to qualified firms to help you with your unique packaging needs:

✔ **Cahners Publishing,** which publishes the excellent trade magazine *Packaging*, Des Plaines, IL, 847-635-8800; in the U.S., 800-662-7776. Order a few back issues and skim them for coverage of specialists in your area of interest, or ask an editor for advice and contact ideas.

✔ **American Society for Testing and Materials,** Philadelphia, PA, 215-299-5585. Try them for technical help if you are exploring alternative packaging materials.

✔ **I.D. (International Design) Magazine,** New York, NY, 212-947-1400. They sponsor an annual contest that includes a packaging category. Try their recent award winners if you are looking for an innovative designer or inspirational ideas for your own designs.

✔ **Institute of Packaging Professionals,** Herndon, VA, 703-318-8970 (in the U.S., 800-432-4085). Publishes *Packaging Matters*, a helpful trade magazine for ideas and contact names, and produces the packaging industry's premier sourcebook

for finding professional help of all sorts. The book is called *Who's Who and What's What in Packaging*, is updated yearly, and — the only hitch — it costs $130 for non-members. (But until IDG Books Worldwide does a full-blown *Packaging For Dummies*, it's your best bet.) Finally, inquire about this organization's seminars, as they have a full program for marketing professionals.

✔ **Package Design Council International,** same address as the preceding. This organization is run by the same management company as the Institute of Packaging Professionals, but it represents packaging and design firms with an international presence. If you are looking for assistance beyond the borders of the U.S., this organization can help you identify candidates.

✔ **Design Firms.** If you are impatient and want to talk to a packaging designer right away, here is a brief selection to get you started: Central Graphics and Container Group Ltd., Mississauga, Ontario, Canada, 905-238-8400; Continental Concepts, Cicero, IL, 708-222-4650; DDB Needham Marketing Communications, Dallas, TX, 214-855-2578; Kell Container Corp., Chippewa Falls, WI, 800-472-7744; Reynolds Guyer Designers, Inc., St. Paul, MN, 612-603-2300; Whitehouse Designs, Inc., Van Nuys, CA, 818-895-8575. In addition, all the big, international ad agencies have packaging expertise — see the listing in Chapter 7.

Chapter 16

Distribution, Retail, and Point of Purchase

· ·

· ·

*I*magine walking into a car dealership and buying whatever car you wanted, not just what they have on the lot or what they can locate at other dealerships in the area. You could literally buy the make and model you want, in your favorite color, with the specific extras you do and don't want. In other words, you could buy the car you want rather than the one they want to sell you. Heck, the car is probably the largest purchase that you'll make all year. You should be able to have it your way, right?

Well, you can't. Not now. And the reason is that the distribution method used to get cars from their producers to their potential customers makes offering that broad of a selection impossible. This, like many marketing problems, turns out to be a distribution problem at heart. Often when customers are unhappy with the product selection or service, the best fix is in the distribution channel and its design rather than in the product and its service support. Frequently, when market share or sales volume disappoints the marketer, the best fix is better distribution rather than a new ad campaign or more sales promotions. Distribution is the bottleneck between the marketer and the customer, and it often hurts performance in hidden ways.

That's why General Motors (GM) is establishing huge regional distribution centers all across the United States. The centers inventory all GM brands in depth, putting a wider selection closer to dealers and their customers. The centers are located so as to be able to offer same-day delivery of any vehicle from stock. Will this innovation in GM's distribution improve customer satisfaction and increase sales? I think so, because GM's marketing research reveals that 35 percent of auto customers cannot find the specific car they want when they visit conventional dealers and, thus, make a compromise purchase. Consumers will be happier under the new plan. Furthermore, GM reports that 11 percent of customers defect to another auto maker when they can't find what they want, so the plan will also increase customer retention.

Amazing what distribution can do. Maybe you ought to give some serious thought to how your organization distributes its products.

Finding and Riding Distribution Trends

At first glance, distribution channels (the paths from producer to customers) generally look pretty stable. But appearances can be deceiving. In truth, every distribution channel is undergoing change — but often at a slow rate. In some channels, new intermediaries (the organizations that help connect producer to customers) are arising to provide new services. In others, intermediaries are being cut out as manufacturers go straight to retailers or even develop direct marketing relationships with end customers (see Chapter 18 on direct marketing if you want to do the same). In still other channels, one type of retailer or distributor is gradually replacing another type. If you can understand such changes, you will be able to get out ahead of them. If not, the changes will run you over. Even though the changes are slow, shifts in distribution are powerful. And you don't want your marketing to get run over by a steam roller!

Let me give you some specific examples, in case you don't take my warning seriously:

- ✔ In the stationery and office supplies industries, independent retailers are being displaced by major retail chains (like Staples). Furthermore, the chains buy direct from manufacturers, cutting out the traditional distributors as well.

- ✔ In the U.S. market for sweet baked goods (worth $16 billion in annual retail sales according to Find/SVP, a marketing research firm), bakery chains and in-store supermarket bakeries are gaining at the expense of freestanding bakeries. Bakers that sell directly to the public are gaining rapidly at the expense of those who retail other bakeries' goods — and the producers and distributors who supply them.

✔ In the U.S. health care industry, more than a thousand managed care providers are jockeying for position as this new form of health care organization displaces traditional hospitals, clinics, medical partnerships, and insurers. *Scale advantages* (lower costs for larger operations) appear to favor HMOs with larger enrollments, so the consolidation trend will continue.

✔ Many industries, such as electric motors, seals, springs, and machine tools, are going global, and companies that used to compete regionally must now cope with low-cost overseas producers as well. That means tougher competition in their home markets and also a greater need to become effective in the export/import arena.

✔ In a wide variety of industrial and consumer product industries, the World Wide Web is putting more power in the hands of buyers, permitting them to easily locate and evaluate offerings from a great many vendors. This trend is putting heat on marketers to make their offerings more competitive in quality and price. The trend is allowing some marketers to go direct via the Web and displace more traditional distributors. For example, semiconductor producers and distributors now put their catalogs on the Web, and many buyers surf the Net to find what they need.

✔ The Web isn't the only way producers are finding to cut out middlemen. Direct marketing is increasingly common in most industries. For instance, the U.S. now has more than 12,000 factory outlet stores and more than 300 outlet malls. The fact that these manufacturer-owned outlets compete with distributors and retailers does not seem to be a deterrent. Producers are increasingly able to go behind their channel partners' backs and create their own direct channels to compete with the traditional intermediaries.

Researching Channels

If you're researching an industry, one of the basic tasks is to figure out who the various players are at each step of the distribution channel. How are goods produced and brought to customers? The better you understand this process, the better you can take advantage of it to shape your own distribution channels to your and your customer's advantage.

Who *produces* the products? Try trade associations (libraries have directories to them) to locate producers in an industry. For example, the Polyurethane Manufacturer's Association in Glen Ellyn, Illinois, lists many major manufacturers of this raw material in its membership directory, as well as a variety of specialized producers of goods that use the product (makers of roller-skate wheels, for example).

Who *distributes* the products? Are wholesalers or other intermediaries in the distribution channel? If so, who are they and how many of them can you locate? Business-to-business telephone directories are published by region for most of the U.S. (call the business office of your local phone company to order them), and they often reference the category of intermediary you seek in their yellow pages sections. You'll also find several helpful trade associations and trade shows specializing in distributors in specific industries. For example, the International Food Distributors Forum puts on an annual conference for food distributors. A couple days at an event like that and you'll know more than you want to about the structure and trends of the distribution channel you're studying.

You may also want to contact the American Wholesale Marketers Association (AWMA), 1128 16th Street NW, Washington, DC, 20036 at 202-463-2124. They publish a directory of intermediaries that is a useful resource for marketers. The AWMA also offers members a special service called MarketPlus, which is an automated database of manufacturer product information that distributors receive on CD-ROM with monthly updates. The purpose of this service is to help intermediaries keep up-to-date with the current lines they carry and to locate new products of interest to them — so if you are a manufacturer or an up-stream distributor, get your products into this database (and consider becoming a member — ask them for details). That way, new companies will find you if they think they can do a good job of selling your products.

Who are the *retailers*? Retail stores are much easier to identify for the simple reason that they are in the business of being easy to find. They are listed in the yellow pages phone directories in any U.S. metropolitan areas of interest to you. They also have their own trade associations (such as the International Council of Shopping Centers (in New York at 212-421-8181). Consult any directory of associations for extensive listings (available in the reference sections of most libraries). Finally, consider wearing out a little shoe leather and tire rubber to find out who the leading retailers are in any specific geographic market. All you have to do is visit high-traffic areas and see what stores are prominent and successful to know who the leading retailers in the area are. (Retail market shares are often obtained by observational research, but can also be calculated from data on shopping habits provided by consumers in marketing research surveys.)

Marketing Channel Structure and Design

Efficiency is the driving principle behind channel design. Traditionally, channels have evolved to minimize the number of transactions, because doing so makes them more efficient.

As Figure 16-1 shows, a channel in which four producers and four customers do business directly has 16 (4 x 4) possible transactions. That's not too bad, but in reality, the numbers would get much higher when you have markets with dozens or hundreds of producers and thousands or millions of customers.

The number of transactions is far less when you introduce an intermediary, because now the math is simple addition instead of multiplication. In the example shown in Figure 16-1, you only need 8 (4 + 4) transactions to connect all four customers with all four producers through the intermediary. Each producer or customer has only to deal with the intermediary, which links him to all the producers or customers he may wish to do business with.

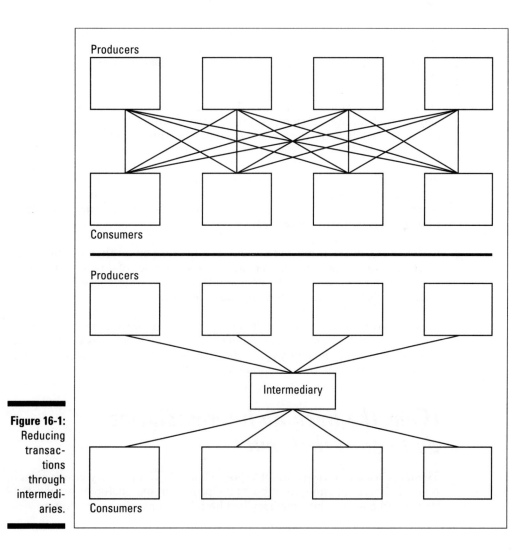

Figure 16-1:
Reducing transactions through intermediaries.

Although intermediaries add their markup to the price, they often reduce overall costs of distribution because of their effect on the number of transactions. Adding a level of intermediaries to a channel reduces the total number of transactions needed for all producers and customers to do business with each other.

I know that this example is simplistic, but you can see how the logic applies to more complex and larger distribution channels. Introduce lots of customers and producers, link them through multiple intermediaries, perhaps adding a second or third layer of intermediaries as well, and you have a classic indirect marketing channel. Odds are that you have some channels like this in your industry.

I have to warn you that I am suspicious of such channels. The longer and more complex they are, the more types of intermediaries they have, and the more times the product is handed from intermediary to intermediary, the less I like the channel.

I don't like these channels because I don't think they are the best way to achieve distribution efficiencies. I think that improved transportation, computerized links between channel members (through *electronic data interchange* or *EDI*), the creation of just-in-time inventory systems in which suppliers bring only what's needed, when needed, and the emergence of direct marketing technologies and practices all make running lean and mean channels much easier. Just as big companies are de-layering to become more efficient and get closer to their customers, so, too, are the big distribution channels in many industries.

In the future, distribution will be simpler and more direct than it is now, and marketers will be better able to handle a large number of customer transactions on their own without the help of intermediaries. Database management techniques alone do much to make this possible.

So think hard about how to get closer to your customer. Can you reduce the layers in your channel or begin to develop direct channels (by mail, phone, or Internet) to supplement your traditional indirect channels? Maybe. But if you don't, I bet some of your competitors will.

What the heck do intermediaries do to earn their cut?

The main reason to try to simplify your channels is that every intermediary takes their markup, and, thus, costs the producer and customer money. For this added cost, the intermediary had better perform some function or functions of value! In fact, they often do, or we wouldn't put up with them for long. Take a look at the various functions you may want your intermediaries to perform:

- Researching customer attitudes and desires
- Buying and selling
- Breaking down bulk shipments for resale
- Setting prices
- Managing point-of-purchase promotions
- Advertising at the local level (*"pull" advertising,* which is designed to bring people to a store or other business)
- Transporting products
- Inventorying products
- Financing purchases
- Locating and qualifying customers
- Providing customer service and support
- Sharing the risks of doing business
- Combining your products with others to offer appropriate assortments

That's a pretty long, and somewhat sobering, list, because you may not have realized how many things your intermediaries do for you. (Unless you don't have any intermediaries, in which case you may be thinking that spreading some of your risk and sharing some of those many tasks would be awfully nice!) The point is that intermediaries can and do perform useful functions, so you want to be sure that you can get the same work done efficiently in some other way before you cut intermediaries out of your channel.

Channel design considerations

Yes, your intermediares can do several useful things for you, as the preceding lists indicate. You need to decide who will do which of these things. But in addition to thinking about those various functions and who should perform them, you may want to consider the following strategic issues. Each is affected by how you set up and manage your distribution channel or channels.

- **Market coverage.** How well does your channel reach your target customers? If you go direct, doing everything yourself, you may be unable to cover the market as intensely as you want to. By adding even one layer of intermediaries, you suddenly have many more warm bodies or storefronts out there. As you add more layers to the channel, the bottom of the channel grows ever larger, allowing you to achieve increasingly good market coverage.

In short, market coverage increases as you add layers and members to your distribution channel. As you increase market coverage, you increase your availability to customers, which in turn maximizes your sales and market share. You can't fight that. So sometimes building a channel, rather than de-layering it, makes sense. Just make sure that you really do get better coverage and that the coverage translates into increased sales. Otherwise, those intermediaries aren't pulling their weight.

✔ **Level of intensity.** Thinking about the issue of market coverage in terms of *intensity*, defined as the extent of your geographic coverage of the market, is often helpful. Conventional wisdom says that three practical strategies exist. An *intensive distribution strategy* attempts to put every customer within reach of your products by using as many intermediaries and layers as needed to create maximum coverage. This strategy is a good idea in mature markets where your competitors are trying to do the same thing, or in markets where the customer makes a convenience purchase — because intensive distribution makes your product convenient. Keep in mind that this strategy is costly and may not be needed in other circumstances.

The second alternative is *selective distribution strategy,* in which you target the most desirable areas or members of your market. For example, the business-to-business marketer may decide to target a geographic region where many users of their technology are headquartered. The consumer products marketer may decide to market to zip code areas or counties where heavy users of their product are found.

The third alternative is *exclusive distribution,* in which you cherry pick to find the best intermediaries and customers. This strategy is appropriate where you don't have any really serious competition, and where you have a specialty product that you want to keep providing at the same profitable level. This method won't grow your market or boost share significantly, but it will maximize profit margins, and that's not bad!

Exclusive distribution is also appropriate as you introduce an innovative new product, whether good or service. You find a limited number of early adopters in any market, so a massive effort to mass-market a new innovative product usually fails. Start with exclusive distribution to those most interested in trying new ideas and then work up to selective distribution as competition builds and the product goes mainstream. Finally, push toward intensive distribution as the market matures and your emphasis shifts from finding first-time users to fighting over repeat business.

REAL WORLD

The incredible expanding company

Ronin, a New York City-based management consulting firm run by three principals, seemingly can't very well handle major projects for ten corporate clients in ten different cities at the same time. The company doesn't have big offices and a large staff in each of those cities.

But, this firm supplements its in-house staff with a database of qualified consultants throughout the country and the world, and is, therefore, able to create project teams for any and all clients, regardless of their locations or the nature of their problems.

In effect, Ronin uses its network of independent consultants as intermediaries. They step in to deliver Ronin's services to its clients when the need arises. And because Ronin has established this unusual distribution channel, it is able to compete with much larger consulting firms without having to maintain expensive staffs and offices in every major city like the others do.

✔ **Speed to market.** The longer the channel, the slower the product's trip from producer to customer. A relay team could never beat an individual runner in a sprint. If your customers need or want faster delivery and service, you'll have to prune the distribution channel until it is fast enough to satisfy the consumers.

Think about the trend toward catalog direct shopping in the clothing industry. Customers can obtain their choice of style and size from a large assortment within a few days if the shipper uses UPS, and the next day if an overnight air service is used. You may think that shopping in a department store is even quicker, because you can walk out with your purchase. But the busy consumer may not have time to visit a department store for days or weeks, whereas a late-night call to Land's End can be taken care of today. And you may need to visit several stores to find what you want, which eats up more days and more lunch hours. However, looking through a stack of catalogs is a simple thing. One reason that catalog clothing sales are gaining over retail sales is that many consumers perceive catalog shopping as the quicker and easier alternative.

Retail Strategies and Tactics

If you study retailing at a business school or bring in a specialized designer, you will soon be drawing *planograms* of your shelves (diagrams showing how to layout and display a store's merchandise) and counting *SKUs* (stock-keeping units — one for each unique item you stock). Perhaps you will also be examining the statistics on sales volume from end-of-aisle displays (higher sales) versus middle of the aisle (lower) and from eye level displays (higher sales) versus bottom or top of the shelf (lower). Great. Go for it. However, I have to warn you that, while a technical approach has its place, this method is not the way to create a retail success story.

The real winners in retail are the result of creative thinking and good site selection, in that order. Those are the two big-picture issues that will determine whether your store has low or high performance. A creative, appealing store concept. In a spot that has the right sort of traffic and lots of it.

Traffic is a flow of target customers near enough to the store for its external displays and local advertising to draw them in. You want a great deal of traffic, whether it is foot traffic on a sidewalk, automobile traffic on a road or highway, or virtual traffic at a Web site. Retailers are dependent upon people walking, driving, or surfing into their stores. Customers won't come in big numbers unless you have plenty of people to draw from.

An old joke about retailing goes like this: "There are three secrets of success in the retail business — location, location, and location." Not very funny, really, unless you've ever tried to market a store that is in a poor location. And then you laugh pretty hard over the joke, but with a certain hysteria! Pick a location carefully, making sure that you have an excess of the right sort of traffic nearby. Think of designing a retail store like digging a pond. You wouldn't dig a pond unless running water was nearby to fill it. Yet people dig their retail ponds in deserts or up steep hills from the nearest flow of traffic all the time.

Nor would you dig a huge reservoir beside a small stream. You must suit your store to the amount and kind of traffic in its area, or move to find more appopriate traffic. In my small town, Amherst, Massachusetts, we have a two-block downtown shopping district. The district has dozens of store-fronts, and at any one time a handful of them are available for rent, because the stores in them have gone belly-up like fish without water. The stores usually stay vacant for a few months, and then another brave soul comes along to try his luck. Sometimes the person is a hapless entrepreneur who is the next to fail. Sometimes the next failure is a big company that ought to have known better (McDonald's came and went recently, unable to generate enough sales from a store to keep it open).

I make something of a game of guessing who will fail and who will make good. Doing so is not hard, really. The reason is that downtown Amherst does not have heavy traffic. The town is small, and even with a large college nearby, not enough people are around to make the sidewalks crowded.

Any retailer has to find a way to appeal to a broad cross-section of that traffic or has to find something so compelling to sell that people flock from out of town to visit the store. This attraction power is termed *draw,* and few retail concepts are so unique as to be able to draw traffic from beyond their immediate area. But some do.

For example, a jewelry store in town has such a good selection of merchandise that it draws far more traffic than the surrounding stores. And its owner is careful to stimulate this traffic through a direct mail program and by giving the store a unique and highly visible appearance — the store is in a huge, ornate, yellow Victorian house on the edge of town. The store's strategy is based on the one thing that old joke about retailing leaves out — the store *concept.* And concept is a creative mix of merchandising strategy and atmosphere that you can use to give your store higher-than-average drawing power.

Merchandising strategies

Whether you retail services or goods, you need to think about your merchandising strategy. You do have one, whether you know it or not — and if you don't know it, then your strategy is based on conventions in your industry and needs a kick in the seat of the pants to make it more distinctive. *Merchandising strategy,* the selection and assortment of products offered, is generally the most important source of competitive advantage or disadvantage for retailers.

I want to encourage a creative approach to merchandising. Innovations in merchandising are the reason for the majority of success stories in retailing. So you ought to be thinking of new merchandising options daily — and trying out the most promising ones as often as you can afford to. Following are some existing strategies, which may give you ideas for your business. Perhaps no one has tried them in your industry or region, or perhaps they will suggest novel variations to you.

General merchandise retailing

This strategy works because it brings together an assortment of products that is both wide and deep, thus allowing customers to easily find what they want — regardless of what the product might be. Department stores and variety stores fall into this category. *Hypermarkets,* the European expansion of the grocery store that includes some department store product lines, are another example of the general merchandise strategy. In the U.S., both Kmart and Wal-Mart are leaders because they offer more variety (and sometimes better prices) than nearby competitors. The warehouse store (like Home Depot or Staples) is also an example of general merchandise retailing. And as this varied list of examples suggests, this strategy can be implemented in many ways.

Limited-line retailing

This strategy emphasizes depth over variety. In New England, the Bread & Circus chain of grocery stores specializes in natural and organic food products; as a result, the chain can offer far greater choice in this area than the average grocery store. Similarly, a bakery can offer more and better varieties of baked goods because that's all a bakery sells.

Limited-line retailing is especially common in professional and personal services. Most accounting firms just do accounting. Most chiropractic offices just offer chiropractic services. Most law firms just practice law. For some reason, little innovation has been seen in the marketing of services.

Perhaps you can combine several complementary services into a less limited line than your competitors. If you can do so without sacrificing quality or depth of offerings, then you will give customers greater convenience and that should make you a winner.

After all, the limited line strategy only makes sense to customers if they gain something in quality or selection in exchange for the lack of convenience. Regrettably, many limited line retailers fail to make good on this implied promise — and they are easily run over when a less limited line is introduced nearby. What makes, say, the local stationery or shoe store's selection better than what a Staples or Kmart offers in a more convenient setting? If you're a small businessperson, then you better make sure that you have plenty of good answers to that question! Know what makes your merchandise selection, concept, and/or location different and better than that of your monster competitors.

Scrambled merchandising

Consumers have preconceived notions about what product lines and categories belong together. Looking for fresh produce in a grocery store makes sense these days, because dry goods and fresh produce have been combined by so many retailers. But 50 years ago, the idea would seem radical, because fresh produce used to be sold by specialized limited-line retailers. When grocery stores combined these two categories, they were using a *scrambled merchandising* strategy, one in which unconventional combinations of product lines are used. Today, the meat department, bakery, deli section, seafood department, and many others combine naturally in a modern grocery store. And gas stations combine with fast food restaurants and convenience stores to offer pit stops for both car and driver. These scrambled merchandising concepts are now widely accepted. But newer experiments such as the introduction of clothing lines or coffee bars and bookshops into grocery stores are less common.

GREAT IDEA

Mix and match

Can you think of the perfect new combination of stores? How about a gym and a laundromat, so people can work out while washing their clothes? Or a "connections" store that offers the combined services of a flower shop, jewelry and gift store, card and stationery store, e-mail/Internet access service, gift wrapping and shipping service, and a computerized dating/introduction service? With all these under one roof, the store could serve any and all needs having to do with making or maintaining personal relationships. See? Coming up with novel combinations isn't hard — give it a try!

Scrambling is a great way to innovate. It gets at the essence of creativity, because many people define creativity as the search for unexpected but pleasing combinations of things or ideas. I hope that you will pursue this strategy. But I want to warn you that this strategy should never be employed just for your convenience as a marketer. Too often, retailers add a novel product line just because doing so is easy. They know someone in another industry who can handle the line for them, or they have a chance to buy a failed business for peanuts. Those are the wrong sorts of reasons. Scrambling only works if you approach it *from the customer's point of view* by seeking new combinations that may have special customer appeal.

For example, several innovators around the U.S. have stumbled independently upon the concept of combining a coffee shop and an Internet access service into one retail store. The result is a natural — a coffee shop where you can enjoy your espresso while cruising the Internet or flirting with another customer online. Here is a new combination that adds up to more than the sum of its parts, giving customers a pleasurable new retail experience.

Atmosphere

A store's *atmosphere* is the image that it projects based on how it is decorated and designed. Atmosphere is an intangible — you can't easily measure or define it. But you *can* feel it. And when the atmosphere feels comforting, or exciting, or enticing, then this feeling draws people into the store and enhances their shopping experience. So you need to pay close attention to atmosphere.

Sophisticated retailers hire architects and designers to create the right atmosphere and then spend far too much on fancy lighting, new carpets, and racks to implement their plans. Sometimes this approach works, but sometimes it doesn't. My biggest concern with this approach is that at any point in time, most of the professional designers are in agreement about what stores should look and feel like. And that means your store will look like everyone else's.

Instead, I think you should develop the concept for your store. If you think the right atmosphere is a virtual tropical forest, then hire some crazy artists and designers to turn your store into a tropical forest! Rainforest Cafe did so a few years ago, creating a fantasy environment they call "a wild place to shop and eat." Their first store, in the Mall of America in Minnesota, was so successful that they are opening others around the country.

Maybe you really like old-fashioned steam engines. Great. Make that the theme of your children's toy store or men's clothing boutique. Run model train tracks around the store, put up huge posters of on-coming steam engines, and incorporate the occasional train whistle into your background music. Some people will love it, others will think you're nuts. But at least nobody will ever forget your store.

The reason atmospherics are important is that consumers increasingly seek more from retail shopping than specific products. In consumer societies, shopping is an important activity in its own right. Surveys suggest that less than a quarter of shoppers in malls went there in search of a specific item. Consumers often use shopping to alleviate boredom and loneliness, avoid dealing with chores or problems in their lives, seek fulfillment of their fantasies, or simply to entertain themselves. If that's what motivates many shoppers, then you need to take such motivations into consideration when you design your store.

Perhaps the most honest and simple thing you can do is to provide some entertainment for your customers. Just as a humorous ad entertains people and, thereby, attracts their attention long enough to communicate a message, so, too, can a store entertain for long enough to expose shoppers to its merchandise.

The Disney Stores use this strategy effectively, because Disney designers have so much experience in the entertainment business. For example, they continuously play movies on a large-screen television in the back of stores. Shoppers often walk back to have a look at the movie, which draws them through the store twice — going in and going out. As a result, they walk past much of the merchandise and are, therefore, more likely to see something they want or need. (Well, something they want. I don't think anybody really *needs* the stuff in a Disney Store. But that doesn't seem to hurt their sales in the least!)

Price and quality strategies

Retail stores generally have a distinct place in the range of possible price and quality combinations. Some stores are obviously upscale boutiques, specializing in the finest merchandise — for the highest prices. Others are middle-class in their positioning, while still others offer the worst junk from liquidators, but sell it for so little that almost anybody can afford it. In this way, retailing still maintains the old distinctions of social class, even though they are hardly visible anymore in other aspects of modern U.S. and European society.

For you as a retailer, this distinction means that customers will get confused about who you are unless you let them know where you stand on the class scale. Does your store have an upper-class pedigree, or is it upper-middle, middle, or lower-middle class? Do you see your customers as white-collar or blue-collar? And so forth.

After you make a decision about how to place your store, then you are ready to decide what price strategy to pursue. In general, the higher-class the store's image, the higher prices the store can charge. But the real secret to success is to *price a step below your image*. That way, customers feel like they are buying first-class products for second-class prices. And that makes them very happy indeed!

Retail sales

Many retailers take a passive approach. They put the products on the shelves or display racks and wait for customers to pick them up and bring them to the counter. Others are a bit more proactive. They have staff walking the aisles or floors, looking for customers who may need some help. But few retailers go all the way and actually put trained salespeople on the floor to work the customers.

Various numbers are thrown around the industry, but the ones I've heard suggest that active efforts to close a sale are made by less than 20 percent of retailers. Probably much less. Even the less active strategy of asking customers if they need help is used only 20 percent of the time. In the majority of cases, nobody even approaches the customer.

Sometimes that makes sense, I guess. But in general, if people walk into a store, they are considering making a purchase, which makes them likely prospects. To me, that means that somebody ought to find out what their wants or needs are and try to meet them! The effort does not need to be pushy — in fact, the effort mustn't be pushy or you'll reduce return visits —

Going in for the close

Retail employees these days are rarely trained or empowered to act as salespeople. They rarely try to close a sale. They hardly ever even get involved in helping the customer make a selection. In part, this problem is because stores have too few employees for them to be able to spend much time with customers. Big mistake. And in part, the problem exists because store managers hire the least-qualified workers for the lowest possible wages, and you don't really want those employees talking with your customers.

What I recommend if you are in the retail business is to try an experiment. One day a week, put extra staff on the floor, and make sure that your most experienced people are in the sales roles. Perhaps managers could do this job for the duration of the experiment. Then compare your sales on those days with comparable days in which you don't have extra staff devoted to sales and customer support. In the majority of cases, I think you'll find that the extra expense is more than repaid by increased sales. And over the long haul, customers may also see your store as more friendly and service-oriented, and, thus, give you increased repeat business, too.

but the effort should be made nonetheless. Find out what customers are looking for, offer them whatever you have that seems relevant, and ask them if they'd like to make a purchase. The last part, asking them for the purchase, is especially important. In selling, that's called the *close,* and when you attempt to close sales, you up the sales rate in every case. See Chapter 17 for more details.

By the way, if you want to get plugged in to a wide variety of publications, conferences, and other events of interest to U.S. retailers, call the National Retail Federation in Washington, DC, at 202-783-7971 and the International Council of Shopping Centers in New York at 212-421-8181. And if you need to learn more about store planning or track down experienced store planners, try The Institute of Store Planners at 25 North Broadway, Tarrytown, NY 10591. Their phone number is 914-332-1806.

POP! How to Stimulate Sales at Point of Purchase

Point of purchase, or *POP,* is the place where customer meets product. It may be in the aisles of a store, or even on a catalog page or computer monitor,

Getting more fizz for your POP

For more information about POP, a directory of POP designers and manufacturers, or a calendar of trade shows and events for the industry, contact POPAI at 1660 L Street N.W., 10th Floor, Washington, DC 20036. You can reach POPAI by phone at 202-293-7000, and their fax number is 202-530-3030. Net surfers may prefer to e-mail them at popai@popai.org. I also recommend POPAI's *Point of Purchase Design Annual*, a book offering color photos and plans of hundreds of displays. Perusing the latest winners of merchandising awards is a great way to come up with your own winning POP or retail concepts. Finally, don't overlook the interactions between package design/labeling and POP (see Chapter 15) and also check out Chapter 10 for details of how to design and use signs and banners.

but wherever this encounter takes place, the principles of POP advertising apply. The Point of Purchase Advertising Institute is particularly relevant to retail design and point-of-purchase marketing, so have a quick look at the numbers in Table 16-1:

Table 16-1	Nature of Consumer's Purchase Decision	
	Supermarkets **% of Purchases**	**Mass Merchandise Stores** **% of Purchases**
Unplanned	60%	53%
Substitute	4%	3%
Generally planned	6%	18%
Specifically planned	30%	26%

Some purchases are planned outside of the store — 30 percent of supermarket purchases and 26 percent of mass merchandise purchases fall into this category. In these cases, customers make a rational decision about what stores to go to in order to buy what they want. Because they have a clear idea of what they mean to purchase, their purchases are not highly subject to marketing influence. Even so, the right merchandise selection, location, atmosphere, and price strategy will help get customers to choose your store for their planned purchases instead of a competing store. And the right store layout and point-of-purchase displays will help customers find what they want quickly and easily. So even with so-called specifically planned purchases, you do have an influence over what happens.

Furthermore (and this is the really good news for marketers), you have a far greater influence over the majority of purchases than you probably realize. All the studies that I've seen, including the preceding one from which I took those statistics in Table 16-1 (and also the statistic saying that three fourths of people visiting malls aren't looking for a specific item) all add up to the startling conclusion that:

> **Shoppers are remarkably aimless and suggestible!**

The fact that *between a half and three-fourths of all retail purchases are unplanned* is really incredible. What happened to the venerable shopping list? How do consumers get their checkbooks to balance with all that impulse buying? And why are they wandering aimlessly through stores in the first place — don't they have jobs or families or hobbies to keep them busy? Evidently not.

I don't pretend to understand our consumer society, I just write about it. While I can't explain the fact that the modern retail shopper is in some sort of zombie-like state much of the time, I can tell you that this fact makes point-of-purchase marketing incredibly important to all marketers of consumer goods and services. Whether you are a retailer, wholesaler, or producer, you need to recognize that an impulse decision will be made — either to buy your product or not to buy it — in the majority of cases. And that suggests you had better do what you can to sway that decision your way at point of purchase. Otherwise, the sale will go to the competitor who does.

When hunter-gatherers go shopping

Actually, I do have a pet theory about why consumers seem so easily influenced at point of purchase. My theory comes from the observation that for most of our history, human beings have made a living by hunting and gathering in natural environments. If you've never tried this, I'll tell you what it was like. You got up when you felt like it, made a nice breakfast out of yesterday's leftovers, rested a while to digest, then said, "Hey, I guess I'd better go find something to eat for dinner." Then the women and children grabbed their digging sticks and sacks, the old men went back to sleep, and the younger men tiptoed off with bows and arrows or spears to try their hand at hunting.

Most days, the hunting party followed tracks and examined spore for a few hours, then got hot and thirsty and so decided to come back to camp. Every now and then, of course, they'd chance upon an antelope or something and return with lots of fresh meat to roast over the fire.

Meanwhile, the women and children filled up their sacks with whatever they found that looked ripe and yummy. Fresh fruit or berries. Grains to pound into meal. Roots and tubers dug up with their sticks, along with the occasional find of fresh bird or turtle eggs and the like.

If you think of this scenario as shopping without the inconvenience of a cash register to fill, then you can understand modern shopping behavior far better, for it is based on this instinctive foraging behavior.

You can't plan foraging, not in a specific way. Sure, you may keep an eye on those berries and plan to come back and pick them when they are ripe — but that sort of preplanned foraging only works in a minority of cases. Most of the time, you have to be a skilled opportunist, acting on the hunch that a spot looks good and trusting your eyes and nose to guide you to a find. Or you have to revisit spots that were productive in the past. When you get home, you dump out your sacks, examine the haul, and decide what you're going to have for dinner.

The data available on how people shop makes little sense in the context of today's tight household budgets, but it's just about right for hunter-gatherers. My advice to marketers is to make product design/packaging, store design, and point-of-purchase display decisions with this hunter-gatherer model in mind. Tap into that ancient instinct of consumers to sniff out likely spots and then wander through them looking for ripe stuff to pop in your sack. Give consumers just enough challenge to make the terrain interesting, but make sure that winning this game is easy by making sure that customers find plenty of good stuff to bring home. Place things within eyeshot and easy reach (people don't carry those big sticks any more), and design and package products so they look ripe and appealing.

Oh, and one other thing. Remember that some shoppers are hunters at heart, not gatherers. These are the people who take great pleasure in the lengthy, dogged pursuit of a particular item. They will stalk one item from store to store, so they show up in surveys as making planned purchases. But they rarely buy the product the first time they see it, because they want to wait for the right opportunity to make their kill. To please these hunters, you need to offer certain high-involvement — versus routine purchase — items in a different way. Hide the products for hunters to discover and offer a special deal (in pricing or by bundling related products) so that they feel that this is indeed a "lucky shot" that they can't pass up.

Designing POP displays

To take the hunter-gather metaphor (from the preceding section) even further, you can boost sales by designing modern-day versions of bushes and trees from which consumers can pick your products. Free-standing floor displays have the biggest effect, but are least likely to be used by retailers. They take up too much floor space. Rack, shelf, and counter-based signs and displays aren't quite as powerful, but are more likely to be used by stores. Any really exciting and unusual display is likely to be used and work very well, because it will have a general impact on store traffic and sales, as well as boosting sales of the products it is designed to promote. Exciting displays add to the store's atmosphere or entertainment value, and store managers like that.

Because creativity is one of the keys to successful store concepts, it follows that creativity also drives POP success. Let me show you what I mean through an example that worked well and won design awards for its originality as well.

When Procter & Gamble introduced a new formulation of the Vicks 44 cough syrup, they created a point-of-purchase display (to be used freestanding or on a wall rack) that featured a rotating frame in which two clear bottles were on display. Each had some red syrup in it — one with Vicks 44, the other with a competing cough syrup. When customers rotated the frame to turn the bottles over, they could see that the Vicks 44 coated the inside of the bottle while the competition's syrup sloshed to the bottom. The point of this interactive display is to prove the unique selling proposition that Vicks 44 coats your throat better. I like this display because it is interactive — giving customers something interesting to do to build their involvement — and because it demonstrates the product's *USP* (its *unique selling proposition* — what makes it different from all competitors). Like a good advertisement, this POP display attracts attention, builds involvement, and then communicates a single, powerful point about the product.

Too often, POP displays don't do everything the Vicks 44 display does. They won't work well unless they

- ✔ **Attract attention:** Make them novel, entertaining, or puzzling to draw people to them.

- ✔ **Build involvement:** Give people something to think about or do in order to build their involvement in the display.

- ✔ **Sell the product:** Make sure that the display tells viewers what's so great about the product. The display must communicate the positioning and USP (hope you have one!). Simply putting the product on display is not enough. You have to sell the product, too, or the retailer won't see the point. Retailers can put products on display without marketers' help. What retailers want help in is *selling* those products.

You may have noticed I keep worrying about whether retailers will like and use POPs. This concern is a major issue according to David Rush, a principal at consumer-products consulting firm KSA, who estimates that between

50 and 60 percent of marketers' POPs never reach the sales floor. If you are a product marketer who is trying to get a POP display into retail stores, you face an uphill battle. The stats say that your display or sign had better be twice as good as average or it will simply be tossed into the nearest dumpster. (KSA, or Kurt Salmon Associates, is in Atlanta, Georgia, at 404-892-3436. Their fax number is 404-873-4834.)

Facts about POP

I've covered the principles of POP — now I'll give you some facts to help you develop and implement your own POP program.

1. Who should design and pay for POP — marketers or retailers?

In some cases, marketers design POPs and offer them to retailers as part of their marketing programs. In other cases, retailers develop their own POPs. The Point-of-Purchase Advertising Institute (POPAI) reports that the industry is about equally divided. In other words, half of all POP displays are purchased directly by retailers, the other half by marketers who then offer their materials to retailers. So the answer is a bit of both.

2. What kinds of POPs do marketers use?

Again, the Point-of-Purchase Advertising Institute is a helpful source of data. Their surveys reveal that spending on POPs is highest for permanent displays (generally, retailers make these purchases). Next in popularity (based on spending) are in-store media and sign options. And third in popularity are temporary displays. Yet marketers generally think about temporary displays first when talking about POP. Maybe marketers need to rethink their approach and redesign their programs to emphasize permanent displays and signs first, and temporary displays second.

3. How much will POP lift your sales?

Lift is the increase in sales of a product attributable to POP marketing. Researchers compare sales with and without POP to calculate lift (it's the difference between the two). You need to estimate lift in order to figure out what return you'll get for any particular investment in POP. First, I can tell you that, in general, accessories and routine repurchases have the highest lifts. Also significantly new products have high lifts if their POPs effectively educate consumers about their benefits. Second, I can give you a range of lift statistics (shown in Table 16-2), based on a detailed study of the question by the Point of Purchase Advertising Institute.

Table 16-2	Lift Statistics
POP Displays/Signs for:	*Typical Lift (%)*
Film/Photo-finishing	48
Socks/underwear/pantyhose	29
Dishwashing soaps	22
Cookies and crackers	18
Videos	12
Butter/margarine	6
Pet supplies	6
Stationery	5
Salty snacks	4
Salad dressing	3

4. How much of your marketing budget should you allocate to POP?

I can't tell you for certain, because every program has to be shaped by its unique circumstances. But I can tell you that POP advertising ranks third in spending among measured media in the U.S., which is a fact that surprised the heck out of me. (Television is first — around $30 billion, print second at about $25 billion, and POP third at $12 billion.) And that means POP is a far bigger medium than most marketers realize. Yet partly because this spending is spread out broadly among retailers, distributors and wholesalers, and producers, POP doesn't get the attention that other media do in most marketing programs and plans. Big mistake. Try to identify who in your distribution channel is involved in POPs that affect your sales, and work toward an integrated strategy and plan so that you can bring this hidden medium into the spotlight and make it work more effectively for your plan.

Chapter 17

Sales and Service Essentials

● ●

In This Chapter

▶ Deciding if personal selling is the key to your marketing

▶ Taking the Sales Ability Test to predict or improve your sales performance

▶ Managing the sales/service process

▶ Organizing a sales force

▶ Compensating a sales force

● ●

*A*t Black & Decker, sales and service to distributors and major retailers is as important as good products. Perhaps more important. According to Bruce Cazenave, a VP at Black & Decker, the *trade* — all those distributors and retailers who resell their products to the end user — has three high level requirements:

✔ Delivery support

✔ Field sales support

✔ Customer service

If the company does these three things well, it retains its trade customers and builds sales through them. If not, the company is liable to lose those trade customers to competitors — and that means losing all the end consumers they reach, too. And so sales and service — perhaps especially the service part of sales — is key to Black & Decker's success.

Black & Decker's requirements are not unlike those of millions of firms. Without close, personal relationships built up through numerous sales calls and strong service and support, this company's marketing would falter. If the same is true of your business — and you can find out by taking the test just a bit later in this chapter — then you need to make sales and service the focus of your marketing efforts.

If so, then you also need to be good at sales — or hire people who are. This chapter also includes a test for diagnosing sales ability and figuring out what areas need improvement. And it goes on to cover the details of managing and improving your sales process, organizing your sales force, hiring outside sales reps, and designing the right compensation plan to keep your salespeople highly motivated.

These are all difficult tasks, fraught with peril. Should you perform them well, however, the payoff is huge. A well-managed, well-organized sales force, with the right leads and a good sales presentation, can sell the dickens out of any decent product, and so I highly recommend a careful read of the topics in this chapter.

When to Emphasize Personal Selling

Sometimes *personal selling* — selling face to face — is essential to the marketing process, and when that is the case, then sales must be the main focus of marketing plans and activities. Any advertising, direct mail, telemarketing, event sponsorships, public relations — or anything else you may think of — has to take a back seat to sales. When sales is important, then it follows that sales is the most important point of influence over customers.

A focus on sales

The importance of personal selling was really brought home to me many years ago when I was invited to join the corporate staff of Consolidated Freightways (CF), a huge company providing transportation and logistics services to other businesses. With the deregulation of trucking and air-freight industries in the U.S. in the early '80s, this company faced a new level of competition and many new opportunities as well. And so its executives decided the company needed to enter the world of modern marketing, and I was asked to help build up a new marketing department as part of this initiative. We threw ourselves into modernizing CF's marketing, bringing modern survey research and planning to all the subsidiaries, initiating aggressive print advertising and publicity campaigns, developing sophisticated telemarketing and direct-mail programs, introducing new products, and so forth.

But after a while, I began to realize that all these new marketing components were not making a big difference. Try as we might, we could not change the customer's focus, which continued to be on their relationships with salespeople. Customers selected CF over the competition largely because of what happened in face-to-face encounters with salespeople. They largely ignored other marketing channels. And they did so for some very good reasons that were beyond our control. For example, whenever they had a problem, the salesperson was the one to call to sort things out. So that relationship is very important to customers, and the rest of the marketing program has to support it.

Are Personal Sales & Service the Key to Your Marketing Program?

❏ yes	❏ no	Our typical customer makes many small purchases and/or at least a few very large ones in a year.
❏ yes	❏ no	Our typical customer usually needs help figuring out what to buy and/or how to use the product.
❏ yes	❏ no	Our typical customer's business is highly complex and imposes unique requirements on our products/services.
❏ yes	❏ no	Our products/services are an important part of the customer's overall business process.
❏ yes	❏ no	Our customer is accustomed to working with sales-people and expects personal attention and assistance.
❏ yes	❏ no	Our competitors make regular sales calls on our customers and/or prospects.
❏ yes	❏ no	We have to provide customized service to retain a customer.

If you read the sidebar "A focus on sales," then you know that personal selling is the dominant influence over Consolidated Freightway's (CF) customers. Why? I think I know the answer:

✔ First, the freight transportation customer often has unique and complex needs because every business operation is different and transportation of raw materials and finished goods is typically critical to the success of a company's operations. Given the unique requirements of each customer, a face-to-face problem-solving and negotiation process is the best way to design and price a service offering for the individual customer.

✔ Second, customers depend on freight transportation on a daily basis, and so want to have a personal relationship with someone who can handle an urgent problem or facilitate a special request.

✔ Finally, CF's customers typically buy a fair amount of shipping — enough that their business is quite valuable, and, therefore, worth the trouble for a competing salesperson to try to steal. If CF didn't empha-size personal selling, its competitors would outsell it and take those customers away — regardless of how many CF ads they saw in magazines!

The same may be true about your business. If it is, then you know something very important, something that will allow you to focus your marketing program on personal selling and service.

All you have to do to gain this invaluable insight is sharpen your pencil and take a quick test. The following section asks you seven questions. If you answer yes to four or more of them, then personal selling has to be the main focus of your marketing. While you will certainly want to do many other things too, be sure to think of the rest of your marketing effort as supporting the personal sales process, because the personal sales process is going to be the key to your success — or failure. And that means *you will need to give careful thought to how you hire, manage, organize, support, and motivate salespeople. Their performance will determine whether your marketing succeeds or fails.*

Retaining Customers through Great Service

The other thing I learned from CF is that sales and service go hand in hand. Where personal selling is important — as it is in many business-to-business markets, and in a variety of consumer markets as well — then you can bet that customer service will also be key. Why? Because while personal selling produces new customers, personal service keeps them. If you don't know how to keep new customers, then you have no reason to produce new customers. You'll just lose them.

If your customer base *churns,* or turns over, at a rate of, say, more than 10 percent a year, then I bet you have a customer service problem. Find out by comparing customer lists from two consecutive years — or asking your salespeople (if you have any) to gather the data if you cannot do so easily from your central customer database or billing records.

Note: Sometimes companies define a lost customer as one whose business has fallen by more than half, which gives you a more conservative measure than one based only on customers who have stopped ordering entirely.

To figure your churn rate, follow these steps:

1. **Compare last year's and this year's customer lists to find out how many customers you lost during the year.**

   Ignore new customers for this calculation.

2. **Count the total number of customers on the first of the two lists.**

   That's your base, where you started.

3. Divide the number of lost customers (from Step 1) by the total number of customers (from Step 2) to get your turnover or churn rate.

For example, if you started the year with 1,500 customers and lost 250, then your turnover rate is $^{250}/_{1500}$ or nearly 17 percent. If that's the case, then you fail my 10 percent test and had better find out what is wrong with your customer service!

Do You Have What It Takes?

Some people seem born to sell, while others are doomed to fail. But the rest of the population, well, they muddle along, struggling to improve their sales ability and wondering if they really have the right stuff. Most people are neither sales stars nor duds, but are somewhere in the middle — capable of great performances, but not so gifted that the performances come naturally.

And so companies are increasingly testing sales ability as a requirement of the job. The available tests are all horribly subjective — and many are extremely poorly written (a variety of printed evaluation instruments are sold to the HR departments of firms, but I don't recommend any of them). Training programs are designed to evaluate sales ability as a way to diagnose areas for improvement. In spite of all this testing and training, companies still seem to hire the wrong people, evidenced by the fact that sales force turnover is as high as 70 percent per year on average according to some studies! Where sales force turnover is high, so is customer turnover — so you need to find and keep the right salespeople.

I cannot recommend any single screening instrument without substantial reservations, but I do believe that a significant benefit comes from assessing sales ability. So, I'm going to follow the old rule that says "If you want something done right, you better do it yourself."

Following is my version of a *test of sales ability*. Take five minutes to answer the questions and then another couple minutes to score them. At the end, you will have some useful feedback about your overall sales ability right now, plus the areas to focus on if you want to improve your overall score in the future.

Employers take note. This test will not guarantee someone's success — your management and the rest of your marketing program are as key to her performance as is her sales ability. But on the other hand, anyone who you think ranks low on most of these test items is definitely *not* ready to take over an important sales territory.

Measure Your Sales Ability

Check any statements that fit you well. If a statement does not fit you, leave it blank.

1 ❑   I feel good about myself much of the time.

2 ❑   I usually say the right thing at the right time.

3 ❑   People seek out my company.

4 ❑   I don't get discouraged, even if I fail repeatedly.

5 ❑   I am an excellent listener.

6 ❑   I can read people's moods and body language with ease.

7 ❑   I project warmth and enthusiasm when I first meet people.

8 ❑   I am good at sensing and bringing out the real reasons behind a negative answer.

9 ❑   I can see many ways to define a problem and understand its causes.

10 ❑   I am skilled at drawing out other people's concerns and problems.

11 ❑   I know enough about business to help others solve their problems with ease.

12 ❑   I am so trustworthy and helpful that I quickly convince people to work with me in true collaborations.

13 ❑   I manage my time so well that I am able to get to everything that is important in a work day.

14 ❑   I focus on the "big picture" goals that matter most to me and my company rather than always reacting to the latest crisis or chore.

15 ❑   I can balance the need for finding new customers with the demands of maintaining and strengthening all existing customer relationships.

16 ❑   I keep looking for and finding ways to be more effective and efficient.

17 ❑   I find that for me, a sense of accomplishment is even more rewarding than money.

18 ❑   My internal standards and expectations are higher than any imposed on me by others.

19 ❑   I don't care how long it takes to succeed at a task — I know I'll succeed in the end.

20 ❑   I feel I deserve the respect and admiration of my customers and associates.

Scoring

A. Positive Personality?

Total number of checks on statements 1 through 4:_____

(Less than 3 checks = Need improvement on personal attitude, emotional resiliency, and self-confidence.)

B. Interpersonal Skills?

Total number of checks on statements 5 through 8:_____

(Less than 3 checks = Need improvement on communication and listening skills, including your ability to control your own nonverbal communications and read others' body language.)

C. Solution-Finding Skills?

Total number of checks on statements 9 through 12:_____

(Less than 3 checks = Need improvement on problem-finding, creative problem-solving, and collaborative negotiating skills.)

D. Self-Management Skills?

Total number of checks on statements 13 through 16:_____

(Less than 3 checks = Need improvement on organization, strategy, and focus skills.)

E. Self Motivation?

Total number of checks on statements 17 through 20:_____

(Less than 3 checks = Need to build your personal motivation and learn how to find rewards in the pleasures of doing a job well and accomplishing a goal.)

F. Overall Level of Sales Ability?

Total number of checks, all statements (1 through 20):_____

Total Number of Checks	*Score*
0 - 5	Guaranteed to fail.
6 - 9	Low sales ability. Not likely to succeed.
10 - 12	Low sales ability. With improvement, may be moderately capable.
13 - 15	Moderate sales ability. Capable of improvement.
16 - 18	High sales ability. Capable of improvement.
19 - 20	Guaranteed to succeed. Superstar potential.

If you checked a total of 13 or more, you have enough ability to be out there on the road making sales calls right now. However, this doesn't mean you're perfect. If you checked a total of less than 19 or 20, you should work on your weak areas — and when you do, your sales success rate should go up.

Making the Sale

Sales is a process — a sometimes painful process. If you think of sales in this way, you can divide and conquer. You can divide sales into multiple steps and then focus on one step at a time as you prepare a sales plan or look for ways to improve your sales effectiveness. As with any complex process, a weak link always exists. When you look at the steps in your own sales process, try to find the one you do worst right now. That's the one to focus on!

Figure 17-1 displays the sales/service process as a flow chart. Note that the chart does not flow automatically from beginning to end. You may be forced to cycle back to an earlier stage if things go wrong. But ideally, you never lose a prospect or customer forever — they just recycle into sales leads, and a new effort is mounted to win them over.

I use Figure 17-1 for real-world training, and so I drew it very differently from the ones in the sales textbooks and company training programs. The biggest difference is that I integrated the sales and service processes. Why? Because that's real-world selling. You can't stop when you close a sale and write the order. Your competitors certainly won't stop trying to win that account! So you need to think of a completed sale as the beginning of a relationship-building process. More sales calls, further presentations and efforts to find new ways to serve the customer — these should be your focus after you close a sale.

Not only that, but you must also *anticipate problems*. You always have a problem at some point — something goes wrong that upsets, disappoints, even angers your customer. Trust me — it happens, no matter how good you think your company is.

Therefore, the sales process has to include a *service recovery* step. That means you have to figure out how to detect a service problem — how good is your communication with that customer? Make sure that the customer knows to call his salesperson when that problem occurs. (If you think you could use even more help in the customer service arena, check out a copy of *Customer Service For Dummies* (IDG Books Worldwide, Inc.) by Karen Leland and Keith Bailey.)

How well can the salesperson respond to a problem? If the salesperson is over-scheduled with sales calls, he or she cannot take the time to solve problems. So budget, say, one in ten sales calls as *service recovery time* to prepare for this contingency. (Over time, you should be able to drive down

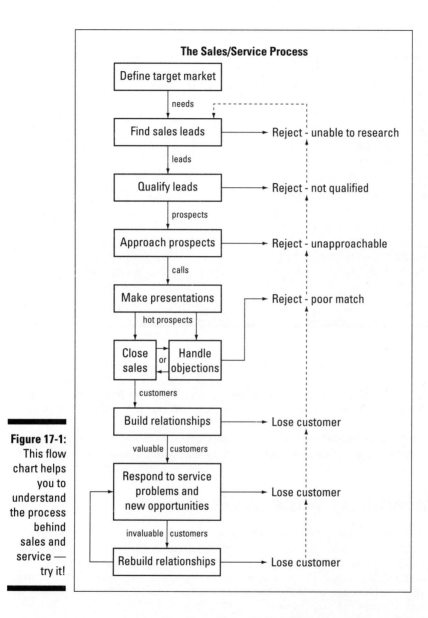

Figure 17-1:
This flow chart helps you to understand the process behind sales and service — try it!

the need for recoveries; perhaps you will only need to budget 1 in 20 calls next year.) And keep in mind that the salesperson needs some resources in addition to time in order to solve customer problems and rebuild relationships. Give the salesperson some spending authority so she can make the customer whole and turn their anger into satisfaction. The most faithful customers are the ones who have had a big problem that you managed to solve in a fair and generous manner, so anything invested in service recovery is time and money well spent!

A card for every occasion?

You know that good communications helps retain customers and is also the key to finding out about problems so that you can begin service recovery efforts immediately.

Some salespeople have discovered that a brief personal note, penned inside an attractive greeting card, is just the thing to build or maintain a customer relationship. Having trouble making an appointment? Try writing the prospect a note on a nice card. Too busy to stop by and thank a client for a recent order or apologize for a late shipment? Try sending a personally-signed card. This quick form of communication is also quite personal.

Your local card shop is a potential source, but you may also want to look into the offerings of IntroKnocks, a fairly new, and quite successful, company specializing in cards for salespeople. The company is located in New York City, at 212-967-6185, and its product line caters to sales-oriented messages like "Thank you for your time" and "I look forward to speaking with you again." (I wish *I'd* thought of that idea! I'd be in the card business today.)

I'm going to look briefly at several other issues that are key to making that sales/service process run smoothly and efficiently. In many companies, the most important steps are those in which sales leads are found and qualified, because — as in any process — the "garbage in, garbage out" rule applies.

Don't throw garbage leads into your sales/service process. Make sure that you feed your sales process with a constant flow of quality sales leads.

Generating sales leads

Lynden Air Freight in Seattle, Washington, uses a new multi-step system to generate qualified sales leads for its 60 salespeople. David Rosenzweig, the firm's director of marketing, says that the close ratio for sales calls improved by 70 percent after the new system was instituted, which is a pretty good advertisement for the system! Here is how it works: Start by pulling the names of potential prospects from a CD database of U.S. companies called *Dun & Bradstreet's MarketPlace*. This source groups companies by SIC code (a U.S. government designation based on product type — see Chapter 6 for a listing), location, and size (as indicated by annual sales), so you can target companies by industry and city and eliminate any that seem too small, for example.

Next, you can use a telemarketing firm (or a temp telemarketer) to call each of these leads, find the appropriate decision-maker, and conduct a brief survey on the industry.

Finally, analyze survey responses to identify prospects who are interested in the kind of services or products that you provide. These leads, now qualified by the telemarketers, are ready for salespeople who can use them to set up personal meetings with the decision-makers.

I hate to argue with success, but one thing about many companies' lead-generation systems troubles me: It is commonplace these days to give the telemarketers a *survey script* for those calls they make to qualify the leads. The reason is that people are more likely to answer a survey than talk to a salesperson. But this is a deceptive practice. As a card-carrying member of the American Marketing Association, I happen to recall that its code of ethics prohibits "selling or fund-raising under the guise of conducting research." Why? First, the practice is deceptive, abusing the respondent's trust. (And deception in sales can run afoul of *fraud laws* — so may be illegal as well as unethical. Please see Chapter 13, Legal and Ethical Issues, in Lewicki, Hiam and Olander, *Think Before You Speak* [Wiley, 1996], to keep out of legal trouble when selling or negotiating a sale.) Second, deceptive prospecting irritates respondents so that if it is widely done, people will stop participating in legitimate marketing research. That would be a big problem for marketers. You can use the same multistep process without deceiving leads just by making sure your sources are good and your telemarketers well-trained.

So do use a multistep screening process to generate qualified leads. Pull company names from any accurate database. And by all means, have somebody call the leads to find out if they qualify for a sales visit. Just don't pretend you are doing something else — like a survey. An honest telemarketing script can work. As long as your questions are short, to the point, and clear, the majority of decision-makers will take time to answer you. You can get the full benefits without any dishonesty. The multistep information gathering and screening makes this method a success.

And remember, telemarketers are the first people from your company to talk with decision-makers at these prospects, so make sure that they are well-spoken and polite. Better yet, have your salespeople select and train your telemarketers so they have control over that vital first impression.

Forget cold calling on households

The classic retail salesperson walks a residential block, ringing doorbells to pitch brooms, encyclopedias, aluminum siding, or other household products.

Forget that. This method no longer works in most North American and European countries. Nobody's home at most houses in the daytime anymore, and the few people who are home are afraid to admit a stranger carrying a large suitcase — or ought to be. Some nonprofit organizations (like Greenpeace) canvas door-to-door at dinnertime with moderate success — if they pick neighborhoods where their name is well known and their cause popular. But this tactic doesn't work for most salespeople. Cold calling door-to-door is dead.

So how do you use personal selling to reach households? At Encyclopaedia Britannica, which eliminated its traditional sales force ten years ago, the answer is to generate leads through advertising and referrals. Then do follow-up by telemarketing, or in person if absolutely necessary. The trick to eliminating cold calling on homeowners is to get really good at generating sales leads — and to use many other marketing program components for the purpose of getting leads.

Another alternative is to use a Web page or on-line newsletter to reach out for prospects and generate visits and inquiries that you can turn into leads. See Chapter 7 for how to use this hot new technique to supply your salespeople with better leads.

Consider following the lead of a couple of the most successful cosmetics companies. At Avon, the solution to reaching households is to *network* through personal and professional contacts in order to set up appointments — usually after working hours. This strategy gets through people's natural suspicions and busy schedules. In North America alone, Avon has 445,000 salespeople — evidence that person-to-person selling is not dead in the retail industry. It just has to been done differently, and with a bit more finesse, than in days of old. Mary Kay uses a similar strategy with success as well. Its salespeople typically schedule a personal showing or a neighborhood event through their network of contacts, allowing sales representatives to sell cosmetic products in the home with success.

Great sales presentations and consultations

The sales presentation is the critical step in which the salesperson must convince the prospect to become a customer, and thus is also a common source of trouble. Only the truly great sales presentation can persuade prospects to become customers at a high rate of success.

What makes a sales presentation great? Success. Any presentation that works, that gets customers to say "yes" quickly and often, is an exceptional presentation. *Any* presentation can be a success — so be prepared to experiment and think creatively about this task.

REAL WORLD

A consultative approach

Here is how Wallace Computer Services, Inc. describes what they do in a recent Annual Report:

> *Wallace manufactures and distributes a wide range of information management products, services and solutions that help companies minimize costs, improve information processing efficiency, and simplify and accelerate business transactions.*

And I thought they were in the business of printing labels and forms. They are, sort of. But they also invest a lot of time in figuring out how to help their customers reduce inventory costs, outsource material distribution, eliminate out-of-stock situations, and get rid of the need for forms and paper records. They deliver benefits like quicker turnaround on their clients' order fulfillment and customer service — real solutions to real business problems. And their customers love it — Wallace's sales and profits keep going up and customer turnover is low. This approach — offering help and expertise to improve your customers' lives or boost their profits — may be right for you. Especially if your product can be adapted to a wide variety of customer needs and problems. (Can it? Give this issue some serious thought.)

For each specific market and company, that great sales presentation will be *different*. Don't believe what's being said these days — that the only way to sell is through a lengthy consultative style in which you do in-depth research on your customer, diagnose your customer's business needs, and then, endless hours or months later, finally show that customer how your products can be used to meet those needs in a creative way. Sure, that works well for some companies — like Wallace Computer Services, Inc. (Hillside, Illinois), where some of my past marketing students work as salespeople. See the nearby sidebar, "A consultative approach," for more details.

But, BUT, consultative selling may not be right for your company. Maybe you can't see any obvious ways to sell valuable business services along with your product. You just want to deliver an excellent product and let the customer worry about what to do with it. If so, the last thing you want your salespeople to do is to pretend that they are management consultants.

Or — and this is increasingly common — perhaps you *could* solve customers' problems, but customers won't give you the time. Bringing a salesperson up to speed about a business in order for him to be able to solve the company's problems takes considerable time. In many markets the buyers can't be bothered, in which case you can forget consultative selling. What you need is a good old-fashioned *canned approach.* You need something like

Key Medical's one-minute sales presentation. Review their approach (in the nearby sidebar, "The 60-second presentation") and see if a similar script might work for you.

A simple, canned approach is just as good as a sophisticated consultative approach, because the approach works in the context for which it is designed. Be sure to tailor your sales style to accomodate your customers' needs.

The 60-second presentation

Key Medical Supply's president, Matt Hession, wanted independent pharmacies to sell his medical equipment to their customers.

Wheelchairs, hospital beds, whatever may be needed for home care, Key Medical can deliver, set up, and teach the customer how to use the equipment. But how to reach patients who need this equipment in their homes? Hession realized that local pharmacies are great distribution channels for his services. But he knew that the independent pharmacist is already scrambling, between the daily demands of his business and the growing competition from big chains. These pharmacists have no time, and no extra money, to add a line of medical equipment from Key Medical in their stores.

So Hession figured out how to make it easy and cheap for the pharmacist to sell medical equipment. All the pharmacist does is display information about Key Medical's equipment and services. If a customer asks, the pharmacy calls Key Medical's free phone number, and Key takes over from there — paying the pharmacy a generous sales commission for finding the customer.

But even with a better product, Hession found making the sale to the pharmacist a difficult task. The pharmacists are too busy to talk to salespeople. The solution is a carefully scripted presentation that takes only *one minute* to deliver. A Key sales representative finds the clerk nearest the counter behind which the pharmacist is working. He says (in a voice loud enough for the pharmacist to hear), "I know the pharmacist is busy, but when he has a moment, I have a one-minute presentation." (Here he starts to unbuckle his watch to show he is serious.) "And he can leave his wallet in his pocket."

With that opening, he generally arouses the interest of the pharmacist, who is amused by this unlikely approach to selling. Within a few minutes, a Key sales representative is invited behind the counter to deliver his one-minute presentation. He introduces himself, holds up his watch to time the presentation, and launches into it. The script is carefully designed to show the pharmacist how he can offer a special service to his customers that those competing chain stores don't, and the script also makes clear that the pharmacist won't be spending significant time or money to get into this new line of business. Then the minute is up, the sales representative leaves a copy of his "partnership agreement" (which includes details of how the pharmacist earns commissions), and gets out of there with the promise of a follow-up phone call next week.

Hundreds of independent pharmacies now offer Key Medical's products across the states of Texas and Louisiana. All because of a sales presentation that turns cold calls into hot prospects in 60 seconds!

Organizing the Sales Force

Who does what, when, and where? Such organizational questions plague many a sales or marketing manager, and they can make a big difference to sales force productivity. Should salespeople be run out of local, regional, or national offices? Should they be based in offices where staff provide daily support and their boss can supervise their activities closely? Or should they be set free to operate on the road, maximizing the number of calls they make — and communicating with the company through high-tech lap-top computers instead of through regional offices? Or — if your business is a small one — should the owner do all the selling or does it make sense to bring in a salesperson on commission? I don't know. Honestly. These decisions depend upon your situation. But I can help *you* decide by giving you an idea of the options available — several exist — and also by sharing some of the conventional wisdom that helps you assess your particular situation.

How many salespeople do you need?

If you have an existing sales force, then you can examine the performance of each territory to decide whether more salespeople would help, or if perhaps you could do with less. Are some territories rich in prospects that salespeople just don't get to? Then consider splitting those territories. Also consider splitting, or adding a second person to create a sales team, if you are experiencing high customer turnover in a territory. Turnover probably indicates a lack of service and follow-up visits. Alternatively, if you see some territories that have little potential (estimating sales potential is covered in Chapter 6), then you may be able to merge them with other territories. (Similarly, the small business owner should consider adding commissioned salespeople if he or she is unable to cover all prospects adequately due to time or travel constraints.)

You can also use another, more systematic approach — this approach is essential when you have to design a sales force from scratch. Study your market in order to decide how many sales calls you want made over a year-long period. The process is not really very complicated and is explained in detail in the nearby sidebar, "How many salespeople does it take to sell a lightbulb?"

Hire your own or use reps?

The most basic choice is whether to do it yourself or subcontract. Good sales companies exist in most industries that take on the job of hiring and managing salespeople for you. Called *sales representatives* (or reps), they usually work for a straight commission of between 10 and 20 percent depending upon the industry and how much room is in the pricing structure for their commission. Also, in areas where more work needs to be done — customer support through consultative selling and customized service — then reps earn, and deserve, a higher commission.

If your company is small or your product line short, I recommend using sales reps. They are the best option whenever you have *scale problems* that make justifying the cost of hiring your own dedicated salespeople somewhat difficult. Scale problems arise when your product line is too short, which means that salespeople don't have very much to sell to customers and each sales call produces such small total orders that they don't cover the cost of the call. What reps usually do is handle many companies' product lines so that they have a larger portfolio of products to show when they call on a client than your own independent salesperson would. Many product lines spread the cost of that sales call over more products, which may make the sales call more valuable for the buyer as well. If you sell too few products, a busy buyer may not be willing to take the time to listen to your salesperson's presentation — so again, the rep has a scale advantage.

How many salespeople does it take to sell a lightbulb?

One to hold it and ten to convince it to turn? I'm not quite sure what the best answer is to this question, but I do know how you can determine the number of salespeople you need to sell your product or service. To find your personal answer to this burning question, follow these steps:

1. **Count how many potential customers you have in your entire market.**

2. **Decide what proportion/how many of those customers you want to call on.**

3. **Decide how many calls you want made over the next year for each customer on average (for example, two a month or 24 per year).**

4. **Multiply Step 2 by Step 3.**

   Doing so gives you the total sales calls needed for the entire year.

5. **Decide how many calls one person can reasonably make in a day.**

The answer depends on the nature of the call and the travel time between customers.

6. **Multiply this daily figure (in Step 5) by the number of working days in your company's calendar.**

7. **Divide the total number of calls needed per year (from Step 4) by the number of calls one salesperson can make per year (from Step 6).**

   Doing so gives you the number of salespeople needed to make all those calls.

For example, 10,000 sales calls needed next year, divided by 1,000 calls per salesperson per year, means you need a sales force of 10 people to execute your plan. If you only have five on staff, you'd better hire five more, or bring on some sales reps to help your staff — if you can't get authority for either plan, scale back your sales goals by half. You'll never sell that lightbulb with only five salespeople.

However, if you can possibly justify hiring and running your own dedicated salespeople, by all means do! You will have much more control, better feedback from the market, and you will find that a dedicated sales force generally outsells a sales rep by between two and ten times as much. Why? Because of the dedicated salesperson's focus and dependence on your product. Often, the rep doesn't care what he or she sells, as long as something is bought. And so reps tend to make the easy sales, which may not be yours!

Finding good sales reps

How do you find sales reps? The obvious doesn't work — you won't find them listed in any telephone directory. I don't know why, but rep firms prefer that you find them by networking. Perhaps doing so avoids their being pestered with lots of requests from companies that don't know the industry and don't have decent products. But if you want to find reps, you have to do it on the reps' terms, which means either getting a word-of-mouth referral or meeting them at a trade show or industry conference.

As far as word-of-mouth referrals go, I recommend asking the companies that reps sell to for their opinions as to who are the best rep firms. After all, these are the customers you need the reps to sell your product to, so their opinion is the most important! You can also get referrals from other companies that sell (noncompeting) products through the same kinds of reps. And if you have some reps already, they can tell you about firms that cover other territories.

I also highly recommend networking for reps at trade shows in your industry. Reps attend the trade shows, and many of them rent booths in order to represent their products there. You can find them just by wandering the exhibition hall, using your eyes and nose, and asking occasional questions.

If you're in the U.S., consider this: American Exhibition Services (AES) has introduced a neat service at the many trade shows it manages; marketers can find reps more easily and vice versa. What you do is call AES before a show (at 205-323-2211 — why don't you call right now to get their show schedule?). Ask them to register your product or product line with EXPOMAGIC, a computerized kiosk that provides information and assistance for reps and those who seek them. EXPOMAGIC displays a list of product categories available by region. Reps select products and then get a printed list of the companies offering them. If you list your products, you are likely to get calls from any reps at the show who wish to add products such as yours to their line.

Manage your reps — with an iron glove!

After you have reps lined up for each territory, your work has only just begun. You must, absolutely *must,* monitor their sales efforts on a regular basis. Which rep firms are the best and worst sellers? Usually 10 or 15 percent of the reps make almost all your sales. If you notice such a pattern developing, you can quickly put the others on notice. And if they don't heat up in a hurry, you can replace them. With constant nourishment and weeding, you can get that 10 percent up to 75 percent or more, which is at least approaching the bottom end of the performance scale for an independent sales force.

Rent a salesperson

Temps are popular these days, so why not temporary salespeople? Temp agencies have been providing telemarketers on a temporary basis for years. They are often used for a few weeks in conjunction with any special project that requires telephone prospecting or follow-up — such as generating leads for a new product or new territory.

Any of the leading temp agencies can fill an order for experienced telemarketers. Look under Employment Contractors — Temporary Help in your local Yellow Pages telephone directory (or try Employment Agencies if your book does not have this listing). One of the big, national temp agencies is likely to have an office nearby as well, so you can also check your directory for Kelly Temporary Services or Manpower Temporary Services (both have offices across most of North America).

Less common, but even more effective, are temporary salespeople. And nowadays you *can* find real pros who will hit the ground running to help you open up a new territory, introduce a new product, or follow up on a backlog of sales leads from that big trade show you exhibited at last month. You probably want to hire these sorts of temps on a monthly basis, to give them time to develop some continuity. And consider teaming them with your full-time salespeople (if you have them) to ease the transition for new accounts when the temporary service period is over.

I know of two major U.S. temp agencies that specialize in experienced salespeople (although other temp agencies may be able to help as well). Try Sales Staffers International, headquartered in Danvers, Massachusetts (508-758-9999), which draws salespeople from a huge database maintained by Management Recruiters International (in Cleveland, Ohio). I also hear that MMD Inc. in New York City is a good resource, especially for medical and technical salespeople. Some people in marketing are now calling temporary salespeople *rent-a-reps,* for what that's worth. But by any name, they may be a useful tool when you have short-term sales needs that exceed your internal sales capacity. Often a burst of sales calls over a few weeks or months is just what a marketing plan needs — and now you have an easy way to do that.

Laptop magic

Many salespeople swear by their laptops, because as salespeople, they can do something nobody else in business has managed to do: They can actually turn their laptop into a virtual office that provides all the support functions they need to do their job well. Scheduling. Detailed databases on customers. Sales reports. Correspondence. Forecasts and projections. The latest business news. E-mail from the home office. All this information is on a laptop, and your salespeople are fully informed and organized everywhere they go.

To accomplish the magic of having a virtual office on a laptop, you probably want to load one of the specialized software programs designed specifically for salespeople. The best, from what I've seen, is ACT! from Symantec Corporation (Cupertino, California, 408-253-9600).

If you want to link salespeoples' laptops through a wireless, satellite-based, telecommunications system, you can do that, too. No need for telephone hookups. Just open the laptop, wherever you may be, and you're linked to the rest of your company and the world. Motorola offers this service, for one, in their EMBARC product. Along with wireless e-mail, you are provided with access to a variety of news services and can also provide reports about companies for your last-minute research needs. Pretty cool! (In the U.S., EMBARC information is available with a toll-free call to 800-EMBARC4, ext. 525.)

Rally Centers replace home offices

If you have a team of sales people working to sell your product, they are likely out in their cars all day, working from their laptops. They don't need to come into a home office before hitting the road, so why pay rent on office space for them?

Rally Center facilities take the place of home offices at MCI, where salespeople now operate out of their laptops and cars. They spend so much time on the road that they don't need to come in to a desk in the morning, so the company is doing away with their desks and offices.

However, sometimes they do need access to office facilities, and so the Rally Center provides them on a share basis. Meeting rooms, a video training area, and computer workstations are available for special events and projects, as well as for entertaining clients or just mingling with other salespeople. The salespeople drop by when they need these facilities, but they do not come in on a daily basis. As a result, you don't need to rent as much office space for your Rally Center as you used to when every salesperson was assigned a personal desk or office.

Compensating the Sales Force

This is one of the toughest and most important management decisions in marketing — how to compensate salespeople. Compensation has a significant impact on the sales staff's motivation and performance, and, of course, salespeople's performance has a big effect on sales. The issue becomes difficult because motivation is a subtle issue and compensation's effect on it is not always obvious.

A good resource for those who want to go deep on this topic is the American Compensation Association in Phoenix, Arizona, at 602-922-2020 (fax: 602-922-2080). This association offers a good introductory one-day seminar called *Designing and Implementing a Sales Compensation Plan,* and they also publish a booklet summarizing the seminar's content titled *Designing Sales Compensation Plans.* Their approach is practical and hands-on, with good formulas for assessing your current compensation plan by using pay/performance data, interviews, questionnaires, turnover analysis, and comparison with other companies. (You can see that redesigning your plan is a great deal of work!) They also teach some basic commission formulas that are a good starting point for your design.

If you want to recruit special salespeople, you may need to offer them a special compensation plan. The idea is to do something sufficiently different from the norm in your industry to make your job openings really stand out. For example, what if you want to make sure that your salespeople take a highly consultative, service-oriented approach, with long-term support and relationship building? What you need is people with patience and dedication, people who are looking for a stable situation and will build business over the long term. So try offering them less commission than they would earn elsewhere. Make your compensation salary-based. If you give them sales incentives, consider bonuses linked to long-term customer retention or to building sales with existing customers. Your compensation plan will stand out from your competitors and send a clear signal about the kind of sales behavior you expect.

Similarly, if you want the hottest, most self-motivated salespeople, offer more commission than the competition. That's what Realty Executives, a Phoenix, Arizona-based real estate firm, does. In an industry in which commissions from home sales are typically split between the agent and their realty firm, Realty Executives gives 100 percent of the sales commission to its realtors. And rather than offer a base salary, it charges its agents a monthly fee for use of the firm's name and facilities. This unusual approach attracts top salespeople, who are able to earn more than $15,000 more annually than the average broker would. And it weeds out low performers who would have slid by on their base salaries and an occasional commission at a more conventional firm.

Chapter 18

Direct Marketing via Advertising, Telemarketing, and Direct Mail

Continental Cablevision has 4.5 million subscribers in the United States. That's a lot of customers. And signing those customers up took a great deal of marketing effort. But how many customers will stay with Continental as competition enters the market and gives them alternatives? Hmm. Don't know. They didn't have to worry about that in the past. But now they (and you!) do. Continental's response to competition is to get into the *direct marketing* business in a big way (direct marketing is when you use media to communicate with and build a relationship with customers directly, instead of through marketing intermediaries like retailers). To do this, Continental hired a corporate direct-mail manager and began mailing its customers special offers and building a database of information about them.

Part of Continental's initiative is a program called Inner Circle, a preferred customer program that offers various incentives and services to members. The program's goal is to build a relationship with each customer, one that gives her more reasons for doing business with Continental Cablevision and thus increases her loyalty. I highly recommend you use the same strategy — that is, to offer customers membership in a program that gives them special benefits, and gives you a direct connection with them.

Perhaps your business relies on indirect or impersonal approaches to marketing. If so, then you probably are reading this chapter because you realize you need to supplement your current marketing efforts with a loyalty-building direct relationship, using media like direct mail/fax, telemarketing, e-mail, and the World Wide Web. You're right. Keep reading. Almost every marketing program needs to integrate some direct marketing with the other elements of its marketing program.

Or perhaps you are in a business that already is a direct marketer. A fast-growing selection of businesses relies on direct marketing to conduct business — and bypasses indirect distribution channels as a result. This strategy is a great one, too, and one that is easier every week as new media and new information-management technologies come on line.

Either way, direct marketing is an important issue — and mastering it to the degree that you can "beat the odds" and obtain higher-than-average response rates is vital. I revisit this concept repeatedly in this chapter as I help you review the varied problems and practices of direct marketing. This chapter focuses on conventional media — print ads, mail, and telephone primarily. Remember these can be integrated with (or sometimes replaced with) Internet-based marketing, which I cover in Chapter 7.

And remember, too, that behind every effective direct marketing program (or personal selling program) is a good, well-managed database of customer and prospect names. If you need some help with yours, see the nearby sidebar, "Using a database."

Using a database

Almost all direct marketers use computerized databases. You should make the transition to this technology eventually if you don't already. But a computerized database is not absolutely necessary unless you have thousands of names in your database, so small-time direct marketers can postpone the transition if they are computer-averse. In fact, the simplest form of database is a box of index cards, which is what marketers used for years, until the computer industry caught up with them and created functional products to do the same job. The following table shows some of the leading brands of database management software for use in direct marketing:

Database Management Programs

Program	Publisher
MS FoxPro	Microsoft
dBase and Paradox	Borland International
Access	Microsoft
Approach	Approach Software
4th Dimension/4D First	ACI Inc.
FileMaker	Pro Claris
Helix Express	Helix Technologies
Oracle	Oracle Corp.

If you are unfamiliar with the use of such programs, you may want to take a workshop on database management for marketing. Or consult the *...For Dummies* product line, which contains reference books on a wide variety of computer programs.

If you are designing or reviewing a database management system, make a list of the things you want the system to be able to do. Write your list in nontechnical terms. You don't care how the program does its magic, just so long as it *does* it. For example, while different programs and in-house systems use different techniques to keep track of past customer sales, all you care is that your system be able to sort customers by frequency or recency of past sales or give you a sales history on specific customers. Some programs will permit this sort of analysis, others may not, so consulting that list of what you want the program to do is essential before you make a purchase.

Following are some of the most fundamental requirements of any marketing database:

✔ Report on or sort by recency of purchase.

✔ Report on or sort by frequency of purchase.

✔ Report on or sort by total value of past purchases in a selected period.

✔ Support list management (merging and purging functions).

✔ Permit integration of new fields (including data from purchased lists or marketing research).

✔ Support name selection (through *segmentation* — dividing the list into similar subgroups, *profiling* — describing types of customers based on their characteristics, and *modeling* — developing statistical models to predict or explain response rates).

✔ Make sorting, updating, and correcting data an easy task.

✔ Make tracking and analyzing individual responses to specific communications easy, in order to either test the effectiveness of a letter or script.

✔ Allow operators at *call centers* to quickly pull up and add to profiles of all customers (or at least customers designated as members of a club or continuity program). Call centers are offices dedicated to handling in-coming customer phone calls — see Chapter 18's coverage of telemarketing for how to set one up.

The preceding list is longer than I meant to write, but when you think about it, you may want to do a great many things with your database. So please think about it and ask the software maker or distributor, or the consultant or in-house programmer you work with, to match a program to your list of requirements. Otherwise, you will spend a great deal of time learning what your database program can't do, and that's not much fun!

What the Heck Is Direct Marketing?

Direct marketing. Relationship marketing. One-to-one marketing. Interactive marketing. They're all the same thing at heart, so I don't care what term you use.

To me, direct marketing occurs whenever you, the marketer, take it upon yourself to create and manage customer transactions at a distance through one or more media.

In many industries, customers are too numerous or far-flung for the producer to want to do business with them directly, or vice versa. I don't want to have to go to San Francisco, headquarters of Levi Strauss & Co., to shop for a pair of jeans, and Levi Strauss doesn't want to have to send a sales rep with a truck full of jeans to my home. So we can't do business in person. Instead, a variety of intermediaries — distributors and retailers — get into the act. Levi Strauss & Co. sends a selection of Levi's clothing to stores near my home, and they get me into those stores to shop for clothes. Distribution channels such as the one used by Levi Strauss & Co. are a solution to the problem of reaching many or remote customers.

But direct marketing offers an alternative solution, a way to extend your reach without using any intermediaries. Sears pioneered the use of a mail-order catalog as a substitute for visiting a store. And today's direct marketer is also a sort of virtual retailer, able to reach out through clever use of media and engage in exchanges with all those hard-to-reach customers.

At least that's how I define direct marketing. If you want the official line on what it is, here is how the Direct Marketing Association defines it: Direct marketing is an interactive system of marketing which uses one or more advertising media to effect a measurable response and/or transaction at any location. I didn't write it, so don't ask me what it means. However, this definition does add two important concepts to my less formal definition.

- ✔ **Interactive:** Don't get too excited about that. Some people preach the Gospel of Interactive Marketing as if an interaction with the customer via Internet, telephone, or mail is some incredible, transformational experience. Balderdash. The simple truth is that in order to make a sale, you have to have some action on the part of the customer. You do something. The customer does something. That's the basis of any marketing exchange. Of course, your direct marketing has to produce some interaction between you and the customer. Otherwise, you're not marketing. However, stimulating that action by the customer at a distance can be hard, so direct marketing focuses on how to get customers to take action.

- ✔ **Measurable response:** The idea behind this concept is that you can — and ought to — keep good records of what you do in direct marketing. Finding out the cost of approaching a prospective customer and what returns result from your efforts is a pretty simple task. That means direct marketing can be based on clear information about what you did and what happened. With this sort of information in hand, you can rapidly learn from experience. Again, measurable response is not really a special feature of direct marketing. All marketing should be measured and controlled to make sure that you know what results you get. But reiterating the importance of measurement and analysis when you talk about direct marketing never hurts.

Even if you have little or no experience in direct marketing, have faith that a small initiative will generate enough information for you to learn how to direct market better and on a larger scale. The best way to become good at direct marketing is to start doing it. Ease into direct marketing with a modest program to minimize your down-side risk, and start learning and growing from there. This principle is true, whether you are big or small, a retailer or wholesaler, a for-profit or not-for-profit. The guideline is even true for Levi Strauss & Co. They just started a direct marketing initiative by including a registration card with each pair of jeans they sell. This technique is well-known to equipment marketers, but hasn't been used very much in other markets. If the approach works for Levi's brand jeans, then Levi Strauss & Co. will build up a database of customers. And once that database is in hand, they can begin direct marketing from it.

A variety of media and strategies are available to the direct marketer. The following sections look at the options.

Direct-Action Advertising

Do you think many potential customers are out there who would love to order your product direct — but don't know they can? Do these potential customers even know that you exist and are they thinking about you at the moment? If not, then you should try to reach out to them through *direct-action ads* — ads that stimulate people to respond with an inquiry or purchase. (Some marketers call them *direct-response ads*. Take your pick.) The registration cards Levi's now includes with each pair of jeans fall into this category, although direct-action ads are more commonly seen in print media — magazines and newspapers — and now on the fax machine and the Internet as well.

The people who respond to such advertising have been self-selected as customers or prospects for your product. You need to do two things with these customers.

 ✔ You need to try your best to close the sale by getting them to buy something.

 ✔ You need to learn as much as you can about them and put the information in your database for future direct-marketing efforts.

Many businesses build a direct-marketing capacity through this very process. They place ads in front of what they hope is an appropriate target market and wait to see who responds. Then they attempt to build long-term direct-marketing relationships with those who respond (for example, by sending them catalogs or direct-mail letters). Over time, respondents are added to the direct-marketing database, information about the respondents builds up, and many of them become regular direct purchasers.

Direct-action advertising is not the only way to stimulate responses. I'll show you how to use direct mail and telemarketing in the same way in up-coming sections (and don't forget the Internet's emerging capabilities in this area, too!). Both print and television advertising also have successful track records in this area — and radio might work, too, but you have to innovate to overcome the problem that people rarely write down what they hear on radio (thus, radio is not very action-oriented).

Beating the odds: The direct ad designer's toughest goal

Because your goal is to stimulate consumers to respond to you, your direct-action (or direct-response) advertising has a pretty difficult task to accomplish. You need to understand that most of the interactions between your ad and your prospects will fail to stimulate the response you desire. Failure is the most common outcome of direct-action advertising! So your real goal is to minimize failure.

Look at the statistics if you don't believe me:

- ✔ A full-page magazine ad typically pulls between 0.05 to 0.20 percent of circulation (the *pull rate* is the percentage of readers who respond to the ad by calling or mailing as per the ad's instructions). The most you can expect from a decent ad is, therefore, two responses per thousand. Pretty bad, huh?

- ✔ A direct-mail letter, individually addressed, typically pulls between 0.5 and 5 percent of names mailed. The most you can expect from a decent letter is, therefore, 50 responses per thousand. Better, but still pretty bad. (By the way, the cost per thousand — CPM — of a letter is also higher, so you don't necessarily get a better deal from direct mail than from magazine ads.)

- ✔ A direct-mail showing of your product in a portfolio of products, as in a catalog or card deck, will pull far less. Divide that 50 per thousand figure by the number of competing products for a rough idea of the maximum likely response rate (although prominent placement will improve the rate, and so will any tendency of customers to make multiple purchases from the catalog). For example, if your product is on one postcard in a shrink-wrapped deck of 50 cards, the maximum response may be 1 per thousand. That's really bad.

- ✔ A telemarketing center making calls to a qualified list can do somewhat better. The center may pull in the 0.75 to 5 percent range for a con-sumer product, but can get as high as 15 percent for some business-to-business sales efforts. However, telemarketing generates far more failures than successes, and its CPM is often higher than direct mail.

In short, direct marketing doesn't work in the vast majority of cases. At least direct marketing is not very good at finding the right customer, in the right mood to respond (which is why we all complain so much about junk mail and aggravating telemarketing calls). That's the dirty secret the industry doesn't want the world to know, but you definitely do need to know the facts before you try to design a direct marketing program or — especially — the initial pull ads to bring in new customers or prospects. However, before you despair, you should also know that good direct marketing programs beat these odds and are highly lucrative. So don't be discouraged — just be dedicated to doing it better than average.

What you can and must do is put a great deal of creative energy and attention to detail into the effort to make the ad a little better than the typical direct-action ad. If you can come in at the high end of those pull ranges mentioned earlier — or even beat them — then the economics of direct-response advertising will be in your favor. But if your ad pulls in the middle or bottom of those ranges, you will have problems making a profit in direct marketing.

The goals of direct-action advertising

The high failure rates make good sense if you consider how much more a direct-action ad must do than the typical image-building or brand-oriented ad. The latter has a tough enough mandate. It must attract attention, build viewer involvement, communicate a compelling message, and by so doing, leave the viewer with a permanently positive impression of your product so as to soften them up for the other elements of your marketing program. But these other elements — often the distribution channel, in particular — have the job of closing a sale. Compare that to the direct-action ad, which has to create enough enthusiasm to get people to close the sale, on their own initiative, right now.

How do you accomplish this goal? I'm going to look at an example of a successful direct-action ad to find out what the secret is. The example I chose is a decades-old, full-page magazine ad for the home music courses of the U.S. School of Music — which was in New York City, but is no longer listed in the Manhattan phone book. (I don't know what happened to them. Maybe they stopped running that ad.) David Ogilvy, co-founder of ad agency Ogilvy & Mather and author of the wonderful book, *Ogilvy on Advertising* (Random House), says the school's ad is one of the best ever written.

The ad shows a pen-and-ink drawing of a group of people in a living room, one of them just sitting down to play the piano for the others. (I guess the replacement of pianos by TVs in American living rooms may explain the disappearance of the U.S. School of Music.) But most of the ad is copy, starting with a large-type header, followed by body copy that tells the protagonist's story in the first person:

> ### They Laughed When I Sat Down
> ### At the Piano
> ### But When I Started to Play! —
>
> *To the amazement of all my friends, I strode confidently over to the piano and sat down.*
> *"Jack is up to his old tricks," somebody chuckled. The crowd laughed. They were all certain that I couldn't play a single note.*
> *"Can he really play?" I heard a girl whisper to Arthur.*
> *"Heavens, no!" Arthur exclaimed. "He never played a note in his life . . . but just you watch him. This is going to be good."*
> *I decided to make the most of the situation. With mock dignity I drew out a silk handkerchief and lightly dusted off the piano keys. Then I rose and gave the revolving piano stool a quarter of a turn, just as I had seen an imitator of Paderewski do in a vaudeville sketch.*
> *"What do you think of his execution?" called a voice in the rear.*
> *"We're in favor of it!" came back the answer, and the crowd rocked with laughter.*
> ### Then I Started to Play
> *Instantly a tense silence fell on the guests. The laughter died on their lips as if by magic.*

The ad goes on to tell the story of how the protagonist's friend, Arthur, "himself an accomplished pianist," thinks he must have been playing for years. But he hasn't, because the U.S. School of Music has "a new simplified method that can teach you to play any instrument by mail in just a few months." This, the ad's claim, would probably be put in the headline by most of us. In this ad, the claim appears in the middle of three columns of text. But people got the point anyway, and in record numbers, because the surrounding story made the ad entertaining and believable.

I don't know if there ever was a Jack, but the ad works because readers identify with his character and imagine themselves benefiting in the same ways. He was as real as any fictional character can be, and the ad was read as carefully as any good story is. The ad ends with a tear-out order form, and a great many readers filled it out and sent for "Our Free Booklet and Demonstration Lesson" by mail.

While this ad's premise, and language, are humorously outdated, its secrets of success still work. Make sure that your direct-response ad does the following:

✔ **Appeals to its target readers.** A good story, a character they can identify with and want to be more like — these are the timeless elements of true appeal.

✔ **Supports its main claim about the product fully.** Because the ad must not only initiate interest, but also close the sale, it has to give sufficient evidence to overcome any reasonable objections on the readers' part. If the product's virtues are obvious, then show them with a close-up view of the product. If not (as in the case of a service), then use testimonials, a compelling story, statistics from objective product tests — in short, some form of evidence that is logically or emotionally convincing — or better yet, both.

✔ **Speaks to readers in conversational, personal language.** The language in the preceding ad is admittedly a bit dated, but at the time, the ad was natural and easy to read and believe. Your ad must be equally natural and comfortable for readers. Don't get fancy! Write well, yes. Polish and condense, yes. Seek better, catchier, clearer expressions, yes. But don't get stiff or formal on me — please. You're not creating a report for your boss, you're writing an ad.

✔ **Targets likely readers.** Your response rate is affected dramatically by your ad's readership. In fact, the same ad, placed in two different publications, can produce response rates at both ends of the range. So the better you define your target consumers, and the more of them that are in the readership, the better your ad will perform.

Highly selective publications are better for direct-response advertising. A special-interest magazine may deliver a readership far richer in targets than a general-interest magazine or newspaper. If you are focusing on women, select a publication read by them. That ups your response rate 50 percent right off the bat! *Good Housekeeping,* for example, reaches almost 5 million readers — most of them women.

✔ **Make responding easy.** Note that the preceding piano ad ends with an offer of a free booklet and demonstration lesson. The ad does not ask for money — only the names and addresses of interested parties. The ad's goal is simply to generate qualified prospects, who can then be turned into paying customers. Why? I'm sure that the advertisers were as eager as you are to land some new customers, but to do so in a single ad would have been too difficult. Not for the advertiser — cashing checks when they come in the mail is no problem — but for the prospective customer. In this case, expecting the customer to make a full commitment to a course of home study without more information is unrealistic. So the ad makes taking action easy for the customer by offering a simpler and less risky intermediate step.

Sometimes this intermediate step is not necessary. When in doubt, try two versions of your ad — one with an intermediate step and one that tries to make the sale on the spot. Then see which one produces the most sales in the long run.

Marketers at Cahners, a Boston-based publisher of trade magazines, use direct-action ads to generate inquiries from advertisers interested in buying ad space in its magazines. They use direct-response ads, such as a recent four-page insert in *Advertising Age,* to reach the people who influence media buying decisions. Their strategy emphasizes choice. They give readers multiple contact options and multiple things to ask for. The multiple options let a wide range of prospects easily take action by allowing them to select the response they prefer.

When direct advertising works, it really works

A modern classic illustrates the ability of some direct ads to close the sale without any intermediate steps. You may still find this small, simple, black-and-white ad running in the back pages of the *New York Times Sunday Magazine.* The advertiser is David Morgan of Bothell, Washington, a distributor of the Cattleman, a "traditional Australian Stockman's hat" made by Akbura of Australia. The ad simply shows a photo of a felt hat, along with a body-copy description that includes information such as "Pre-shaped in Akbura's Imperial Quality pure fur felt, fully lined, $3\frac{1}{4}$" brim, ornamental band." And the ad gives an article number and the price: $85.00 plus $5.00 for shipping and handling. The copy also mentions that David Morgan carries a wide range of products, from "Celtic Jewelry" to "Maps of Britain." A toll-free number is listed for ordering, an address is provided for those who prefer to write, and an e-mail address is given as well.

I've seen this ad, without alterations, in dozens of magazines in recent years. That means it works. And works. And works. Why? Well, the ad stars a product that somebody evidently wants. I don't wear those things, but men who like unusual hats probably know about them and want to find a source. The copy is stark and simple — no stories here — but the ad is engaging to those who can see themselves wearing that hat. And just enough information is provided about the company's other products to tantalize readers with the impression that here is a truly unusual retailer, a potential source of products you can't get anywhere else.

Finally, this ad also provides an easy way for readers to make contact. Three different options are given: phone, mail, and e-mail. The ad makes clear that you can call to request a catalog, not just to order the hat, so the reader is given two follow-up options. All this is an inexpensive back-section advertisement. Perhaps I should qualify my earlier statement: Direct marketing doesn't work very often, but when it does, it really works!

Direct Mail

Direct mail is the classic form of direct marketing — in fact, the whole field used to be called direct mail until the experts changed the term. *Direct mail* is the use of personalized sales letters, and it has a long tradition all its own. I review what I think are the best ideas from this tradition in a minute, but first I want to point out that direct mail is really no more nor less than a form of print advertising. So before you design, or hire someone to design, a direct mail piece, please think about it in this context (and see Chapters 4 and 5).

Actually, a direct mail piece is not like a print ad. It's like two print ads.

- ✔ The first ad is the one the target sees when the mail arrives. An envelope, usually. And that ad has to accomplish a difficult action goal: to get the viewer to open the envelope instead of recycling it. Most direct mail ends up in the recycling pile without ever getting opened or read! Keep this fact in mind. Devote extra care to making your envelope (a) stand out — it needs to be noticeable and different, and (b) give readers a reason to open it (sell the benefits or engage their curiosity or, even better, promise a reward!).

- ✔ The second ad goes to work only if the first succeeds. The second ad is what's inside, and its action goal is to get the reader to respond with a purchase or inquiry. In that respect, this ad is much the same as any other direct-action ad. The same rules of persuasive communication apply — plus a few unique ones.

The secrets of great direct mail

A great many so-called formulas exist for successful direct-mail letters. None of them work. At least, nothing about your letter should be formulaic. Your letter must be creative copy writing and design at its best. It needs to use the secrets of direct advertising design as described above. Your letter needs to employ the principles of creative marketing and good communications as covered in Chapters 4 and 5.

However, certain strategies can help you employ these principles of good design in a direct-mail piece. Following are several approaches that may help.

First, the most effective direct mail letters generally include several elements, each with its own clear role:

- ✔ **Bait:** Some sort of bait should be present that is designed to catch the readers' eye and attention so as to get them to read the letter in the first place.

- ✔ **Argument:** You then need to provide a sound argument — logical, emotional, or both — as to why what you offer is such a great thing for the reader and will solve some specific problem for him. The bulk of many letters is devoted to making this case as persuasively as possible, and this is a sound practice.

- ✔ **Call to action:** Finally, you should make an appeal to immediate action, some sort of hook that gets readers to call you, send for a sample, sign up for a contest, place the order — or whatever. As long as they act, then the letter has been successful. So this hook is really the climax of the letter, and everything must be designed to ensure that it works.

These three essential elements can be described in various ways. One favorite of many copywriters is the *Star, Chain,* and *Hook.* If you can't find and mark all three of these elements in your own letter, it isn't any good:

- ✔ **The Star:** A lively opening to your letter. It attracts attention and generates interest.

- ✔ **The Chain:** This part of the letter is your argument — the benefits of the product and your claim about what it will do to make the reader's life better.

- ✔ **The Hook:** This part is the ending of your letter, and it asks the reader to do something immediately. If the letter doesn't make a purchase request, then it should offer an incentive for readers to send in their name or call for more information.

These formulas refer specifically to the text of your letter itself. Remember to think hard about what else goes into your mailing as well. The outside of the envelope needs to entice readers to get them to open the letter in the first place. Following are some techniques to make your envelope enticing enough to open:

- ✔ **The stealth approach envelope:** You disguise your letter so that it looks like a bill or personal correspondence — or just cannot be identified at all. Hopefully, the reader will open the envelope just to find out what's inside.

- ✔ **The benefits approach envelope:** You include a headline, perhaps a little supporting copy, even some artwork, to let people know what the mailing is about and summarize why you think your offer is worthy of their attention. I like this approach best, because it is honest and direct — and this is direct marketing after all! Furthermore, this method ensures that those who do open the envelope have self-selected based on interest in your offer. But this technique only works if you have a clear benefit or point of difference to advertise on your envelope. If you can't say "Open immediately for the lowest price on the XYZ product ranked highest in *Consumer Reports,*" then this ploy may not work.

✔ **The special offer envelope:** This envelope entices with the hook — never mind the offer. By letting consumers know that they can enter a sweepstakes to win a billion dollars, or get free samples, or find valuable coupons or a dollar bill enclosed, this envelope gives them a reason to read the inside letter. But the envelope doesn't try to sell the product — it leaves that to the carefully crafted letter inside.

✔ **The creative envelope:** If your mailing is unique enough, everyone will want to open it just to find out who you are and what you are up to. An oversized package in an unexpected color. An envelope with a very funny cartoon or quote on the back. A window teasing readers with a view of something interesting within. You can make your envelope the most exciting thing in someone's mailbox by using any number of creative ideas. Yet this strategy is the least common, probably because creative envelopes cost more. But don't be penny wise and pound foolish. If you spend 25 percent more to double or triple the response rate, then you've saved your company a great deal of money on the mailing by spending more on the envelope!

What else should go into your mailing? In general, a letter combined with a *circular* — a simple catalog-style description of your product(s) — pulls more strongly than a letter alone. Circulars don't work for all products (don't bother for magazine subscriptions), but do work well for any product or service the consumer sees as expensive or complex. In other words, use circulars where purchase involvement is likely to be high — because the circular gives the reader a way to get involved. And make the circular more elaborate, involving, glossy, colorful, and large where involvement should be higher. Big circulars for big-ticket items, little ones for simple items.

Also include reply forms. Allow readers to easily get in touch with you in multiple ways. Give readers some choices about what offers they want to respond to if possible. Postage-free (or prepaid) reply forms generally ensure a higher response rate and so justify their cost many times over. Don't skimp on the form, because, after all, getting that response is the whole point of your mailing.

The final design issue is how to send the letter. Third class versus first class via the U.S. Postal Service? Should you use an overnight air service for an offer to business customers? Or maybe send the letter by e-mail or fax? The fax is emerging in business-to-business marketing as a useful new medium — especially for time-sensitive offers such as a new product announcement. But in general, the postal service is still best. And on average, third class pulls as well as first class, so save your money.

I do recommend sending direct mail to your in-house list by first class mail once in a while, because that way you'll get any incorrectly addressed envelopes back in the return mail. Doing so provides an easy way to clean up or evaluate your database.

Do these principles apply to e-mail? Yes, but with two adaptations. First, think screens, not pages, when writing the body copy of an e-mail sales letter. It takes as much effort (and involvement) to click on the next screen as it does to turn the page, yet a screen holds less than a page. So be more precise and less wordy or your e-mail won't pull as well as the same letter in printed form. Second, think hard about how to package your e-mail in an enticing virtual envelope. Most e-mail messages start with a bunch of really boring junk the software throws on — stuff about the path or distribution of the message, for example. Can you suppress this stuff? Or if not, can you slip something enticing into it, for example, by sending from an e-mail address that says something about your offer? It's not too much trouble to create a unique address with an enticing or interesting name just for one mass e-mailing. And this may help boost readership, just like a good envelope does.

How to get your letter mailed

One little detail often puzzles first-time direct mailers: how to actually get your mailing printed, folded, stuffed, and mailed. If you don't know, the best thing to do is hire someone who does. Your local telephone directory will list some companies that do this under "mailing" or "marketing" headings, and often commercial printers do this type of work as well. Printers can often handle anything from a small envelope to a major catalog. Talk to various printers to get an idea of the range of services and prices.

If you are planning small-scale mailings — say, less than two thousand at a pop — then you may find doing the work in-house is a cheaper and quicker route. Many local businesses and non-profits do small-scale mailings, and using printers is not economical for them. If you want to set up this capability, talk to your local post office to find out how to handle metered or permit mail. And consider purchasing mailing equipment, such as the following (all of these are capable of processing standard-format mailings): feeders, sealers, scales to weigh the mailings, meters, and sometimes additional features. Combine this equipment with your local photocopy shop's ability to produce, fold, and stuff a mailing, and you have an efficient small-scale direct-mail center! Table 18-1 shows some of the leading equipment makers.

Table 18-1	Mailing Equipment Makers
Company	*Phone Number*
Ascom Hasler Mailing Systems	800-243-6275
Francotype-Postalia	800-341-6052 or 630-241-9090
Neopost	800-624-7892 or 510-475-6317
Pitney Bowes	800-672-6937 or 203-356-5000

Telemarketing

In the U.S., three-fourths of all consumers use a toll-free number at least once each year. And more than $500 billion in sales takes place over the phone. Telemarketing has emerged in the last 15 years as a major medium for direct marketing. (Telemarketing is also an important accompaniment to direct selling, especially in business-to-business marketing — see Chapter 17 for details.)

While telemarketing requires nothing but a telephone, it is usually most effective when combined with toll-free, in-bound calling. In the U.S., this service is available for all 800 numbers since their introduction in 1967 and now for 888 numbers as well; toll-free numbers are increasingly available in similar forms in other countries as well. The idea is for you, the marketer, to pick up the cost of the customer's telephone call so as to remove a possible objection to calling. Of course, a local phone number is just as good, if not better (many people prefer to do business locally), but currently, the toll-free number is most popular with marketers because it allows all calls to be routed to one centralized *call center* (an office dedicated to handling incoming calls) for answering.

By the way, you can also arrange with most phone companies to list a local number in each local market you wish to, and then have the phone company bill you the added cost of transfering that call to your non-local office. That way, people pay only for their local call, and feel that they are dialing a local business rather than an impersonal national business. List the local number in local Yellow Pages or other phone directories for effective local advertising! This alternative to the toll-free number is less well-known, but may be more effective for you.

The toll-free number is only useful in one form of telemarketing: *inbound telemarketing,* in which customers call you in response to direct-action advertising. And every direct-action ad should have a phone number as one of the contact options — with a trained telemarketing sales force or an eager entrepreneur at the other end.

Actually, I have to qualify that statement, because recently, computers have been pushed to the front lines at some call centers. Using new *interactive voice response (IVR) technologies,* computers can solicit information from callers, route their calls appropriately, and even take orders for products or follow-up information. If your call center is constrained by a high volume of routine calls, then consider exploring this new technology — doing so can reduce the cost and increase the speed of each call. But remember that many callers still prefer a real person on the other end of the line, so be sure to make this option available in the initial menu!

The other form of telemarketing is *outbound telemarketing,* in which salespeople make calls in order to try to get prospects on the phone — and then *pitch* them (or try to make a sale; see Chapter 17 for how to design a good sales presentation). Like personal selling, outbound telemarketing yields plenty of rejections.

The percentage of rejections is often terribly high in outbound telemarketing operations. The reason is that phoning someone costs so much less than visiting him or her in person that marketers don't bother to develop good quality call lists. They just hire a bunch of college kids at hourly rates to make random calls in the hopes of finding a few good prospects for each hundred calls made. That type of marketing isn't smart. Please, don't waste your time and consumers' good will by dialing numbers from the phone book!

You can improve the *hit rate* (number of successes per number of calls) of outbound telemarketing dramatically by developing a good list before you start calling. (See my following coverage of this topic.) If you do, then you can afford to put competent salespeople on the phones so that your company is not represented by blithering idiots. I don't know why most telemarketers haven't figured out that the first contact between their company and a prospective customer should not be in the hands of a temp worker who cannot pronounce the name of the product correctly. To avoid such problems, you need to develop lists (see Chapter 20) and a script that are good enough to give your callers at least a 15 percent hit rate. I estimate that target is ten times the average for consumer telemarketing operations right now.

By the way, I'm not going to cover those darn computers that actually make outbound telemarketing calls. What an awful idea! If you decide to use one, just make sure that you don't give it my number. And be forewarned that they are illegal in many states in the U.S.

"Hello, sir; I'm calling from (company name), which has been retained by (prestigious economics magazine publisher) to see if you are receiving your copy of (magazine name) on time and in good condition." So said the female caller when I picked up the telephone at my office the other day. And my "abusive marketing antennae" immediately sounded a warning.

Profiling telemarketing programs

Let me illustrate the uses of outbound telemarketing with two very different examples of telemarketing programs.

The first is a company (I dare not name names) that sells what they say is a highly superior vacuum cleaner. The machine sells for a highly superior price as well — one that includes a much higher margin than is typical of the product category — and it is only available through their direct marketing organization.

Their marketing program uses outbound telemarketing to names from local phone books in order to generate prospects who are interested in the product. These prospects are then visited by a salesperson for a full-blown sales presentation and closing effort.

The telemarketers are by-and-large young women with pleasant telephone manners. They are paid (in cash) at $5 per hour, making 200 calls per five hour shift. Most people hang up right away, but about 25 out of these 200 are interested enough to listen to the telephone pitch. Of these, about five qualify financially (they must have full-time work, a credit card, and own their own home).

Out of this pool, several actually end up receiving an in-home demonstration, and one or two ultimately make the purchase. Thus, the closure rate is about 1 percent. However, the (illegal) use of cheap, cash-only labor keeps the calling costs so low that the operation is sustainable — at least until somebody from the Department of Labor or the IRS busts them for back payroll taxes.

The second is a story more to my liking, as its approach is more responsible and sustainable. The Steppenwolf Theatre in Chicago prefers to sell subscriptions. Doing so guarantees an audience (or at least a box office take) for each show in its season.

Theatre marketers discovered that a 16-week phone campaign to its *in-house list* (a list of current and past customers and qualified leads), supplemented with any other appropriate names they could find, was very effective at selling subscriptions. The telemarketing effort is done in-house by properly trained, knowledgeable staff and has a fairly high hit rate.

Note that this telemarketing program is successful at generating sales, and it does not risk legal and financial liability or expose prospects to incompetent — and possibly rude — telemarketers.

Furthermore, this program actually completes the sale, instead of requiring a follow-up sales visit. This approach is, therefore, far better than the first example. Outbound telemarketing contains a wide range. Plan to be at the top of that range, not the bottom!

When I pointed out that I thought she was really calling for some other purpose, she admitted that she wanted to offer me "an opportunity" to extend my subscription because "prices are going up" but she could give me a multiple-year subscription at the price I currently pay.

When I then observed that her opening line was a good example of an illegal sales call — it was designed to deceive me into thinking the call had another, more altruistic purpose — she quickly hung up. And so denied me the opportunity to point out another potentially illegal aspect of the call. Did you catch it? Yes, the assertion that prices are going up was probably not factual. When I checked my records, I learned that the company's price for subscriptions had actually dropped slightly in recent years, not gone up. And since I received the call, the prices have gone down, not up.

The bottom line is that this telemarketing script is improper, and has at least the potential to lead to legal complications. But so do lots of telemarketing scripts these days. Why? Because the pressure is on. Selling anything over the phone is much harder than it used to be — be it a magazine or a long distance telephone service. People are getting sick of these sales calls. So, marketers are experimenting with stealth techniques (these techniques are explained in the section, "The secrets of great direct mail," earlier in this chapter), and that is leading them into dangerous ethical and legal territory.

What's really happened is that a formerly new distribution channel has matured. Desirable consumers became jaded to junk mail, print ads, billboards, and radio and television ads decades ago. But telemarketing's rise in the '80s gave marketers something new and different to experiment with. It was great fun — for a while. But now, most prospects have received hundreds, if not thousands, of telemarketing calls. I get at least six a day at my office, and if I make the mistake of staying home on a weekday, I get a dozen more. Catching my attention by phone is just as difficult as it is by mail or other media.

That means today's telemarketers have only two choices. One, they can go on doing what they've always done, and that will lead to increasingly desperate and shady practices as their medium matures and their industry shakes out. Or two, they can wake up and smell the coffee, and realize that their little bubble has just burst. Telemarketers need to find new strategies for their newly mature medium. Some of these strategies include:

✔ **Don't overuse the phone:** Save calls for issues that really deserve personal contact from the prospect's perspective. And if you have something truly important to talk about, then you don't need a misleading hook to keep people on the phone. Remember that every marketing program should use a balanced mix of media and methods. You can't do all jobs with one tool. And also remember that even where telephoning is appropriate, your customers and prospects won't want you to call constantly. Give them a little breathing room.

✔ **Be respectful:** You are interrupting anyone you reach by phone.

✔ **Compensate telemarketers for building relationships, not frying them:** If telemarketers are paid only by the *kill* (commission on sales), then they will get frustrated and start berating and hanging up on your prospects and customers. Note that this rule means that you ought not to use *subcontractors* (specialized companies that telemarket for you) if they pay by the kill — and most of them do!

✔ **Guard existing customers:** After the call I received from the economics magazine, I wrote to complain and cancel my subscription. Deceptive, high-pressure, or irritating phone sales tactics may produce a good-looking end-of-day sales report, but they are guaranteed to increase customer turnover. Why? They bring in deal-prone customers, who will be taken away by the next telemarketer, and they irritate your loyal customers instead of rewarding them. At the very least, use two different strategies and scripts: one for existing customers and one for deal-prone prospects. At best, focus your telemarketing on building existing customer loyalty, for example, by really calling to see if you can improve the product or service quality.

✔ **Learn from other media:** Holding someone's attention long enough to deliver a marketing message is a major problem in every medium, not just telemarketing. And clever solutions have been developed in other media. Why not try some of them in telemarketing? You could write a script that includes entertainment — a very short story, a good joke, or other opener may build interest far better than a deceptive claim about the purpose of the call. Similarly, a sales promotion tie-in can hold attention. For example, your script can start with the offer of a contest or free sample give-away, and then go on to a pitch for the product.

In theory, any engagement device that works in other media can be adapted to the phone. Yet nobody has tried such devices. Time for some creativity!

Establishing and Running a Call Center

The *call center* is the place where telephone calls from your customers are answered. It can be a real, physical place — a big room full of phones staffed by your employees. It can also be a virtual place, a telephone number that rings to whatever subcontractor you are currently using to handle telemarketing for you.

Whether in-house or out, your call center needs to do several things very well, as described in the following sections:

Be accessible to desirable customers when they want to call you

If you service businesses, then business hours will be fine (but make sure that you cover business hours in the business' time zones, not just your own). If you service consumers, however, be prepared to take calls at odd hours. Some of clothing catalog's best customers do their shopping late at night, just before bed, for example.

And remember, being accessible means more than just having staff by the phones. You need to make sure that nobody gets a busy signal (your local phone company has a variety of services to help solve this problem — ask them for details).

You also need to measure and minimize customer wait time. Don't leave people sitting on hold for more than what they perceive to be a moderate amount of time. Depending upon the nature of your product and customer, that time limit is probably less than two perceived minutes. A *perceived minute* is the time period a customer on hold thinks is a minute of waiting — and that time is typically more like 40 seconds when measured on the clock. You have to convert actual wait times to perceived wait times in order to appreciate the customer's perspective.

A hidden advantage of keeping the control center in-house, according to Ted Furguson of Taos Computers (Palo Alto, California) is that managers can keep an eye on the accessibility issue and add more lines and staff quickly if a problem arises (according to a helpful article on telemarketing in *Sales & Marketing Management,* Dec. '96, p. 58-62).

Capture useful information about each call and caller

One of the most important functions for your call center is to field inquiries or orders from new customers as they respond to your various direct advertisements — such as magazine ads, letters to purchased lists, and responses to your Web page. These callers are hot leads. You don't want their order as much as you want their *data.* Don't let them escape from your call center. Make sure that your operators ask every caller for her full name and address, how she heard of your company, and perhaps a few other qualifying questions as well.

The best way to "capture" call-ins for your customer database is to have your operators online, so that they can enter the data directly into your database as they obtain it.

Recognize, and take care of, repeat customers

Putting your operators online also solves the related problem of recognizing repeat customers. Their names will pop up on screen for the operator's reference. That way, the operators won't have to ask stupid questions, and they will be able to surprise customers with their knowledge.

Gather data on the effectiveness of direct marketing ads

I'm often amazed by how little information marketers gather about the effectiveness of their own work. What you don't know does hurt you in marketing, that's for sure! Finding out which direct ads pull the best, and which pull the worst, is so easy, and by doing so, your direct marketing program can grow more efficient over time. The simplest way to accomplish this goal is to tell your operators to ask every caller where they heard about you (ask repeat customers what prompted this latest call).

Many direct mail marketers use a unique code number on each mailing to help them trace a call to a particular mailing. This technique can be broadened to all written promotions if you wish — even ones on the Internet. An identifying code links calls to specific ads, allowing easy analysis of their effectiveness.

You can also use codes for each ad to support customized sales promotions. For example, one mailing may offer a special two-for-one price over a two-month period — with the code, your operator can quickly display the terms of this offer on screen.

If you don't want to set up a call center yourself, you can hire a consultant to design a call center for you — or a service firm to perform the function for you. One such service provider is SITEL Corp. in Omaha, Nebraska. They provide both services, and their phone number is 402-963-6810.

The Importance of Civility in Direct Marketing

Many marketers are rushing to direct marketing in the often-mistaken belief that they can handle their customers better than any intermediaries can. But if you aren't accustomed to dealing directly with customers, you are likely to mess direct marketing up. The most common way to mess it up is to be too direct.

If you are "in your customers' face," then you are probably on their nerves as well. The point of direct marketing is to build a bridge between you and the customer. But the way some companies go about doing so, you'd think that the point was to hit customers over the head with the building materials and then drag their corpses under the bridge for later consumption. (I call this the *Troll Strategy.*)

How do you know where to draw the line between assertive marketing and irritating invasion? The answer is harder to discern in direct marketing because the marketing isn't really direct. That is, you aren't dealing with individuals on a personal level. You are reaching them through impersonal media instead. But because you are trying to create a sort of artificial personal contact through these media, let the rules of personal social contact be your guide.

In other words, don't do anything in direct marketing that would be considered rude in person. It's that simple. And if you follow this elementary rule, you'll alienate fewer customers (which means fewer defections and much less negative word-of-mouth), and you'll be more likely to create the kind of long-term relationships with customers that you truly want and need.

An occasional reality check of your approach is also helpful, and you can get one by surveying a fairly small sample of your target customers (from 25 to 50 will do). This sort of survey is not very scientific, so don't expect to make subtle statistical discriminations from it. But the survey can tell you if a *perception problem* exists (you don't want any negative attitudes about your telemarketing in the minds of your customers). Ask targets how they feel about your contacts (mailings, telephone calls, or whatever). Give them questions that easily allow them to express any negative feelings.

The open-ended question, "Do you want us to change anything about the ways we contact you?" is a pretty good probe, for example. If you get several of comments like "Stop having those rude callers interrupt me during dinner," or "Why don't you spell my name right in the junk mail you send me?," then you know you have some problems to fix.

Part IV
The Part of Tens

The 5th Wave   By Rich Tennant

IN A BIZARRE SET OF CIRCUMSTANCES, DOUG'S FAUCETS BECOMES THE FOCUS OF A SMALL CULT LOOKING FOR ANSWERS.

DOUG'S FAUCETS

PREPARE TO MEET YOUR MAKER

In this part . . .

1'd give you ten good reasons to read this part, but why bother — it already contains more than 20! Here is where you find warning of how to avoid many common mistakes and causes of failure. I intend to read this section once a month, just to make sure my marketing inoculations are up-to-date.

Oh, and one other thing. I bet you want to save as much money as you can on marketing. Believe me, almost every marketer shares this wish. But few accomplish it, at least without ruining next year's revenues and profits and sending customers away angry. So please consult this part of the book to find out how to save money — and how not to!

Chapter 19

(More Than) Ten Ways to Save Money in Marketing

. . . .

In This Chapter

▶ Think small

▶ Cut your fixed costs

▶ Plan your marketing program

▶ Target your audience

▶ Use creativity

▶ Concentrate your resources

▶ Introduce your product region by region

▶ Integrate

▶ Focus wisely

▶ Spend wisely

▶ Use new channels and media

▶ Be a cost cutter

▶ Spend money

. . . .

*E*veryone wants to know how to do marketing on the cheap. In general, the advice out there on this topic is worthless. Sure, it's pretty cheap to place photocopied fliers under people's windshields (although it's illegal in some towns). But when you compare the impact of a cheap flier under the windshield wiper with a well-produced TV spot, you can easily justify the difference in price. In general, you get what you pay for in marketing. The cheapest consultants, designers, and researchers may be brilliant professionals on their way up — but they usually aren't. And free exposures usually don't reach your target market or, if they do, don't make a favorable impression on them. It's hard to do good marketing on the cheap.

However, you can find ways to save money in marketing. Real money. Lots of it. They aren't as obvious or easy as some would have us believe, but they can work. In general, they involve doing real marketing, rather than substituting some cheap alternative. The approach that really saves money is to do the right things — better. Here are some good ways to save money without reducing your effectiveness or embarrassing yourself.

Think Small!

I bet this header catches more eyes than any of the others in this chapter — simply because it's so much smaller. Sometimes you can make a big impact in marketing media by being smaller than anybody else. A little print ad sometimes outpulls a big one. Not on average, to be sure. But sometimes. And that's all you need to know, because that means you should be able to develop a great small ad of your own if you work at it hard enough.

Same is true in other media. Especially media where the size of an ad is measured in time. Most radio spots run 30 seconds. And most of the time, their writers struggle to hold the listener's attention for the full 30 seconds. Why not give up that battle and just make a 10-second radio ad?

The same strategy works on TV. In early 1997, ABC Sports ran a series of 10-second TV ads to encourage viewers to tune into their coverage of the upcoming 1997 U.S. Figure Skating Championships. The ads were incredibly simple and powerful. They were shot from high above a skating rink, and each one showed figure skaters carving a number into the ice — to count down the days til the championship. Developed by Leonard/Monahan, a Providence, Rhode Island agency (Damon Williams was the art director), these promos were remarkably effective at catching the eye and delivering the reminder message. And because they were only 10 seconds long, they cost only a fraction of what a more conventional daily schedule of ads would cost.

Another way to think small in advertising is to use less expensive media than you have used in the past or than your competitors do. Following are some ideas to consider:

- ✔ If your industry does a lot of TV advertising, try a print campaign instead. Even if you spend only a third or a quarter of what you would have on a TV campaign, that money will make a big splash in national magazines.

- ✔ If your competitors do flashy print and billboard ads, consider side-stepping an expensive showdown in those media by using radio for your message. Or the Internet.

- ✔ Create a fascinating newsletter and develop a database of prospects to send it to via direct mail.

- ✔ Switch from commercial radio advertising to sponsorship of syndicated public radio programs. It's cheaper, and for some audiences has much more impact and a better image.

- ✔ Abandon national brand-building ads entirely, and put all your limited resources into a great package design and a series of brilliant point-of-purchase displays.

- ✔ Stop giving away money with all those coupons and sponsor a neat contest instead. Most consumers are more motivated by the chance to go to Hawaii for ten days next winter than by 20 cents off their next purchase — and yet the 20 cents off offer typically costs the marketer much more!

- ✔ Put together a "road show" like Rollerblade did — with a team of incredibly skilled in-line skaters touring the country by van to put on shows featuring their stunt skating.

- ✔ Cancel your print advertising in industrial magazines in order to afford larger booths at the major trade shows, with telemarketing and direct mail follow-up for all who visit the booths (as some clever business-to-business marketers have done).

- ✔ Give away more free samples than any other competitor. If your product really is better, then samples are by far the cheapest way to get that message out.

There is *always* a less expensive media alternative. It just takes creativity and a risk-taking spirit to find it.

Another way to think small is to focus on a smaller market area in order to concentrate your resources. In essence, this makes you a bigger fish in a smaller pond. Many entrepreneurs use this strategy successfully, for example, by distributing, (at first) in a single metropolitan area. Once they gain significant market share in a small area, then they can afford to roll out to other areas. The trick to this strategy is understanding the effects of *scale* in your business. There is a minimum profitable market size in most industries, and it varies dramatically. So, do some back-of-the-envelope calculations. Will a 10-percent or 20-percent share of the market in a single region, state, or city be enough to cover your fixed costs as well as variable costs and get you significantly above your break-even point? It will — *if* your fixed costs aren't too high for that market. So businesses with high fixed costs — a factory, for example — usually have to think bigger when choosing a market.

Cut Your Fixed Costs

Consider getting your *fixed costs* down. That, while it sounds more like accounting or operations management than marketing, is in fact an incredibly powerful marketing strategy!

Apply your marketing imagination to cost management for a change, and see if there is a smaller-scale way to produce that product or perform that business process. If so, it makes it possible for you to do small-scale and local marketing activities that your competitors can't profit from — but you can. For example, if you are trying to figure out how to introduce a new product on a shoe-string budget, consider searching for a low-cost supplier who can make the product for you in small batches. Even if the total costs are slightly higher, your fixed costs will be much lower because you won't have to advance-order in quantity, and then inventory extra units. And so you will then be able to *boot-strap* (or grow on your own cash flow) by making and marketing a small batch in a small market, then plowing your profits into a slightly bigger second batch, and so forth.

Plan on Planning

Marketing is probably the least well planned of all the major business activities. My guess is that half of all marketing expenses are unplanned in the sense that the money is spent without thinking about how it fits into the big picture of the marketing program. Companies often reprint their four-color brochures, renew their sales reps' contracts, buy expensive display ads in phone directories and trade magazines, inventory large quantities of poor-selling products, or spend money on fancy packaging without any idea of whether these are good marketing investments. If you and your organization will make a commitment to spend nothing on marketing without knowing why — and considering alternatives — then you will avoid wasting money on marketing activities that don't have much impact on sales. Because many of them don't. The more time you spend on developing strategy and designing your program based on it, the more cost-effective and economical your marketing will be.

Target Your Audience

Most marketing programs waste much of their effort on people or organizations who will never become good customers because they aren't in the target market — or shouldn't be. Think about the waste involved in running an ad that thousands or millions view, when only a small fraction of that audience is your target. And think of the waste involved in direct marketing to a list that generates a 1-percent response rate.

Be Creative

All things being equal, the more you spend on marketing, the more you sell. Competitors with the largest marketing programs get more attention and sales. It's no wonder that winning the marketing war can get pretty expensive. However, one of the wonderful things about marketing is that you *can* escape this spending war — by being more creative than your competitors. Every year, one or two of the most effective ad campaigns has a shoestring budget, but succeeds because of its great creative concept.

 When the California Raisins TV commercials first aired, using claymation singers, it rose to the top of the ad industry's charts in spite of having a far smaller budget than other top-ten ads. Similarly, a creative new product concept or package design, a clever approach to point-of-purchase advertising, a new way to distribute the product — any such innovations can help you achieve big-money returns from small-time investments. Getting big results on a shoe-string budget is possible, but it's gonna take some creativity!

Concentrate Your Resources

Don't spread yourself thin. Concentrate your salespeople, or your stores, or your direct marketing, or whatever you do in your program into certain areas or periods of time so as to cash in on these *economies of scale.* Economies of scale means that your costs per ad or other marketing task go down as you do more. So make sure you do each marketing activity on a large scale so that it is economical. Take advantage of discounts from printers, mailing list houses, and the media that sell ad time and space.

Roll Out Sequentially

Rolling out sequentially is a good way to concentrate your resources. Even the biggest consumer marketers often use this strategy to concentrate their resources. The idea is to roll out a new product region by region, rather than trying to introduce it everywhere at once. The roll-out strategy is a variant on the concentration strategy. Use it by doing one market at a time, and make a big impact there before going to the next market. This strategy works for other things too, not just new product introductions. You can roll out an expensive advertising campaign in one or two markets, and then wait for your returns from this investment before funding the program in additional markets. If you are patient, you will be able to fund a much higher level of advertising and achieve a far higher share of voice than your annual budget would seem to permit.

Integrate Your Efforts

Most marketers use many communication channels to reach their customers — they use many points of influence (see Chapter 1). They also tend *not* to use these multiple channels in a coordinated manner. The messages are often inconsistent in content and style and, as a result, their communications are relatively ineffective.

In the Japanese approach to quality management, you sometimes hear the expression "too many rabbits" to describe the situation in which lots of initiatives are under way without sufficient coordination. Marketing programs usually have too many rabbits when what they want is one really big rabbit — or better yet, a powerful bull that pulls the company along behind it! To solve the "too many rabbits" problem, you need to integrate all your marketing communications by doing the following:

1. **Identify all the channels of communication with your market (some of them you don't control right now — see Chapter 1).**

2. **Design an overall message strategy that says what your organization should communicate through any and all channels and that also defines a general feel or style for those communications.**

You will communicate far more effectively using integrated marketing communications, and may find you can cut back your budget and still get your point across.

Focus on the Right Objective

Many marketers spend their money on raising awareness of their brands when this is not their problem. If consumers already know about the brand, then exposing them to it more often may not help sales — or at least not very much. More likely, marketing needs to work on the brand's image so that more of those who do know about it will decide to try it. Or maybe the problem is that lots of people try it, but too many of them give up on it without becoming regular users. Then the problem may lie in the product itself, and marketing should spend its money on an upgrade rather than expensive sales or advertising. If you don't know what your bottleneck is, then you aren't spending your money wisely. Make sure you focus hard on one objective at a time, and be sure that objective is appropriate! (Chapters 2 and 3 contain further advice on setting your marketing objectives.)

Don't Give Away Money

I can't believe how eager most marketers are to give away their money. Many marketers devote half or more of their budgets to price-oriented promotions, and I can't tell you the number of times I have heard managers say things like, "Sales seem to be off this month. Let's cut prices and see if that helps." Discounts and price cuts have their role, to be sure — but should never be used unless you have clear evidence that the net result will be profitable. And it usually isn't, as I demonstrate in Chapter 13. Sometimes customers are highly price-sensitive, competitors undercut you, and you have no choice but to slash your prices too. But in general, you don't want to compete on price. Making a profit (and staying in business) is far easier when you compete on some aspect of your product's quality, something that makes it different and better. Yet many marketers volunteer to compete on price, pushing coupons and discounts at their customers until the customers learn to treat the category as a commodity and shop for the cheapest priced goods or services. This strategy always makes it more expensive to do business. It cuts profit margins to the bone and uses up your marketing budget so that you have little left to spend on differentiating your brand.

Use New Channels and Media

Doing direct marketing on the Internet is cheaper than doing so on the telephone, mostly because the Internet is a relatively new and unproven medium. Take advantage of that by being one of the innovators who proves that the Web can work. Or be one of the first in your industry to switch from mailings to faxes for new product announcements. Or be one of the first to experiment with direct marketing as a replacement for the traditional intermediaries in your industry. Also, when selecting media, favor new magazines with growing readership, because the rates of these magazines always lag behind their circulation and give you more exposures for your money.

Whenever possible, find the new thing, the up-and-comer, and hop on for the ride. Your marketing money goes much farther for two reasons. First, new means unproven and prices are generally lower as a result. Second, new means smaller, so you can be a big fish in a little pond. Your share of voice is much higher in a new medium than in an overcrowded mature medium.

Help Your Company Cut Costs

Marketers have access to a vital perspective that others don't — the customer's viewpoint — and to a customer, many of the line items in a company's budget seem unimportant. Yet nobody asks the customer — or the marketers, whose job is to represent the customer perspective — what they think about the company's budget. If they did, they might cut back on many expenses that don't affect the product's quality or availability in ways that matter to customers. From the customer's perspective, the landscaping outside the headquarters building matters not (many of those inside that building feel the same way!). Even some of the marketing department's expenses are wasted on customers, who may not notice or care, for example, whether the department's letterhead is printed in two colors or one, or whether salespeople drive new or old cars.

The campus daily newspaper at the school where I teach circulated a survey to find out what customers care about. The survey asked students to rate the importance of things like "national news coverage" and "accuracy of reporting on administrative actions." Some of these things will receive higher ratings than others, and so the managers will decide to invest in them. But what if the survey left something important out? This one did — it never asked people to rank the importance of the paper's entertainment value. And yet that is probably the key to its readership. If someone really wants to follow a national news event, they won't rush out to get the campus newspaper. But they *will* pick it up if it provides an entertaining ten-minute read. Does your company make similar mistakes? Are you investing in relatively unimportant aspects of your product instead of improving its core attributes? I bet you are.

Spend Money

This advice may seem out of place in a chapter on how to save money, but remember that well-designed marketing programs are an investment in future sales. The most obvious way to save money on marketing is to cut the marketing budget, but across-the-board cuts rarely work. They save money this year, but hurt sales and profits disproportionately next year. If you don't reach out to customers, they won't reach out to you! So remember to view marketing as an investment in future revenues and profits. You save money by making smarter investments, not by stopping the investments entirely.

Chapter 20

Ten Common Marketing Mistakes

*I*n marketing, lots of people waste time reinventing the wheel. That's too bad — and I hope you will avoid the mistake by using this book to find out about other people's solutions to your problems. But reinventing the wheel isn't nearly as bad as falling into the same pit as someone else. You should never repeat other people's mistakes — but you will! We all do, sometimes. It's just not possible to know enough about other people's experiences to be able to learn from all that might be relevant.

Even so, you can feasibly minimize the number of times you reinvent marketing mistakes. It may happen occasionally, but don't make a regular practice of it. In this chapter, I outline some of the most common mistakes, ones that I see over and over. Take a good look. They are pretty big pits, so you need to know about them if you don't want to fall into them.

Not Listening to Your Customer

"So," I often say to managers, "What do your customers think of this idea?" And too often I get a blank stare in return. Most new marketing ideas (and business plans in general) come from within the business. Some manager or employee came up with the idea. That's fine. Who else cares enough about your success to give it their undivided attention? But the problem is that customers may not like your ideas. Consider the company that tried to introduce French-fried vegetables. Great idea, except nobody would eat them. And so you can avoid an incredible number of mis-steps and wasted efforts by running ideas by your customers before you implement them.

Listening to Your Customer

Not listening to your customer is a big mistake. Consider the following, though: Sometimes *listening* to your customer is an even bigger mistake! Sometimes you have to go on instinct. The time to trust your instinct is when you think you have an insight that will allow you to lead your customer and market in bringing about a positive change.

For example, you may believe that if lawyers could give clients real-time advice via chat rooms on the Internet, they would avoid many mistakes requiring costly legal bills later on. Now, this idea sounds good — to a visionary. But to the average lawyer, who's used to picking up the pieces later on rather than participating in preventive medicine, and who never does business on the Internet, it sounds crazy. And many customers will agree with this assessment at first blush. They aren't used to the idea either, and to use such a service, they would have to change not only their attitude toward lawyers but their decision-making behavior as well. So almost everyone you try the idea on will laugh in your face. Yet the idea may just be hot. Some day, people may subscribe to legal advice services on the Internet and routinely pop online to get a few opinions before making any important decisions. So it may be a big mistake to give up on this idea, just because customers laughed at it.

Sometimes you have to trust your vision and go on instinct. It's a mistake not to try your hand at market leadership every now and then.

Not Using Marketing Research

This is a variant of the "not listening to your customer" mistake. And it is amazing how many marketers design their programs without doing any marketing research. Unless you are an alien with special powers, you can't possibly know enough to make any decisions until you've done some research.

The field of marketing research offers many ways to listen to your customers and markets (see Chapter 6), but often the simplest approach is the best. At the very least, just ask some customers what they think of your ideas. Then listen carefully to what they say, trying not to interrupt them with "But you don't understand" and "But the engineering department says . . ." You already know your organization thinks the idea is sound. Let the customer give you his or her gut reaction to it. Because if it doesn't seem like a winner from the customer's uneducated perspective, then it *isn't*.

Believing the Numbers

If you do any formal marketing research, or even read any reports about your industry, you will soon find yourself deluged with numbers. "X percent of customers don't like their current brand and are willing to switch for the right offer." "Y percent of customers say they would switch to your brand if the price was lower." And so forth. Each and every table and percentage tells its own story, and many of these stories are actionable. You could do something *because* the numbers suggest it is a good idea. Yet I guarantee that I could perform another research study and come up with a different finding, a contradictory number. Too much depends on how you construct your samples, how you phrase your questions, how you analyze the data, and even how you interpret the results. You can't do without marketing research, but on the other hand, you can't take it too seriously either!

Before you reach any conclusion or take any action, put on your skeptic's hat and try to find alternative explanations and interpretations for the result. Until you've considered them, you shouldn't rely on any findings. Even if your initial interpretation seems the most likely one, go one step further toward certainty. Verify your interpretation in two more ways that are independent of your original source. Find other sources or other ways to test your conclusion. If your interpretation still holds water after all this, then perhaps you can believe the numbers. But be careful — the numbers often lie.

Doing the Wrong Thing Well

This is certainly the most common problem I see when I go out into the real world to do consulting work. (In fact, I find it occurs in all aspects of management, not just marketing.) The root cause of this error is the management philosophy that says employees should *do* their work and not waste too much time *thinking about it.* In theory — although it's a poor philosophy — only the boss needs to know *why*. Everyone else is supposed to focus on knowing *how*.

The reality of business — and especially of marketing — is that many employees have to make on-the-spot decisions about what to do. Senior managers don't generally know about three-fourths of the decisions their company makes. (And they may mess up the other quarter, but that's another story.) So what you get are lots of people doing things as carefully as they can, without thinking about whether those things make sense or not.

In marketing, the majority of people do their job a certain way today because they were done that way the day before. Stop! Never do something just because it's "what we do" or "how we do it." Rethink your marketing practices and assumptions regularly. It will keep you from getting bored on the job, and it will save your company from wasting its precious resources on next-to-useless or positively destructive activities.

Doing Too Many Good Things at Once

Even the largest marketing budgets are too small to support more than one or two major initiatives at the same time. Large corporations may be able to deal with two projects, but your budget is probably much smaller than Procter & Gamble's, so this mistake is especially dangerous for you.

Don't undertake more than one major new marketing project at the same time if you can possibly avoid it. (If you can't avoid it, circulate your resume quietly, just in case.) I don't care what the reasons — they always *seem* good, but you should resist them. If your company has invented a great new product, and has just acquired another firm in the industry, then you have a good excuse to undertake two major projects at once. But trust me, there is no way you can integrate your sales force with theirs and introduce the new product at the same time. Neither effort will go well. Decide which project is more important and do it first. (I suggest launching the product first; merging the sales forces second.)

Failing to Ask for the Sale

I talk about the importance of closing the sale in Chapters 16 and 17. Closing the sale is a frequent weak point for salespeople and retailers alike. Yet the mistake is more widespread than that. Many ads, for example, fail to include a *call to action* — advertising's version of the sales close. It asks the audience of the ad to do something like call a toll-free number or go to a specific store where the product is in stock.

Co-op advertising, which is cooperatively designed and paid for by product marketer and retailer, is often better than general brand-oriented advertising because it asks people to come to a specific store or chain to buy the product.

Sometimes marketers find it difficult to include a call to action because they haven't thought through how to handle inquiries or purchases. This is often the case in situations where the marketing channel is lengthy and somebody else makes the sale. But even if other organizations normally handle sales, you need to try to close sales in all your marketing efforts. Send customers to the right retailers or build a direct marketing capability.

And instruct *all* your employees, at least once a month, in how to handle customers. That way, if they find themselves talking to a customer, they are sure to ask for their business instead of chasing it away. If you don't think employees chase business away, try calling up any big consumer products company. If you can even get through the telephone computer to reach a real person, that person does his best to get rid of you. Many large companies just don't seem to get the fact that the whole point of their work should be to close sales.

Making Too Big a Deal out of a Minor Product Difference

Remember when clear beverages were all the rage? Just a few years ago, clear sodas and beers seemed like they were going to take over the industry. Huge marketing programs supported these innovative new products. And consumers were — briefly — enchanted with them. After a while, though, they faded away.

This fad died because the whole thing was based on a pretty minor issue. So what if you can make a soda that looks like water? What does that have to do with the core benefits of the product? Very little, as consumers soon realized. You shouldn't have too high expectations for differentiation strategies unless your product differs *significantly* from competitors, and in an area that matters highly to customers. The core product is most important, not peripheral stuff like color or packaging. Customers aren't stupid, so you can't afford to be, either.

Trying to Sell Anything You Can't Explain in Five Words or Less

Well, maybe I'll give you twelve words, because that's how many it took to write the header for this section. But no more! The point is, even the most advanced and important products must eventually be reduced to sound bites in order to succeed in the marketplace. The same holds true with your marketing messages. Don't bother trying to design advertisements, for example, until you can write the claim in five (well, okay, twelve at the most) words. Otherwise, your thinking won't make it through the many hurdles and into customers' minds. The old KISS rule applies to everything in marketing (that stands for "Keep it simple, stupid!").

Ignoring the World Beyond Your Own Industry or Market

Wow. This is a common error. And most people never realize they've made it. Because it is natural to focus on what your competitors are doing, and judge yourself against them. But most of the things you do, in marketing and in the rest of your business, too, are also done in many other industries. Very little is unique from industry to industry. This becomes clear when you take a *process perspective* — that is, when you identify the processes which your department or company performs.

You make sales calls and provide service and support. You inventory and deliver products. You handle incoming customer calls. You maintain and market from a customer database. You hire and motivate salespeople. You display at trade shows to generate leads. You design marketing programs. You get the idea. But many thousands of other companies, most of them in other industries and perhaps even in other countries, do the same things. So what are the odds of someone in your industry being the best at any of those processes? Pretty slim. Then why do you benchmark your performance against your competitors? Why not pit yourself against the best?

Time to broaden your horizons, to seek out companies in other industries that are better at those common processes than anyone in your industry — and to learn from them. By doing this, you will soon be way ahead of your industry instead of being held back by it.

Appendix

Writing a Marketing Plan

• •

*M*ost simply, you can think of a *marketing plan* as a summary of your marketing goals and strategies — covered in Part I of this book — and the components of your marketing program — covered in Part III of this book. If you have already worked on your strategies and your program, then you have done all the prep work necessary to start writing.

If, however, you aren't quite sure how to put together your program, read Chapter 1 and use the sample programs in it as your guide.

Marketing plans vary significantly in format and outline from company to company, but all have core components, described in the following sections:

Executive Summary

Write this part last, but place it first. Summarize the main points of your plan and make clear whether the plan is efficiency oriented or effectiveness oriented. If the former, then say that your plan introduces a large number of specific improvements in marketing practice. If the latter, then say that your plan identifies a major opportunity or problem and adopts a new strategy to respond to it. Make sure that you summarize the bottom-line results — what your projected revenues will be (by product or product line unless you have too many to list on one page) and what the costs are. Also show how these figures differ from last year's figures. Keep the whole thing under one page in length.

If you have too many products to keep the summary under one page in length, you *can* list them by product line. But a better option is to do more than one plan. Any plan that can't be summarized in a page is too complex to be clearly thought out. Divide and conquer!

Objectives

The *objectives* are what your plan is supposed to accomplish. For example, will the plan increase sales by 25 percent, reposition a product to make it more appealing to upscale buyers, introduce a direct marketing function via the Internet and phase out direct mail as a result, or launch a new product? Maybe the plan will combine several products into a single family brand and build awareness of this brand through print and radio advertising so as to gain market share from several competitors, or cut the costs of marketing by eliminating inefficiencies in coupon processing, media buying, and sales force management? These are the sorts of things to say in the objectives section of the plan. They give the plan its focus.

If you write clear, compelling objectives, you will never get too confused about what to write in other sections, because when in doubt you can always look back at this section and remind yourself what you are trying to accomplish and why.

I try to write this part of the plan first — but all the while I know I will rewrite it often as I gather more information and do more thinking. And in the long run, I still end up reworking it at the very end. Objectives are such a key foundation for the rest of the plan that you can't ever stop thinking about them. However, for all their importance, they don't need a lot of words. A half page to two pages at most.

Situation Analysis

What's happening? That's the question your *situation analysis* must answer. The answer can take many forms, so I can't give you a formula for preparing the situation analysis. You should analyze the most important market changes, as these are the sources of problems or opportunities. (See Chapter 5 for formal research techniques and sources.)

But what *are* the most important changes since you last examined the situation? The answer depends on the situation. See the difficulty? Yet somehow you must gain sufficient insight into what's happening to see the problems and opportunities clearly.

In fact, your goal is to see the changes *more clearly than the competition*. Why? Because if your situation analysis is worse than the competition, you'll lose market share to them. If your analysis is about the same, then you may hold even. Only if your situation analysis is better will you gain on the competition.

What you want from your situation analysis is

✔ *Information parity,* which is the term I use to describe the state where you know as much as the leading competitors know. If you don't do enough research, or the right kind of analysis, then your competitors will have an information advantage. Therefore, the first goal is to gain enough insight to put you on a level playing field with your competitors.

✔ *Information advantage,* which I define as an insight into the market that your competitors don't have. The purpose of an information advantage is to put you on the uphill side of an uneven playing field. That's an awfully good place from which to design and launch a marketing program or advertising campaign!

Most marketing plans and planners don't use these terms and don't think about their goals this way. I'm telling you one of my best-kept secrets, because I don't want you to waste time on the typical *pro forma* situation analysis, in which the marketer rounds up the usual suspects and parades information that everybody ought to know before reading the plan. That approach, while common, does nothing to make the plan a winner. If all *you* wanted to do was the minimum, then I don't think you would have bothered to buy this book in the first place.

Marketing Strategy

Many plans use this section to get specific about the objectives by explaining how they will be accomplished. Some writers find this task easy, while others keep getting confused about the distinction between an objective and a strategy. An objective sounds like this:

Solidify our leadership of the home PC market.

A strategy sounds like this:

Introduce hot new products and promote our brand name in order to solidify our leadership of the home PC market.

Note that the second, the strategy, emphasizes the general approach to accomplishing an objective. It gives some good pointers as to what road you'll take. But some people view the difference between objectives and strategies as a pretty fine line. If you are comfortable with the distinction, then write a separate strategy section. If not, combine this section with the objectives section and title it Objectives and Strategies; then what they're called won't matter as long as they are good.

For more details about how to develop and define marketing strategies, see Chapters 2 and 3.

Overview of a Marketing Program

A *marketing program* is the combination of marketing activities you use to influence a targeted group of customers to purchase a specific product or line of products. I show you how to develop or analyze marketing programs in Chapter 1. A marketing program starts, in my view, with an analysis of what your *influence points* are — in other words, what ways your organization has to influence customer purchases. And the program ends with some decisions about how to use these influence points.

In Chapter 1, I suggest that you prioritize by picking a few primary influence points — ones that will dominate your program for the coming planning period. The main reason for this approach is that it concentrates your resources, giving you more leverage than otherwise (and maybe more leverage than less-focused competitors) at certain points of influence. Make the choice carefully, trying to pick one to three legs for your marketing program to stand on. Then use the (usually many) other influence points in secondary roles to support your primary points by filling in around them. (You'd think the plan would become stronger as you add legs, but it doesn't. It just gets shorter.)

If you follow my advice in Chapter 1 (and it's still not too late!), you already have identified your influence points and you have a good idea of what your organization spent on them last year. Pick some to focus on (if you aren't sure which, review the coverage of program components in Part III to find influence points that seem best suited to your needs and market). Then, still consulting Part III chapters as needed to clarify how to use the various program components, begin to develop specific plans for each.

For example, say that you are considering using print ads in trade magazines to let retail store buyers know about your hot new line of products and the in-store display options you have for them. That's great, but now you need to get specific. You need to pick some magazines (call their ad departments for details of their demographics and their prices — see Chapter 8 for details). You also need to decide how many of what sort of ads you will run, and then price out this advertising program.

Do the same analysis for each of the items in your list of program components. Work your way through the details until you have an initial cost figure for what you want to do with each component. Total these costs and see if the end result is realistic. Is the total cost too big a share of your projected sales? Is it higher than the boss said the budget could go? If so, adjust and try again. After a while, you should be able to get a budget that looks acceptable on the bottom line and also makes sense from a practical perspective.

A spreadsheet is a great aid to this process. Figure A-1 shows the format for a very simple one. All you have to do is build formulas that sum the costs to subtotals and a grand total, and then subtract the grand total from the

Figure A-1:
This program budget, prepared on a spreadsheet, gives a quick and accurate overview of an annual wholesale marketing program for a line of gift products.

Overview of Program to Target Retail Store Buyers	
Program Components	**Direct Marketing Costs ($)**
Primary Influence Points:	
– Sales calls	$450,700
– Telemarketing	276,000
– Ads in trade magazines	1,255,000
– New product line development	171,500
	Subtotal: $2,153,200
Secondary Influence Points:	
– Quantity discounts	$70,000
– Point of purchase displays	125,000
– New Web page with online catalog	12,600
– Printed catalog	52,000
– Publicity	18,700
– Booth at annual trade show	22,250
– Redesign packaging	9,275
	Subtotal: $309, 825
Projected Sales from this Program	$23,250,000
Minus Total Program Costs	- 2,463,025
Net Sales from this Marketing Program	**$20,786,975**

projected sales figure to get a bottom line for your program. In this figure, I've shown what a program looks like for a company that wholesales products to gift shops around the U.S. This company uses personal selling, telemarketing, and print advertising as its primary program components. It also budgets some money in this period to finish developing and to introduce a new line of products.

This company's secondary components don't use much of the marketing budget compared to the primary components (which are 87 percent of the total budget). But the secondary components are important, too. A new Web page is expected to handle a majority of customer inquiries and act as a virtual catalog, permitting the company to cut way back on its catalog printing and mailing costs. Also, the company plans to introduce a new line of floor displays for use at point of purchase by selected retailers. This display unit, combined with improved see-through packaging, is expected to increase turnover of the company's products in retail stores.

If your marketing plan covers multiple groups of customers, then you'll need to include multiple spreadsheets (such as the one in Figure A-1), because each different group of customers may need a different marketing program.

For example, the company whose wholesale marketing program is illustrated in Figure A-1 sells to gift stores — that's what that program is for. But they also do some business with stationery stores. And even though the same salespeople call on both, the products and promotions are different for these two groups of customers. They buy from different catalogs. They don't use the same kinds of displays. They read different trade magazines. Consequently, the company has to develop a separate marketing program for each, allocating any overlapping expenses appropriately. (For example, if two-thirds of sales calls are on gift stores, then the sales calls expense for the gift store program should be two-thirds of the total sales budget.)

Similarly, if you need to market different products or product lines differently, then you need to prepare a separate marketing program for each. Even if a single plan covers all of your products and lines, be sure to break out each into a separate program overview for this section of the plan.

Marketing Program Details

In this part of your plan, you need to explain the details of how you will use each component in your marketing program. You should devote a section to each component, which means that this part of your plan may be quite lengthy (give it as many pages as you need to lay out the necessary facts). You have to think these things through in detail anyway, so no harm is done by writing them down. The more of your thinking you get on paper, the easier implementing the plan will be later — as will rewriting the plan next year.

Although this portion is the most lengthy part of your plan, I'm not going to cover it in length here for the simple reason that Part III of this book does the job already. Each chapter goes into detail about how to use specific components of a marketing plan. Review the relevant chapters for ideas as you write this section of your plan.

At a minimum, this part of the plan should have sections covering the *four Ps* — the product, pricing, placement (or distribution), and promotion (how you communicate with and persuade customers). But more likely, you will want to break these categories down into more specific issues — as I do in the chapters making up Part III of this book.

Don't bother including any sections in your marketing plan on program components that you cannot alter. Often the person writing the marketing plan can't change pricing policy, or order up a new product line, or dictate a shift in distribution strategy. Explore your boundaries, try to stretch them, but in the end, admit they exist or your plan won't be practical. If you can only control promotion, then this section of the plan should be all about the ways that you'll promote the product. In this case, never mind the other three Ps. You do what you can do.

Management of the Marketing Program

This section of the plan is not mandatory, but including it is often a good idea. The management section summarizes the main activities that must be performed in order to implement your marketing program(s). The section then assigns these activities to individuals, justifying the assignments by considering issues such as their capabilities, capacities, and how they will be supervised and controlled. The main purpose of this section of the plan is to simply make sure that enough warm bodies are in the right places at the right times to get the work done. Sometimes this section gets more sophisticated, by addressing management issues like how to make the sales force more productive or whether to decentralize the marketing function.

Now you need to put on your accounting and project management hats. (Neither fits very well, I know, but you can bear them for a day or two.) You need to

- ✔ Estimate future sales, in units and dollars, for each product in your plan.

- ✔ Justify these estimates and, if they are hard to justify, create "worst case" versions, too.

- ✔ Draw a timeline showing when your program costs are incurred and program activities performed (doing so will help with the preceding management section and will also get you prepared for the unpleasant task of designing a monthly marketing budget).

- ✔ Write a monthly marketing budget that lists all the costs of your programs for each month of the coming year and also breaks out sales by product or territory and by month.

Passing the buck

I say that you have to do these unpleasant tasks now, but I should qualify that a bit. Some of the plans I've worked on have been *strategy oriented* — which lets the author off the hook for these details! The idea is for the marketing people to figure out what the goals and strategies are, and suggest ways of using the marketing program to implement them. Then the plan is passed on to the "experts" in sales, advertising, and other functional areas for them to develop detailed implementation plans. But even if you delegate these parts of planning, supervise and check the work carefully. It's your plan, and the numbers better be right.

You can increase buy-in (and even protect your neck) by getting participation on the revenue and profit figures for your plan. But sometimes it's hard to get other people, especially from other departments (if you are in a big company), to help you out. You can try telling them I said that having the advertising people design the ad budget is a good idea, as is having the sales managers design the sales budget, if you think that will help convince them. And you might also point out that they have a personal interest in seeing that these parts of your plan are practical from their perspective — thus participation makes sense for both you and them.

Making the buck — how to forecast sales

Take the worst case scenario — that you are indeed stuck with writing a full-blown marketing plan and won't have any help from specialists or participation from other departments. If so, then I'm most worried about your sales projections. I think you'll muddle through the rest of it, the cost side that is, because after all, figuring out how to spend money is not very hard. Just go shopping for a bunch of likely sounding marketing activities — ads, a PR agency, brochures, whatever — and sum these expenses to get your totals. The math part of that is trivial, and because you're in marketing (and are armed with this book), I think I can trust your judgment on the rest of it. But how about those sales projections? Unless you have a crystal ball, I recommend that you make a bit of a study of forecasting before you commit to any numbers on paper.

The secret to marketing projections, forecasts, and budgets, in a nutshell, is to look at them from a return-on-investment perspective. What matters is not how much you spend, but how much your expenditures return to the company.

It might be that a 50 percent cut in overall spending will give you a better return on a percentage basis. Or that a 200 percent increase will. Or that the same budget, allocated differently to be more effective and efficient, will give you a 25 percent increase in yield. If you devote sufficient care to your market forecasts, to your sales projections, and to your budgets, then you will be able to predict and measure returns on marketing investments well enough to gain such insights. Just make sure you carefully link specific marketing programs with specific results (as Figure A-1 shows). Then you'll know what you are spending your money on, and can estimate (and later substantiate) what your returns on your marketing expenditures are.

Estimating sales

Several helpful techniques are available for projecting sales. I'm going to review them so you can pick the most appropriate. If you are feeling nervous, just use the technique that gives you the most conservative projection. And a common way to play it safe is to use several of the techniques and average their results.

✔ **Buildup forecasts:** These go from the specific to the general, or from the bottom up. If you have sales reps or salespeople, have each one project next period's sales for her territories and justify her projections based on what changes in the situation she anticipates. Then aggregate all the sales force's forecasts to obtain an overall figure.

If you have few enough customers that you can project per-customer purchases, build up your forecast this way. You may want to work from reasonable estimates of the amount of sales you can expect from each store carrying your products or from each thousand catalogs mailed. Whatever the basic building blocks of your program, start with estimates for them and then add these estimates up.

✔ **Indicator forecasts:** This method links your forecast to economic indicators that ought to vary with sales. For example, if you are in the construction business, you will find that past sales for your industry correlate with GDP (gross domestic product; national output) growth. So you can adjust your sales forecast up or down depending upon whether the economy is expected to grow rapidly or slowly in the next year.

✔ **Multiple scenario forecasts:** These are based on what-if stories. They start with a straight-line forecast in which you assume

that your sales will grow the same percentage next year as they did last year. Then what-if stories are made up and their impact on that projection are estimated to create a variety of alternative projections.

For example, you might try the following scenarios:

- What if a competitor introduces a technological breakthrough?
- What if our company acquires a competitor?
- What if Congress deregulates/ regulates our industry?
- What if a leading competitor fails?
- What if our company has financial problems and has to lay off some of our sales and marketing people?
- What if our company doubles its ad spending?

For each scenario, think about how customer demand might change. Also about how your marketing program would need to change in order to best suit the situation. Then make an appropriate sales projection. For example, if a competitor introduced a technological breakthrough, you might guess that your sales would fall 25 percent short of your straight-line projection.

The trouble with multiple scenario analysis is that it gives you multiple scenarios. What your boss wants is a single sales projection, a one-liner at the top of your marketing budget. One way to turn all those options into one number or series of numbers is to just pick the option that you think is most likely. That's not very satisfying if you aren't at all sure which, if any,

(continued)

(continued)

will come true. So another way is to take all the options that seem even remotely possible, assign each a probability of occurring in the next year, multiply each by its probability, and then to average them all to get a pretty fancy number.

For example, Scenario A projection = $5 million and Scenario B projection = $10 million. The probability of A = 15%, probability of B = 85%. The Sales projection = [($5 mil x .15) + ($10 mil x .85)]/2 = $4,630,000.

✔ **Time period projections:** To use this method, work by week or month, estimating how much sales will be in each time period and then summing them across the entire year. This approach is helpful when your program or the market is not constant across the entire year. Ski resorts use this method because they get certain types of the revenues only at certain times of the year. And marketers who are planning to introduce new products during the year or to use heavy advertising in one or two *pulses* (concentrated time periods) also use the method because their sales will go up significantly during those periods. Finally, entrepreneurs, small businesses, and any others on a tight cash-flow leash need to use this method, because it gives them a better idea of what cash will be flowing in by week or month. An annual sales figure doesn't tell them enough about when the money comes in to know whether they will be short of cash in specific periods during the year.

Controls

This section should be the last and shortest of your plan — but in many ways the most important. The section's purpose is to permit you and others to track performance.

Identify some performance benchmarks and state them clearly in the plan. For example

✔ All sales territories should be using the new catalogs and sales scripts by June 1.

✔ Revenues should grow to $XXX by the end of the first quarter if the promotional campaign works according to plan.

These statements give you (and, unfortunately, your employers) easy ways to monitor performance as you implement the marketing plan. Without them, no control exists over the plan. Nobody can tell whether or how well the plan is working. With them, unexpected results or delays can be identified quickly — in time for appropriate responses if you have designed these controls properly.

Planning and Budgeting Templates

Having some model plans to refer to is helpful. Unfortunately, most companies won't release their plans — they rightly view them as trade secrets. Fortunately, a few authors have compiled plans or portions of them, and you can find some good published materials to work from.

I recommend that you look at sample marketing plans and templates in several different books. These show you alternative outlines for plans and also include budgets and revenue projections in many formats — one of which may suit your needs pretty closely:

- *The Vest-Pocket Marketer* by Alex Hiam, published by Prentice Hall
- *How to Really Create a Successful Marketing Plan,* by David Gumpert, published by *Inc.* magazine
- *The Marketing Plan,* by William Cohen, published by John Wiley & Sons

You should be able to order any of these from your local bookstore for delivery within the week, as major book distributors do stock them. However, they are rarely kept on bookstore shelves because most people don't pick marketing plans as a topic for casual reading.

Index

IDG BOOKS WORLDWIDE REGISTRATION CARD

RETURN THIS REGISTRATION CARD FOR FREE CATALOG

Title of this book: **Marketing For Dummies®**

My overall rating of this book: ❑ Very good [1] ❑ Good [2] ❑ Satisfactory [3] ❑ Fair [4] ❑ Poor [5]

How I first heard about this book:

❑ Found in bookstore; name: [6]

❑ Advertisement: [8]

❑ Word of mouth; heard about book from friend, co-worker, etc.: [10]

❑ Book review: [7]

❑ Catalog: [9]

❑ Other: [11]

What I liked most about this book:

_____

_____

What I would change, add, delete, etc., in future editions of this book:

_____

_____

Other comments:

_____

_____

Number of computer books I purchase in a year: ❑ 1 [12] ❑ 2-5 [13] ❑ 6-10 [14] ❑ More than 10 [15]

I would characterize my computer skills as: ❑ Beginner [16] ❑ Intermediate [17] ❑ Advanced [18] ❑ Professional [19]

I use ❑ DOS [20] ❑ Windows [21] ❑ OS/2 [22] ❑ Unix [23] ❑ Macintosh [24] ❑ Other: [25]_____

(please specify)

I would be interested in new books on the following subjects:
(please check all that apply, and use the spaces provided to identify specific software)

❑ Word processing: [26]

❑ Data bases: [28]

❑ File Utilities: [30]

❑ Networking: [32]

❑ Other: [34]

❑ Spreadsheets: [27]

❑ Desktop publishing: [29]

❑ Money management: [31]

❑ Programming languages: [33]

I use a PC at (please check all that apply): ❑ home [35] ❑ work [36] ❑ school [37] ❑ other: [38] _____

The disks I prefer to use are ❑ 5.25 [39] ❑ 3.5 [40] ❑ other: [41]_____

I have a CD ROM: ❑ yes [42] ❑ no [43]

I plan to buy or upgrade computer hardware this year: ❑ yes [44] ❑ no [45]

I plan to buy or upgrade computer software this year: ❑ yes [46] ❑ no [47]

Name: _____ Business title: [48] _____ Type of Business: [49] _____

Address (❑ home [50] ❑ work [51]/Company name: _____)

Street/Suite# _____

City [52]/State [53]/Zipcode [54]: _____ Country [55] _____

❑ **I liked this book!** You may quote me by name in future
IDG Books Worldwide promotional materials.

My daytime phone number is _____

IDG BOOKS

THE WORLD OF
COMPUTER
KNOWLEDGE

❑ YES!

Please keep me informed about IDG's World of Computer Knowledge.
Send me the latest IDG Books catalog.

SECRETS™

...FOR DUMMIES™
COMPUTER
BOOK SERIES
FROM IDG

MACWORLD
MW
AUTHORIZED
EDITION

AUTHORIZED
PC WORLD
EDITION

BUSINESS REPLY MAIL
FIRST CLASS MAIL   PERMIT NO. 2605   FOSTER CITY, CALIFORNIA

NO POSTAGE
NECESSARY
IF MAILED
IN THE
UNITED STATES

IDG Books Worldwide
919 E Hillsdale Blvd, STE 400
Foster City, CA 94404-9691